Ideology, Politics,
and Political Theory

Ideology, Politics,
and Political Theory

edited by Richard H. Cox
State University of New York at Buffalo

Wadsworth Publishing Company, Inc.
Belmont, California

Preface

This book is intended primarily as a textbook for use in both undergraduate and graduate courses on modern political theory. It should also be useful in courses on comparative politics, on the scope and method of political science, and on political sociology. In addition, it is intended as an interpretive sourcebook of materials for scholars and students interested in the concept of ideology.

While the organization and scope of the book, and above all, the content of the introductory materials, reflect my own interpretation both of the problem of ideology and of the means by which to understand it, the selections have been chosen to present alternative interpretations of that problem. In short, I have tried to combine some of the features of an original book on the topic with the features of a "reader." The nature of that attempt, in addition to the constraints imposed by limitations of space, largely explains the book's contents.

Many people and a number of institutions have contributed to the making of this book and a word of public thanks is therefore due to them.

William T. Bluhm and David Lowenthal made helpful critical comments on the content and organization of the book in its various developmental stages. A number of others—most notably, David Minar, W. J. Stankiewicz, and Dante Germino—contributed pre-publication reviews of part or all of the book. Carol Cotton, David Esmond, John Gunnell, Heather Johnston, Jerry Meadows, Peter Melvin, Marcus Raymond, Edwin Stromberg, and Ross Thrasher, as graduate research assistants, lightened the load of sheer labor and, more importantly, made useful suggestions. The State University of New York Research Foundation at Albany provided two summer Faculty Research Fellowships. The Naval War College at Newport, Rhode Island provided time and assistance during the final stages of editing the selections and writing the introductory materials. And the Graduate School at the State University of New York at Buffalo supplied funds for the final preparation of the manuscript.

Buffalo, New York   R.H.C.

Contents

Introduction

Ideology is the science of Idiocy. . . . It is the bathos, the theory, the art, the skill of diving and sinking in government. It was taught in the school of folly; but alas Franklin, Turgot, Rochefoucauld, and Condorcet, under Tom Paine, were the great masters of that academy. (John Adams, on the original concept of ideology.)[1]

Few concepts play a larger part in present-day discussion of historical and political topics than does that of ideology. . . It is here intended to clarify the theme by examining the different significations attached to the term "ideology," and the shifting status of the phenomenon itself. . . It is hoped that the term "ideology" will be shown to possess both a definite meaning and a particular historical status: the history of the concept serving as a guide to the actual interplay of "real" and "ideal" factors whose dialectic is obscurely intended in the formulation of the concept itself. . . (Sociologist George Lichtheim, on the contemporary concept of ideology.)[2]

The word "ideology," or what that word signifies in contemporary theoretical and practical discourse on politics, is the subject of this book.

[1]John Adams, *The Life and Works of John Adams* (Boston: Charles C. Little and James Brown, 1851), Vol. VI, 403.

[2]George Lichtheim, "The Concept of Ideology," *History and Theory*, Vol. 4 (1965), p. 164.

Where should this investigation begin? A number of concrete examples of the contemporary usage of "ideology" can be culled from the text of contemporary speeches and publications:

A *New York Times* news article reported that U Thant, Secretary-General of the United Nations, compared the "ideological intolerance of today" to the "religious intolerance which prevailed not so long ago."[3] The transcript of a hearing held by the House Committee on Un-American Activities has been published as a pamphlet entitled "The Ideology of Freedom vs. The Ideology of Communism,"[4] while Secretary of Defense Robert McNamara testified before a Congressional Committee that the Communist threat "is political, it is ideological, it is economic, it is scientific; and it extends even into the cultural spheres."[5] Former Republican President Dwight Eisenhower said in his Farewell Address to the nation, "We face a hostile ideology—global in scope, atheistic in character, ruthless in purpose, and insidious in method."[6] John F. Kennedy, Eisenhower's Democratic successor, told the nation: "If we can contain the powerful struggle of ideologies and reduce it to manageable proportions, we can proceed with the transcendent task of disciplining the nuclear weapons which shadow our lives. . ."[7] An article in *The Reporter* analyzed a project of the U.S. Joint Chiefs of Staff to fight Communism with a "stronger *dynamic* ideology."[8]

A professor of philosophy and a professor of sociology engaged in a rather passionate debate in the pages of the scholarly journal, *Commentary*. The question at issue was whether—in spite of the rhetoric of an Eisenhower and a Kennedy—the advanced Western democracies had not begun to experience the "end of ideology," and if so, what were the implications for democracy.[9] A professor of economics and a professor of political science presented a study of the "ideologies" of the "major groups which largely determine

[3] The occasion was the United Nations' observance of the twentieth anniversary of the formation of that organization. See *New York Times* (June 27, 1965), 3:1.

[4] House of Representatives, 85th Congress, Second Session (Washington: U.S. Government Printing Office, June 5, 1958).

[5] Committee on Foreign Affairs, House of Representatives, 88th Congress, Second Session (Washington: U.S. Government Printing Office, March 25, 1964), pp. 83-84.

[6] *The Department of State Bulletin* (February 6, 1961), p. 180.

[7] *Ibid.*, (June 5, 1961), p. 842.

[8] William H. Hale, "Militant Liberty and the Pentagon," *The Reporter* (February 9, 1956), pp. 30-34.

[9] These two articles appear in Part II.

public policy in America."[10] A professor of political science rendered an historical sketch of the interaction of modern political ideas and political events, beginning with the contention that, "For the past two centuries the Western world has been living through a time of troubles that might well be called the Age of Ideologies."[11]

An historian set forth a "Concept of Ideology for Historians."[12] Another historian used that concept as a critical tool for the evaluation of the American tradition in a work entitled *Individualism and Nationalism in American Ideology.*[13] A professor of political science treated the problem of how to utilize the "concept" of "ideology" as a device in "empirical research."[14] A professor of philosophy tried to show the essential nature of "ideology" by subjecting it to "logical analysis."[15] And a professor of theology discussed the theoretical relationship of political "ideologies" to "religion."[16]

The purpose of these brief and diverse examples is to dramatize (1) the ubiquity and (2) the protean character of the word "ideology" in contemporary American discourse. What is true today of American discourse is also largely true in most other parts of the world, as a comparable set of examples from England, France, India, Japan, or Russia would readily show. There are indications of the awareness of "ideology" that permeates the style of thought we experience today. This fact may suggest certain questions: Is this style of thought historically characteristic of theoretical and practical discourse on politics? If not, when and why did it develop? What are its theoretical and practical implications?

This book does not contain complete answers to these questions, but it does contain a variety of introductory essays and readings designed to help the

---

[10]R. J. Monsen, Jr. and Mark W. Cannon, *The Makers of Public Policy: American Power Groups and Their Ideologies* (New York: McGraw-Hill Co., 1965), p. vi.

[11]Frederick M. Watkins, *The Age of Ideology—Political Thought, 1750 to the Present* (Englewood Cliffs, New Jersey: Prentice-Hall, Inc., 1964), p. 1.

[12]Richard V. Burks, "A Concept of Ideology for Historians," *Journal of the History of Ideas,* X (April 1949), 183-198.

[13]Yehoshua Arieli, *Individualism and Nationalism in American Ideology* (Cambridge, Mass.: Harvard University Press, 1964).

[14]David Minar, "Ideology and Political Behavior," *Mid-West Journal of Political Science,* V (1961), 317-331.

[15]Gustav Bergmann, "Ideology," *Ethics,* LXI (April 1951), 205-218.

[16]James L. Adams, "Religion and the Ideologies," *Confluence,* IV (1953), 72-84.

reader think about the questions. It may help in the sense in which John Stuart Mill, in *On Liberty*, attributed merit to the ancient "Socratic dialectics." To Mill, those dialectics were essentially a "contrivance" to aid in the

discussion of the great questions of philosophy and life, directed with consummate skill to the purpose of convincing any one who had merely adopted the commonplaces of received opinion that he did not understand the subject . . . in order that, becoming aware of his ignorance, he might be put in the way to obtain a stable belief, resting on a clear apprehension both of the meaning of the doctrines and of their evidence.[17]

This book on "ideology" is in its own way a contrivance too—a device to help the reader examine his own received opinions concerning the nature and significance of what is one of the commonest terms in contemporary political vocabulary.

The readings treat both the theoretical and political aspects of ideology. This division is somewhat artificial, because the distinction between the *theoretical* and the *political* aspects of "ideology" is often difficult to discern in reality. Still, a persistent pattern of contemporary usage tends toward a double focus around the theoretical and political aspects of the term, a pattern discernible even in the above examples, where a brief analysis yields the following observations.

First, political leaders sometimes use "ideology" in an emphatically political way, to unleash polemical broadsides against the principles of an opposing political society. But they also use it impartially in describing both their own and their opponents' political principles, i.e. the "ideology" of democracy or the "ideology" of communism. Second, scholars either use "ideology" in a theoretical sense, to categorize a set of political principles, or politically, to criticize these principles or political trends. Thus *both* groups use the term in polemical and impartial ways. It is one of the term's intriguing and perplexing qualities to be able to serve in all of these senses. The extremes evident in usage, though, tend to be the poles of political and theoretical meaning. I have, therefore, assembled the readings around those two poles, in the expectation that the reader will see, as he proceeds, that in the real world the political and the theoretical senses often meet and blur.

One further word concerning the order of treatment: The material on the theoretical aspect of ideology is presented first for two reasons. First, much contemporary analysis of the political aspect of ideology presupposes some

[17]J. S. Mill, *On Liberty* (Great Books Foundation Edition, Chicago: Henry Regnery Co., 1949), p. 55.

understanding of various ideological theories. The second reason is that, historically, the political aspect of ideology has arisen from such theories. But the exact nature of the interaction of these two aspects of ideology is too complex to reduce to a simple formula; this interaction is itself one of the intriguing problems of ideology.

Part One

**Ideology and Political Theory:
An Historical-Critical Survey**

This part is the most important in the book because it supplies the basis for a correct understanding of the problems raised in the other two parts. Its purpose is to demonstrate the validity of five propositions: First, theories of ideology are essentially modern. Second, the original theory of ideology appeared in Europe at the end of the eighteenth century. Third, it was part of a philosophical conception of politics critical of all pre-modern theoretical and political conceptions. Fourth, all later theories of ideology are attempts to resolve the basic theoretical and practical problems posed by that original theory. Fifth, the contemporary ideological climate of thought is largely the result of the dissemination and vulgarization of theories of ideology.

The current interest of American scholars and intellectuals in theories of ideology is a recent development and stands in contrast to the satirical, scornful dismissal of ideology by John Adams. During most of the history of the American republic, its scholars and intellectuals knew little of and cared less about theories of ideology. Earlier attempts had been made, however, to arouse interest in them. The original theory of ideology was introduced to America by Thomas Jefferson. He had become interested in the writings of Destutt de Tracy, a French philosopher who was one of the propounders of the original theory. Jefferson attempted to have Tracy's theory incorporated

in the original curriculum of the University of Virginia,[1] but was
unsuccessful. And after Jefferson's death, interest in the theory of ideology
waned. Destutt de Tracy's conceptions retreated into the pages of dusty
volumes, and the term itself seems to have disappeared from American
political and intellectual discourse until well into the twentieth century.

An interest in ideology reappeared in America in the wake of the Soviet,
Fascist, and Nazi political revolutions in Europe. At first its reappearance was
more a reflection of these events than of theoretical concern on the part of
American scholars and intellectuals. A striking indication of this fact is
provided by the fifteen-volume *American Encyclopedia of the Social
Sciences*, an authoritative work first published in the early and middle 1930s.
The articles are not dated, but internal evidence would suggest that most were
completed not long prior to publication. It is revealing, then, that there is no
article on "ideology" nor any entry for the term in an index of some 12,000
items. Furthermore, the key articles on political topics—"Revolutions," "The
State," "Nationalism," "Political Parties," and "Government"— reveal little
theoretical concern with "ideology." Thus, nearly twenty years after the
Soviet Revolution, and several years after the appearance of Karl
Mannheim's influential *Ideology and Utopia* (1929) in Germany, explicit
awareness of or interest in the theoretical aspect of "ideology" among
American social scientists was rare.

This perspective of American social scientists in the early 1930s stands in
sharp contrast to their perspective today. The difference is easily illustrated
by the new American *International Encyclopedia of the Social Sciences*
(1968: 17 volumes). It contains two articles on ideology: "The Concept and
Function of Ideology" (Edward Shils) and "Ideology and the Social System"
(Harry M. Johnson). Together, these articles cover nearly twenty pages—one
of the longest treatments of any topic in the entire *Encyclopedia.* The two
articles also cite seventeen cross-references to other articles relevant to the
treatment of the concept, including "Consensus," "Democracy," "Fascism,"
"Karl Mannheim," "Marxism," "Political Theory," and "Values." The general
index to the *Encyclopedia* lists fifty-five cross-references, mostly to separate
articles, in which the concept is used.

The contrast between the lack of American theoretical interest in ideology in
the early 1930s and the very great interest in the middle 1960s may be of the

[1] See, for example: Herbert B. Adams, *Thomas Jefferson and the University of Virginia*
(Washington: Government Printing Office, 1888), pp. 63, 65, 83, 95; Roy J. Honeywell,
The Educational Work of Thomas Jefferson (New York: Russell & Russell, Inc., 1964),
pp. 110-111, 121, 124-125, 163-165; Adrienne Koch, *The Philosophy of Thomas
Jefferson* (Gloucester, Mass.: Peter Smith, 1957), pp. 45, 54, 56-57, 58-63.

greatest significance for understanding the contemporary low status of traditional political theory. As theoretical interest in ideology has increased, serious interest in and respect for traditional political theory has decreased. But to grasp the nature and the significance of this transformation, it is necessary to look first at the historical evolution of the theory of ideology, and next at the way its relationship to traditional political theory appears in contemporary theoretical discourses on politics.

The readings in Part I do not present a sweeping and superficial historical review of theories of ideology since 1800. Rather, they present a concentrated review of three key theories, by means of introductory essays and excerpts from the original works. In order to point up the difficulties of each theory, the excerpts are then paired with a critical commentary.

The theories of ideology contained in this part are from (1) Destutt de Tracy's *Élémens d'Idéologie*; (2) Karl Marx's and Friedrich Engel's *The German Ideology* and Marx's *Capital*; and (3) Karl Mannheim's *Ideology and Utopia*. These works have been chosen first, because together they span the whole period, from the origins of a theory of ideology to the outburst of contemporary interest in the middle 1930s; second, because they were written at different times in that period; third, because each has been most influential in developing a theoretical—and often a political—consciousness of ideology; and fourth, because they are sufficiently different to suggest the general variety of such theories in the history of ideology.

Chapter One

The Original Concept of Ideology

Our English word "ideology" is an Anglicized version of the French *idéologie*, which was invented toward the end of the eighteenth century, by the school of thinkers called *idéologues*, to designate their new, fundamental "science of ideas." The nature, purpose and fortunes of this original form of ideology are our present concern.

The *idéologues* were conscious of basing their new science on prior philosophical developments. More specifically, they were conscious of building on the great early-modern philosophers: Francis Bacon, Thomas Hobbes and John Locke in England, and René Descartes in France. The *idéologues* felt that these earlier thinkers had, in two ways, opened the way to a restoration of learning and to the firm establishment of truth. First, they had made an all-out, reasoned attack on medieval and ancient philosophy—above all, on its purposes and methods. Second, they believed they had laid the foundations for a true understanding of the world by discovering the definitive importance and the main principles of the true "method" of all science. The *idéologues* called their method *analyse*, or analysis. By this they meant the intellectual process of deliberate, systematic reduction of every idea pertaining to every phenomenon into its simplest, irreducible elements, followed by a synthesis of those elements. This process was held to result in a clear, exact knowledge of each idea; and science was held to be the end product of this two-way process.

The *idéologues'* fascination with analysis is illustrated by their categorical application of this method to every aspect of the world—natural or social, physical or spiritual, animal or human. The words of P. J. G. Cabanis (1757-1808), one of the well-known, influential *idéologues,* provide an example:

> Since Locke, Helvétius and Condillac [the latter two were French followers of Locke], metaphysics is essentially the knowledge of the procedures of the human mind, the enunciation of the rules that man must follow in the search for truth. . . . It is equally applicable to the physical and moral sciences, and to the arts. . . . True metaphysics is, in a word, the science of methods, which it bases upon knowledge of the faculties of men, and which it applies to the nature of the different objects of the world.[1]

These remarks indicate first that the classical conception of metaphysics as the first philosophy or "science of being" had been decisively overturned; second, that the new metaphysics was essentially analysis, in the sense propounded by the *idéologues*; and third, that analysis of ideas is the fundamental science. For if the particular sciences—physics or chemistry or psychology—try to operate without having first clarified the exact content of their basic ideas, they will never overcome the difficulties into which ancient and medieval philosophy had fallen. This is equally pertinent to the science of morality or that of politics. Each profoundly depends on the more fundamental science of ideas. Thus in every case the object is to proceed, through analysis, away from the unclear, inexact, unexamined ideas of common discourse to the clear, exact, wholly scrutinized ideas of science.

The *idéologues* believed that their understanding of analysis went beyond that of the early-modern philosophers in two respects. First, even though Bacon and others had discovered the method of analysis, they had not succeeded in developing it into a real science, as the *idéologues* were confident they could. Second, even though Bacon and the others recognized that everyone would eventually benefit from the new science, they had not disseminated either analysis or the substantive findings of the new forms of particular sciences. The *idéologues* were at pains to accomplish this dissemination. In short, the *idéologues* felt that their philosophical ancestors had stopped short of the ultimate goal: the universal, direct transmission of the entire corpus of

---

[1] This passage appeared in a letter on the perfectibility of human understanding. It is quoted in P. J. Picavet, *Les Idéologues* (Paris: F. Alcan, 1891), p. 592. (Translations of this and other passages from Picavet were made by the editor.)

science, as well as the detailed methods of its procedures, to the entire citizenry.

Our main concern in this discussion of the *idéologues* is the application of their line of thought to the political sphere. They felt that, by failing to start from the true science of ideas, every previous political theory was absolutely defective and that all past and existing political practice was wholly or largely in error. A certain regime might have stumbled on some correct principles, but this was unlikely and, in any event, the principles were unscientific and therefore invalid.

The *idéologues* were deeply concerned with many political ideas: the political and intellectual equality or inequality of men, the nature of liberty, and the right to property. But to them, *all* such existing political ideas were essentially prejudices—whether encountered in the writings of the medieval or ancient philosophers, in the laws of the land, or in the political discourse of rulers and subjects. This meant that because the technique of analysis had not been applied to these prejudices, they existed in the minds of men only as muddled and incoherent images. The practical consequence of this was that men failed to understand each other, fell into disputes, and often ended by killing each other. In short, the root of civil discord was the prejudicial quality of men's ideas about the nature and objects of political life.

How, then, could these prejudices be eradicated and replaced with scientific —clear, exact, universally acknowledged—ideas? A new and comprehensive education based on the science of ideas was to provide the answer, and there were to be actual attempts to put such an education into practice. But the *idéologues* perceived a great general problem in making the transition to that new kind of education. They felt that the traditional intellectual, political, and religious authorities were so attached to the prevailing, centuries-old prejudices that they had a common interest in resisting any transition to a new kind of education. Most difficult was the obstacle of religion; the religious authorities clung most strongly to prejudices, and their quarrels over theological dogma became fanatical political-religious conflicts.

The real issue was the tension between ideal politics (only prospective, but scientific and enlightened), and actual politics (despotic, ignorant and fanatical). A comparison of the actual reign of ignorance and the prospective reign of enlightenment is stated in these terms by Cabanis:

Ignorance perpetuates the misery and the dependence of the poor. It establishes between them and other men relations of abasement and domination, respectively, which even the wisest of laws are impotent to make disappear. Here, then, is that which has been well understood only by the modern philosophers, who have made a true science of liberty. For they have taught us that liberty, although it may sometimes be the product of a happy instinct of a nation, can never be conserved or perfected except by the enlightenment of men.[2]

The enlightenment projected by the *idéologues* was not merely a speculative scheme. A limited but important attempt to put it into practice took place during the French Revolution under the auspices of the new National Institute, which was established by law in the National Convention (August 22, 1795). Three classes of subjects were to be taught in the National Institute: mathematical and physical sciences, moral and political sciences, and literature and fine arts. The second class was divided, in turn, into six sections: analysis of sensations and ideas, morals, social sciences and legislation, political economy, history, and geography. A number of *idéologues* were among the original members of the Institute, and their influence on the content of the second class is readily perceived from both the title and the primary position of the first section.[3]

The object of the National Convention was, according to Professor M. Picavet, a late-nineteenth-century French scholar, to "destroy [the] inequality of enlightenment" by the application of analysis to every idea in every school. It was expected that this would produce a large number of students capable of "executing a plan, which has for its goal . . . the regeneration of the human understanding." Thus, according to Picavet, "in pedagogy, as in philosophy, the *idéologues* opened the road on which we still try to proceed."[4]

However, this retrospective judgment by Picavet did not reflect the fortunes of the *idéologues* in their own time. Then, they were caught up in the intellectual and political struggles of the French Revolution. For some years after the establishment of the second class at the National Institute, their influence was considerable. They even persuaded Napoleon to become an honorary member of the Institute and he indicated approval of their aims and methods to the extent of occasionally speaking their language: "the only true conquests, the only conquests which give rise to no regrets, are those which one makes of ignorance."[5]

[2]Quoted by Picavet, *op. cit.*, p. 594.

[3]See Jules Simon, *Une Académie Sous le Directoire* (Paris: Michel Levy Frères, 1895), pp. 63-68, 76; Le Comte de Francqueville, *Le Premier Siècle de L'Institut de France* (Paris: J. Rothschild, 1896), I, pp. 60-64.

[4]Picavet, *op. cit.*, pp. 32, 68.

[5]Quoted in Hans Barth, *Wahrheit ünd Ideologie* (Zurich: Manesse verlag, 1945), p. 25. (Translated from the French by the editor.)

But as the cumulative upheavals of the troubled era unfolded, mounting attacks were made on the various schools of philosophy. The central issue was whether philosophy itself, especially the form which had lately developed in France, was the cause of the worst excesses of the Revolution. Even Napoleon had concluded by January of 1803 that the *idéologues'* theories were in fact pernicious doctrines. He closed down the second class of studies of the National Institute and waged a long, polemical war against the *idéologues.* That war is epitomized in this statement Napoleon made in 1812, after his crushing defeat in the Russian campaign:

It is to ideology, that obscure metaphysics, which searching after first causes, wishes to found upon them the legislation of nations, instead of adapting the laws to the knowledge of the human heart and to the lessons of history, that we are to attribute all the calamities that our beloved France has experienced.[6]

The powerful political opposition engendered by the *idéologues'* attempt to transform morals and politics through the teaching of their science of ideas thus directly contributed to an early and significant transformation of the meaning of the term "ideology." For the original, strictly theoretical meaning was now joined by a profoundly political meaning: "ideology" is a visionary, abstract type of theorizing which is intent on utterly overturning traditional political practice by subverting the settled opinions of men. It is in the latter sense that John Adams referred to the term; whereas Jefferson generally referred to it in the former sense.

But the opposition to ideology and other schools of Enlightenment philosophy was not simply confined to the political sphere. An intense controversy also took place among the intellectuals. Men such as Antoine Rivarol attacked both the theoretical premises and the practical effects of the doctrines of such schools as the *idéologues'.* Rivarol felt that the real issue was the nature of modern philosophy as such. He argued that modern philosophy's deliberate and wholesale rejection of ancient philosophy—and particularly its attempts to repudiate the ancient distinction between theoretical and practical philosophy—is rooted in a profoundly mistaken conception of the nature and purpose of theorizing. The practical effect of that mistake is to undermine the very basis of political life by attempting to transform political principles and beliefs, which are basically *non*-theoretical, into universally held theoretical principles. It is a savage irony to Rivarol that what began as an attack on the fanaticism of traditional religious-political conflicts ended as a fanatical defense of theoretical principles.

---

[6]Part of Napoleon's speech appears, in translation, in John Adams, *The Life and Works of John Adams* (Boston: Charles C. Little and James Brown, 1851), VI, pp. 401-402.

The propounders of the original theory of ideology were deeply aware of joining in a great intellectual and political struggle. To them, it was a desirable, even an inevitable, struggle. Its great purpose was to give practical effect to theories derived from the critique of ancient philosophy and traditional politics so gloriously begun by Bacon, Hobbes, Locke and Descartes. But, on the other hand, the political and theoretical criticisms of their purpose indicate that, from the beginning, the idea of ideology has been part of a comprehensive contest—a contest which has come to be known as the "battle of the ancients and the moderns."[7]

Destutt de Tracy (1754-1836) was one of the most active and influential of the *idéologues.* An English journal, the *Monthly Review,* noted in 1796 that Tracy had read a paper at the French National Institute in which he "proposed to call the philosophy of mind, ideology." The development of his project took many years, culminating in his extensive presentation of the "System of Ideology" in *Elements of Ideology* (1801-1815).

The first volume—*Ideology, Strictly Defined*—treats thinking, sensations, and the formation and effects of ideas. In the introduction, Tracy praises John Locke's *Essay Concerning Human Understanding* in these terms: "He was the first man who tried to observe and to describe human intelligence just as one observes and describes a property of a mineral or a vegetable, or a notable condition in the life of an animal. He also made this study part of physics."[8]

Volume II—*Grammar*—treats the principles of language as they pertain to thinking, sensations and ideas. Language is conceived as the link between ideology and logic.

Logic is the title of Volume III. Here Tracy pays great attention to the work of Francis Bacon and Thomas Hobbes. In the appendix to the volume, Tracy gives a resumé of Bacon's *Great Instauration,* and a translation of those parts of Hobbes' *De Corpore* which treat subjects such as propositions and syllogisms. The extent of Tracy's admiration for Hobbes' treatment of these matters is revealed in this passage from Volume III:

That political principles are derived from knowledge of the motions of the mind; and knowledge of the motions of the mind from the study of sensations and ideas. For this sentence alone, Hobbes should be considered as the founder of Ideology, and the renovator of the moral sciences.[9]

[7] For a satirical presentation of this battle, see Jonathan Swift's *Battle of the Books.*

[8] Tracy, *op. cit.,* I, p. xv. (Translations of this and other passages from Tracy used in the Introductory Essay were made by the editor.)

[9] *Ibid.,* III, p. 102.

This praise is particularly interesting in light of the remarks which Tracy adds in a footnote:

Hobbes, like Bacon, has often been reproached with being sincerely in favor of arbitrary authority. This may be, but it is none the less true that it has done him a great deal of harm. It is not necessary today to enter into lengthy arguments to prove that whoever helps to ensure the advance of man's reason, strikes at the root of all forms of oppression, and even that he attacks them in the only really effective manner. This is a constant truth there is no danger in revealing, for it is better known to the oppressors than to the oppressed.[10]

Finally, Volume IV is entitled *Treatise on the Will and its Effects.* This is an application of the ideas of the first three volumes to the problem of the nature and operation of the will. The premise is that once these matters are correctly understood through the analytic technique, a comprehensive understanding of human actions, as in political affairs, is within reach.

Curiously enough, Tracy never presents the substantive treatment of the moral and political sciences which was admittedly his ultimate goal. He was aware of this limitation, but he justified the publication of the "System of Ideology" without it on the grounds that it laid adequate foundations. All that remained to be done by others was to make a more detailed application. And to critics who might claim that he had spent a great deal of time and space in producing a very "metaphysical" introduction to the moral and social sciences, Tracy replied:

It is precisely because it is very metaphysical that there is no bad metaphysics in the rest of the work; because there is nothing like beginning by fully clarifying the principal ideas to prevent one from falling into sophisms and illusions.[11]

The first selection from Tracy's work is from Volume III, *Logic.* It illustrates (1) Tracy's criticism of existing conceptions or ideas concerning the main parts of the moral and political sciences (political economy, ethics, legislation, etc.), and (2) the way in which he conceives of re-establishing these sciences on the foundation of the science of ideas, which he also calls "first philosophy."

The second selection is more revealing of the substance of Tracy's treatment of political ideas. It shows how he applied the science of ideas to what was for him the most important political idea—liberty.

Antoine Rivarol (1753-1801) received ecclesiastical training but then forsook an intended career in the church for a literary one. He won attention in 1784

[10]*Ibid.*

[11]*Ibid.,* III, p. 441.

by receiving a prize from the Academy of Berlin for his *Discourse on the Universality of the French Language.* Later, he translated Dante's *Inferno.* But as political events in France moved toward the Revolution, he turned increasingly to intellectual and political matters. He contributed often to the *Political and National Journal,* and compiled a *Small Dictionary of the Great Men of the Revolution* (1790). Although critical of Louis XVI and the regime, he ultimately threw in his lot with the Royalists, a decision which eventually placed him in jeopardy. He emigrated to Brussels, then to London, Hamburg, and finally Berlin, where he died.

The selection included here is from the first part of a vast, unfinished work projected by Rivarol: *Preliminary Discourse of the Dictionary of the French Language.* The pamphlet from which the following extract is taken was published in 1797, but its scathing tone barred its distribution in France. Rivarol's polemic against modern philosophy and in defense of ancient philosophy does not explicitly treat the work of Tracy or the other *idéologues.* But this is less significant than the fact that his critique focuses on (1) the technique of analysis characteristic of the "science of ideas," and (2) the attempt to disseminate that technique and its fruits through universal enlightenment. Rivarol's defense of ancient philosophy is also joined to a defense of religion and of the traditional political order. As such, it is a good example of the alliance of authorities attacked by the *idéologues.*

From *Elements of Ideology**

Destutt de Tracy

1. On Logic

Logic as the Basis of the Moral and Political Sciences

If, from [the] very general sciences, which include all existing beings, we pass on to those which have as their particular object the human species, we find they are even less certain in their procedures, even more disconnected, and equally devoid of the primary notions on which they should be founded.

The one which we quite improperly call *political economy,* no doubt possesses precious truths on the effects of property, of industry and of the

*The selections printed here are taken from M. Destutt Comte de Tracy, *Elémens d' Idéologie,* 3iéme édition (Paris: 1817), 4 volumes. The exact citations are as follows: III, pp. 339-343, 344, 345-347, 377-386; IV, pp. 98-106. Joyce Loubere prepared the original translation. Final editing and revision of the translation was done by the editor.

causes which favor or oppose the formation and increase of our wealth. But since it is really, or should be, the history of the utilization of our energies toward the satisfaction of our needs, it should go back to the genesis of these needs and to the source of our power to act. Consequently, it should go back to the origin of the rights which the former give us and the duties imposed on us by the exercise of the latter.

Shall we say that this is rather the object and the special obligation of the science known to us by the name of *ethics*? I shall first reply that ethics considers our needs and our desires, in a word, all our feelings not yet reduced to acts, rather with the intention of evaluating and regulating them, than with that of satisfying them; and that, as far as our actions are concerned, it is more aware of the rights of others than of our own direct and immediate interests. Secondly, I shall not fear to state that, no more than political economy, does it go back to that primary cause of all need and all power, of all rights and all duties. Up to now, it deserves more than any other human science the reproach of being only a collection of empirical principles, deduced from scattered observations. The practice of these principles, although quite imperfect, is still very superior to the theory, because fortunately we are so disposed that at least the most essential of these principles are easier to feel than to prove. This is so true that we are still arguing about the fundamental basis which should be given to ethics, about the purposes it should have in view, and whether we should seek for its main principle within our own nature or outside of it. And it is so true that even many philosophers maintain that any idea of utility whatsoever, any relationship of any kind with ourselves, is a design unworthy of ethics, which degrades and debases it. Indeed, it is impossible to imagine a branch of knowledge less advanced and less certain than one about which such questions are raised.

Since the two sciences which we have just mentioned are incomplete, the science of *legislation* cannot fail to be even more so. This word, taken in its widest sense, means the knowledge of the laws which should govern man in all circumstances and at all periods of his life. Thus it includes the science not only of the laws which govern the interests of individuals, of those which determine social organization, and those which decide the relationships of society with foreign nations, but also of those which should control childhood. The science of legislation includes the science of government and that of education. For government is nothing but the education of adult men, and education is the governing of children. But in the first, most attention is given to acts, because they have an immediate effect; and in the second we apply ourselves to the formation of opinions, because actions are as yet not very important.

Since the aim of the science of legislation is to govern the opinions and acts of men, it is necessarily without any solid foundation, as long as the actions and the opinions of men, and the consequences of one and the other, have not been appraised and evaluated with accuracy and precision. Besides, we are so ill-aware of the meaning of *police, policy*, or the science of the *city*, that we often give one of these names, which ought to be synonyms, to the vilest form of espionage, and the other to a system of trickery both so false and so outworn that it only catches those who make use of it.

I am not speaking of the *science of law*, which is separate from the science of legislation. It consists only of the knowledge of what has been decreed, without reference to what should have been decreed. So it is evident that it has neither theory nor principles. It is simply the history of what exists.

If, from these sciences, that may be called particular, we go back to the one which claims to govern them all and to point out the way to truth, I mean *logic*, I find that it can be reduced to teaching us how to draw conclusions, and that it has as a principle that one should never discuss principles, that is to say, that it has no self-created ones of its own, which it could justify . . .

Going back, then, or rather descending step by step to the foundations of it all, I discovered that the superb construction of our knowledge, which first of all offered me such an imposing facade, was weak at the base, and was built on quicksand. This dismal truth, which filled me with sorrow and fear, has proved to me that the great renewal so often demanded, but not carried out by Bacon, had only superficially taken place; that the sciences had indeed begun to advance in a more regular and wiser fashion, starting from certain points that were either given or agreed upon without sufficient elucidation, but that all of them were in need of a beginning which was nowhere to be found. . . .

I therefore thought that I should, in my turn, apply myself to primary philosophy, and make it the subject of all my meditations. It took but little concentration to discover that it should not be, as it was believed, a positive and explicit science, dogmatizing upon such and such a species of beings in particular, or on certain general effects of the existence of each one of them, and of their common relationships: for these are results, the elements of which must first be discovered. It was therefore easy for me to recognize that the true primary philosophy could only be true logic, the science which teaches us how we know, judge, and reason; and that Hobbes was quite right to make logic the first part of the first section of his Elements of Philosophy, and to place it before what he himself inopportunely calls primary philosophy, although quite justly he only gives it a subordinate place in his work.

But, as I have often said, logic, as it has always been known, was nothing but the art of drawing legitimate conclusions from recognized principles. It was not therefore what it should have been if it were true logic, or the beginning of everything. It was only an art, it should have been a science. It was based on accepted principles, when it should show us the cause of all principles; and it is this very imperfection which was the source of the widespread and mistaken belief that there could have been something preceding it which deserved to be called primary knowledge.

Yet how could this logic be perfected? How could it be completed? How could it be turned into a real science, the first of them all? It is obvious, or I am completely mistaken, that this could only be done by making it consist of the study of our means of knowledge. The art which claims to teach us judgment and reasoning can scarcely depend on anything else; and the science which aspires to direct this art, which would and must preside over and precede all the other sciences, cannot be anything else. Thus I saw myself by necessity induced to examine our intellectual operations, their properties and their consequences.

Desires as the Operative Force in the Will

Desires have two essential properties, which give rise to two distinct sciences, two different systems of knowledge. One of these properties is to make us rejoice or suffer; the other is to make us act. They correspond to the two great phenomena of animal economy, the action of the nervous system on itself, and its reaction on the muscular system. Consequently, to be really acquainted with our faculty of will and its results, we have to study separately, on the one hand, these desires themselves, their properties, their consequences, and on the other hand the direct or remote effects of the actions which result from them, and which all have the purpose of satisfying one or other of these desires. These two sorts of knowledge combined form, according to me, the part of Ideology which concerns the will.

I admit that I do not know what name should be given to these two branches of research. One could be called *ethics* and the other *economics*. But then these two words would have to be given a meaning very far removed from that usually attributed to them. Here not only do I encounter once more the difference between science and art—a difference which, I noted, exists between my way of considering logic, and that in which it has always been treated—but even the very fashion in which I conceive the subject, and classify things, is quite different from the usual one. Generally, we understand by ethics—if we have any clear idea whatever of what it means—a sort of legal code derived from reason, which should control our behavior on every occasion when legitimate authority, human or superhuman, has explicitly decided and delivered its verdict. When a philosopher has engaged in research on the justice and the rightness of our feelings, on the legitimacy of our actions and their consequences, we do not say that he has created an ethic. We say only that he has engaged in moral reflections or considerations relating to that code which we call *ethics*; and that these reflections or considerations are apt to reform or perfect the laws of this code, which governs not only our opinions, but also our actions.

Now I myself begin by totally separating our actions from the science in question. After that I make the latter consist solely in the examination of those of our perceptions which contain a desire, of the way in which they are produced in us, of their conformity or opposition to the true conditions of our being, of the soundness or weakness of their incentives, of the advantages and disadvantages of their consequences, but without allowing myself to impose any law on them. This imposition should result from reflections of another kind.

The meaning of the word economics would undergo an even greater change, perhaps, in order to adjust to my way of thinking. According to its etymology, it means the governing of a household. In popular usage it means chiefly the liking, or the talent for ordering any resources at one's disposal, above all pecuniary resources. And when we speak of political economy, we mean almost always only the science of creating and managing the wealth of a political society. Instead of that, in the plan I have in mind, just as the science called *ethics* would be a detailed study of our desires, inasmuch as they constitute all our needs, the science called *economics* would consist in the circumstantial examination of the effects and consequences of our actions considered as a means of providing for our needs of all kinds, from the most material to the most intellectual. If these two subdivisions were effectively filled out, then and then only would we have a complete picture of the effects of our faculty of will, since from it alone arise equally all our needs and all our means of action.

But from the two sciences conceived in this fashion, a third must necessarily come into being. Just as from the knowledge of the formation of our ideas, and that of their symbols, arises naturally the knowledge of how to combine them, which leads the thinking being towards truth; so also the reasoned knowledge of our tendencies and our actions results directly in the science of directing them in such a way as to produce the happiness of the being who wills. For happiness is the aim of the will, as truth is the aim of the intellect.

Is this last science then so new that there does not exist any name suitable for it, and that we do not yet know even how to designate it? I am afraid so. For the science generally known as the *science of government*, rarely has in view the aim that we have just mentioned, and that which is known under the title of *social science* only deals with a portion of that subject, since it does not include education, or even, perhaps, all the branches of legislation. Now, a system of principles best suited to guide men to the highest degree of well-being, should include the principles of behavior and control of men of all ages, and in all circumstances. So here we have yet another science to be named. However, taking suitable precautions, we can use the accustomed expressions; but here we come to a more important subject for deliberation.

Is the order in which we have just set forth the different parts which make up a complete examination of our faculty of will, really that in which these parts should be considered? It is at least very doubtful. At first glance it seems that we should first discuss our needs, then our means of action, and finally the way in which we can best use the latter to the greatest satisfaction of the former. But if we give more serious thought to our desires, we soon see that they are not all well motivated; that several are based on false judgments, and imperfect assessments; that their satisfaction would not lead us to the objective which was proposed; that it would be better to refrain from, or undeceive oneself about them, rather than have them succeed; that the most important thing is for us to judge them correctly; in short that we must be careful to evaluate them before we can think of satisfying them. For we have made more progress in this world when we know what we should wish for, than when we know how to attain what we wish for. Now the way to evaluate these desires is to know the consequences and the results of the actions to which they lead. Thus it follows that we should examine our means of action before we examine our needs. That too is my conclusion.

I believe, then, that the first part of a treatise on will should be devoted to the examination of the effects of our actions of all types, not only in respect to the satisfaction of our physical needs, and the creation of our private and public wealth, but also with respect to their moral and intellectual consequences, and their influence on the happiness of the individual, of society and of the species in general. This way of considering our actions is, as we can see, beyond the limits of ordinary economic science; it makes us perceive them in a far wider perspective. It teaches us to measure not only the effects of work properly so called, and its different varieties, but also the effects of all our behavior whatever it may be. It teaches us to measure the effects of the whole of our conduct, and even the effects of the different estates, associations, or corporations formed within the framework of society, from the family to the numerically greatest group. It teaches us, finally, to measure the effects of their action, both on the individual who is part of them, and on the entire mass. In a word, it will help us to find the results of all and every employment of our resources, from their most immediate effect, to their most remote consequences. Such a work properly carried out—and it never has been, it has not even been undertaken on this level—would not yet give us the theory of social science. But it would give us a table of all the elements of which it is composed, without which this science can only be constructed haphazardly, and in a completely hypothetical manner.

Once we suppose this first part adequately carried out, the second part would follow quite naturally: for it is very easy to estimate their different degrees of merit and demerit, when we have clearly recognized all the consequences of the actions to which they lead. The very ease with which it is done proves . that this is indeed the way to undertake a thorough treatment of such a subject. In fact, our actions are always the symbols of our ideas. But just as when we have to determine their value as symbols, we must first examine the ideas that they represent; in the same way when, on the contrary, it is a question of evaluating the worth of these ideas as opinions, we must necessarily begin by observing the effects of the actions to which they lead. Therefore this second part of the *Treatise on Will*, thus situated, cannot fail to lead us to positive results, though perhaps they will be very different from many well-established opinions; and it offers anyone who undertakes it no real difficulty, except that of properly distinguishing how our different feelings, our different passions, in short, our different affections, arise one from the other, propagate and combine with one another.

But also, once this difficulty is overcome, the third part, of which we have spoken, will already be done for us: for as soon as we know how our feelings are engendered, we know the way to cultivate some and eradicate others. Consequently, the principles of education and legislation become obvious; and the science of man as a being who wills and acts is completed. This is how I should like to see it treated, and how I imagine it fittingly rounding out the history of our intellectual faculties. Happy the man who will have the honor of doing this! And happier yet those whose judgment and will, from their earliest years, will be formed and directed according to the principles resulting from this exhaustive history of our faculties.

Such a treatise on the will and its effects would, in my eyes, be the most
important work that anyone could undertake, and the one which is the most
urgently required, in the present state of our understanding. For it would
contain the germ of a methodical and precise theory of *all* the moral sciences.

2. On Liberty

The Ideas of Liberty and of Constraint Arise
from the Faculty of Will

Nothing would be easier than to arouse interest in all generous minds by
beginning . . . with a species of hymn to this first of all the blessings of
sentient nature: *liberty*. But these explosions of feeling only aim at electri-
fying the speaker or rousing the emotions of the audience. However, a man
who is sincerely dedicated to the search for truth is sufficiently encouraged
by the aim that he has set himself, and relies on the same state of mind in all
those by whom he is happy to be read. The love of the good and the true is a
real passion. This passion is, I believe, quite a new one. At least it seems to me
that it could only have existed in its full vigor since it has been proved, by
reasoning and by facts, that the happiness of man is proportional to the mass
of his enlightenment, and that one and the other increase and can go on
increasing indefinitely. But since these two truths have been demonstrated,
this new passion which characterizes our era is not at all rare, whatever people
may say; and it is as forceful and more constant than any other. Let us not
therefore seek to stimulate it, but to satisfy it, and let us speak of liberty as
coolly as though the very word did not stir up our most powerful feelings.

I say that the idea of liberty arises from the faculty of the will. For, with
Locke, I understand by liberty, the power to carry out one's will, to act in
conformity with one's desire. And I maintain that it is impossible to attribute
any clear idea to this word if we wish to give it any other meaning. So, there
would be no liberty, if there were no will; and liberty cannot exist before the
birth of the will. It is therefore truly nonsense to claim that the will is free to
come into being; and so were all the well-known dictums which dominated
people's minds before the true study of human intelligence came into existence. Furthermore, the conclusions which were drawn from these supposed
principles, and particularly this one, were mostly completely absurd.

Without any doubt, we cannot say it too often, the sensitive being cannot
exercise his will without a reason; he can only use his will according to the
way he is moved; and so his will derives from his previous impressions; just as
necessarily as any effect derives from the cause which has the necessary

properties to produce it. This necessity is neither good nor evil for the sensitive being; it is a consequence of his nature; it is the condition of his existence; it is the datum which he cannot change, and which must be the starting point of all his speculations.

But when a desire is conceived in a living being, when he has come to some determination, this feeling of will, which is always painful as long as it is unsatisfied, has, to make up for this, the admirable property of acting on our organs. It does so by regulating most of their movements and by governing the use of almost all our faculties. In this way, it creates every means of enjoyment and power in the sensitive being, when no outside force prevents this—that is to say, when the being who wills is free.

Liberty, taken in this most general of all meanings (and the only reasonable one), signifying the power to carry out our will, is therefore the remedy for all our ills, the accomplishment of all our desires, the satisfaction of all our needs, and consequently, the first of all our blessings, that which is a source of all others and which contains all others. It is the same thing as our happiness. It has the same limits. Or rather, the scope of our happiness cannot be greater or lesser than that of our liberty, that is to say, than our power of satisfying our desires. Constraint, on the contrary, whatever it may be like, is the opposite of liberty; it is the cause of all our sufferings, it is the source of all our evils. Strictly speaking, it is our only evil; for every evil is always the thwarting of a desire. . . .

The constraint from which we suffer, or rather, which we suffer, since it is constraint itself which constitutes all suffering, can attain different degrees. It is direct and immediate, or only mediate and indirect. It comes to us from animate and inanimate beings. It is invincible or it can be overcome. The kind which is the effect of physical forces which curb the action of our faculties, is immediate, while the kind which results from various combinations of our intelligence, or from certain moral considerations, is only indirect and mediate, although also very real. One and the other, according to circumstances, can be insurmountable or likely to yield to our efforts.

In all these different cases, we have different ways of behaving to escape from the suffering caused by constraint, to achieve the fulfillment of our desires; in a word, to attain our satisfaction, our happiness; for, once again, these three things are one and the same. From these diverse fashions of reaching the unique goal of all our efforts, of all our desires, of all our needs and of all our abilities, we should always choose those which are the most apt to help us to

it. This is also our unique duty, the duty which includes all others. The way
to carry out this unique duty is first, if our desires are capable of being satisfied, to study the nature of the obstacles which lie in their way; and to do
everything that is in our power to overcome them. Secondly, if our desires
can only be fulfilled by our submitting ourselves to further evils, that is to
say, by giving up other things that we desire, to weigh the disadvantages, and
to decide on the lesser. Thirdly, if the success of our desires is quite impossible, we must give them up, and retreat without complaint within the limits
of our powers. Thus, everything comes down to the exercise of our intellectual faculties, first in judging our needs, then in using our abilities to the
utmost extent, and finally by submitting to the necessities of our nature, to
the unsurmountable conditions of our existence. . . .

[I thus believe to have shown, first] that since all our means of achieving
happiness consist in the voluntary use of our faculties, liberty, the power of
acting according to our will, is the sum of all that is good, our sole good.
[And second], that our sole duty is to increase that power, and to use it well,
that is to say, to use it in such a way as not to hamper or restrict its later use.

Should we, before we leave the subject, apply to this first of all good things,
liberty, the idea of value which, we have seen, arises necessarily from the idea
of *good*? And should we ask what is the value of liberty? It is evident that the
total liberty of any being possessed of feeling and will, being nothing but the
power to use his own faculties as he pleases, the total value of this liberty is
equal to the total value of the faculties of this being. It is also evident that if
we withdraw from him only a portion of that total liberty, the value of the
portion withdrawn is equal to the value of the faculties which he is prevented
from using, and that the value of what liberty remains to him is the same as
that of the faculties which he can still use. It is evident, finally, that however
weak may be the faculties of any animate being, the loss of his liberty is for
him a truly infinite loss. He cannot estimate the cost of its loss, for it is everything to him. It is the extinction of all possibility of happiness. It is the loss
of his entire being. It can allow of no compensation, depriving him of the
right to dispose of anything that he might receive in return.

These general notions are sufficient for the moment. I will add only one
reflection. It is commonly said that man, on entering the social state, sacrifices a portion of his liberty in order to secure the rest. After what we have
just said, this statement is not correct. It does not give a true idea either of
the cause or of the effect, or even of the birth of human societies. To begin
with, man never lived completely alone; he could not live thus, at least in
early infancy. So a state of society does not begin for him on a certain date

and with a set purpose; it establishes itself imperceptibly and by degrees. Secondly, man, in closer and closer association with his fellows, binding himself to them more and more each day by tacit or express agreements, never intends to lessen his former liberty, to weaken the total power (which he had previously), of carrying out his will. His goal is always to increase it; if he gives up a few ways of using it, it is in order to be aided, or at least not to be opposed, in other uses he would make of it, and which he judges more important for him. He allows his will to be somewhat hampered, in certain cases, by that of his fellows. But it is in order that it may become much more powerful with regard to all other beings, and even, on other occasions, with regard to his fellows. So that the total sum of power or of liberty which he possesses will be increased. That, I think, is the idea which we must hold concerning the effect and the goal of the gradual establishment of the social state. Whenever it does not have this result, it does not fulfill its object. But it always fulfills it, more or less, in spite of its universal and enormous imperfections.

From *On Modern Philosophy**

Antoine Rivarol

The Nature of Philosophy and Its Corruption

Philosophy has always been divided into two branches: that which is concerned with the study of nature, and which includes physics, chemistry, natural history and astronomy; and that which only studies the intellectual and moral aspect of man. In one and the other of these divisions, philosophy seeks and always finds new reasons to admire nature, and new ways to serve men. If philosophy had not strayed from this honorable mission, it would have contributed towards the perfecting of mankind, to the peace and glory of the world; and its name, the warranty, reminder and augury of happiness, would be the sweetest hope of the human race. But it is the essence of philosophy to make rare minds greater and vulgar souls bolder; to rouse an enlightened admiration in the first, and blind audacity in the second. Like the profession of war, which turns to theory in the head of the true warrior, and becomes the science which protects empires, while for ordinary men it is only

*The selections printed here are taken from Antoine Rivarol, *De La Philosophie Moderne*, 2iéme édition (Paris: 1802), pp. 3-14, 16-22, 28-29, 35-37, 65-67, 68-71, 73. Joyce Loubere prepared the original translation. Final editing and revision of the translation was done by the editor.

a school of barbarism and brigandage, philosophy has had the misfortune to breed arrogant minds whose excesses have dishonored its name.

By philosopher today we mean, not the man who is learning the great art of mastering his passions, or of increasing his understanding, but the man who combines a spirit of independence with despotism in making decisions; who doubts everything that exists, and is affirmative in everything that he says; the man, in short, who shakes off prejudice, without acquiring virtue.

The outcome of this has been that a first-class but devout physicist, like Pascal or Newton, was no philosopher; and that any brash and ignorant man was a great philosopher. This consequence did not surprise our era.

Since it is above all the analytical attitude which predominates in philosophy, its latest disciples have everywhere been engaged in dissolving and decomposing. In physics, they have found nothing but objections to make to the author of nature. In metaphysics, they have found nothing but doubts and subtleties. Ethics and logic have provided them with nothing but harangues against the political order, against religious ideas and against the laws of property. They have aspired to nothing less than the reconstruction of everything, by means of a revolt against everything. And without remembering that they themselves are in the world, they have torn down the pillars that support the world.

How was it that they did not see that their analyses were methods of man's mind and not one of nature's means? That this same nature is made up of relationships, proportions, harmony and wholeness? That it always connects, assembles and composes, even in decomposition? For its laws are never dormant; while analytical man, either the chemist or the rationalist, can only observe and suspend, decompose and kill. What would we say of an architect who, commissioned to raise a building, were to break up the stones in order to find minerals, air and earthen base, and offer us in this way an analysis instead of a house? The prism which dissects light spoils our view of the spectacle of nature.

Thus they have constantly abused the most subtle instrument of man's mind, I mean analysis or metaphysics. They have not sensed that truths are in harmony, and that they must be presented in order. . . . Real philosophy is to be an astronomer in astronomy, a chemist in chemistry, and a politician in politics. And yet these philosophers believed that defining men was better than bringing them together; that emancipating them was better than governing them; and finally that rousing them was better than making them happy. They have over-thrown states in order to regenerate them, and dissected living men, in order to know them better.

It is in vain that Plato (for Greece also suffered from the intemperance of this philosophy) warned them that it was not their business to write poetry and music, but to comment on them, since their philosophy was argumentative. In vain Zeno declared that the real philosopher is only a good actor; equally suitable for the part of king and subject, master and slave, rich man and poor man. For in fact the nature of real philosophy is to do everything well, not to find everything ill. It is in vain, I say, that men were well advised on the nature and difference of the two philosophies. A change took place in all men's minds preparatory to the revolution of which the philosophers suddenly became the promoters, guides and victims—a revolution in which they imagined that everything could be perverted without anything being destroyed, or that everything could be destroyed without danger, and the human race be imperilled without misdeed.

In society, people used to scoff at philosophers. The philosophers, in their turn, scoffed at everything society adores; they scorned riches, rebuked the passions, and demonstrated the emptiness of honors. And people scoffed at them for the same reason that our philosophers scoff at saints: because they did not believe in them.

But if the ancient philosophers sought only the sovereign good, the new ones have sought only sovereign power. And so society adapted itself at first to this philosophy which adapted itself to all the passions. It had an appearance of boldness and loftiness that enchanted youth and conquered mature men, a readiness and a simplicity that obtained everyone's approval and eliminated all resistance. Indeed, instruments of destruction are so very simple! These philosophers seemed to have the privilege of liberty and understanding, which they honored or vilified as they pleased. They enlisted or dismissed from their records great men of every century, according to whether they found them favorable or not to their design. They so successfully captivated, engaged and involved the self-esteem of the public, the administrators, the courtiers and kings, that it was necessary to rally to their standard in order to be in the same camp with reason. So was formed an alliance with them against the yoke of religion, against the refinements of morality, against the hesitations and timorousness of politics and experience; in a word, against our former society. And philosophy was thus no longer to be distinguished from the latest fashion.

We recall the prodigious joy of the philosophers on seeing the success of their books, the mass of conversions, and the unanimity of approval. They were dazzled by it to the extent of believing that at the sound of their voice nations would begin to stir, like the stones of Thebes to the strains of Amphion. They did not see that the applause came to them from a still intact existing order, and that approval was given them by all ranks of society. When we put on a play about chaos, the house rings with applause. But the author of the play does not conclude from his success that he must with all speed sow chaos, death, and annihilation throughout the world.

Yet this is what the philosophers attempted and succeeded in doing. Instead of letting their fancy run loose in a vacuum, they said: "Since we have the power, let us make our fancies reality. Let us build between the tombs of our fathers and the cradles of our children. Let us place our hopes on other generations. Let us save our love for the future and the unknown, and our protection for the universe. Let us reserve our hatred and our curses for our contemporaries, and for the ground we tread upon. May our colonies perish, may the world perish, rather than a single one of our principles!". . .

Here are their words, here is the spirit, the heart, the doctrine and the oracles of these friends of man! Hypocritical defenders, they have loved the poor, and the negroes, with all the strength of their hatred for the white and the rich. World legislators, they have made a mockery of the rights of property, the anxieties of morality, the suffering of religion and the cries of humanity . . . Oh! how many blows have they struck against wretched humanity, which will only resound for posterity!

But their laughter did not last. The sect to which they gave birth crushed them first of all under the consequences of their own principles. "Alas!" cried one of them, as he took his own life, "we found only a labyrinth at the bottom of an abyss!" The others have perished on the scaffold, and their ashes bathe in the tears and the blood of a million victims. Some, more unfortunate perhaps, drag their miseries throughout Europe, without remorse (for all fanatics die without remorse). They demand to return to their prey, or some other land to regenerate. They cannot imagine the appalling mistakes of their proselytes. "What," they cry, "are our disciples and our satellites become our executioners?"

They have already been answered by the man [John Milton] who best de- scribed the devils in hell. It is because in a kingdom of anarchy you were building a bridge over chaos. But when you wished to pass over, monsters disputed your approach to it. Terrified by this apparition, you retreated, and the monsters said to you: "Why do you retreat? You are our fathers!"

It is sad, perhaps, that such metaphors should be only pale imitations of what we have to see and endure. And I cannot help remarking here how well-timed were the deaths of Rousseau, Helvétius, Diderot, d'Alembert and Voltaire. By leaving us on the eve of our misfortunes, they carried with them the approval of their times. They do not have to weep over the revolution which they brought about, they do not have to blush to receive the compliments of the Convention. If they were still alive, they would be cursed by the victims who once praised them, and massacred by the executioners who speak of them as gods.

The most eloquent of these philosophers [Rousseau] said that children were of necessity little philosophers; therefore philosophers must of necessity be grown-up children. But Hobbes has proved that the wicked man is only a lusty child: therefore our philosophers are wicked men.

The Fallacy of Enlightenment

All their fallacies can be reduced to one only: to the miracle of a sudden enlightenment of everyone's mind, and of a universal propagation of understanding amongst all peoples. They said: "We shall eliminate national differences by means of commerce; political boundaries by means of philanthropy; high rank and condition by means of equality; governments by means of liberty; and all religions by means of incredulity. Philosophy has only its torch for a scepter, and the great families of the human race will walk in its light."

But the everlasting nature of things at once showed itself contrary to these vast pretentions. Enlightenment is lofty, not broad in scope. It moves ever upwards, not along the surface of things. It becomes known to the vulgar by increasingly numerous effects, never through theories. And like Providence, the arts spread greater and greater benefits, without becoming less difficult. On the contrary, the light they shed comes from an increasingly lofty source. And so knowledge which reaches too great heights is finally treated by the people as magic, as much admired as it is little understood. Balloons have roused in ordinary people no conjectures about atmospheric theory; lightning rods none about electricity; pendulums none about the laws of motion; finally, the discoveries of geometry did not turn the people from the four rules of arithmetic, and the almanac teaches nobody astronomy. It is therefore certain that as science reaches greater heights it escapes the common folk.

And so it is progress in concentration, and not the spread of enlightenment, which should be the aim of sound minds. For in spite of all the efforts of a century of philosophy, the most civilized kingdoms will always be as close to barbarism as the most polished blade is to rust: nations, like metals, shine only on the surface. The people reject or adopt scientific methods as they would reject or adopt their opposites: always lacking in convictions, they give to truth, as well as to error, an approval born of imitation, an obedience born of captivation, and an enthusiasm born of novelty. The educated man is right to think and say about the people what the people cannot say or think about him: for he knows the people and the people do not know him. Therefore the man of science should be consulted about the people and not the people about the man of science. The will of the people may be to burn the public library or the collections of natural history. But the will of the man of science will never be to destroy the workshops and storehouses of the people.

It can be stated as a principle that, in this world, the ignorant and the weak render tacit consent to knowledge and power. The philosophers were well aware of this. But they believed that knowledge and power would never be separated, and that the gun and the printing press would always be in the same hands. Experience has cruelly disabused them: from the day the philosopher Robespierre had power, he oppressed knowledge. His murderers abhor his name, but they adore his principles, and still profit from his crimes. The world is still threatened with one of those intervals of darkness so fatal to the human race; a time of interrupted progress, of kingdoms refashioned, of new men and strange superstitions; an unhappy time, in which destructive savagery is mingled with speculative subtlety; when the ancient constructions of the arts are combined with the bizarre and fleeting emblems of change. . . .

The Fallacy of Absolute Equality

Instead of ordaining that the law should be equal for all men, they decreed that men were naturally equal, without restriction. But what can never be made equal by decree are condition, rank and fortune. If they had said that all conditions should be equal, they would have been laughed at; so they only decreed the equality of men, thus preferring danger to ridicule. I say danger, for men being declared equal, and conditions remaining unequal, the result had to be a fearful conflict. Fortunately, the decrees of philosophers are not laws of nature: nature desired men to be equal, but of unequal state and fortune, as we desire unequal rings for unequal fingers, which leads to general harmony. In the same way, the addition of uneven numbers in geometry results in even ones, while uneven plus even numbers would never produce anything but uneven ones. How does it help men to be declared equal if their conditions must remain unequal? On the contrary we should rejoice to see

men of very little ability in very inferior positions; just as we should be distressed if brutish men were placed in the highest position and men of genius
pushed back into base, mechanical employment. Inequality is thus the
moving spirit of the body politic, the efficient cause of regular function and
order. But the word equality dissolves both politics and humanity: therefore
it weakens the two fundamental supports of the social order.

Moreover, this sophistry, although it has been the source of endless evils,
deludes nobody. If you say to some disciple of the revolution, "You are not
my fellow-man, nor my neighbor," he will laugh. But if you say to him, "You
are not my equal," he will slaughter you. This is because he believes in the
resemblance which is obvious, and does not need to be proved; and because
he does not believe in equality, so has to prove it by violence. . . .

Not only would it be impossible for the philosophers to found a social order
on the dogma of equality, but they could not even make a stage play, which
is but a pale imitation of life, out of it. Let us never forget that any principle
from which we cannot or dare not draw the consequences, is not a
principle. . . .

The Nature of Ethics and Religion

The radical vice of philosophy is its inability to speak to the heart. Now the
mind is only a part of man, but the heart is everything. The mind has often
been compared to fire. But the intelligence can only possess light. Warmth is
in the heart. The mind can only illuminate things. Only the heart can enter
into and identify them. That is why ethics, which speaks to the heart, owes so
little to the philosophical spirit. Conscience does not make discoveries: vice
and virtue are its two poles, it touches them at every moment. The ancients
prescribed ethics for everyone, and kept their theoretical mysteries for their
disciples; the moderns prescribed philosophy for everybody, and ethics for
no-one.

So religion, even the most ill-conceived, is infinitely more favorable to political order, and more adapted to human nature in general, than philosophy,
because it does not ask man to love God with all his mind, but with all his
heart. It approaches the generous and sensitive side of us, which is much the
same in all individuals; and not the reasoning, unequal, and limited side,
which we call the mind. Even if religions were regarded as a body of superstitions, they would nevertheless be benefactors of the human race. For there
is in the heart of man a religious fiber that nothing can eradicate, which is
always stirred by hope and fear. It is a question, then, of giving man stabilized
fears and hopes. Vague superstition would only cause misfortunes: this is a

weakness which stability changes into strength. Metals are to be found all
over the world. Each government marks them with its stamp, which produces
a feeling of confidence born of stability. In the same way, superstition is
everywhere; every nation marks it with its stamp and so stabilizes it. And
what so many religions have in common that is good and admirable, is the
feeling they encourage, the relationship between man and God. If, through a
happy combination of too rare causes, there were to be established on this
earth a more universal cult, the human race should consider itself blessed, as
it would do if it had more universal coins and measures.

Nothing is good but what is unified and stabilized, nothing harmful but what
is novel and diversified. Public opinion, that bugbear which the philosophers
of our day have used to scare governments, has its home in fact amongst the
public, that idle, uncertain and changeable portion of the political body. The
opinions of the people are peaceable, universal and always shared by the
government: whether they be judgments or prejudices, it does not matter;
they are good, because they are stable. And that is why custom so successfully upholds law. In the conflict of ideas, plans and projects spawned by
men, victory is not called truth, but stability. Therefore the people need not
reasoning but decision; not demonstrations but authority. Genius in politics
consists not in creating but in preserving; not in changing but in stabilizing. It
consists, in short, in making up for truths by use of maxims, for it is not the
best, but the most stable law, which is the good one. Take a look at philosophical opinions: one by one they are placed on Time's grindstone, which
first gives them edge and brilliancy, and ends by wearing them away. Look at
all the brilliant founders of so many sects! Their theories are barely numbered
amongst the dreams of the human mind. And their systems are only variations in a tale which varies continually. . . .

The Primacy of the Political

We know that there have been men who, from the standpoint of the physical
order, have drawn conclusions for the moral order: "God," they say, "does
not punish crimes. Therefore, he is indifferent to them. A murder in the eyes
of nature is only a piece of steel plunged into some drops of blood. A lie is
only an empty sound which strikes the air." These and a host of other
sophisms are as fearful in their consequences as they are horrible in their
design.

We know the noble answer of Cicero and Cato to Caesar, who allowed himself
to make such arguments in favor of Catilina and his accomplices. Caesar,
speaking like a true philosopher of our time, said that nothing was less certain
than the immortality of the soul, the greatest evil that could befall man being

the loss of life. Cato and Cicero rose. Without discussing the immortality of the soul, they observed to the senate that Caesar was professing a doctrine that would be fatal to the republic and to the human race. They answered like real philosophers, because they were speaking like statesmen. Caesar wanted the senate to become a school of philosophy. He was establishing metaphysical principles, in order to draw political conclusions, which is a sophistry we have already denounced. . . .

Let us not therefore be surprised that governments so readily come to an agreement with religion. But between them and the philosophers there can be no treaty. To please the latter, governments either have to abdicate or allow them to stir up the people. In a word, philosophy divides men through their opinions, religion unites them in the same dogma, and politics in the same principles. Therefore there is an everlasting contract between politics and religion. Every state, if I may say so, is a mysterious vessel anchored in heaven.

The true philosopher who understands this mystery leaves faith in the place of knowledge, and fear in the place of reason. He does so because he cannot undertake to educate the people. He can neither bend by force of habit, nor elevate by improvement of the faculties, the minds and hearts of a multitude destined to labor and sensation, not to leisure and reasoning. He would gain nothing by saying to the people: "Be just, because there reigns a mighty harmony in the universe." This is not the way politics deals with the passions. It considers man, not only with the eye of the law, but with the eyes of morality and religion. It makes use of *everything* in the difficult art of governing. It requires instruction from morality and strength from religion. It borrows enlightenment even from philosophy. Finally, it takes the reins in both hands.

The crime of the modern philosophers is to have made the gift of incredulity to men who would never have discovered it by themselves. For those who have the misfortune to reach that point by meditation or by long study, either are rich people, or calm and lofty minds, kept in their place by the general harmony. Their education and their fortune serve as guarantees to society. But the people, incited by everything around them to be restless, and unaware of the order to which they belong, are left without fear and without hope, as soon as they are without faith.

I appeal even to our philosophers: when philosophy began its revolution in their minds, did it not find them inured by government and religion to good conduct and good principles? It is certain therefore that modern philosophy has been gleaning in the fields of religion and politics: if it found men as it thinks they are, or as it would like to fashion them, it would soon discover only monsters. So the limitations of its outlook, its confusion and its inadequacy have never appeared more obvious than at a time when it became all-powerful and realized its dream of a nation of philosophers. It then became only too obvious that in order to live in ease and leisure, one must be surrounded by hard-working men. And to live without prejudice, one must be surrounded by a nation of believers. Incredulity is a fearful luxury. . . .

It is in vain that Aristotle defined law as a mind without passion. The philosophers, once they had become supreme, listened only to the voice and spoke only the language of the passions. They saw the world, reason and posterity as actors on the narrow and turbulent stage of their tribunes. They took contagiousness for success. They admired everything until the day they became afraid. Death and exile caught them between what they had wished to do and what they had done—I mean between their ambitious dreams and their foolish performances. Vanquished, they deserved their defeat without it being possible to say that their conquerors deserved their success: one cannot speak of them with justice without appearing to speak of them with scorn. What can we think, indeed, of a legislature that persistently declared: "Ah! if only nature and necessity had allowed us to do as we wished!"

Will they now allege that time and good fortune failed them during their government? It was marked by four years, I will not say of submission, but of enthusiasm. Will they complain of lack of understanding and of warnings? We can cite for them all the predictions that they laughed at, the clamors and tears of the landowners that they made mock of, the efforts and plans of the monsters that they knew and favored. Was it not in the revolutionary assemblies that the daily laws and decrees were drawn up? Was it not there that the people's representatives went to bolster up the authority which they displayed in the legislative body? Had not the titles of patriot and revolutionary become synonymous? "But we cut no one's throat!" they will say. A fine humaneness, to leave life to those from whom you take away the means of living! You forgot to cut throats: in your criminal progress this is the only omission that we know of, and we are reduced to explaining away the evil that you did not commit. If you claim not to be responsible for the inordinate crimes of your allies, posterity which, better than we do, knows where to direct its scorn and hatred, will pronounce sentence. It will judge between those who prepared the victim, and those who sacrificed it; between those who planned the crime, and those who carried it out. It will discover whether principles are not always more to blame than consequences (and modern philosophy is nothing but passions armed with principles). . . . Only the brute beast bites the stone which is thrown at it: but man can see the hand which strikes him, and the philosophers will not be able to trick us out of our suffering. In the end, posterity will say to what extent the people themselves deserved their misfortunes. For they were the instruments before they became the victims, inhuman before they became wretched. And prosperity had blinded them even before power had led their leaders astray.

Others, not I, will describe that reign of terror, in which, to the eternal humiliation of ambitious men without genius, we saw the most obscure disciple of modern philosophy [Robespierre] rise to supreme power along a path which the philosophers themselves had opened to him with their own hands, and paved with their heads. . . This fearful crisis was called the revolutionary government: an undefinable expression, a monstrous coupling of words, prepared by the philosophy of our times!. . . The signal is given: no more constitutional authority. Everything must be a committee or a revolutionary tribunal. The sovereignty of the people is suspended. Its representatives are chosen for life, but are no longer inviolable; for one must die and another must govern. The entire nation finds itself irresponsible and conspiratorial, a minor in its actions, and of age when it comes to punishment. It sinks and struggles under the knives of a hundred thousand assassins. . . .

What is this huge, mysterious vehicle, whose innumerable wheels travel everywhere, loaded with scaffolds, with severed heads and broken scepters? It is the juggernaut of the revolution. And these hideous, ragged people, with haggard eyes and bloody hands crowding around the juggernaut? This is a revolutionary people . . . But the juggernaut advances, crushing everything. It drives onwards through the public squares, through the streets, before the gates, traversing France, dragging down or crushing a thousand victims a day, and night cannot slow its course. On the juggernaut sits Revolution, brandishing suspicion, the axe in her hand. The dismal sound of her advance drowns that of war, and the cannon which slaughters in the distance seems gentle and splendid to the imagination profoundly disturbed by the mighty, continual, muffled thudding of the guillotine. . . .

Modern philosophy, whither have you led us? Into whose hands have you delivered us? Are these your saturnalia, your triumphs, and your orgies?. . . Black night descended in the name of enlightenment! Widespread tyranny in the name of liberty! Profound delirium in the name of reason! Bloody outrages, calculated insults, inhuman indignities, we cannot describe you too faithfully, if it is to serve a purpose, nor speak of you with too much restraint, if we are to be believed!

Chapter Two

Karl Marx's Concept of Ideology

A common modern notion is that men's values reflect their economic position in society; that they are rationalizations of economic interests. This is essentially a vulgarized version of Marx's concept of ideology. Like most vulgarizations of theoretical concepts, it catches something of the central meaning of the original, but over-simplifies that meaning; and what is worse, it ignores the reasoning that was basic to the original. This introduction and the readings by Marx are designed to reveal both the complexity of the original and the reasoning by which it is supported.

The simplest version of Marx's concept of ideology is the one which appears in the *Communist Manifesto* (1848). It takes the form of a dramatic rhetorical question: "Does it require deep intuition to comprehend that man's ideas, views, and conceptions, in one word, man's consciousness, change with every change in the conditions of his material existence, in his social relations, and in his social life?"[1] The proposition that man's ideas are but reflections of the changing modes of his material and social existence appeared, in 1848, to be both clear and obvious. But this proposition had been neither clear nor obvious to Marx a few years earlier. Indeed, he was

[1] Lewis S. Feuer, ed., *Basic Writings on Politics and Philosophy: Karl Marx and Friedrich Engels* (Garden City, N.Y.: Doubleday & Co., Inc., 1959), p. 26.

well aware that it was a highly simplified statement of his own maturing understanding of the relation between physical existence and thinking, an understanding which had evolved only in the course of a lengthy, complex criticism of preceding and contemporary philosophers. It is impossible to state here the full scope and significance of that criticism. But it is necessary to sketch those aspects of it which are most relevant to his concept of ideology.

This criticism was part of an epic struggle between philosophical idealism and philosophical materialism. To Marx idealism was the view that thinking or spirit is primary, while materialism held that being or nature is primary. Idealism posits the subordination of material existence and man's physical existence to thinking or spirit, and it concludes that man's consciousness ultimately determines his existence. Conversely, materialism posits that thought is dependent upon material existence, above all upon man's physical relations with nature and with other men. Its conclusion is that these conditions determine his consciousness.

Marx was caught up in this philosophical struggle at an early age. As a law student, in Bonn and then in Berlin, he at first came under the influence of the philosophical idealism of Immanuel Kant (1724-1804) and Johann Gottlieb Fichte (1762-1814). But even at this stage he complained that in attempting to construct a "philosophy of law" derived from idealism, he had experienced ". . . the disturbing influence of that opposition between what is and what should be which is the special characteristic of idealism. . . ."[2] Troubled by this sense of opposition, he increasingly felt the need to clarify his philosophical position.

This process of clarification was helped by Marx's participation (1836-1837) in the discussions of a philosophical club—discussions that probed the very questions that troubled him. Simultaneously it was hindered because most members of the club were followers of the most formidable philosophical idealist of them all, G. W. F. Hegel, who had died only recently, in 1831. Marx appreciated the stimulation of the discussions yet resisted the necessity of carrying them on within the framework of the very idealism he felt was somehow defective. He was also handicapped at first by his relative ignorance of Hegel's thought, which he had once satirically dismissed as a "grotesque melody of the grottoes."[3] Now, under the challenge of these discussions, he

[2]H. P. Adams, *Karl Marx In His Earlier Writings* (New York: Russell & Russell, Inc., 1965), p. 22.

[3]*Ibid.*, p. 23.

plunged into ferocious study of Hegel's works, with the intention of coming to terms with this paradigm of idealism.

The study of Hegel was decisive, and it supplied the germs of Marx's concept of ideology. First, it supplied the germ of the notion that man's ideas about himself and his social world are not static but evolutionary. It did so by introducing Marx to the dazzling power of Hegel's conception that the world and all its parts must be understood historically, as a developmental process. And Hegel introduced Marx to the method of analysis by which that process must be understood: the dialectic. That method is the technique of analyzing a given phenomenon into developmental stages. In the dialectic, the motive power for the transition from stage to stage is supplied by the inherent internal conflicts or contradictions in each developmental stage. Each successive step goes beyond yet retains the elements of each preceding stage.

In later years, Marx recognized the profound influence of Hegel's historical conception of philosophy and of the dialectic method by which that conception is brought to bear. In the preface to the first edition of his master-work, *Capital: A Critique of Political Economy* (1867), Marx said that his standpoint was to view the "economic formation of society" as a "process of natural history."[4] And in the preface to the second edition (1873), he makes clear both his debt and his opposition to Hegel:

My dialectic method is not only different from the Hegelian, but is its direct opposite. To Hegel, the life-process of the human brain, i.e., the process of thinking, which, under the name of "the Idea," he even transforms into an independent subject, is the demiurgos of the real world, and the real world is only the external, phenomenal form of "the Idea." With me, on the contrary, the ideal is nothing else than the material world reflected by the human mind, and translated into forms of thoughts.[5]

Marx's study of Hegel also produced the germ of the notion that man's ideas are the product of material existence. It did this indirectly and ironically by leading Marx into the study of materialism. For in reading Hegel's *History of Philosophy*, Marx noticed that the later Greek philosophers received more cursory treatment than the earlier ones. Marx thus conceived the project of a doctoral dissertation which would compare the philosophy of nature of two Greek materialists, Democritus (c. 460-370 B.C.) and Epicurus (c. 340-270 B.C.).

---

[4] Karl Marx, *Capital: A Critique of Political Economy*, Modern Library Edition (New York: Random House, Inc., n.d.), p. 15.

[5] *Ibid.*, p. 25.

The character of Marx's treatment of these philosophers was heavily influenced by Hegel.[6] But the materialism of the ancient Greek philosophers —particularly that of Epicurus—powerfully appealed to Marx. It is possible that Marx conceived of himself as a modern Epicurus, whose materialism would stand in a dialectical relationship to the idealism of Hegel, just as he conceived that Epicurus' materialism stood in such a relationship to Plato's idealism.

From this time Marx was increasingly attracted to materialist philosophy, especially to materialist criticism of Hegelian philosophy. Such "criticism" consisted of internal and external analyses of the Hegelian system. Its purpose was to show that Hegel, for all his genius, had misunderstood the nature of human consciousness; and its main weapons were concepts and arguments derived from what Marx understood as modern English and French materialism.

Marx saw such materialism in the philosophies of Francis Bacon, Thomas Hobbes and John Locke in England, and Condillac, Helvétius, and Holbach in France. The sense in which he considered such philosophy materialist is conveyed in passages such as these:

The real ancestor of *English materialism* and all *modern experimental* science is Bacon. For him natural science is true science and *physics* based on sense perception is the outstanding part of natural science. *Anaxagoras* with his *homoeomeria* [simple substances] and Democritus with his atoms are frequently quoted as his authorities. According to his doctrine, the senses are infallible and the *source* of all knowledge.

In his essay on the origin of human understanding *Locke* provided the basis for Bacon and Hobbes' principle [that our knowledge and ideas originate from the world of the senses.]

In *Helvetius*, who . . . took Locke for his starting point, materialism received its real French character . . . Sensuous qualities and self-love, pleasure and enlightened self-interest are the bases of all morality. The natural equality of human intelligence, the unity between the progress of reason and the progress of industry, the natural goodness of man, the omnipotence of education are the principal features of his system.[7]

The content and brevity of these remarks reflect the sweeping character of the larger thesis being elaborated—that there is a dialectical development in modern philosophy and that this development is the external or theoretical expression of the dialectical development of modern modes of life. Marx

[6]See Adams, *op. cit.*, pp. 27-41.

[7]Loyd D. Easton and Kurt H. Guddat, translators and editors, *Writings of the Young Marx on Philosophy and Society* (Garden City, Doubleday & Co., Inc., 1967), pp. 391, 392, 393. Reprinted by permission of Doubleday & Company, Inc.

argues that the eighteenth-century French philosophical materialism of Helvétius and the others is "explained [by the] practical form of French life at the time." In other words, the "anti-theological, anti-metaphysical, materialistic practice" required the appearance of theories which corresponded to it.[8]

The materialist criticism that had attracted Marx was directed, first, against Hegel's understanding of religion. Men such as Ludwig Feuerbach had attempted to show that, contrary to Hegel, "man makes religion" rather than vice versa. Hegelian idealism conceives of religion as a spiritual manifestation of man's development, but to his critics this is an illusion which conceals from man the truth of his existence in this world. Marx, in an early work which criticizes Hegel's *Philosophy of Right*, called religion ". . . only the illusory sun about which man revolves so long as he does not revolve about himself."[9]

This criticism of religion shows the illusory character of man's ideas about his gods, but it is only the preliminary stage of criticism. The definitive stage of materialist criticism deals with the equally illusive quality of man's ideas concerning this world—above all his ideas concerning politics, law, and economic relations. It shows the fundamental deficiencies in the Hegelian and other idealist understandings of these ideas. It is here that Marx's understanding of Bacon, Locke, and Helvétius as materialists is brought fully to bear. And it is here that Marx's later, elaborate economic studies have their root. As he worked through the early versions of his criticism, Marx came to the conclusion that only by means of such studies could the actual relations of ideas to material existence—summarized in the proposition that men's ideas are essentially reflections of their material conditions—be revealed in detail. Marx had to examine this proposition with respect to the dominant mode of production in the modern era—capitalism.

The German Ideology (1845-1846) was written in collaboration with Engels. It is a lengthy polemical work, undertaken as part of that criticism of Hegelian idealism which forms the basis of later, more specifically economic works by Marx—*A Contribution to the Critique of Political Economy* (1859), and *Capital* (1867).

---

[8]*Ibid.*, p. 389. Reprinted by permission of Doubleday & Company, Inc.

[9]Karl Marx, "Contribution to the Critique of Hegel's Philosophy of Right," in T. B. Bottomore, translator and editor, *Karl Marx: Early Writings* (New York: McGraw-Hill Book Co., 1964), p. 44.

The title of *The German Ideology* is revealing; Marx treats German philosophy of the first part of the nineteenth century in terms of the concept of ideology, and thus foreshadows the twentieth century tendency to equate ideology and philosophy. The reasoning behind his equation of ideology and philosophy is presented in detail in this work, in contrast to Marx's statements in *Capital* or in the *Communist Manifesto*.

The first selections are from the first part of *The German Ideology*, entitled, "Feuerbach: Opposition of the Materialistic and Idealistic Outlook." It criticizes Feuerbach and others for their failure to extend the materialist critique to secular ideas, and also contains lengthy statements on Marx and Engels' conception of the evolution of human society and ideas.

Marx's *Capital* presupposes the validity of the concept of ideology set forth in earlier works such as *The German Ideology*. *Capital* contains many specific applications of that concept, even though they are not always identified by that term.

The selection from *Capital* is a revealing example of the mature Marx's application of this concept, because it occurs in the context of a discussion of a fundamental Marxian economic concept—value. It also provides insight into the way Marx applied the concept of ideology to a classical philosopher's thought.

In the passage, Marx is discussing the nature of commodities, particularly whether, and in what sense, commodities can be said to possess an abstract value. Marx's argument is that the concept of value is dependent on the prior appearance of the capitalist mode of production of commodities. In the course of this argument, Marx turns briefly to comment on a passage in Aristotle's *Ethics* (Bk. V, ch. 5, 13-15). Marx's reduction of Aristotle's understanding of value to the "consciousness" of a man who lived in a society "founded upon slavery" is in sharp contrast to his praise of Aristotle as "the great thinker who was the first to analyse so many forms, whether of thought, society, or nature."

The last selection in this chapter, from Karl Federn's *The Materialist Conception of History* (1939), is an historian's critical analysis of Marx's basic theory. Federn states that theory in a series of 15 propositions, then criticizes each individually. He advances general arguments against the "single-cause" quality of the theory and presents a number of historical examples which he feels undercut the basis of the theory.

Federn singles out Marx's proposition that man's ideas are determined by the material modes of production as the key problem. He then seeks to show that with respect to religion, law, politics, art, science, and so on, the historical facts defy the categorization of Marx's concept of ideology.

From *The German Ideology**

Karl Marx
and Friedrich Engels

Ideology in General, German Ideology in Particular

German criticism has, right up to its latest efforts, never quitted the realm of philosophy. Far from examining its general philosophic premises, the whole body of its inquiries has actually sprung from the soil of a definite philosophical system, that of Hegel. Not only in their answers but in their very questions there was a mystification. This dependence on Hegel is the reason why not one of these modern critics has even attempted a comprehensive criticism of the Hegelian system, however much each professes to have advanced beyond Hegel. . . .

It has not occurred to any one of these philosophers to inquire into the connection of German philosophy with German reality, the relation of their criticism to their own material surroundings.

The premises from which we begin are not arbitrary ones, not dogmas, but real premises from which abstraction can only be made in the imagination. They are the real individuals, their activity and the material conditions under which they live, both those which they find already existing and those produced by their activity. These premises can thus be verified in a purely empirical way.

The first premise of all human history is, of course, the existence of living human individuals. Thus the first fact to be established is the physical organization of these individuals and their consequent relation to the rest of nature. Of course, we cannot here go either into the actual physical nature of man, or into the natural conditions in which man finds himself—geological, orohydrographical, climatic and so on. The writing of history must always set out from

*Karl Marx and Friedrich Engels, *The German Ideology*, edited by R. Pascal (New York: International Publishers Co., Inc., 1939), pp. 4, 6-7, 13-15, 19-21, 22-23, 39-43.
Reprinted by permission of International Publishers Co., Inc. Copyright © 1939.

these natural bases and their modification in the course of history through the action of man.

Men can be distinguished from animals by consciousness, by religion or anything else you like. They themselves begin to distinguish themselves from animals as soon as they begin to *produce* their means of subsistence, a step which is conditioned by their physical organization. By producing their means of subsistence men are indirectly producing their actual material life.

The way in which men produce their means of subsistence depends first of all on the nature of the actual means they find in existence and have to reproduce. This mode of production must not be considered simply as being the reproduction of the physical existence of the individuals. Rather it is a definite form of activity of these individuals, a definite form of expressing their life, a definite *mode of life* on their part. As individuals express their life, so they are. What they are, therefore, coincides with their production, both with *what* they produce and with *how* they produce. The nature of individuals thus depends on the material conditions determining their production. . . .

The fact is, therefore, that definite individuals who are productively active in a definite way enter into these definite social and political relations. Empirical observation must in each separate instance bring out empirically, and without any mystification and speculation, the connection of the social and political structure with production. The social structure and the State are continually evolving out of the life-process of definite individuals, but of individuals, not as they may appear in their own or other people's imagination, but as they really are; i.e. as they are effective, produce materially, and are active under definite material limits, presuppositions and conditions independent of their will.

The production of ideas, of conceptions, of consciousness, is at first directly interwoven with the material activity and the material intercourse of men, the language of real life. Conceiving, thinking, the mental intercourse of men, appear at this stage as the direct efflux of their material behaviour. The same applies to mental production as expressed in the language of the politics, laws, morality, religion, metaphysics of a people. Men are the producers of their conceptions, ideas, etc.—real, active men, as they are conditioned by a definite development of their productive forces and of the intercourse corresponding to these, up to its furthest forms. Consciousness can never be anything else than conscious existence, and the existence of men is their actual life-process. If in all ideology men and their circumstances appear upside down . . . this phenomenon arises just as much from their historical life-process as the inversion of objects on the retina does from their physical life-process.

In direct contrast to German philosophy which descends from heaven to earth, here we ascend from earth to heaven. That is to say, we do not set out from what men say, imagine, conceive, nor from men as narrated, thought of, imagined, conceived, in order to arrive at men in the flesh. We set out from real, active men, and on the basis of their real life-process we demonstrate the development of the ideological reflexes and echoes of this life-process. The phantoms formed in the human brain are also, necessarily, sublimates of their material life-process, which is empirically verifiable and bound to material premises. Morality, religion, metaphysics, all the rest of ideology and their corresponding forms of consciousness, thus no longer retain the semblance of independence. They have no history, no development; but men, developing their material production and their material intercourse, alter, along with this their real existence, their thinking and the products of their thinking. Life is not determined by consciousness, but consciousness by life. In the first method of approach the starting-point is consciousness taken as the living individual; in the second it is the real living individuals themselves, as they are in actual life, and consciousness is considered solely as *their* consciousness.

This method of approach is not devoid of premises. It starts out from the real premises and does not abandon them for a moment. Its premises are men, not in any fantastic isolation or abstract definition, but in their actual, empirically perceptible process of development under definite conditions. As soon as this active life-process is described, history ceases to be a collection of dead facts as it is with the empiricists (themselves still abstract), or an imagined activity of imagined subjects, as with the idealists.

Where speculation ends—in real life—there real, positive science begins: the representation of the practical activity, of the practical process of development of men. Empty talk about consciousness ceases, and real knowledge has to take its place. When reality is depicted, philosophy as an independent branch of activity loses its medium of existence. At the best its place can only be taken by a summing-up of the most general results, abstractions which arise from the observation of the historical development of men. Viewed apart from real history, these abstractions have in themselves no value whatsoever. They can only serve to facilitate the arrangement of historical material, to indicate the sequence of its separate strata. But they by no means afford a recipe or schema, as does philosophy, for neatly trimming the epochs of history. On the contrary, our difficulties begin only when we set about the observation and the arrangement—the real depiction—of our historical material, whether of a past epoch or of the present. . . . [Four "moments" or "aspects" of "fundamental historical relationships" are now stated: (1) men must be able to live in order to "make history"; (2) as soon as one need is satisfied, new needs arise; (3) men make things, but they also make other men, thus producing familial (social) as well as natural (physical) relations; (4) the mode of production of man's physical needs constantly undergoes change.]

Only now, after having considered four moments, four aspects of the fundamental historical relationships, do we find that man also possesses "consciousness"; but, even so, not inherent, not "pure" consciousness. From the start the "spirit" is afflicted with the curse of being "burdened" with matter, which here makes its appearance in the form of agitated layers of air, sounds, in short of language. Language is as old as consciousness, language is practical consciousness, as it exists for other men, and for that reason is really beginning to exist for me personally as well; for language, like consciousness, only arises from the need, the necessity, of intercourse with other men. Where there exists a relationship, it exists for me: the animal has no "relations" with anything, cannot have any. For the animal, its relation to others does not exist as a relation. Consciousness is therefore from the very beginning a social product, and remains so as long as men exist at all. Consciousness is at first, of course, merely consciousness concerning the immediate sensuous environment and consciousness of the limited connection with other persons and things outside the individual who is growing self-conscious. At the same time it is consciousness of nature, which first appears to men as a completely alien, all-powerful and unassailable force, with which men's relations are purely animal and by which they are overawed like beasts; it is thus a purely animal consciousness of nature (natural religion).

We see here immediately: this natural religion or animal behaviour towards nature is determined by the form of society and *vice versa*. Here, as everywhere, the identity of nature and man appears in such a way that the restricted relation of men to nature determines their restricted relation to one another, and their restricted relation to one another determines men's restricted relation to nature, just because nature is as yet hardly modified historically; and, on the other hand, man's consciousness of the necessity of associating with the individuals around him is the beginning of the consciousness that he is living in society at all. This beginning is as animal as social life itself at this stage. It is mere herd-consciousness, and at this point man is only distinguished from sheep by the fact that with him consciousness takes the place of instinct or that his instinct is a conscious one.

This sheep-like or tribal consciousness receives its further development and extension through increased productivity, the increase of needs, and, what is fundamental to both of these, the increase of population. With these there develops the division of labour, which was originally nothing but the division of labour in the sexual act, then that division of labour which develops spontaneously or "naturally" by virtue of natural predisposition (e.g. physical strength), needs, accidents, etc., etc. Division of labour only becomes truly such from the moment when a division of material and mental labour appears. From this moment onwards consciousness *can* really flatter itself that it is something other than consciousness of existing practice, that it is *really* conceiving something without conceiving something *real*; from now on consciousness is in a position to emancipate itself from the world and to proceed to the formation of "pure" theory, theology, philosophy, ethics, etc. But even if this theory, theology, philosophy, ethics, etc. comes into contradiction with the existing relations, this can only occur as a result of the fact that existing social relations have come into contradiction with existing forces of production; this, moreover, can also occur in a particular national sphere of relations through the appearance of the contradiction, not within the national orbit, but between this national consciousness and the practice of other nations, i.e., between the national and the general consciousness of a nation.

Moreover, it is quite immaterial what consciousness starts to do on its own: out of all such muck we get only the one inference that these three moments, the forces of production, the state of society, and consciousness, can and must come into contradiction with one another, because the division of labour implies the possibility, nay the fact that intellectual and material activity—enjoyment and labour, production and consumption—devolve on different individuals, and that the only possibility of their not coming into contradiction lies in the negation in its turn of the division of labour. It is self-evident, moreover, that "spectres," "bonds," "the higher being," "concept," "scruple," are merely the idealistic, spiritual expression, the conception apparently of the isolated individual, the image of very empirical fetters and limitations, within which the mode of production of life, and the form of intercourse coupled with it, move . . .

This crystallization of social activity, this consolidation of what we ourselves produce into an objective power above us, growing out of our control, thwarting our expectations, bringing to naught our calculations, is one of the chief factors in historical development up till now. And out of this very contradiction between the interest of the individual and that of the community the latter takes an independent form as the *State*, divorced from the real interests of individual and community, and at the same time as an illusory communal life, always based, however, on the real ties existing in every

family and tribal conglomeration (such as flesh and blood, language, division
of labour on a larger scale, and other interests) and especially, as we shall
enlarge upon later, on the classes, already determined by the division of
labour, which in every such mass of men separate out, and of which one
dominates all the others. It follows from this that all struggles within the
State, the struggle between democracy, aristocracy and monarchy, the
struggle for the franchise, etc., etc., are merely the illusory forms in which the
real struggles of the different classes are fought out among one another . . .

The ideas of the ruling class are in every epoch the ruling ideas: i.e. the class,
which is the ruling material force of society, is at the same time its ruling
intellectual force. The class which has the means of material production at its
disposal, has control at the same time over the means of mental production,
so that thereby, generally speaking, the ideas of those who lack the means of
mental production are subject to it. The ruling ideas are nothing more than
the ideal expression of the dominant material relationships, the dominant
material relationships grasped as ideas; hence of the relationships which make
the one class the ruling one, therefore the ideas of its dominance. The individuals composing the ruling class possess among other things consciousness,
and therefore think. In so far, therefore, as they rule as a class and determine
the extent and compass of an epoch, it is self-evident that they do this in
their whole range, hence among other things rule also as thinkers, as producers of ideas, and regulate the production and distribution of the ideas of
their age: thus their ideas are the ruling ideas of the epoch. For instance, in an
age and in a country where royal power, aristocracy and bourgeoisie are
contending for mastery and where, therefore, mastery is shared, the doctrine
of the separation of powers proves to be the dominant idea and is expressed
as an "eternal law." The division of labour, which we saw above as one of the
chief forces of history up till now, manifests itself also in the ruling class as
the division of mental and material labour, so that inside this class one part
appears as the thinkers of the class (its active, conceptive ideologists, who
make the perfecting of the illusion of the class about itself their chief source
of livelihood), while the others' attitude to these ideas and illusions is more
passive and receptive, because they are in reality the active members of this
class and have less time to make up illusions and ideas about themselves.
Within this class this cleavage can even develop into a certain opposition and
hostility between the two parts, which, however, in the case of a practical
collision, in which the class itself is endangered, automatically comes to
nothing, in which case there also vanishes the semblance that the ruling ideas
were not the ideas of the ruling class and had a power distinct from the power
of this class. The existence of revolutionary ideas in a particular period

presupposes the existence of a revolutionary class; about the premises for the latter sufficient has already been said above.

If now in considering the course of history we detach the ideas of the ruling class from the ruling class itself and attribute to them an independent existence, if we confine ourselves to saying that these or those ideas were dominant, without bothering ourselves about the conditions of production and the producers of these ideas, if we then ignore the individuals and world conditions which are the source of the ideas, we can say, for instance, that during the time that the aristocracy was dominant, the concepts honour, loyalty, etc., were dominant, during the dominance of the bourgeoisie the concepts freedom, equality, etc. The ruling class itself on the whole imagines this to be so. This conception of history, which is common to all historians, particularly since the eighteenth century, will necessarily come up against the phenomenon that increasingly abstract ideas hold sway, i.e. ideas which increasingly take on the form of universality. For each new class which puts itself in the place of one ruling before it, is compelled, merely in order to carry through its aim, to represent its interest as the common interest of all the members of society, put in an ideal form; it will give its ideas the form of universality, and represent them as the only rational, universally valid ones. The class making a revolution appears from the very start, merely because it is opposed to a *class*, not as a class but as the representative of the whole of society; it appears as the whole mass of society confronting the one ruling class. It can do this because, to start with, its interest really is more connected with the common interest of all other non-ruling classes, because under the pressure of conditions its interest has not yet been able to develop as the particular interest of a particular class. Its victory, therefore, benefits also many individuals of the other classes which are not winning a dominant position, but only in so far as it now puts these individuals in a position to raise themselves into the ruling class. When the French bourgeoisie overthrew the power of the aristocracy, it thereby made it possible for many proletarians to raise themselves above the proletariat, but only in so far as they became bourgeois. Every new class, therefore, achieves its hegemony only on a broader basis than that of the class ruling previously, in return for which the opposition of the non-ruling class against the new ruling class later develops all the more sharply and profoundly. Both these things determine the fact that the struggle to be waged against this new ruling class, in its turn, aims at a more decided and radical negation of the previous conditions of society than could all previous classes which sought to rule.

This whole semblance, that the rule of a certain class is only the rule of certain ideas, comes to a natural end, of course, as soon as society ceases at last to be organized in the form of class-rule, that is to say as soon as it is no longer necessary to represent a particular interest as general or "the general interest" as ruling.

Once the ruling ideas have been separated from the ruling individuals and, above all, from the relationships which result from a given stage of the mode of production, and in this way the conclusion has been reached that history is always under the sway of ideas, it is very easy to abstract from these various ideas "the idea," "die Idee," etc., as the dominant force in history, and thus to understand all these separate ideas and concepts as "forms of self-determination" on the part of *the* concept developing in history. It follows then naturally, too, that all the relationships of men can be derived from the concept of man, man as conceived, the essence of man, *man*. This has been done by the speculative philosophers. Hegel himself confesses at the end of *The Philosophy of History* that he "has considered the progress of *the concept* only" and has represented in history "the true theodicy." Now one can go back again to the "producers of the concept," to the theoreticians, ideologists and philosophers, and one comes then to the conclusion that the philosophers, the thinkers as such, have at all times been dominant in history: a conclusion, as we see, already expressed by Hegel. The whole trick of proving the hegemony of the spirit in history . . . is thus confined to the following three tricks.

1.   One must separate the ideas of those ruling for empirical reasons, under empirical conditions and as empirical individuals, from these actual rulers, and thus recognize the rule of ideas or illusions in history.

2.   One must bring an order into this rule of ideas, prove a mystical connection among the successive ruling ideas, which is managed by understanding them as "acts of self-determination on the part of the concept" (this is possible because by virtue of their empirical basis these ideas are really connected with one another and because, conceived as *mere* ideas, they become self-distinctions, distinctions made by thought).

3.   To remove the mystical appearance of this "self-determining concept" it is changed into a person—"self-consciousness"—or, to appear thoroughly materialistic, into a series of persons, who represent the "concept" in history, into the "thinkers," the "philosophers," the ideologists, who again are understood as the manufacturers of history, as "the council of guardians," as the rulers. Thus the whole body of materialistic elements has been removed from history and now full rein can be given to the speculative steed.

Whilst in ordinary life every shopkeeper is very well able to distinguish between what somebody professes to be and what he really is, our historians have not yet won even this trivial insight. They take every epoch at its word and believe that everything it says and imagines about itself is true.

This historical method which reigned in Germany (and especially the reason why), must be understood from its connection with the illusion of ideologists in general, e.g. the illusions of the jurists, politicians (of the practical states-men among them, too), from the dogmatic dreamings and distortions of these fellows; this illusion is explained perfectly easily from their practical position in life, their job, and the division of labour. . . .

From *Capital**

Karl Marx

[Certain peculiarities of the forms in which "value" may appear will] . . . become more intelligible if we go back to the great thinker who was the first to analyse so many forms, whether of thought, society, or nature, and amongst them also the form of value. I mean Aristotle.

In the first place, he clearly enunciates that the money form of commodities is only the further development of the simple form of value—*i.e.*, of the expression of the value of one commodity in some other commodity taken at random; for he says

5 beds = 1 house . . . is not to be distinguished from
5 beds = so much money. . .

He further sees that the value relation which gives rise to this expression makes it necessary that the house should qualitatively be made the equal of the bed, and that, without such an equalization, these two clearly different things could not be compared with each other as commensurable quantities. "Exchange," he says, "cannot take place without equality, and equality not without commensurability". . . Here, however, he comes to a stop, and gives up the further analysis of the form of value. "It is, however, in reality, impossible . . . that such unlike things can be commensurable" *i.e.*, qualitatively equal.

---

*Karl Marx, *Capital: A Critique of Political Economy*, Modern Library Edition (New York: Random House, Inc., n.d.), pp. 68-69.

Such an equalisation can only be something foreign to their real nature, consequently only "a make-shift for practical purposes."

Aristotle therefore, himself, tells us, what barred the way to his further analysis; it was the absence of any concept of value. What is that equal something, that common substance, which admits of the value of the beds being expressed by a house? Such a thing, in truth, cannot exist, says Aristotle. And why not? Compared with the beds, the house does represent something equal to them, in so far as it represents what is really equal, both in the beds and the house. And that is—human labour.

There was, however, an important fact which prevented Aristotle from seeing that, to attribute value to commodities, is merely a mode of expressing all labour as equal human labour, and consequently as labour of equal quality. Greek society was founded upon slavery, and had, therefore, for its natural basis, the inequality of men and of their labour powers. The secret of the expression of value, namely, that all kinds of labour are equal and equivalent, because, and so far as they are human labour in general, cannot be deciphered, until the notion of human equality has already acquired the fixity of a popular prejudice. This, however, is possible only in a society in which the great mass of the produce of labour takes the form of commodities, in which, consequently, the dominant relation between man and man, is that of owners of commodities. The brilliancy of Aristotle's genius is shown by this alone, that he discovered, in the expression of the value of commodities, a relation of equality. The peculiar conditions of the society in which he lived, alone prevented him from discovering what, "in truth," was at the bottom of this equality.

From *The Materialist Conception of History**

Karl Federn

We shall not deny that this idea has the appeal of a certain simplicity and even grandeur; it reveals man in his perennial efforts to make the earth and its

*Karl Federn, *The Materialist Conception of History* (London: Macmillan & Co., Ltd., 1939), pp. 13, 16, 17, 32, 56-59, 62, 63, 72, 73, 76-82, 89-91, 95-97. Reprinted by permission.

forces subservient to his own ends; it shows how, with man's constant endeavour to utilise these forces, ever more complicated social systems arise and ever new thoughts spring up in men's heads.

One may, however, raise the question whether such simplifying generalisations in which the immensity of the real world is condensed into a few short sentences, the countless facts of history into a few words, do convey any real knowledge. A still more important question is whether, in examining the concatenation of events in history, the formation of institutions and opinions, we shall find that the theory holds good. . . .

It is the development of the human mind that determines the development of the productive forces. No productive force ever discovers itself, none applies itself to economic production; it is the human mind that discovers and applies them. Human minds are so constituted that they will observe the forces at work in nature. Some minds are qualified to divine or to discover the possibility of using these forces to satisfy human needs, and some persons endowed with such minds are able to persuade others to do this. Everything must be present in thought before it can be present in action. This fact is so evident and commonplace that it is constantly overlooked and neglected. Yet unless it is constantly borne in mind, neither human life nor human history can be properly understood.

It is human minds that play the active part in social evolution, whereas the productive forces play only a passive part. In the expression "development of the productive forces" the word "development" has an active sense. The productive forces do not develop: they are being developed. . . . This was the prevailing theory in former times when the course of history was regarded as being shaped to a large extent by the human mind and the evolution of mankind as proportioned to the human mind's development. . . .

[The Nature and the Difficulties of Marx's Proofs]
. . . Marx stated his meaning with perfect clarity; translated into the language of our time, it would read as follows: economic activity and the social order do not result from man's intelligence, from their thoughts and feelings; rather are their thoughts and feelings determined by their economic activity and the ensuing social order.

The proofs produced to substantiate this thesis were of two kinds. Either they were taken from prehistoric times, which is to say that one hypothesis was based on another hypothesis—the writers who did so assumed that people in prehistoric times lived in such and such a state, and then adduced their living in this state as a proof of the theory. Or, when taken from history, the proofs were furnished by sweeping statements conformable with the theory but not with reality, statements which had not been arrived at by inferences from the particular to the general, but the reverse . . .

[The Problem of Christianity]

According to the Marxist theory, the rise of Christendom can be rationally explained by the economic misery in the Roman Empire, which made mankind look forward to a blissful state in a future life as a redeeming hope, while the union of so many nationalities in one and the same Empire and the free accordance and subsequent extension of Roman Citizenship had made an international ideal acceptable to the inhabitants of the antique world.

The propagation and diffusion of the Christian religion offers an excellent opportunity to apply, so to speak, a crucial test to the truth of the Marxist theory of history.

The diffusion of Christianity in the Old World was accomplished, approximately, in the time from the middle of the first century to the twelfth century, that is, more than a thousand years.

It must be said, in the first place, that the economic misery which, it is asserted, was one of the sources from which the Christian religion derived its origin, did not exist. The larger part of the population of the Roman Empire were at no time so well off and happy as during the first two centuries after the fall of the Republic. Never before had the ancient world enjoyed such a long and unbroken period of peace; the imperial governors were not allowed by the emperors to exploit and oppress the provinces, as the Roman aristocracy had done under the republican regimen, and riches and general well-being increased accordingly. During this time, the Christian religion expanded slowly and gradually over the Empire.

About the end of the second century after Christ, this general prosperity began to decline. Continuous civil wars brought about increasing misery, made worse by invasions of barbaric tribes. The military organisation of the Empire decayed and crumbled. The so-called migration of peoples, which at bottom was but an accelerated influx of the barbarians who until now had been repelled by Roman legions, completed the general ruin. The civil population of the Empire was, at this period, perhaps more miserable than ever afterwards. Yet the diffusion of Christianity proceeded with unabated force.

The uncivilised or half-civilised German tribes conquered the Empire, divided it and established new feudal kingdoms in its stead, whose laws, customs and economics were widely different from those of the Ancient World. The diffusion of the new religion, however, continued unimpaired.

It spread in times of peace and opulence as well as in centuries of war, misery and decay; it spread in periods of high civilisation, among a refined and sceptical aristocracy, as well as among rude peasants and slaves. It was disseminated by preaching and writing, by the flames of martyrdom, by secret propaganda from door to door and from mouth to mouth. It spread among the barbarians, now owing to the zeal of fearless and fanatical preachers—as among the Anglo-Saxons and in Germany at the time of Boniface—and now because a barbarian king adopted it for political reasons or out of admiration of Roman superiority, and his whole tribe followed his example—as in the case of Clovis, King of the Franks. At other times it was imposed upon an entire people by force of arms, as on the Saxons in the ninth century by Charlemagne, and on the Wends in the twelfth century by King Waldemar of Denmark and Bishop Absalon of Roeskilde.

The Christian religion spread in times of highly developed economic systems —for the period of its origin was one of large estates, great industry and a complicated financial system, a period which may well be called one of capitalism—and it spread in times of natural economy among savage warriors and rude peasants.

If, therefore, the mode of production were indeed to be considered as the real basis determining the whole "superstructure" and religion as a part of the super-structure, we should be forced to conclude, on the one hand, that the most different modes of production cause exactly the same spiritual move-ments and, on the other hand, that the same mode of production gives origin to the most different institutions and opinions. We might ask what strange causes these are whose effects are so uncertain and incalculable? Or should we rather not say that there obviously exists no inter-dependency of cause and effect between the conditions of production and religion, and that those who asserted its existence, did so regardless of logic as well as of history? For so much is clear: either a historical movement of such importance as the diffu-sion of Christianity was altogether independent of the economic system and had nothing whatever to do with it, or if economics had any influence upon it, this influence was modified and counter-balanced by others to such an extent as to make its effect on the movement appear insignificant. . . .

[The Problem of Civil and Penal Law]

Nobody will deny that civil as well as penal law, be it in primitive or in civilised times, is largely framed for the purpose of protecting existing economic conditions, as expressed in rights of property and of succession, in contracts and obligations. It is, however, just as undeniable that many, and not the least important, laws derive their origin from sexual or religious motives, or from motives of personal fear, from the need of the individual to be protected from physical violence and moral constraint. Now all these considerations are in no immediate, and often not even in a distant, connection with economic matters. It is further undeniable that many considerations of a non-economic nature did, in many cases, influence laws and customs in the economic sphere. We need only mention mediaeval laws against interest and usury, a good many matrimonial laws, large sections of canonical law, and many other instances.

We shall, however, admit that, law and order being a condition required for the existence of society, they belong, in a broad interpretation of the term, to the conditions of what Engels called the "production and reproduction of material life." But that does not imply that his and Marx's theory accounts in any way for the various legal systems in force in different ages and among different nations.

Much less does it explain their religions and philosophies, their arts and sciences, in short, what is termed by Marx the ideological superstructure.

We did not need Marx's theory to tell us that the intellectual life of a period is to a large extent determined by the prevailing conditions, including economic conditions; we knew that anything that is of importance in men's lives will occupy their thoughts and their imaginations, and that environment influences their opinions. It stands to reason and needs no explanation that an untravelled Englishman does not share the habits and opinions of an Indian, nor a Malay those of a Greenlander. These are truisms.

The question raised by Marx is whether the environment, the *milieu*, and the conditions of production in particular, exert such an exclusive influence on the entire social and intellectual life of the different strata as well as of the single individuals of any society that, given the environment, their intellectual life is bound to take a predetermined form and must go on developing in a predetermined manner? Or are there other factors to influence and to determine it? And, secondly, is it possible to prove Marx's thesis by pursuing an

unbroken chain of causes and effects from the economic basis up to the
simplest and most trivial as well as to the most extraordinary occurrences? . . .

[The Problem of Greek Art and Culture]

At the time when Marx wrote his propositions, he and Engels—as already
observed—joined issue with Hegel. It was against his conception of history
that their polemics were intended in the first place. Engels was right in calling
Hegel's sentence that "Greek history is essentially an elaboration of the fine
personality" an empty phrase and a mere assertion. Yet his and Marx's
explanation of Greek art and culture as derived from the mode of economic
production is likewise a mere assertion and no better than an empty phrase.
The mode of production of a great number of nations was perfectly similar to
that of the Greeks, yet none of them produced an art and a civilisation in any
way comparable to theirs. In the same place, Engels says that "it is not
inconsistent to believe in ideal impulses and driving forces, but it is inconsistent not to carry the investigation any further until the motive causes
behind those driving forces and impulses are discovered." That, however, is
just the inconsistency with which we reproach Engels and all Marxist historians: they never attempt really to dive into the matter and to carry the
investigation further until the motive causes are discovered. It is true, they
assert that these last causes are already discovered, giving out that the economic facts, the forces and the conditions of production are these last causes,
but this is not carrying the investigation back to these causes, being nothing
more than a mere assertion. They give us, so to speak, their word of honour
that it really is the case. A word of honour, however, is no scientific proof.
We are not satisfied. Had they, in any real case, pursued the investigation
back to the economic causes, they would be able to pursue the way in the
opposite direction. If their theory was more than a mere hypothesis, they
would be in a position to demonstrate how the economic conditions create
the ideology, by exposing to view the causal chain, link for link. . . .

[The Problem of the Ideas of Different Classes]

We do indeed find that the opinions of men belonging to the same class, and
brought up under exactly the same conditions, are nevertheless quite different. How is it that from the same class of the Roman Optimates there
arose men like Scipio and Opimius who advocated aristocratic rule and
interest, and men like the Gracchi? That in the French nobility of the Ancien
Régime we find conservative, liberal and revolutionary members? How is
it—the question has often been put—that the founders of Socialism and the
leaders of the modern labour movement have for long years come almost
without exception from the bourgeoisie, that is, from an environment which,
if there were any truth in the theory, would necessarily have implanted in

them directly opposite views? We may even go still further and find the influence of environment still more questionable, seeing that men procreated by the same parents, brought up in the same house and educated by the same teachers, nevertheless develop widely differing views and opinions.

If anybody should say that these are but exceptions, we should reply that where there are exceptions, there is no law in the scientific sense of the word, least of all when the exceptions are so frequent as to be noticeable every-where and every day. We shall see, too, that it is these exceptions which are of the greatest, and even of the only real, importance in the evolution of mankind. If environment did determine their ideology, all men living in the same environment would necessarily have the same ideas and pursue the same ends. It would be impossible that from the same class, the same set and even the same family, there should arise, by the side of brothers and sisters who follow the common track, some original and revolutionary thinker. Either environment determines ideology or does not determine it, but an environ-ment that in some cases determines men's ideology and in other cases fails to do so, is either no causal factor at all, or else there must needs exist other factors which suspend or counteract its effects in numerous cases. If there are exceptions there must be a cause that accounts for them. We know that these exceptions are in part determined by innate qualities of the individual, and in part by special and purely personal impressions and experiences during the individual's lifetime. Of these the first, belonging to the enigmatic phenomena of heredity, are up to this time hidden from our knowledge, while the latter are but rarely discernible other than to the individual experiencing them. It was thought for some time that the individual is the result of two elements: heredity and environment. It has been rightly said that this is trying to explain an unknown value by means of two still less known. For heredity, especially as far as the transmission of the subtle qualities of the intellect is concerned, is an unexplored field of which we know next to nothing. And the environment, the *milieu* of a person, consists of such an enormous and incalculable mass of facts, events and impressions as to be quite beyond the range of our insight and knowledge. In no single case is it possible for us really to determine it. That man is influenced by his environment is not to be doubted. But we are quite unable to tell in what way he is influenced by it, nor can we know which, of the countless component parts of a man's envi-ronment, will exercise or has exercised a decisive influence. There are, no doubt, cases in which we are able to state such influences *ex post* when the effects are clearly seen, but even then we can do so, as a rule, only in rough outlines and with no real certainty. The influence of the environment on the individual depends, besides, to a great extent on the latter's personality, different individuals being very differently impressed and influenced by the same facts. Some individuals react with great force to certain impressions while others exposed to the same conditions do not react at all. There are persons who, though grown up in the country and living surrounded by natural scenery, yet derive no pleasure from it. Some of the persons bred up amidst books and by scholars will grow up to be scholars themselves, whereas others will develop an aversion to science and books. There are people without any artistic taste or inclination who passed their childhood in houses decorated with consummate art, whereas the same environment will imbue others with an eternal longing for beautiful surroundings. In the same way, there are persons in whom the conditions of production will create opinions answering to their economic interest, or what they believe to be their economic interest, while the same conditions of production will induce in others the opposite opinions, based on their moral sense. Possibly the latter will indignantly demand that the existing conditions of production be changed: they may start a propaganda to this end and create an intellectual and political movement. Their moral indignation is perhaps to be traced back to obscure hereditary influences, to certain impressions made on their forefathers in a remote past. It may be so, but we have not the slightest proof of it, and we are not entitled to draw conclusions from uncertain suppositions and unauthenticated beliefs, or if we do so, our conclusions will be void of any scientific value.

Thus, socialistic or revolutionary ideas sprang up in the heads of men belonging to the aristocracy or the middle classes.

To this a Marxist might make the following objection: History, he would say, is an uninterrupted struggle of classes, fought out in ideological forms. The reasons and arguments which men allege in fighting it out, are but the ideal forms in which this struggle appeals to their consciousness. "New ideas will spring up in the heads of that part of the population that is affected by a change in the condition of production: they are, so to speak, an ideological precipitate of the conditions of production." Among the Roman proletarians dispossessed of their native soil, or among the workmen defrauded of the surplus value produced by the work of their hands, discontent spreads and an effervescent state of mind, and at the same time, in the heads of intelligent and educated persons like the Gracchi in ancient Rome, or Marx and Engels in our time, new ideas will germinate and plans of reform. The effervescence in the heads of the proletarians and the new programmes in those of the leaders are both reflections created in men's brains by the conditions of production. If economic conditions were not in a bad state, there would neither be an effervescence in the class affected by them, nor would new ideas be born and take shape in men's brains.

We shall admit the truth of this argument in that particular case. Obviously, feelings and new ideas concerning the conditions of production could not well have come into existence unless the state of these conditions had called them forth. It is, however, noteworthy, that even in this case the new ideas did not arise from among the class affected by the change but, on the contrary, from that part of the population which was not, or certainly much less, affected or even profited by it. And if our opponent should reply: All strata of a population are affected by a change in the conditions of production, all Romans felt the disastrous consequences of the changed mode of production in the last two centuries of the Republic, the exploitation of the conquered nations, the large estates and the usurious practices of the Optimates, the misery of the masses, one part of the population having grown immoderately rich and the other intolerably poor, the whole social system was put out of gear, the new ideas were bound to come; in what heads they first arose depended on the necessary degree of intelligence.

All right, we should say, this proves only what an important part is played in all historical movements and changes by personal gifts and by intelligence. Moreover, the Romans themselves knew perfectly well that everybody is affected by great economic changes. They knew from experience that discontented masses are apt to be riotous and that, whenever this happened, persons were found who proposed some plan for redress, plans which, in some cases, led to important consequences and in others proved abortive. And all educated persons in the nineteenth century knew as much as this. We did not need Marx and Engels to tell us. Marx and Engels, however, enunciated a doctrine different from this hackneyed wisdom, they asserted that all opinions and ideologies are *determined* by the conditions of production, which is to say that given conditions of production will of necessity produce a certain corresponding ideology. But neither Marx nor Engels nor any of their followers was ever able to demonstrate that this is really the case. The episodes from Roman and from our own history which he quotes as cases in point, prove, like the instances given before, that the same conditions of production are liable to produce quite different ideologies in different minds. Nor could any of these writers ever explain why and how this influence of economic production on men's ideologies takes effect. . . .

[The Problem of Science]
Let us consider another case. If there ever was a scientific discovery whose consequences shook the world, it was that of the Canon of Frauenburg, Nicolas Copernicus, who established the truth of the earth revolving round the sun. It took him some fifteen years of intricate calculations to substantiate it. Now, in what connection these calculations stood to the mode of

production in the sixteenth century we should be curious to know. We shall admit that a certain development of economic conditions is required to make scientific research possible. It is obvious that, in a primitive state of agriculture or nomadic life, the intellectual faculties of individuals are not sufficiently differentiated to enable a number of them to devote themselves to scientific studies, and, moreover, centuries of continual scientific application have to pass before men are likely to become capable of such subtle and difficult calculations. Admitting this, we do not imply that the economic changes are the basic fact in this development. We know that in the early Middle Ages, at a time when economic production was primitive enough, once the Franks had outgrown their first barbaric state and acquired a varnish of Roman culture, science and a subtle philosophy was cultivated under the Carolingian emperors. We may even go so far as to admit that without the economic development of modern times, those comprehensive studies and investigations in every domain of human thought and experience which constitute modern science, would have been impossible. It is, however, obvious, from the very nature of the human mind, that, once begun, scientific discoveries had to be continued and developed. . . .

[The Problem of Thought Affecting Later Times]

. . . thoughts may have an existence independent of the society, or form of society, which gave them birth. The existence of books, which may be read five thousand years after having been first conceived and written, is a sufficient proof. People may die, races become extinct, but tradition or written documents will carry on their thoughts and deliver them to future generations, living under conditions of production that have little or nothing in common with those prevailing in such bygone times. And none can tell what influence those thoughts of a nearly forgotten society may have upon the living. A few ancient treatises, rediscovered by chance in the eighth and ninth centuries of our era, not only determined the course of studies in schools and universities during the Middle Ages, but the trend and character of all mediaeval philosophy and, to a large extent, that of modern philosophy also. The *Isagoge* of Porphyrius, found among these manuscripts, gave rise to the endless controversy between Nominalists and Realists. A grammatical treatise having been found among them, grammar lessons have formed a part of instruction in languages to this day. The treatises discovered then and there had been composed at different times between the fourth century before and the fifth after Christ, yet they influenced the studies and the school teaching of nearly all white nations for more than a thousand years.

But how about the origin of these thoughts outliving generations and systems? There are individuals in whom the intellect of mankind manifests itself, as it were, in concentrated form. Here, Marx's theory of history is found to be hopelessly at fault. The appearance of those men who opened new outlooks to their generation or who successfully took the lead in some critical situation, is in nowise connected with, or dependent on, the conditions of production. If anybody would contend that it was owing to the development of the productive forces and to the existing conditions of production that such men as Kant and Newton, Rousseau and Mirabeau, Goethe and Napoleon were born, men whose influence extended over a great part of the earth and far into the unknown depth of time, he is bound to prove it and to demonstrate why and how the conditions of production caused the birth of these men at this particular time; otherwise his assertion is idle talk and nothing but an arbitrary hypothesis. . . .

Chapter Three

Mannheim's Concept of Ideology

Karl Mannheim was a professor of sociology in Germany until 1933. After Hitler came to power, he went to England, where he taught at the London School of Economics and Political Science until his death in 1947.

Mannheim's most influential book contains the most explicit statement of his concept of ideology: *Ideology and Utopia: An Introduction to the Sociology of Knowledge*. The book was published in Germany in 1929. It immediately created a stir, and several of the German intellectuals who wrote critical reviews were destined shortly to go into exile and become leading intellectual figures in America: Hannah Arendt, Herbert Marcuse, and Paul Tillich.

English and American scholars at first paid little attention to Mannheim's book. However, as the political crisis in Germany deepened, and particularly after the Nazis came to power in 1933, a large number of German scholars made their way to the western democracies. These emigres—especially those who had been trained in the social sciences in Germany—brought with them a deep awareness of the theory of ideology. One of the practical effects of the communication of that awareness was the appearance of an English translation of *Ideology and Utopia* (1936). Louis Wirth, an American sociologist

who collaborated on the English translation, wrote a special preface directed
to English and American scholars. In it he developed his own interpretation
of the significance of the theory of ideology. He said: "What was once
regarded as the esoteric concern of a few intellectuals in a single country has
become the common plight of the modern man."[1] The "common plight" he
refers to is the intellectual and political effect of an undermining of the
traditional belief in the objectivity of human thought. Wirth goes on to praise
Mannheim's work as a major contribution to (1) understanding how and why
this condition has developed, and (2) producing a new basis for society.

Wirth's judgment of Mannheim's book agrees, essentially, with the author's
own evaluation of his purpose. To Mannheim, contemporary society is in a
state of deepening crisis that can be resolved only by a new "science of
politics" based upon the "sociology of knowledge." His concept of ideology
is an integral element in this larger conception.

Mannheim theorizes that modern society emerged from the progressive disintegration of medieval society, and that contemporary society emerged from a
radicalization of tendencies inherent in modern society. Thus today's great
crisis is not the beginning of the end of contemporary society, but the penultimate stage in the dissolution of medieval society. The ultimate stage of this
dissolution should be the creation of a new form of society based on a new
form of understanding.

Mannheim applies this general thesis to the evolution of modern thought.
Medieval society, he argues, was unitary—a highly integrated, hierarchical
organization which was believed by its inhabitants to be the only natural
organization of mankind. This belief was derived from the domination of the
clergy, whose world view was of a knowable, hierarchical, harmonious order of
things, human and divine. But the unitary character of thought was questioned as medieval society began to disintegrate and the domination of the
clergy was challenged by the emergence of early modern philosophy and
science.

Mannheim believes that the questioning of medieval thought has gone
through three stages. The first was the emergence of early modern philosophy
as a reaction against scholastic philosophy. The central concern of this phase
was the development of epistemology, or the science of knowing. The most
significant aspect of modern epistemology, Mannheim argues, is that it shifted

[1] Karl Mannheim, *Ideology and Utopia*, translated by Louis Wirth and Edward Shils
(New York: Harcourt, Brace & World, Inc., 1939), p. x.

philosophical attention from the world to man. More precisely, it replaced the problem of the order of the world and man's place in it with the problem of the knowing subject's perceptions. Major works presenting this concern with the human faculty of understanding are John Locke's *An Essay concerning Human Understanding* (1690) and Immanuel Kant's *Critique of Pure Reason* (1781) and *Critique of Practical Reason* (1788).

The second stage was the emergence of modern psychology as an extension of early modern epistemology. Its object was to resolve epistemological difficulties concerning the genesis and operation of the individual psyche. Mechanistic psychology focused on the operation of the parts of the psyche and treated them as parts of a mechanism, like a machine. Genetic psychology focused on the genesis of the parts of the psyche and the relationship of that genesis to the content of conscious thought and action. Notable examples of the mechanistic psychology would be the various theories of the utilitarians; and examples of the genetic psychology would be the early forms of psychoanalysis.

The third stage of modern questioning was the emergence of sociology. This took place, Mannheim believes, because both epistemology and psychology had unexpected difficulty in giving a satisfactory account of the individual understanding and consciousness. The basic difficulty, he argues, was that both of the earlier forms of theory had failed to grasp the significance of the social situation's effects on the individual. Hence the new science of sociology came into being as a corrective to this limitation. Its object was to provide a comprehensive analysis of the social relations of man, particularly as they affect his perceptions and actions. Important examples of what Mannheim means by sociology are the theories of Karl Marx and Max Weber.[2]

Within this third stage, Mannheim says, there was a belated development of the branch of sociology called the "sociology of knowledge." This branch emerged as a result of the modern democratization of politics. Until this democratization occurred, the epistemological, psychological, and sociological insights of modern thought remained the property of the intelligentsia. But they were increasingly shared by all strata of society as this process proceeded, and as vertical class mobility transformed the make-up of the intelligentsia. As participation in political life spread, men of all strata became increasingly aware of fundamental differences in their ways of perceiving reality. Even more important, they learned from sociology to attribute those differences to a bias created by men's social position and interests.

[2]See Ch. 1, Part 3 of Mannheim, *op. cit.*

Mannheim saw the net result of this democratization of the insights of modern thought as the increasing fusion of politics and science. All political parties—the organized segments of the different social strata—increasingly "strove to provide their conflicts with philosophical foundation and systematization."[3] The positive effects of this fusion were first, to cause more men to think about society and politics "with the categories of scientific analysis"; and second, to help political and social science to "gain a concrete grip on reality" by focusing attention on the real events of political conflict. The negative effects were first, to produce a tension between the experimental character of science and the interested and fighting character of political parties; second, to transform crises in political thinking into crises of scientific thought.[4]

In its first phase, the fused form of politics and science is what Mannheim calls ideology. Its purpose is to unmask political opponents' principles. Its method is to show that such principles are but reflections of the opponents' social position. But because of the critical operations of an increasingly large "socially unattached intelligentsia," the theory of ideology in its second phase is transformed into the "sociology of knowledge." Its purpose is to produce an objective account of how the social setting decisively controls the content and purpose of thinking. It differs from ideology in that it does not use this understanding to gain political advantage, but rather seeks to subject the "irrational factors" which underlie thinking to scientific control. It resembles the method of ideology in analyzing thought in terms of social position. But it goes beyond ideology by tracing the entire historical sequence of social thought and showing the universal character of its social determination.

Mannheim's general perspective can be reformulated as follows. The contemporary crisis in society is a crisis produced by the political effects of ideology, that is, all parties now use ideological criticism as a weapon in political fights. This criticism strains, then shatters, the bonds of society; for men destroy the common beliefs which held the society together to the same extent that they destroy each other's claims to objectivity. At this critical junction the new insights of the purified form of ideology—the "sociology of knowledge"—indicate a way out of the crisis. The proposed solution would incorporate the partial but important truth of the concept of ideology into the evolving principles of society to produce ever newer syntheses of all

[3]*Ibid.*, p. 36.

[4]*Ibid.*, pp. 37-38.

political points of view. Thus, the "socially unattached intelligentsia" have it in their power to create a "science of politics" which will provide a new means of understanding for all men.

The following selections are from Chapter II of Mannheim's book, where, though the concept is used in important ways in other parts of the work, the main definitions and analyses of ideology are presented.

The critique which follows these selections concentrates on two aspects of Mannheim's concept: the nature of the historical evidence used to establish the validity of the concept, and the implications for politics and philosophy of the acceptance of that concept and its incorporation into the new "science of politics" based on the "sociology of knowledge."

From *Ideology and Utopia**

Karl Mannheim

1. Definition of Concepts

In order to understand the present situation of thought, it is necessary to start with the problems of "ideology." For most people, the term "ideology" is closely bound up with Marxism, and their reactions to the term are largely determined by the association. It is therefore first necessary to state that although Marxism contributed a great deal to the original statement of the problem, both the word and its meaning go farther back in history than Marxism, and ever since its time new meanings of the word have emerged, which have taken shape independently of it. . . . In general there are two distinct and separable meanings of the term "ideology"—the particular and the total.

The particular conception of ideology is implied when the term denotes that we are sceptical of the ideas and representations advanced by our opponent. They are regarded as more or less conscious disguises of the real nature of a situation, the true recognition of which would not be in accord with his interests. These distortions range all the way from conscious lies to

*From *Ideology and Utopia* by Karl Mannheim, trans. by Louis Wirth and Edward Shils (New York: Harcourt, Brace & World, Inc., 1939), pp. 55-69, 71-78, 105. Reprinted by permission of Harcourt, Brace & World, Inc.

half-conscious and unwitting disguises; from calculated attempts to dupe others to self-deception. This conception of ideology, which has only gradually become differentiated from the common-sense notion of the lie is particular in several senses. Its particularity becomes evident when it is contrasted with the more inclusive total conception of ideology. Here we refer to the ideology of an age or of a concrete historico-social group, e.g. of a class, when we are concerned with the characteristics and composition of the total structure of the mind of this epoch or of this group.

The common as well as the distinctive elements of the two concepts are readily evident. The common element in these two conceptions seems to consist in the fact that neither relies solely on what is actually said by the opponent in order to reach an understanding of his real meaning and intention. Both fall back on the subject, whether individual or group, proceeding to an understanding of what is said by the indirect method of analysing the social conditions of the individual or his group. The ideas expressed by the subject are thus regarded as functions of his existence. This means that opinions, statements, propositions, and systems of ideas are not taken at their face value but are interpreted in the light of the life-situation of the one who expresses them. It signifies further that the specific character and life-situation of the subject influence his opinions, perceptions, and interpretations.

Both these conceptions of ideology, accordingly, make these so-called "ideas" a function of him who holds them, and of his position in his social milieu. Although they have something in common, there are also significant differences between them. Of the latter we mention merely the most important: —

(a) Whereas the particular conception of ideology designates only a part of the opponent's assertions as ideologies—and this only with reference to their content, the total conception calls into question the opponent's total *Weltanschauung* (including his conceptual apparatus), and attempts to understand these concepts as an outgrowth of the collective life of which he partakes.

(b) The particular conception of "ideology" makes its analysis of ideas on a purely psychological level. If it is claimed for instance that an adversary is lying, or that he is concealing or distorting a given factual situation, it is still nevertheless assumed that both parties share common criteria of validity—it is still assumed that it is possible to refute lies and eradicate sources of error by referring to accepted criteria of objective validity common to both parties. The suspicion that one's opponent is the victim of an ideology does not go so far as to exclude him from discussion on the basis of a common theoretical frame of reference. The case is different with the total conception of ideology. When we attribute to one historical epoch one intellectual world and to ourselves another one, or if a certain historically determined social stratum thinks in categories other than our own, we refer not to the isolated cases of thought-content, but to fundamentally divergent thought-systems and to widely differing modes of experience and interpretation. We touch upon the theoretical or noological level whenever we consider not merely the content but also the form, and even the conceptual framework of a mode of thought as a function of the life-situation of a thinker. . . .

[The] particular conception of ideology operates primarily with a psychology of interests, while the total conception uses a more formal functional analysis, without any reference to motivations, confining itself to an objective description of the structural differences in minds operating in different social settings. The former assumes that this or that interest is the cause of a given lie or deception. The latter presupposes simply that there is a correspondence between a given social situation and a given perspective, point of view, or apperception mass. . . .

As soon as the total conception of ideology is used, we attempt to reconstruct the whole outlook of a social group, and neither the concrete individuals nor the abstract sum of them can legitimately be considered as bearers of this ideological thought-system as a whole. The aim of the analysis on this level is the reconstruction of the systematic theoretical basis underlying the single judgments of the individual. Analyses of ideologies in the particular sense, making the content of individual thought largely dependent on the interests of the subject, can never achieve this basic reconstruction of the whole outlook of a social group. . . .

2. The Concept Ideology in Historical Perspective

Just as the particular and total conceptions of ideology can be distinguished from one another on the basis of their differences in meaning, so the historical origins of these two concepts may also be differentiated even though in reality they are always intertwined. We do not as yet possess an adequate historical treatment of the development of the concept of ideology, to say nothing of a sociological history of the many variations in its meaning. Even if we were in a position to do so, it would not be our task, for the purposes we have in mind, to write a history of the changing meanings in the concept of ideology. Our aim is simply to present such facts from the scattered evidence as will most clearly exhibit the distinction between the two terms. . . .

The distrust and suspicion which men everywhere evidence towards their adversaries, at all stages of historical development, may be regarded as the immediate precursor of the notion of ideology. But it is only when the distrust of man toward man, which is more or less evident at every stage of human history, becomes explicit and is methodically recognized, that we may properly speak of an ideological taint in the utterances of others. We arrive at this level when we no longer make individuals personally responsible for the deceptions which we detect in their utterances, and when we no longer attribute the evil that they do to their malicious cunning. It is only when we more or less consciously seek to discover the source of their untruthfulness in a social factor, that we are properly making an ideological interpretation. We begin to treat our adversary's views as ideologies only when we no longer consider them as calculated lies and when we sense in his total behaviour an unreliability which we regard as a function of the social situation in which he finds himself. The particular conception of ideology therefore signifies a phenomenon intermediate between a simple lie at one pole, and an error, which is the result of a distorted and faulty conceptual apparatus, at the other. It refers to a sphere of errors, psychological in nature, which unlike deliberate deception, are not intentional, but follow inevitably and unwittingly from certain causal determinants.

According to this interpretation, Bacon's theory of the *idola* may be regarded to a certain extent as a forerunner of the modern conception of ideology. The "idols" were "phantoms" or "preconceptions," and there were, as we know, the idols of the tribe, of the cave, of the market, and of the theatre. All of these are sources of error derived sometimes from human nature itself, sometimes from particular individuals. They may also be attributed to society or to tradition. In any case, they are obstacles in the path to true knowledge. There is certainly some connection between the modern term "ideology" and the term as used by Bacon, signifying a source of error. Furthermore, the realization that society and tradition may become sources of error is a direct anticipation of the sociological point of view. Nevertheless, it cannot be claimed that there is an actual relationship, directly traceable through the history of thought, between this and the modern conception of ideology.

It is extremely probable that everyday experience with political affairs first made man aware of and critical toward the ideological element in his thinking. During the Renaissance, among the fellow citizens of Machiavelli, there arose a new adage calling attention to a common observation of the time—namely that the thought of the palace is one thing, and that of the public square is another. This was an expression of the increasing degree to which the public was gaining access to the secrets of politics. Here we may observe the beginning of the process in the course of which what had formerly been merely an occasional outburst of suspicion and scepticism toward public utterances developed into a methodical search for the ideological element in all of them. The diversity of the ways of thought among men is even at this stage attributed to a factor which might, without unduly stretching the term, be denominated as sociological. Machiavelli, with his relentless rationality, made it his special task to relate the variations in the opinions of men to the corresponding variations in their interests. Accordingly when he prescribes a *medicina forte* for every bias of the interested parties in a controversy, he seems to be making explicit and setting up as a general rule of thought what was implicit in the common-sense adage of his time.

There seems to be a straight line leading from this point in the intellectual orientation of the Western world to the rational and calculating mode of thought characteristic of the period of the Enlightenment. The psychology of interests seems to flow from the same source. One of the chief characteristics of the method of rational analysis of human behaviour, exemplified by Hume's *History of England*, was the presupposition that men were given to "feigning" and to deceiving their fellows. The same characteristic is found in contemporary historians who operate with the particular conception of ideology. This mode of thought will always strive in accordance with the psychology of interests to cast doubt upon the integrity of the adversary and to deprecate his motives. This procedure, nevertheless, has positive value as long as in a given case we are interested in discovering the genuine meaning of a statement that lies concealed behind a camouflage of words. This "debunking" tendency in the thought of our time has become very marked. And even though in wide circles this trait is considered undignified and disrespectful (and indeed in so far as "debunking" is an end in itself, the criticism is justified), this intellectual position is forced upon us in an era of transition like our own, which finds it necessary to break with many antiquated traditions and forms.

3.   From the Particular to the Total Conception of Ideology

It must be remembered that the unmasking which takes place on the psychological level is not to be confused with the more radical scepticism and the more thoroughgoing and devastating critical analysis which proceeds on the ontological and noological levels. But the two cannot be completely separated. The same historical forces that bring about continuous transformations in one are also operative in the other. In the former, psychological illusions are constantly being undermined, in the latter, ontological and logical formulations arising out of given world-views and modes of thought are dissolved in a conflict between the interested parties. Only in a world in upheaval, in which fundamental new values are being created and old ones destroyed, can intellectual conflict go so far that antagonists will seek to annihilate not merely the specific beliefs and attitudes of one another, but also the intellectual foundations upon which these beliefs and attitudes rest.

As long as the conflicting parties lived in and tried to represent the same world, even though they were at opposite poles in that world, or as long as one feudal clique fought against its equal, such a thoroughgoing mutual destruction was inconceivable. This profound disintegration of intellectual unity is possible only when the basic values of the contending groups are worlds apart. At first, in the course of this ever-deepening disintegration, naive distrust becomes transformed into a systematic particular notion of ideology, which, however, remains on the psychological plane. But, as the process continues, it extends to the noological-epistemological sphere. The rising bourgeoisie which brought with it a new set of values was not content with merely being assigned a circumscribed place within the old feudal order. It represented a new "economic system" (in Sombart's sense), accompanied by a new style of thought which ultimately displaced the existing modes of interpreting and explaining the world. The same seems to be true of the proletariat to-day as well. Here too we note a conflict between two divergent economic views, between two social systems, and, correspondingly, between two styles of thought.

What were the steps in the history of ideas that prepared the way for the total conception of ideology? Certainly it did not merely arise out of the attitude of mistrust which gradually gave rise to the particular conception of ideology. More fundamental steps had to be taken before the numerous tendencies of thought moving in the same general direction could be synthesized into the total conception of ideology. Philosophy played a part in the process, but not philosophy in the narrow sense (as it is usually conceived) as a discipline divorced from the actual context of living. Its role was rather that of the ultimate and fundamental interpreter of the flux in the contemporary world. This cosmos in flux is in its turn to be viewed as a series of conflicts arising out of the nature of the mind and its responses to the continually changing structure of the world. We shall indicate here only the principal stages in the emergence of the total conception of ideology on the noological and ontological levels.

The first significant step in this direction consisted in the development of a philosophy of consciousness. The thesis that consciousness is a unity consisting of coherent elements sets a problem of investigation which, especially in Germany, has been the basis of monumental attempts at analysis. The philosophy of consciousness has put in place of an infinitely variegated and confused world an organization of experience the unity of which is guaranteed by the unity of the perceiving subject. This does not imply that the subject merely reflects the structural pattern of the external world, but rather that, in the course of his experience with the world, he spontaneously evolves the principles of organization that enable him to understand it. After the objective ontological unity of the world had been demolished, the attempt was made to substitute for it a unity imposed by the perceiving subject. In the place of the medieval-Christian objective and ontological unity of the world, there emerged the subjective unity of the absolute subject of the Enlightenment—"consciousness in itself.". . .

The second stage in the development of the total conception of ideology is attained when the total but super-temporal notion of ideology is seen in historical perspective. This is mainly the accomplishment of Hegel and the Historical school. The latter, and Hegel to an even greater degree, start from the assumption that the world is a unity and is conceivable only with reference to a knowing subject. And now at this point, what is for us a decisive new element is added to the conception—namely, that this unity is in a process of continual historical transformation and tends to a constant restoration of its equilibrium on still higher levels. . . . It should be noted, however, that the historically changing nature of mind was discovered not so much by philosophy as by the penetration of political insight into the everyday life of the time.

The reaction following upon the unhistorical thought of the period of the French Revolution revitalized and gave new impetus to the historical perspective. In the last analysis, the transition from the general, abstract, world-unifying subject ("consciousness in itself") to the more concrete subject (the nationally differentiated "folk spirit") was not so much a philosophical achievement as it was the expression of a transformation in the manner of reacting to the world in all realms of experience. . . .

The final and most important step in the creation of the total conception of ideology likewise arose out of the historical-social process. When "class" took the place of "folk" or nation as the bearer of the historically evolving consciousness, the same theoretical tradition, to which we have already referred, absorbed the realization which meanwhile had grown up through the social process, namely—that the structure of society and its corresponding intellectual forms vary with the relations between social classes. . . .

Two consequences flow from this conception of consciousness: first we clearly perceive that human affairs cannot be understood by an isolation of their elements. Every fact and event in an historical period is only explicable in terms of meaning, and meaning in its turn always refers to another meaning. Thus the conception of the unity and interdependence of meaning in a period always underlies the interpretation of that period. Secondly, this interdependent system of meanings varies both in all its parts and in its totality from one historical period to another. Thus the re-interpretation of that continuous and coherent change in meaning becomes the main concern of our modern historical sciences. . . .

[The] two currents which led to the particular and total conceptions of ideology, respectively, and which have approximately the same historical origin, now begin to approach one another more closely. The particular conception of ideology merges with the total. This becomes apparent to the observer in the following manner: previously, one's adversary, as the representative of a certain political-social position, was accused of conscious or unconscious falsification. Now, however, the critique is more thoroughgoing in that, having discredited the total structure of his consciousness, we consider him no longer capable of thinking correctly. This simple observation means, in the light of a structural analysis of thought, that in earlier attempts to discover the sources of error, distortion was uncovered only on the psychological plane by pointing out the personal roots of intellectual bias. The annihilation is now more thoroughgoing since the attack is made on the noological level and the validity of the adversary's theories is undermined by showing that they are merely a function of the generally prevailing social situation. Herewith a new and perhaps the most decisive stage in the history of modes of thought has been reached. . . .

4. Objectivity and Bias

. . .To determine the exact nature of the new criterion of reality which superseded the transcendental one, we must subject the meaning of the word "ideology" also in this respect to a more precise historical analysis. If, in the course of such an analysis, we are led to deal with the language of everyday life, this simply indicates that the history of thought is not confined to books alone, but gets its chief meaning from the experiences of everyday life, and even the main changes in the evaluations of different spheres of reality as they appear in philosophy eventually go back to the shifting values of the everyday world.

The word "ideology" itself had, to begin with, no inherent ontological significance; it did not include any decision as to the value of different spheres of reality, since it originally denoted merely the theory of ideas. The ideologists, were, as we know, the members of a philosophical group in France who, in the tradition of Condillac, rejected metaphysics and sought to base the cultural sciences on anthropological and psychological foundations.

The modern conception of ideology was born when Napoleon, finding that this group of philosophers was opposing his imperial ambitions, contemptuously labelled them "ideologists." Thereby the word took on a derogatory meaning which, like the word "doctrinaire," it has retained to the present day. However, if the theoretical implications of this contempt are examined, it will be found that the depreciative attitude involved is, at bottom, of an epistemological and ontological nature. What is depreciated is the validity of the adversary's thought because it is regarded as unrealistic. But if one asked further, unrealistic with reference to what?—the answer would be, unrealistic with reference to practice, unrealistic when contrasted with the affairs that transpire in the political arena. Thenceforth, all thought labelled as "ideology" is regarded as futile when it comes to practice, and the only reliable access to reality is to be sought in practical activity. When measured by the standards of practical conduct, mere thinking or reflection on a given situation turns out to be trivial. It is thus clear how the new meaning of the term ideology bears the imprint of the position and the point of view of those who coined it, namely, the political men of action. The new word gives sanction to the specific experience of the politician with reality, and it lends support to that practical irrationality which has so little appreciation for thought as an instrument for grasping reality.

During the nineteenth century, the term ideology, used in this sense, gained wide currency. This signifies that the politician's feeling for reality took precedence over and displaced the scholastic, contemplative modes of thought and of life. Henceforward the problem implicit in the term ideology —what is really real?—never disappeared from the horizon.

But this transition needs to be correctly understood. The question as to what constitutes reality is by no means a new one; but that the question should arise in the arena of public discussion (and not just in isolated academic circles) seems to indicate an important change. The new connotation which the word ideology acquired, because it was redefined by the politician in terms of his experiences, seems to show a decisive turn in the formulation of the problem of the nature of reality. If, therefore, we are to rise to the demands put upon us by the need for analysing modern thought, we must see to it that a sociological history of ideas concerns itself with the actual

thought of society, and not merely with self-perpetuating and supposedly
self-contained systems of ideas elaborated within a rigid academic tradition. If
erroneous knowledge was formerly checked by appeal to divine sanction,
which unfailingly revealed the true and the real, or by pure contemplation, in
which true ideas were supposedly discovered, at present the criterion of
reality is found primarily in an ontology derived from political experience.
The history of the concept of ideology from Napoleon to Marxism, despite
changes in content, has retained the same political criterion of reality. This
historical example shows, at the same time, that the pragmatic point of view
was already implicit in the accusation which Napoleon hurled at his adversaries. Indeed we may say that for modern man pragmatism has, so to speak,
become in some respects, the inevitable and appropriate outlook, and that
philosophy in this case has simply appropriated this outlook and from it
proceeded to its logical conclusion. . . .

We are carried a step further in our analysis, and are able to bring out another
aspect of this problem by referring to the example just cited in another
connection. In the struggle which Napoleon carried on against his critics, he
was able, as we have seen, by reason of his dominant position to discredit
them by pointing out the ideological nature of their thinking. In later stages
of its development, the word ideology is used as a weapon by the proletariat
against the dominant group. In short, such a revealing insight into the basis of
thought as that offered by the notion of ideology cannot, in the long run,
remain the exclusive privilege of one class. But it is precisely this expansion
and diffusion of the ideological approach which leads finally to a juncture at
which it is no longer possible for one point of view and interpretation to
assail all others as ideological without itself being placed in the position of
having to meet that challenge. . . .

Marxist thought attached such decisive significance to political practice
conjointly with the economic interpretation of events, that these two became
the ultimate criteria for disentangling what is mere ideology from those
elements in thought which are more immediately relevant to reality. Consequently it is no wonder that the conception of ideology is usually regarded as
integral to, and even identified with, the Marxist proletarian movement.

But in the course of more recent intellectual and social developments, however, this stage has already been passed. It is no longer the exclusive privilege
of socialist thinkers to trace bourgeois thought to ideological foundations and
thereby to discredit it. Nowadays groups of every standpoint use this weapon
against all the rest. As a result we are entering upon a new epoch in social and
intellectual development. . . .

It is interesting to observe that, as a result of the expansion of the ideological concept, a new mode of understanding has gradually come into existence. This new intellectual standpoint constitutes not merely a change of degree in a phenomenon already operating. We have here an example of the real dialectical process which is too often misinterpreted for scholastic purposes—for here we see indeed a matter of difference in degree becoming a matter of difference in kind. For as soon as all parties are able to analyse the ideas of their opponents in ideological terms, all elements of meaning are qualitatively changed and the word ideology acquires a totally new meaning. In the course of this all the factors with which we dealt in our historical analysis of the meaning of the term are also transformed accordingly. The problems of "false consciousness" and of the nature of reality henceforth take on a different significance. This point of view ultimately forces us to recognize that our axioms, our ontology, and our epistemology have been profoundly transformed. . . .

. . .[When] one is interested merely in a sociological analysis of the opponent's ideas, one never gets beyond a highly restricted, or what I should like to call a special, formulation of the theory. In contrast to this special formulation, the general form of the total conception of ideology is being used by the analyst when he has the courage to subject not just the adversary's point of view but all points of view, including his own, to the ideological analysis.

At the present stage of our understanding it is hardly possible to avoid this general formulation of the total conception of ideology, according to which the thought of all parties in all epochs is of an ideological character. There is scarcely a single intellectual position, and Marxism furnishes no exception to this rule, which has not changed through history and which even in the present does not appear in many forms. Marxism, too, has taken on many diverse appearances. It should not be too difficult for a Marxist to recognize their social basis.

With the emergence of the general formulation of the total conception of ideology, the simple theory of ideology develops into the sociology of knowledge. What was once the intellectual armament of a party is transformed into a method of research in social and intellectual history generally. To begin with, a given social group discovers the "situational determination" (*Seinsgebundenheit*) of its opponents' ideas. Subsequently the recognition of this fact is elaborated into an all-inclusive principle according to which the thought of every group is seen as arising out of its life conditions. Thus, it becomes the task of the sociological history of thought to analyse without regard for party biases all the factors in the actually existing social situation which may influence thought. This sociologically oriented history of ideas is destined to provide modern men with a revised view of the whole historical process. . . .

Only when we are thoroughly aware of the limited space of every point of view are we on the road to the sought-for comprehension of the whole. The crisis in thought is not a crisis affecting merely a single intellectual position, but a crisis of a whole world which has reached a certain stage in its intellectual development. To see more clearly the confusion into which our social and intellectual life has fallen represents an enrichment rather than a loss. That reason can penetrate more profoundly into its own structure is not a sign of intellectual bankruptcy. Nor is it to be regarded as intellectual incompetence on our part when an extraordinary broadening of perspective necessitates a thoroughgoing revision of our fundamental conceptions. Thought is a process determined by actual social forces, continually questioning its findings and correcting its procedure. (It would be fatal on that account to refuse to recognize, because of sheer timidity, what has already become clear.) The most promising aspect of the present situation, however, is that we can never be satisfied with narrow perspectives, but will constantly seek to understand and interpret particular insights from an ever more inclusive context. . . .

A Critique of Mannheim's Concept of Ideology*

Richard Cox

1. The Problematic Character of the Historical Evidence

There is, I believe, a profound disproportion between the bold sweep of Mannheim's thesis and the quality of the concrete historical evidence he presents to support it. Indeed, it seems to me that his insistence on the intrinsic importance of achieving a sense of historical *perspective* leads, almost

*Adapted from Richard H. Cox, "Karl Mannheim's Concept of Ideology," an essay prepared for a conference on "Ideology and Politics" (1967), sponsored by the International Institute of Political Philosophy. An expanded version of the essay will appear in a forthcoming volume of the *Annales de Philosophie Politique*, published by the International Institute of Political Philosophy. Permission to reprint part of my essay in this volume has kindly been granted by Professor Raymond Polin, on behalf of the Institute.

paradoxically yet inevitably, to a fundamental depreciation of the problem of historical accuracy. I can give but a few particulars here, but there are many others that could be cited, given more space.

The validity of Mannheim's thesis depends on the validity of his conception that there is a necessary, continuing historical-political transformation in and of the world. If that transformation is indeed propelled by the political motive to dominate, coming necessarily into fusion with the philosophical motive to understand the nature of thinking and its relation to reality, then the evidence of that emergent fusion must, I should think, be given in great detail and with great care. And yet, Mannheim himself starts from the observation that: "We do not as yet possess an adequate historical treatment of the development of the concept of ideology, to say nothing of a sociological history of the many variations in its meaning." Furthermore, as if to document the validity of this latter proposition, he offers perhaps twelve pages of argument, and a mere handful of specific historical examples, to support his thesis. The net consequence is that the concrete historical validity of the thesis appears to me to be largely presupposed, or at very least to be posited in spite of the admitted lack of an adequate set of historical data. The explanation for this curious state of affairs lies, I believe, in Mannheim's uncritical acceptance of the notion that the emergence of the "historical perspective" was, itself, a mark of decisive progress over all previous modes of understanding. The elaboration of the precise historical evidence is then a mere function, it appears, of applying the established "insight" of the "historical perspective."

A second striking thing concerning the historical evidence is the doubtful quality of the interpretation that derives from the actual application of that alleged insight. For without exception, the interpretation is rather simplistic, derivative, and forced. I will illustrate what I mean first by taking for examination the only three specific examples Mannheim gives in Section 2 of Chapter 2, the section entitled "The Concept of Ideology in Historical Perspective."

The examples all refer to writers or "thinkers" as contrasted to political leaders, and are presented as illustrations of the general thesis that original distrust has evolved, historically, into ideological unmasking on a universal scale. The examples consist of a few passages from Francis Bacon's *Novum Organum*, Machiavelli's *Discorsi*, and Hume's *History of England.* . . .

There are several troubling aspects of Mannheim's use of these examples. First, the interpretations appear to me to be rather simplistic because they are deduced from a pervasive, yet never clearly established principle. The principle is that since the theory of ideology was destined historically to appear at a certain stage, the works of leading writers on politics must reflect that development. From that principle, then, it is all-too-easy a deductive leap to conclusions such as these: Bacon's discussion of the idols of the mind "may be regarded to a certain extent as a forerunner of the modern conception of ideology." The passage in Machiavelli which contrasts the thought of the palace to that of the public square is "an expression of the increasing degree to which the public was gaining access to the secrets of politics." The passage in Machiavelli prescribing a strong medicine indicates that Machiavelli "seems to be making explicit and setting up as a general rule of thought what was implicit in the common sense adage of the time." Finally, Hume's remark about men "feigning" is the Enlightenment version of, and direct precursor to, twentieth-century historians' use of the particular concept of ideology.

Second, in two of the three cases Mannheim relies not on the original works, but on German historians' secondary works, for the substance of the passages. This practice is probably consistent with Mannheim's emphasis on the "historical perspective" but it results in an essentially derivative, therefore problematic, type of interpretation. For even if one supposes, for the sake of argument, that Meinecke and Meusel themselves tried to understand Machiavelli and Hume in a very exact way, their effort is hardly a substitute for a similar effort on Mannheim's part. His thesis is independent of theirs. His evidence ought, therefore, to be independently generated.

Third, the three examples cited are all taken from the period after 1500. Although Mannheim does not explicitly say so, the drift of his argument is that even though the tendency to ideological criticism is universal in politics, it became explicit and methodical for the first time only in the modern period. Exactly why this should be so remains unclarified, as does the exact relationship of modern to classical thought. On this latter point, it is worthwhile to observe that Mannheim makes few references of any kind to classical thought. And such references as he does make are characterized by the same simplistic qualities to be found in his use of Bacon, Machiavelli and Hume. Thus elsewhere in his book the thought of the Greek Sophists and of Socrates is disposed of, in two paragraphs, as an ancient manifestation of "skepticism," which, in turn, is explained as a product of "vertical mobility" within Greek Society [pp. 6-10]. Plato's *Republic* is treated, in two lines, as an example of Utopian "mentality," which arises out of the "Greek tradition" of positing a "primal model of things" [p. 219].

Thus far, I have concentrated on the problematic character of Mannheim's historical evidence as that evidence is said to be drawn from the political thought of men known primarily as thinkers and writers. I want, next, to concentrate on his treatment of the political thought of men known primarily as political leaders. For this purpose, the most important example is Napoleon Bonaparte, whom Mannheim singles out as a truly epochal figure in the explicit emergence of a fusion of politics and philosophy in modern times.

Mannheim's interpretation of Napoleon's attack on the *idéologues* is worth examining in some detail, both because of its substance and because of what it reveals about his historical method. As for substance: Mannheim interprets Napoleon's attack as the beginning of a wholly new understanding of an age-old problem: What is the nature of reality? Hitherto, Mannheim contends, that problem had been understood either in terms of an appeal to divinely revealed truths or to rational but "contemplative" modes of thought. Henceforth, it would increasingly be understood in terms of an "epistemology" and an "ontology" derived directly from "political experience." Napoleon, by being the first publicly to subject the doctrines of theoretical men to the stringent test of experiences gained directly in the political arena, is the archetype of truly modern man; for in our era, according to Mannheim, "the criterion of reality is found primarily in an ontology derived from political experience."

Now as for his historical method in producing this interpretation: First, the interpretation is singularly brief, as we found in the case of his treatment of Bacon, Machiavelli and Hume. Second, there is no citation of the actual remarks by Napoleon, nor any analysis of the context of events and circumstances. Third, in order to demonstrate an emergent fusion of political and theoretical treatments of the problem of reality, Mannheim is obliged to stretch the evidence fairly far. Thus, instead of carefully examining the explicit objections made by Napoleon, and then trying to relate these to other views of Napoleon on the conduct of political affairs, Mannheim resorts immediately to the device of seeking out the alleged "theoretical implications" of Napoleon's statements. Quite specifically, Mannheim finds that Napoleon's criticism *must* be "at bottom, of an epistemological and ontological nature" because it depreciates the *idéologues'* doctrines as being "unrealistic."

Now this contention of Mannheim's seems to me to constitute an enormous leap from a single bit of ambiguous evidence to a sweeping and definitive conclusion. Among other things, it imputes to Napoleon a very "real," yet apparently largely "unconscious," concern with the theoretical question of the nature of reality. It also imputes to him a role in the alleged necessary fusion of politics and philosophy which has vague overtones of the Hegelian doctrine concerning epochal political figures, but which is all the worse, for that, by being presented as a solid finding of political sociology. And finally, it imputes to him, on the basis of hardly any explicit evidence, either a stupendous ability to transform the entire course of events, political and intellectual, or the role of a puppet on history's vast stage. In either case, the historical accuracy of Mannheim's treatment is, I believe, extremely suspect.

But whatever the merits of that interpretation, if we now combine it with the parallel interpretation of the writings of Bacon, Machiavelli and Hume, we find that there is a common premise at work: eminent modern political figures and eminent modern thinkers progressively articulate the historically-destined fusion of politics and philosophy. More precisely, epistemology comes to be a function of the political struggle. Conversely, the political sphere comes to utilize the theoretical modes of that originally philosophic science as a necessary device, even as a weapon.

2. Some Reflections on Mannheim's Thesis Concerning Ideology

Now whether Mannheim's historical evidence for his concept of ideology is adequate or not, the fact remains that he understood that concept as a vital historical step in producing a fusion of politics and philosophy. This being the case, I think it is necessary to consider certain implications of his general thesis, independently of the strict accuracy of the alleged historical evidence.

For my purposes, the main point of this discussion is that the historical fusion is what makes the new *science* of politics eventually possible. It does this by providing the combination of practice and theory necessary to an on-going "science of becoming." The conclusion seems to be that ineluctable historical forces have been at work for centuries to produce that science of practice which men have always needed, yet searched for in vain. Historical necessity thus seems to benefit politics and philosophy alike.

But the new science is, by Mannheim's own account, still only in prospect, not actual. This is because the historical process has not quite reached the stage in which the transcendence of the universal partisan use of the theory of ideology in the direction of the scientific use of that theory can be accomplished. Perhaps the single most important condition of that transformation is that the "socially unattached intelligentsia" must achieve an ever-deeper understanding of the historical fusion of politics and philosophy. Stated negatively, such men must no longer succumb to the temptation to revert to "intellectualist" modes of thought. Secondly, one of the means to the end of such understanding appears to be the elaboration of that "sociological history" of the theory of ideology that Mannheim views as still only embryonic; it is a means in that it would directly involve the emergent political scientists in the "historical perspective" on ideology. Thirdly, it is extremely doubtful that such understanding among the political scientists can influence the course of events unless it is widely disseminated to political as well as to other theoretical men in society. It must be disseminated to the political men in order for them to be guided by its precepts. And it must be disseminated to other kinds of theoretical men in order that they, too, may lend their support to the use of its precepts in the guidance of practice.

The widespread diffusion of the historical understanding that a necessary fusion of politics and philosophy has taken place is thus a necessary condition of the operation of the new science of politics. Conversely, once that diffusion is accomplished, political and theoretical men will join, it seems, in protecting the fundamental tenet of the new political science from being challenged: political power and the aura of science will cooperate to ensure that politics and philosophy henceforth may not claim to be distinguished from each other.

The prospective realization of such cooperation seems to Mannheim to be the decisive indicator that the theory of ideology, as a partisan weapon, has been transcended by being incorporated in the science of politics. The similarity of this formulation to present day theses alleging the "end of ideology" is, to me, striking. To cite only one well-known example: Seymour M. Lipset's argument, in *Political Man*, is that ideological politics are being replaced, in advanced western countries, by political sociology. The growing respectability of such views in present-day social science in the United States makes it all the more desirable to examine certain implications of Mannheim's version of the "end of ideology"—for that, in fact, is what his argument comes down to: the theory of ideology is transformed into a political sociology that is the province of the intellectuals who, in turn, educate the political leaders. The implications I have in mind concern the status of politics and philosophy in a society where Mannheim's version of political science would reign.

First, then, let us have a look at the implications for the status of politics. Politics would continue, it seems, essentially as struggle or conflict. But there would be two decisive differences compared to all previous experience. For one thing, the guidance of politics would be transferred from political leaders *per se* to a combination of such leaders with those members of the "socially unattached intelligentsia" who profess political sociology. Second, the quality of the guidance would thereby be transformed. From having been only a crude "art" based on mere "practical knowledge," it would become a "science of creativity" based on an understanding of the entire course of historical development.

The specific quality of this second anticipated change is reflected most acutely in Mannheim's views on political education. Traditional political education, according to Mannheim, included "factual" studies such as political history, constitutional law, statistics, history of political ideas, and perhaps, in more recent times, social psychology [p. 110]. These studies were designed to prepare future leaders for the practical direction of affairs—that is to provide "practical knowledge." But in Mannheim's view, the very idea of practical knowledge as being possibly a self-sufficient basis for the direction of political affairs is obsolescent. It has been made so by the discovery that there is an historical process which gives rise to the "science of becoming." Now, and henceforth, the political man's judgment must be derivative of or controlled by the judgments of the political sociologist. The practical question, "What is best to be done given these concrete circumstances and alternatives?", is joined to this question: "What stage have we reached in the historical process of the transformation of the world?" But in order to answer this question, the previous, practically-oriented studies will no longer suffice. What is needed, now and henceforth, is immersion in topics such as the sociology of history and the sociology of knowledge.

Mannheim's purpose, in sum, is to transform political practice by transforming the political education of men. But the premise that such a dual transformation is possible and desirable is not itself to be subject to dispute by future political leaders. Indeed, their political education is to be so thoroughly rooted in the conviction that the concept of ideology is a true proposition that they presumably cannot find a reason to question the premise. Now it is true that the *exact* degree and nature of the transformation of practice which might result from such a political education is hard to specify. But what one can say with reasonable assurance is that future political leaders are intended, by the very terms of Mannheim's version of political education, to be cut off from any serious consideration of conceptions of political practice which do not harmonize with the concept of ideology.

This point may be illustrated by a brief consideration of how Mannheim treats a rather famous passage from Edmund Burke's *Reflections on the Revolution in France*. The context in which Mannheim quotes Burke is a discussion of different conceptions of theory and practice; and the passage runs as follows:

> The science of constructing a commonwealth or renovating it or reforming it, is like every other experimental science, not to be taught *a priori*. Nor is it a short experience that can instruct us in that practical science[p.120].

Mannheim's interpretation of Burke's conception of politics is revealing: that conception is held to be a rationalization of an aristocratic class's right to govern. In other words, the important fact of resistance to abstract theorizing which lay behind Burke's stout defense of politics as a "practical science" is wholly ignored by Mannheim in favor of ideology-hunting.

My conclusion, then, concerning the implications for politics of Mannheim's concept of ideology is this: What begins, in Mannheim's vision, as a project for increasing political men's awareness of the limitations of their own as well as of their adversaries' thought, is likely to end in a decisive narrowing down in the conception of what political practice of the highest sort may possibly be. For to the extent that the concept of ideology is effectively inculcated in the minds of future political leaders, to that extent there is likely to be a dogmatic rejection of the possibilities of practice as portrayed by all the great political leaders who lived and acted *prior* to the era of ideological self-consciousness. It would not be the first time that what begins as an assault on prejudice ends as a monument to that vice.

I wish to turn, finally, to say a few words about the implications of Mannheim's concept of ideology for the status of philosophy. Those implications can be most sharply revealed by assuming, once again, that Mannheim's projected scheme of education is effectively operative within political society.

The most general implication is that Mannheim's concept, once generally disseminated, stands a good chance of becoming a new intellectual orthodoxy which will preclude any serious return to philosophy in its earlier forms. I think this is so for two reasons.

First, Mannheim's own treatment of philosophy consists essentially of viewing it through the lens of the concept of ideology. And we have seen a few examples, earlier, of what that lens does to both classical and modern thinkers: it reduces their thought to steps on the way to ideological self-consciousness, which is to say to consciousness that thought is but a function of action. Thus even in Mannheim's own work, the concept tends to solidify into a conceptual tool which amounts to a dogma.

Second, the concept performs a dual function with respect to the new intellectual elite, the "socially unattached intelligentsia": on the one hand, it justifies their intellectual and political position; and on the other hand, it explains the status of their thought. As for the effect of the latter point: the status of their thought is defined essentially in terms of a transcendence of previous "contemplative" or "intellectualist" modes of thought; and the transcendence consists of an overcoming of the antithesis of thought and action. Human thought henceforth is intended to be understood as reflective of the profound and inescapable involvement of thought *in* action, and as a guide to action. In effect, then, philosophy in the classical sense of the desire simply to know—as suggested, for example, in the first sentence of Aristotle's *Metaphysics*—is also henceforth to be understood as merely an outmoded phase in the historical development of the intelligentsia's own brand of action—based on thought.

Now this discovery by the intelligentsia that their own thought is a higher stage of thought is certainly not likely to appear to them as capable of becoming an orthodoxy. On the contrary, the guarantee that it cannot be such is that part of the concept of ideology which shows that the new intelligentsia is a classless class, historically destined to transcend all previous orthodoxies. In short, the shared conviction of being in possession of a guaranteed position as transcenders of orthodoxy is presumed to serve as a mighty bulwark against any reappearance of orthodoxy among the intelligentsia.

My general point, then, is this: Even in Mannheim's own work the concept of ideology tends to solidify into a dogmatic conceptual tool for "explaining" all prior philosophy. But in the society he projects that solidification is destined to become a generalized and institutionalized feature of intellectual life. One must be immensely more optimistic than I am able to be to conclude that the idea of philosophy as the unqualified desire to know is likely to receive very serious attention there.

I want to move a step further now to observe the implication of Mannheim's concept for the status of political philosophy in particular. The main implication is that the traditional distinction between political philosophy, strictly speaking, and other kinds of political thought is virtually obliterated. Thus the thought of Plato and Machiavelli is quoted in essentially the same manner as the thought of Napoleon and Mussolini: each kind of thought is equally subject to the interpretive tools produced by the purified concept of ideology, which is to say the sociology of knowledge. This leveling down of political thought is, of course, not peculiar to Mannheim's view—indeed, we are all aware that it is fairly common today for the terms "political philosophy" and "ideology" to be used interchangeably. But the difference between the present situation and the situation projected in Mannheim's republic of the "socially unattached intelligentsia" is an important one, and is therefore worth specifying in greater detail.

The present situation in the Western countries is one in which a fair amount of discussion still takes place about the status of political philosophy. In the context of that discussion, there still occasionally is vigorous and informed criticism of the dominant but not yet universal tendency to reduce political philosophy to ideology. On the other hand, the present situation is one in which the projected supremacy of the "socially unattached intelligentsia" has not yet been realized. But in the political society sketched by Mannheim, that supremacy is taken as a basic condition. The really interesting question, then, is what is likely to happen were that supremacy to become a reality—that is, were the concept of ideology to be universally held as a true proposition.

Since we are here operating in the realm of speculation no answer can be more than probable. But to me, the logic of Mannheim's conception suggests that it would be virtually impossible, in such a situation, for members of the intelligentsia seriously to conceive that the reduction of political philosophy to ideology is a profound error. And what applies to the question of the status of political philosophy applies with equal force to the central substantive problems treated by political philosophers, whether ancient or modern. Consider, as one brief example, the applied effect of the universally-disseminated concept of ideology on the old question whether justice is by nature or by convention. The effect almost surely will be to reduce the original terms of the problem to questions such as what "interests" were served by the making of that distinction, or by the choosing of one of the alternatives. And yet, even the recognition that such a reduction is taking place is precluded by the conviction that the purified concept of ideology is intrinsically superior to the perspective of the original form of the problem.

The image which most readily comes to my mind to describe the condition of political philosophy in Mannheim's projected political society is the old but still suggestive image of the cave, in Plato's *Republic*: The men in the cave cannot conceive that the things they see are but shadows cast upon a wall. Similarly, the intelligentsia in Mannheim's projected society cannot conceive that what they understand of political life is but a shadow of what the great political philosophers have aspired to and, on occasion, even achieved. The men in the cave cannot conceive that the light which produces the shadows is but an imitation of the sun. Similarly, the intelligentsia in Mannheim's projected society cannot conceive that the allegedly profound insight of the concept of ideology may be only an illusion of wisdom concerning the relation of thought to action.

Whether or not all men are destined to start out in the cave—as Socrates seems to suggest—is a good question. But an even better one, for our present purposes, is this: Is it reasonable to suppose that the concept of ideology can guarantee men's escape from the cave? It is in the hope of stirring up this latter question that my remarks on Mannheim are presented.

Part Two

**Ideology and Traditional
Political Theory:
Contemporary Perspectives**

The materials in Part One suggest four conclusions concerning the history of the concept of ideology. First, the concept has had theoretical and political meanings from the very beginning. The starting point was its strictly theoretical meaning, revealed in Destutt de Tracy's conception of ideology as the only true foundation of all other sciences. But this was shortly followed by the political meaning, revealed in Napoleon's and Rivarol's polemical attacks on ideology as a monstrous theorizing about politics. Second, these meanings, once established, have continued throughout the history of the concept. Third, even though there may be a rather clear analytical distinction between the two meanings, they often merge in reality. Throughout its history the theoretical meaning has had a political application, and the political meaning has referred to or depended on theoretical reasoning. Fourth, the persistence of these two meanings and their continual blurring reflect the two persistent conflicts which gave rise to them: the philosophical conflict concerning the nature and status of theory; and the political conflict concerning the effects of theory on political practice.

The form and the terms of these conflicts generally have reflected contemporary developments. This is true, as we shall see in this part, of contemporary treatments of the relationship between ideology and traditional political theory.

Today, within political science, the philosophical conflict concerning the nature and status of theory often takes the form of a debate over the merits of the scientific versus the traditional approach to the understanding of politics. In this debate, the champions of the scientific approach make a distinction between empirical theory, which is modeled on theory as it is understood in modern physical science, and normative theory, which is the formulation and projection of value preferences. The proponents of the traditional view question the validity of this distinction and argue that empirical theory modeled on the physical sciences is inapplicable to the understanding of politics.

The question now arises: How does this debate affect contemporary formulations of the relationship between ideology and theory? The scientific approach generally considers only empirical theory to be truly theoretical—that is, to possess such qualities as exactness, verifiability and predictive capacity. Normative theory, on the other hand, is considered to be rooted in non-exact, non-verifiable, ultimately subjective preferences. Such theory is usually distinguished from the ordinary citizen's principles. But both are understood to be *ultimately* subjective in character; they are understood, that is, as ideological rather than scientific. Furthermore, this distinction between ideology and science is used to categorize previous thought, in such a way that the essential element—if not the whole—of traditional political theory (Plato's *Republic*, or Hegel's *Philosophy of Right*) is understood as ideology.

Many critics of the scientific approach to politics feel that a major consequence of that line of reasoning is the understanding of normative theory, traditional political theory, and ideology as essentially synonymous. They say that this blurring of conceptions undercuts—even jettisons—serious study of the traditional theory in two ways.

First, they claim, it places a serious, perhaps insuperable psychological obstacle before the student who approaches the study of traditional political theory. For if he is convinced, even before he opens Hegel's *Philosophy of Right*, for instance, that the thoughts it contains are simply equivalent to ideology with its contemporary connotations of subjectivity, then what incentive is there to read it carefully? Thus the prior equation of traditional political theory with ideology amounts to a dogmatic categorization which forecloses serious reconsideration of the classic works of political theory.

Second, this equation has the effect of pre-empting the positive ideas of science, empirical, and understanding for the scientific approach to politics.

Here, the question is whether the scientific approach's conception of theory is ultimately true or false. The answer depends on an objective statement of the alternative conception, as contained in the classical works. A detailed comparison is the only valid way to judge between the two conceptions of theory. But for this comparison to be scientific or empirical, we must suspend judgment and question the prior equation that has been made.

This philosophical debate merges with, or forms an important aspect of, the contemporary political conflict over the effect of theory on political practice. This conflict takes the form, today, of a debate concerning the nature and desirability of ideology as a guide to political action. The parties to this debate generally agree that much of the fanaticism of twentieth-century politics can be traced to dogmatic adherence to certain ideological principles or theories: to the Communist theory of inevitable revolution, to the Nazi theory of Aryan racial superiority, and to the Capitalist theory of the right to private property. There is also general agreement that this adherence and the resultant fanaticism are great political evils. Yet there is considerable disagreement on whether ideology is dispensable as a guide to political action—a disagreement which revolves around the meaning of ideology.

At this point the two forms of debate—on the nature and status of theory, and on the effect of theory on practice—merge. Both are influenced by twentieth-century experiences of fanatical ideological conflict, and they both make explicit reference to traditional political theories.

One important effect of this contemporary consciousness of ideological politics is a reaction against the serious study of classic works on political theory. The reaction is sometimes extreme, even to the point of tacitly or explicitly rejecting political theory on the grounds that it leads to fanatical ideologies. Still, political life requires some principles as guides to conduct, and alternative sources of principles are offered today. Though they are different in what they advocate, they all are defined with respect to and held superior to traditional political theories.

In the following articles, two alternative sources of political principles are presented. First is that of the late Albert Camus. To him, traditional political theory is generally an excessive form of man's revolt against his condition in a meaningless world. Camus' alternative—his existential solution—is a non-theoretical sense of moderation in this revolt, and a dedication to respect for the value of every human being. A second alternative is presented by Professor Daniel Bell. He turns to a pragmatic combination of effective traditions and the findings of social science, especially sociology.

A second important effect of the contemporary consciousness of ideological politics is that it has directly contributed to highly problematic categories for the classification of traditional political theory. On one hand, there is negative categorization, which is derived from the equation of totalitarianism with rigid ideology, and of rigid ideology with highly systematic and abstract theorizing, especially where the latter also involves metaphysical considerations. This categorization places works such as Hegel's *Philosophy of Right* and Plato's *Republic* under the shadow of being connected to, if not actually responsible for, the modern forms of totalitarian ideology. On the other hand, there is positive categorization. This is stated in such terms as pragmatism and pluralism, and is conceived of as being anti-metaphysical, hence opposed to rigid theories which may become rigid ideologies. The effect, here, is that modern thinkers such as John Dewey, Alexis de Tocqueville, and John Stuart Mill and classical thinkers such as the Greek Sophists are presented in an initially favorable light.

The net effect of these categories is to create preconceptions which are bound to influence the study of traditional political theory. At their worst, they reduce such study to an exercise in classifying theories to fit the categories. And even at their best, they skew the inquiry away from an objective study of the theory toward a search for precursors and influences.

These preconceptions are often blended today with those drawn from the scientific approach to the study of politics. Thus it is not unusual today for traditional political theory to be viewed both as the cause of ideological politics and as the unscientific precursor of a scientific study of politics. Nor is it easy to tell which of these aspects is decisive in shaping the resultant image of traditional political theory. It is therefore important, in reading the following articles, to be aware of the prevalence of these different currents of thought and of their roots in the two conflicts over theory, which have been continuous since the French Revolution.

The question of the validity of traditional political theory as a subject of serious study thus proves to be entangled today with the question of the meaning and importance of ideology. In fact, the latter question tends to be the dominant one and to set up a screen between contemporary man and the body of thought contained in the classics of political theory. But will this screen prevail in its effects? That is an unresolved question. However, a careful examination of the readings in this part and a comparison of them with the readings in Part One point to this conclusion: Understanding the nature of ideology ultimately requires an understanding of the philosophical and political developments which gave rise to it; and understanding those developments requires an understanding of the attempt of modern philosophy to make a decisive break with classical philosophy. In this sense, the need to reconsider the respective claims of modern and classical political philosophy seems to underlie any comprehensive examination of ideology.

Chapter Four

**The Effect of Ideology on the
Contemporary Status of
Political Theory:
Two Perspectives**

The two essays which follow were written by Dante Germino and P. H.
Partridge, both professors of political science. Each author is concerned with
rendering a critical evaluation of the contemporary effect of ideology on the
status of political theory, and they both conclude that the decline of political
theory is more apparent than real. Yet what is striking is the degree of divergence between their respective understandings of the nature of ideology and
political theory. This divergence reflects different understandings of the
relationship between different aspects of traditional political theory and
between this theory and the modern empirical theory concerning politics.
Taken together, the two essays reveal something of the range and complexity
of the theoretical problems posed by the past development of the concept of
ideology and the effects of modern ideological politics.

The Revival of Political Theory*

Dante Germino

With appalling swiftness, the judgment that political theory is on the verge of extinction has spread through the political science profession. Heading the professional mourners is Alfred Cobban, who has done as much as anyone to establish the allegation that political theory is in lamentable decline as a virtually unchallenged cliché. Cobban's essay of almost a decade ago[1] obviously captured the mood of a sizeable body of political scientists, some of whom have actually resorted to funereal metaphors to describe the present condition of political theory. I propose to argue that this thesis is seriously in error and that its continued acceptance only obscures the fact that an extensive and significant effort is being made at the present time to restore political theory as a tradition of inquiry. My contention is that what Cobban has described as a decline in political theory is actually a crisis in positivist political science. He has chronicled the inevitable demise of political theory within the positivist universe of discourse, where the "fact-value" dichotomy reigns as dogma. The Cobban position fails to recognize that political theory is an experiential science of right order in human society and that theory can never be redeemed or intellectually legitimized by indulgence in subjective "value" speculation. Only by virtue of the recovery of a sound ontology and an adequate epistemology will political theory be able to flourish as it once did; this will require an abandonment of the physicalist interpretation of experience that has for decades been dominant in political science. Such a major philosophical reconstruction is now under way in our discipline and already has produced sufficiently significant results to warrant the judgment that we may now be entering a period that will witness the renaissance of political theory in the grand manner. These are sweeping contentions, but I do not make them lightly.

Meta-Theory

First of all, it will be necessary to engage in an activity which Cobban and many other scholars find reprehensible: meta-theory, or theory about theory. For one cannot answer the question regarding the present *condition* of political theory without initially answering the question about the *nature* of

*Dante Germino, "The Revival of Political Theory," *The Journal of Politics*, 25 (August 1963), 437-460. Reprinted by permission.

[1] Alfred Cobban, "The Decline of Political Theory," *Political Science Quarterly*, vol. lxviii, no. 3 (1953).

political theory. The fact that this latter question is the subject of considerable disagreement among contemporary political scientists makes it all the more necessary to plumb the depths of meta-theory. The matter cannot be left to a jovial eclecticism, for the differences of interpretation between writers who use the term political theory as if it were synonymous with ideology, those who equate it with scientific methodology, and those who regard it as a science of the principles of right order—to cite three of the current approaches culled from the mammoth existing literature—are so vast as to be unbridgeable.

On the question of meta-theory, Cobban has something useful to say. In the guise of an attack upon the meta-theoretic enterprise itself, he actually enunciates an important principle relevant to such an inquiry: *viz.*, that the *nature* of political theory cannot be discovered apart from its *history*. ("Fortunately, we have not to *invent* political theory; that was invented long ago. If there is a right way of considering its problems, I think we should be modest enough to believe that it might possibly be the way of all the greater political thinkers of the past. . . . ") For political theory is a human activity differentiated and developed under specific historical circumstances. Political theory, then, has no "essence" in the strict philosophical sense; it is not a reality with ontological status. It is an activity which, through the articulation of critically refined symbols, describes and points to such realities insofar as they bear upon the problems of human order in society.

Cobban is right in calling upon scholars to examine the writings of the great political theorists of the past with a view to distilling the meta-theory contained in their analyses. It would indeed be presumptuous and pointless to assume that we must start with a *tabula rasa*, as if no tradition of theoretical inquiry into politics existed at all. But at this point Cobban errs in failing to make a necessary fundamental distinction—the distinction between different levels of political thought. There are obvious differences of rank among thinkers in terms of the range of problems explored, the attitude of mind brought to bear upon the analysis, and the critical sophistication of the concepts that are utilized. Between a Plato and an Antiphon, a Thomas and a Marsilius, a Rousseau and a Voltaire, a Hegel and a Burke, a great gulf is fixed. This gulf, I would argue, is that which separates the political theorist proper from the publicist. This is the cardinal distinction which Cobban ignores.

The refusal to recognize the existence of the different levels of political thought leads Cobban to include all political thinkers, theorists not excepted, under the category of publicists. Thus, the unifying bond of all previous political thinkers of distinction becomes the supposed fact that "they all wrote with a practical purpose in mind" and were, indeed, essentially "party men." Now publicists such as Bentham, Burke, and Laski—Cobban's most frequently cited examples of great "political theorists"—did of course write from a practical vantage point. They wished primarily to influence the course of affairs through advocating or opposing specific institutional reforms hotly debated in their own times. The elaboration of the metaphysical and anthropological principles upon which they based their proposals for political action was their secondary pre-occupation (and, as a result, this metaphysical part of their work was done rather badly). I would contend that this order of priorities is reversed in the work of genuine political *theorists*.

Thus, I would argue, the "paradigmatic thinkers" who provide us with the "touchstones" (Matthew Arnold's suggestive word) by which to distinguish political theory from other modes of thinking about politics and who should be our guides in the contemporary effort of political theory to rediscover itself, are the creators of the great scientific treatises rather than the authors of the famous polemical tracts. There should be no serious disagreement if at the top of the list of the great political theorists, we place Plato, Aristotle, Aquinas, Machiavelli, Hobbes, Rousseau, and Hegel. (It may legitimately be argued that certain other figures also belong within this charmed circle, but surely *at least* the above-mentioned seven thinkers must be placed there.)

Accordingly, we can concur with Cobban that "if there is a right way of considering . . . [political theory's] problems [it is] the way of all greater political thinkers of the past." But we must be more discriminating in the exercise of our critical faculties in judging the different ranks of political thinkers and in singling out the men of first rank as our paradigmatic individuals. Do these great political thinkers in fact possess a common conception of political theory's task? Is there a *consensus magnorum* respecting the nature and end of political theory? I hold that there is.

Political Theory as a Tradition of Inquiry

It is to the Greeks that we owe the distinction between theoretical, practical, and productive activity. Philologists tell us that the word *theōria* initially stood for the activity of people called *theōroi*, who went on "visits of inspection" to the religious festivals of neighboring *poleis*. A *theōros* was a "spectator" or an "onlooker." The verb *theōrein* meant to behold or "take in" a "spectacle," in the sense of physically seeing it. With the gradual emergence of meta-physics, *theōria* was given a wider meaning: it was applied to the act of knowing, or inward seeing, through the "eye of the mind."

Theôria, Plato informs us in the *Republic*, is what the philosopher is engaged in when he breaks his chains and escapes the darkness of the cave to "behold" the vision of the *agathon*. Through the inward seeing of the *nous*; the *theôros* is able to pierce the veil of appearance and to arrive at *epistēmē*, as opposed to *doxa*, respecting the nature of reality. From Aristotle we learn that theoretical knowledge is knowledge for its own sake, rather than for the sake of some utilitarian end, and that the *bios theôretikos*, a life whose principal activity is philosophic contemplation, is the highest, most distinctively human, life. In contrast to the aim of practical knowledge, which is action, the aim of theoretical knowledge is understanding.

But how did the founders of political science conceive of *political* theory? Here the curious fact must be noted that Plato and Aristotle did not employ the specific term "political theory" but always used the phrase "political science" (*epistēmē politikē*). As Professor Leo Strauss has pointed out, "political theory" is not used with reference to the study of politics until the nineteenth century. Must we then go along with Strauss in asserting that Plato and Aristotle conceived of the study of politics as a practical rather than a theoretical discipline? The issue is indeed a complicated one, as can be seen from the perplexities it caused later commentators such as Aquinas and John of St. Thomas. The difficulty is caused by the hybrid nature of theoretical reflection on the practical activity of politics: political theory is amphibious, inhabiting the realms of both theory and practice at once.

Plato and Aristotle were aware of the kinship which *epistēmē politikē* has with theoretical inquiry. In the *Statesman* (258-260) Plato permits the Eleatic Stranger to discuss this problem and to conclude that the "royal science" is a species of theoretical knowledge which is designed to "rule" as well as "judge." Aristotle, while refusing to rank *epistēmē politikē* among the purely theoretical sciences—these including only physics, mathematics, and theology —clearly did conceive of the "master science" as being more than merely practical.

Obviously, the *epistēmē politikē* handed down to us in Plato's *Republic* and *Laws* and Aristotle's *Ethics* and *Politics* is not knowledge aimed in the first instance at affecting human action for a practical purpose. Plato and Aristotle did not compose manuals of practical politics within the walls of their academies. Instead, they sought to "observe" the activity of politics and to report everything which they discovered to be essential for the understanding of this phenomenon. While they were about their business they created political theory—that peculiarly hybrid study which is speculative and

practical at once, because it is a theoretical examination of a practical
activity. Like ethics, political theory is a form of what Maritain has called
"speculatively-practical knowledge"; or, in the words of John of St. Thomas,
political theory treats a "subject which is a matter of action . . . not as a
matter of action but as an object of science and an instance of truth."

The term "political theory," then, recommends itself as the most faithful
rendition of the classical *epistēmē politikē*. Let us note carefully that originally "political theory" and "political science" were synonymous with each
other. *Theōria* (theory) was the activity of searching out intellectually the
principles that comprised *epistēmē* (science). Science was simply the reporting of the results of the theoretical probings of the mind. Plato and Aristotle
(and the great masters of political theory after them) were incapable of
thinking in terms of the contemporary distinction between political theory
and political science. Political theory *was* political science, and there could be
no science without theory. Just as we frequently speak of theory as either the
activity of theorizing or the recorded results of the theorizing, so political
theory may legitimately and accurately be used as synonymous with
political science.

As with any other science, political theory claimed to base its results on
observation of a delineated aspect of reality. Or, to put it another way,
political theory was grounded on human experience, and should be considered an *experiential science*. The propositions of political theory were not
to be treated as the subjective opining of an idiosyncratic philosopher, but
were to be regarded as objectively verifiable through the meditative
re-enactment of the experiences to which the propositions referred. Political
theory was a science of man—an anthropological science—and its conclusions
were based on the observation of human nature in its constant and universal
aspects. Every man participated in this common human nature and was
potentially able to verify the teaching of political theory regarding the nature
of man in the political context by exercising his reason, through the rational
exploration of the various dimensions of his own individual experience. The
latter word is significant: experience was the control, but it was multi-
dimensional, comprising in addition to the world of sense impression the
realms of ethical and metaphysical experience—the search for the source and
end of human existence. Each experiential layer would have to be investi-
gated with the organ appropriate to its exploration: phenomena of sense
experience would be explored by the physical organs, but ethical and metaphysical experience could be grasped only by the *nous*, or the eye of the
mind. It is through the possession of the cognitive faculty of the *nous* that

man is able to theorize—to ask the questions of what and why—and man, as the only living being who possesses this faculty, is supremely the theoretical animal, who alone is puzzled by the riddle of existence.

Thus, we are able to extricate from the seminal Platonic-Aristotelian formulation certain distinctive features of political theory and the political theorist. The political theorist is one who seeks in the first instance knowledge about political reality for its own sake, rather than for some immediately practical end, although his knowledge can be used for the guidance of the statesman and the citizen in practical affairs. He bases his political knowledge on his understanding of man's essential human nature, since the natural political order will be a reflection of the order within the psyche of the representative human type. In accordance with his experiential understanding of human nature, he will construct a model of the paradigmatic society, or best regime, and will explore the relation between this "natural" order and the types of regimes which appear in history, establishing to what degree they deviate from and ignore the principles of the natural order, and describing or at least intimating the consequences which ensue to the unnatural regimes with regard to their own internal disorder. The political theorist is characterized, then, by his theoretical attitude or "set," by the range of problems with which he deals, by the fact that his investigation relates politics to the totality of human experience, and by his claim to have arrived at a knowledge of principles which have cognitive status, and are therefore universally applicable to all men at all times.

It is impossible within the confines of this article to offer more than a few succinct illustrations supporting the thesis that political theory in the grand manner of its Greek founders managed to survive and to constitute itself as a tradition of inquiry which stretches well into the modern period. In conformity with the already announced principle of seeking guidance on the question "What is political theory?" by having recourse to the works of the commonly acknowledged "greats" in the history of political thought, further discussion will be confined to a consideration of the five remaining paradigmatic individuals mentioned above: Aquinas, Machiavelli, Hobbes, Rousseau, and Hegel. Despite the obvious differences in the conclusions of their philosophical anthropologies and in their resultant extrapolations of the best regime, all these men conceived of political theory as an experiential science of order in human society. To revise Cobban's formulation, they all wrote with a theoretical purpose in mind and with the objective of enunciating certain perennially valid principles. They all held their propositions to be "verifiable" in the interior experience of their readers, and they sought the deep-knowing of the philosophic theorist rather than the much-knowing of the "empirical" scientist or the know-how of the ideological social engineer. Accordingly, the unity of political theory as a tradition of inquiry will be found to consist not so much in the conclusions reached as in the kinds of questions asked, the attitude of mind in which they are framed, and the method followed for their exploration.

The continuity of the Platonic-Aristotelian conception of political theory is easily visible in the works of Thomas Aquinas, whose theoretical gifts are amply revealed in his analysis of the nature of law in Questions 90ff. of the *Prima Secundae Partis* of the *Summa Theologiae*, as well as in lesser treatises such as the *De Regimine Principum*. In the works of Machiavelli the continuity is less evident, chiefly because he was in revolt against the teaching of classical and Christian political theory regarding the *summum bonum*, or highest good, for man. Essentially, Machiavelli substituted power or glory for virtue as the highest end in human affairs, and so presents us with a conception of the nature of politics radically opposed to that which we find in previous analyses on the subject. However, if we turn away from these conclusions to consider his objectives, his methods, and the range of problems explored, we find that Machiavelli was actually continuing the very tradition against which he was revolting. He declared in the dedicatory epistle to his principal work, the *Discorsi sopra la Prima Deca di Tito Livio*, "I have expressed everything that I know, and everything that I have learned." That is, he announced his quintessentially theoretical intention of placing politics in the totality of his experience and of writing on the broadest possible canvass. The philosophical side of Machiavelli's writing has been too long neglected. Machiavelli does present a fully developed teaching regarding the nature of man and the ends which he pursues in society in conformity with that nature.

With Thomas Hobbes, we are clearly in the presence of one of the master political theorists of all time. Hobbes was so devoted to the disinterested pursuit of knowledge about politics that the appearance of the *Leviathan* brought down the wrath of both the royalist and anti-royalist factions in England upon his head. ("I know already, by experience, how much greater thanks will be due than paid me, for telling men the truth of what men are," he had mused in the dedication of his *Elements of Philosophy*.) This was a remarkable achievement, effectively illustrating how the theorist, as opposed to the publicist, often goes against the grain of *all* the prevailing currents of opinion of his time. For the theorist is not a man who panders to mass movements; in tension with his environment, he is much more frequently a loner or outsider than a team man.

Hobbes has provided us with an unparalleled interpretation of the nature of politics based upon the finding that the avoidance of the *summum malum*, violent death, rather than the pursuit of the *summum bonum*, is the natural goal of man. In the introduction to the *Leviathan*, Hobbes directs our attention to the experiential basis for the claims of his political theory to verifiability as knowledge. To test his views, he says, "read thyself." The universality of human nature makes it possible for those who are willing to engage in intense reflection to test the propositions of the Hobbesian *epistēmē politikē* in terms of their own experience.

The importance of distinguishing between theorist and publicist or ideologist is nowhere more apparent today than with respect to the controversy which still rages over the proper interpretation of Rousseau. Viewed as a manufacturer of utopian schemes for universal social revolution, Rousseau plausibly becomes father to the excesses of the French Revolution and perhaps even of contemporary totalitarianism. But if his work is understood on its own terms, then such a line of argument is, *nolens volens*, reduced to absurdity. On its own terms, Rousseau's intellectual exploration stands as a monument to political theory in the grand manner.

All the leitmotifs that together make up the theoretical pattern are present in Rousseau's writings. His *magnum opus*, the *Contrat Social*, was not a trumpet call for immediate social renovation on a global scale, but a quiet and sober treatise, written to elucidate the perennial *"principes du droit politique."* In the author's own words, the *Contrat Social* was to be *"un livre pour tous les temps."*

The bulk of the *Contrat Social* is devoted to the sketch of the paradigmatic society, based on a thoroughly conceived anthropology. Like every true political theorist, however, he knew that a yawning gap exists between the political order in its theoretical essentiality and universality, and concrete individual political communities in the condition of actual historical embodiment. As did Plato and Aristotle, he saw the inevitable necessity for diluting the paradigm in the name of historical "realism"; consequently, he was able to offer the ruling class of Poland a model constitution which, in its federal structure, was vastly removed from his own paradigmatic construction in the *Contrat Social.*

The final master theorist and "touchstone" of great political theory to be considered here is Hegel and his *Philosophie des Rechts*. Surely, if anyone is the political theorist's theorist, Georg Wilhelm Friedrich Hegel is that man.

No thinker has ever made more explicit that political theory is not subjective ideology but experiential science, and that its *raison d'etre* is to understand rather than to transform, to make out rather than to make over, the political world. Hegel's unmistakable fidelity to theory and his contempt for utopian social engineering were clearly set forth in the *Vorrede* to his afore-mentioned masterpiece:

> This book, then, containing as it does the science of the state, is to be nothing other than the endeavor to apprehend and portray the state as something inherently rational. As a work of philosophy, it must be poles apart from an attempt to construct a state as it ought to be; it can only show how the state, the ethical universe, is to be understood.

This is about as far as one can get from Mr. Cobban's "party man," who writes for the purpose of agitating for social reform. And it is about as close as one can get to the spirit of political theory properly comprehended.

The Assault upon Political Theory

Many political scientists today have lost the historic meaning of the term political theory. Instead of being viewed as an experiential science of right order in society, political theory is more frequently equated with "ideology." Courses in political theory become surveys of the "history of ideas" reflecting the various "climates of opinion" of the particular historical epochs. If we look at its meaning, ideology turns out to be the obverse of what political theory as a tradition of discourse had conceived itself to be. Ideology is societally conditioned; political theory claimed to have made perennial insights. Ideology is a projection of subjective "value judgments"; theory put itself forward as scientific observation of experiential facts. Ideology is an action-related system of ideas employed by participants in the political struggle to attack or justify a given institutional pattern; theory has aspired to be a matter for the spectator, or detached observer, who in the first instance at least sought to know truth rather than to shape the course of political action. Ideology is propagated typically in the form of a catechism for mass circulation; theory had appeared between the covers of difficult treatises likely to be read by only a narrow circle of philosophically inclined persons.

Such a far-reaching transformation of the way in which serious political thought had formerly been conceived could have occurred only after an extensive and well-prepared assault upon the theoretic enterprise itself. The roots of this anti-theoretical movement which sought to bury political theory as it had been developed as a tradition of inquiry are to be found in the intellectual situation in post-revolutionary France. The anti-theoretical attack from within the "social sciences" was first mounted by Antoine Destutt de Tracy, and subsequently by Auguste Comte. . . .

The contraction of "experience" to sense experience and the consequent confinement of social science to propositions capable of verification by sensory perception that we find in Tracy was elevated by Comte to the cardinal tenet of positivist methodology. Just as Tracy invented ideology as the weapon with which to emasculate political theory, so Comte invented the term positivism to replace the older concept of *epistēmē politikē*. The positivist current of thought, which became dominant in twentieth century social science, has its origins in Comte's fertile mind. In his *Discours sur l'Esprit positif*, of 1844, Comte informs us that the positivist, or genuinely scientific, method of analysis is based upon "real," as distinct from "chimerical" (i.e., "metaphysical") experience. Metaphysical speculation, under which heading all previous political theory came, would be relegated to the rubbish heap by the positivist priests of the new dispensation. Somewhat similar conclusions were reached at about the same time by the young Marx, who maintained that all pretended ethical, religious, and metaphysical experience was *ersatz* in nature, the product of a "false," or alienated consciousness. Indeed, in the same year that Comte published the *Discours*, Marx was writing in his manuscript now entitled *Nationaloekonomie und Philosophie* that the very posing of questions about the origin and end of man and society is a reflection of an irrational and alienated social environment. In the transformed environment of the final Communist society, it will not even occur to the new "socialistic man" to ask such questions. He will understand that theory is at one with practice and that human practical-productive activity both is, and creates, reality. Philosophers, Marx wrote later in *Die Deutsche Ideologie*, had hitherto been preoccupied with *interpreting* the world; now they must see that their mission is to *change* it.

The impact of the above doctrines on nineteenth century political thought was enormous. During the course of the century, political theory as an inquiry into the nature and end of political activity grounded on a multi-dimensional as opposed to a physicalist interpretation of experience was all but lost. Political thought became increasingly concerned with problems relating to organizational means rather than with questions of ends, which were assumed without critical examination. Within political science itself, the rise of positivist methodology was so rapid that by the turn of the century it had become the dominant approach among European scholars. The positivization of the American political science profession was delayed a bit—not until the '20's and '30's did it become firmly established in the United States. With the change, political "science" was reinterpreted to mean something quite distinct from the *epistēmē politikē* of Aristotle and the great thinkers. Political science was modelled after the physical or biological sciences in order to illuminate causal relations which would afford the observer exact predictions of political behavior. Armed with the experiential reductionism of Tracy and Comte, the new political science would not admit into the corpus of science most of the work of the "greats": their thought was "meta-physical," therefore non-empirical, unverifiable, "senseless," unreal. Indeed, the term "experience," within the positivist universe of discourse, came to mean sense experience alone. To the positivist, metaphysical and ethical state-ments were "not capable of cognition but only of confession"; only those propositions were scientific which were verifiable through the experimental, as opposed to the experiential, method. The world of physically observable "fact" was the real world; science could give us no information about the relative validity of the different goals men might espouse, for their "opinions" about the good referred to subjective emotions rather than to objective facts. In the words of Max Weber, whose own research did so much to prove the inadequacy of the concept which he fought to see established, the ultimate achievement of social science would be to construct a *wertfrei Wissenschaft*, a "value-free science."

The triumphant positivist orientation could not fail to destroy political theory as it had been known, and, in the name of methodological "purifi-cation," to reduce theory to the lowly role of handmaiden to political science conceived in behavioristic terms. Theory became equated with experimental hypothesis and only those propositions capable of being tested in terms of sense experience were admitted into the theoretical sanctuary. Thus, there could be "theories" of voting behavior, decision-making, social change, and the like, but no theories of the principles of right action in politics, because the latter would be "unverifiable" with reference to sense observation. It is scarcely surprising that, as the positivist concept of political science gained ascendancy, political theory as it had traditionally been known was eclipsed.

Not all social scientists were happy with this situation, however, and even some of those who accepted the basic positivist assumptions thought that it was necessary to restore to political theory the significant and relevant ques-tions with which it had dealt before the positivist "purification." An early attempt was made in Europe, where a sizeable school of neo-Kantian writers began to insist on the inevitability of value-judgments in scientific investi-gation and the *Wertbezogenheit* of factual statements. In the United States, only since World War II has there been a major effort along similar lines to solve the dilemma posed by the emasculation of political theory that accom-panied the positivist ascendancy.

This attempt may be described as a rescue operation from within positivism itself. The "solution" begins by accepting the dogma of the "fact-value" dichotomy. Thus, David Easton, whose book, *The Political System*, made a major impact on the current intellectual scene, states flatly that he accepts the "working assumption . . . generally adopted in the social sciences," to wit, that "values can ultimately be reduced to emotional responses conditioned by the individual's total life-experiences." Facts and values are "logically heterogeneous." . . .

The principal contention of the Easton position (which might be called the axiological-positivist position) is that the fact-value dichotomy need not and should not mean that the political scientist *qua* "political theorist" will eschew value judgments in a bootless chase for the *wertfrei Wissenschaft*. On the contrary, political theorists should gladly seize the opportunity to throw off the encumbrance of having to claim cognitive status for their ethical reflections, a necessity under the old, pre-positivist dispensation. The theorist will now be free to become an "imaginative moral architect." In addition to producing "causal theory" he can indulge in "moral theory." Political theory in the latter sense will be a "projection of an individual's total scheme of preferences." The Eastonian axiological position has been expressed by Dwight Waldo, who, also subscribing to the notion that "value" is a "positive or negative preference," has insisted that "Political theorists should undertake 'imaginative moral architecture,' and indulge their creative imaginations in utopia-building. . . . Whose function is it, if not the political theorist's, to project ways of organizing the political aspects of our lives?"

Contemporaneously with Easton (although Easton goes into the matter much more deeply), Alfred Cobban propounded the same remedy for the rejuvenation of political theory in his previously cited essay. Cobban sharply separated political "science" from "theory." ("The object of science is to show how things happen, and why, in the nexus of cause and effect, they *do* happen. . . .") "What I mean," he wrote in the 1953 article, "is simply that it is not the function of science to pass ethical judgment. . . . The political theorist, on the other hand, is essentially concerned with the discussion of what ought to be. His judgments are at bottom value judgments."

The only difficulty with the proposed solution is that it perpetuates the very intellectual crisis which it is designed to alleviate. Whatever comes of this axiological revisionism (and positivists like Arnold Brecht are by no means disposed to accept it), it cannot possibly have the effect of restoring political theory, because true political theory has nothing to do with value "projection" and utopia-construction. As an experiential science, political theory undertakes to *discover* the place of political activity in the structure of reality as a whole. Like his behaviorist counterpart, the theorist must "test" his propositions by recourse to "experience," only the range of the experience which he regards as suitable for control is broader than the single plane of physical sensation and tactile visibility. One can search the vocabulary of political theorists from Plato to Hegel but he will not find a single reference to the specific term "value judgment" or to the concept for which it stands under some other name. As one of the leading members of what may loosely be called the "movement" to restore political theory as an experiential, if not experimental, science, has expressed it, the terms "value-judgment" and "value-free" science

were not part of the philosophical vocabulary before the second half of the nineteenth century. The notion of a value-judgment (*Werturteil*) is meaningless in itself; it gains its meaning from a situation in which it is opposed to judgments concerning facts (*Tatsachenurteile*). And this situation was created through the positivistic conceit that only propositions concerning facts of the phenomenal world were 'objective' while judgments concerning the right order of the soul and society were 'subjective.' . . . This classification made sense only if the positivistic dogma was accepted on principle. . . .[2]

The theorist is not at liberty to advocate any preferences which, for whatever obscure reason, may strike his fancy (or, in more "sophisticated" language, have an emotive appeal for him), for he takes his bearings from his understanding of the reality in which he participates. All the great political theorists of the past would have subscribed in principle to the Thomistic dictum that *bonum et ens convertuntur*, and they would have agreed that the answer to the axiological question of what ought to be is contained within the answer to the ontological question of what essentially is. When the theorists offered their propositions about the good or "natural" life for man in society, they were, it is true, speaking about what he "ought" to do, but this "ought" was not regarded as a subjective preference or "value judgment" but as an experiential fact; the "ought" is the "experienced tension between the order of being and the conduct of man." (The differences among the various political theorists concerned their divergent reading of what experience teaches about the ontological structure itself.)

The axiological positivist position can never succeed in rescuing political theory from the oblivion to which "value-neutral" positivism has consigned it. If it accomplishes anything, it can only be to turn "political theorists" into opinionated ideologists. The axiological approach, while aspiring to redeem political theory, can only consummate its destruction. If a scholar really

[2]Eric Voegelin, *The New Science of Politics* (Chicago, 1952), p. 11.

accepts the dogma that all speculation about right order in society and psyche is hopelessly subjective, ultimately nothing more than a reflection of his unique "total life experiences," what justification does he, as a scholar and an aspiring scientist, have for engaging in such speculation? If he believes his conclusions on such matters to have no more foundation than his ultimately arbitrary personal preferences, he will as a scientist leave most of what used to be the field of political theory to demagogic exhibitionists, and concentrate on a topic for investigation that will be sanctioned by the profession as a scientific endeavor. Indeed, it was precisely for the reason that he was distressed over social science becoming a battleground for competing subjective value-systems (i.e., ideologies) that Max Weber issued his plea for "value-free" social science in the emotion-drenched university atmosphere in Munich after 1918. Surely the answer to political theory's difficulties—brought on by the victory of the positivist orientation—does not lie in heeding the siren-call of those who say that political theory must become frankly ideological and subjective. The answer can only lie, rather, in the questioning of the positivist dogma itself. For it is the dogma, after all, with its experiential reductionism, that is at the root of the aforementioned difficulties.

The Revival of Political Theory

It is true that a survey of the history of political thought for the last one hundred and fifty years must, for the most part, record the precipitous decline of political theory on the one hand and the proliferation of aggressive ideologies on the other. As we have seen, what has remained of the theoretical impulse to achieve a detached observation of politics has been siphoned off by an increasingly more restrictive positivism to concentrate upon an ever narrower range of problems and phenomena.

However—and this is my main bone of contention with Cobban and others who write about the "decline" of political theory—when we turn to the immediate past, especially the years since World War II, we are compelled to notice a countervailing trend which must be described as an extensive and increasingly significant movement of resistance to the dominant positivist orientation. Among its ranks are thinkers, who, although adhering to different philosophical perspectives, are united in their dedication to restore political theory in its traditional range and depth. While it would be patently impossible to discuss adequately or even to list here all the scholars who are making significant contributions to the restorative effort, a few of them deserve attention.

Perhaps the most original and profound writer in this group is Eric Voegelin of the University of Munich, who is at present engaged in a five-volume study which joins political theory with the principles of a philosophy of history. The author of numerous other books and countless articles in German and English, Voegelin is the most unjustifiably neglected political philosopher in the world today. While it would be premature to evaluate his place in the history of political thought, it is possible that in time Voegelin will emerge as the greatest political theorist of this century and one of the greatest of all time.

Voegelin has labored with enormous learning and impressive philosophical prowess to demonstrate that "political theory" and "political science" are not distinct from but are inseparably bound up with one another. The theoretical activity of the *nous* results in the formulation of the propositions of political science, which should be defined as the science of the principles of right order in the soul and in society. Like Leo Strauss, another prominent figure in the resistance movement, Voegelin is aware that, in order for further decisive theoretical advances to be made, it is necessary to regain the classical thinkers' understanding of *epistēmē politikē* as the science of right order. Much of his work would no doubt be attacked by Cobban, Easton, *et al.* as "historicist" dabbling in the sources to escape the hard tasks of "doing" constructive political theory. In actuality, this portion of his writing is wholly necessary and is, indeed, a brilliant and creative re-interpretation of the basic texts that have comprised the *epistēmē politikē* of the past. The Munich philosopher has salvaged the philosophical anthropology, or ethical theory, and the theory of the right political order (*aristē politeia*) of Plato and Aristotle, applying these insights creatively to current conditions; and he has gone decisively beyond the Greek fathers of political science in discoursing upon the third *topos* of the classic "political science": *i.e.*, the philosophy of history.

Building on the raw material unearthed by Toynbee, Voegelin has discovered the major symbolic forms whose succession makes up what we know as the process of history at its substantive level, and he has evaluated each one in terms of rigorously established critical standards. He has also worked out a profound and original analysis of the structure of the basic "experience of existence" which must serve as a prerequisite to any valid theorizing respecting the human condition. Indeed, his discussion of the requirements for participation in the theoretical debate may well prove to be his most important single contribution to political theory at this critical juncture of its history. His detailed refutation of the widespread idea that utopia construction and political theory have anything in common is another signal service for political theory.

Another key representative of the contemporary resistance movement is Leo Strauss, whose masterful studies of Hobbes, Machiavelli, and the problem of natural right are likely to remain as monuments of painstaking scholarship for decades to come. Although Strauss rejects Voegelin's transcendental realism and embraces the perspective of anthropocentric, as opposed to theocentric, humanism (to use Maritain's fruitful distinction), Strauss resembles Voegelin in that he also is seeking to recover political ethics as an objective science accessible to human reason. Strauss is convinced, as are many other contemporary political scientists, that the rise of totalitarianism revealed the bankruptcy of the positivist teaching, demonstrating that, for all its accumulation of factual information, positivist political science was helpless when it came to the crucial matter of providing standards for distinguishing between just and tyrannical regimes. . . .

In actuality, then, political theory today is hardly in a state of decline, or death. It has been in decline, to be sure, for a century or more, but during recent years, the dominant positivist orientation has been challenged by a number of highly gifted theorists. One might even say that at the present moment we are on the verge of a renaissance in political speculation, a truly creative flowering of this age-old tradition of inquiry. But why, one asks, is there then so much talk of "decline" in contemporary political theory? Two principal reasons suggest themselves. First, and most important, the hard-pressed positivist majority in political science has been unwilling and unable to recognize the extent and importance of the resistance movement. Given the interpretation of theory as *either* behaviorist methodology *or* value-laden ideology (which, I have attempted to show, is unfounded), the positivists are incapable of recognizing genuine political theory when they see it. Non-axiological positivists view the new scientific political theory as simply more of the same old opinionated ideology, lacking any claim at all to scientific, cognitive status. The axiological school, whose spokesmen fail even to mention the representatives of the new political theory, can only be presumed to regard its writings as excessively "academic" and "historicist." To Cobban, who thinks of political theorists as publicists who in the west have the function of shoring up the democratic civil theology, or to Waldo, who sees them churning out utopian reformist tracts, the new political theory must seem irrelevant and intractable for the primarily practical and ideological purposes that they have in mind for it. But political theory has always seemed this way to those who would spend most of their time in the cave of political combat. A second reason for the thus-far rather muted reception of the new political theory is the curious inability on the part of some of the resisters—or restorers—themselves to perceive the extent of their influence or to recognize that other scholars with whom they disagree on some points are actually cooperating with them in a more fundamental sense.

Like the proverbial phoenix, political theory is today rising from the ashes of its own destruction. Instead of acceding to the wishes of those who would schedule its funeral, we should instead be joyously commemorating its rebirth. But such celebration might perhaps be premature, for the success of the restorative movement is by no means guaranteed. The motivation for preserving the positivist taboo on metaphysics is strong: it is discomforting to face fundamental existential problems which do not go away when officially banished. And metaphysical and ethical knowledge is less precise and certain than knowledge gained from sense experience. For the positivists are correct when they argue that metaphysical propositions are more difficult to "verify intersubjectively," and they are right when they point out that even among the great theorists there are displutes of the most fundamental kind, different readings of multi-dimensional experience.

That the theoretical enterprise is difficult is true, but the knowledge sought is of such ultimate importance that the difficulties should not deter us from seeking it. The alternative to political theory is a decapitated science of politics—a science that knows means and methods but is ignorant of ends. Without a fully developed political science, we are left in the jungle of unjustified opinion about the goals of political life, thrown to the mercy of the ideologists. For any thoughtful person, and not only professional political theorists, the effort to resurrect political theory in our time is a matter of pressing concern.

To leave it at this, however, would be to conclude on a non-theoretical note. Theory, after all, is to be engaged in for its own sake. It is a sad fact of our technologically oriented culture that the joys of the *bios theōretikos* are so little regarded even among the *Soi-disant* intellectuals. Possibly the time has come for us to turn inward on ourselves and to recapture the glories of that life.

Politics, Philosophy, Ideology*

P. H. Partridge[1]

My object is to comment upon what seem to me to be some typical trends in current English and American political theory, having in mind the view that has recently been constantly asserted, that political theory has been in decline or may even have expired during the last few decades.[2] I will argue that the report of death, even of decline, is grossly exaggerated, that in fact the present period is unusually fertile in thinking about politics that is not only original and important, but is also, at any rate in many significant respects, entirely in the traditions of 'classical' political theory. That is one half of my thesis; the other half is that during the past few years some very important shifts in interest, approach, and emphasis have certainly occurred; and I shall make some suggestions about the character of these shifts, and the reasons for them.

Unfortunately, those who have been announcing the decay or death of classical political theory have as a rule taken less trouble to establish the fact of death or decay than to assert its causes. I do not know what kind or amount of evidence is necessary to prove that political theory has declined in volume or quality, but the assertion does not seem to be very plausible on its face. For one thing, changes of this somewhat radical kind do not occur quite so dramatically as this one is sometimes supposed to have occurred. Or, again, if we call to mind the very large number of books that have dealt quite recently with such central problems as the nature and conditions of

*P. H. Partridge, "Politics, Philosophy, Ideology," *Political Studies*, 9 (1961), 217-235. Reprinted by permission of The Clarendon Press, Oxford, England.

[1] The writer is very deeply indebted to Professor Wilfrid Harrison for many suggestions for the improvement of the form of this article.

[2] This is a selection from some of the more recent books and articles which have discussed the present condition of political theory: A. Cobban, "The Decline of Political Theory," *Pol. Sc. Q.*, vol. lxviii, no. 3 (1953); J. C. Rees, "The Limitations of Political Theory," *Pol. Studies*, vol. ii, no. 3 (1954); P. Laslett (ed.), *Philosophy, Politics and Society* (1956); G. C. Field, "What is Political Theory?" *Proc. Arist. Society*, vol. liv; G. E. G. Catlin, "Political Theory: What is It?" *Pol. Sc. Q.*, vol. lxxi, no. 1 (1957); D. Braybrooke, "The Expanding Universe of Political Philosophy," *Review of Metaphysics*, vol. xi, no. 4 (1958); J. P. Plamenatz, "The Use of Political Theory," *Pol. Studies*, vol. viii, no. 1 (1960); H. R. Greaves, "Political Theory Today," *Pol. Sc. Q.*, vol. lxxv, no. 1 (1960); A. Brecht, *Political Theory* (1959); H. V. Jaffa, "The Case against Political Theory," *Journal of Politics*, vol. 22, no. 2 (1960); L. Strauss, *What Is Political Philosophy, and Other Studies* (1959).

democracy, the group theory of political action and structure, and the theory of bureaucracy, one might have thought that there has never been a time when so much theoretical speculation about politics has been going on. Clearly, when writers nevertheless maintain that political theory is in decline, they must have something else in mind. Hence, we should perhaps begin by considering briefly what are some of the different things that political theory has meant, what different sorts of thinking about politics the name has been applied to. Some kinds may have become unfashionable, while others have continued to flourish.

I

Classical political theory has usually been a mixture of different kinds of inquiry or speculation. One could distinguish three different impulses— philosophical, sociological, ideological. This paper will be mainly about the third, but I want to say something first about all three. The political specula- tion of Plato, Hobbes, Locke, or Hegel is philosophical chiefly because each of these writers has tried to connect his conclusions about political organiza- tion, or about the 'ends' of political life, with a wider philosophical system. He has tried to derive political and social conclusions from more general beliefs about the the nature of reality, to show that every sphere of reality, including the political, possesses certain common features or 'categories', that all these spheres can be spoken about in the same logical language, that, in short, political conclusions follow from or are supported by more general logical and metaphysical principles. And one obvious reason for the current impression that classical political theory is in decay is that there is not so much of this sort of argument now: many philosophers now insist that one cannot deduce the 'rightness' or 'rationality' of a form of political organi- zation, or of a political policy, from more ultimate principles. For example, that section of Weldon's *Vocabulary of Politics* which deals with what he calls 'foundations' has this main philosophical purpose.

As I have said, one special form of the traditional connexion between philos- ophy and politics starts from the conception that it is the task of philosophy to exhibit what is common between the social and other 'spheres' of reality. Historically, of course, this has been a most important link between philos- ophy and politics; for instance, philosophical atomism has lent support to social individualism, the dialectic and the concrete universal are as important in Hegel's social theory as in the more philosophical parts of his work; and more recently some of the earlier political pluralists gained some support from the criticisms of philosophical monism developed by William James and others.

But clearly, a great deal of political theory has not been philosophical in this sense. Although de Tocqueville or Graham Wallas discussed some of the problems that political philosophers also discussed, their political views were not systematically connected with a philosophical position. A lot of de Tocqueville's writing we should now describe as sociological; he asserts generalizations, including causal generalizations, about the behaviour of social phenomena. Naturally, this is not only true of the de Tocquevilles, Bagehots or Maines; even in the writings of the political philosophers in the more technical sense, there is much sociological generalization—Hobbes is a notable example. Political philosophy was, of course, one of the parents of contemporary sociology. And no one doubts that the development of sociology as a specialized, altogether more rigorous, subject has also affected general political and social speculation.

By the ideological impulse I mean merely the form of political thinking in which the *emphasis* falls neither on philosophical analysis and deduction, nor on sociological generalization, but on moral reflection—on elaborating and advocating conceptions of the good life, and of describing the forms of social action and organization necessary for their achievement. Of course one cannot draw a sharp line between ideological and philosophical political writing: almost all political philosophy has been 'practical philosophy' in that it has had the practical object of persuading readers of the 'rationality' or moral superiority of some specific form of social organization. Even the *Leviathan* has such a practical aim, although Hobbes's practical conclusions are grounded upon philosophical and other argument which has usually been taken to be of greater interest than the practical purpose. But Rousseau, unlike Hobbes and Hegel, was not primarily a philosopher. The *Social Contract* introduces some general distinctions and conceptions of a philosophical kind, the significance and limitations of which were more developed by later writers, including Green and Bosanquet. But one would not expect much to be said about Rousseau in a history of philosophy—not, at least, in one written by an Englishman. In his case it would be very easy to detach and stress the ideological element. In fact, this is what seems to have happened: the image or model of democratic society drawn from the *Social Contract* has been very much more influential historically than any philosophical conceptualization or argument that the book contains.

But no matter how we choose to classify any theorist, I think it will be agreed that we can distinguish these three different impulses and interests, and these three 'orders' of political thinking. Nor will anyone dispute that one very powerful interest throughout the course of European social thinking has been the 'ideological'—moral argument about ends and ways of life, and about the institutional conditions of the good life.

II

Possibly each one of these impulses has grown weaker in recent years. Undoubtedly the progress of detailed empirical political and social inquiry has shaken the habit of speculative sociological generalization of the 'philosophical' kind, the concoction of what Dahl has called 'macro-theory' in politics.[3] Part of what is to be found in classical political philosophy has now been absorbed into political science and sociology. Again, many philosophers now reject the conception of philosophy, and of the resulting connexion between philosophy and politics, on which most of classical political philosophy (in the strict sense) rests. I cannot here discuss the technical reasons for the rejection: I shall make just one remark—addressed to many political writers who have been lamenting the decay of traditional political philosophy: this lament is idle if you have no answer to the technical philosophical arguments which can be deployed against the practice of supporting conclusions about the 'functions' of the State or about the rational ordering of social life by resting upon 'higher' or 'more ultimate' logical and philosophical principles.

But does it follow that these philosophical arguments have produced a decay of philosophical political theorizing? I should argue that there has not been such a decay. While philosophers have been disclaiming competence in political discussion, political scientists have been delighted to accept their disclaimer; and it can be argued that what is now happening is only an example of the familiar separation of a distinct subject from the parent philosophical stem. Political science, like economics, and other sciences, has reached the point where the specialists must themselves deal with the very general matters, including conceptual analysis, popularly or traditionally called 'philosophical'; and they do so at a level of sophistication and complexity which the philosopher *qua* philosopher could hardly approach. The boundaries between philosophy and politics are being redrawn. A number of twentieth-century philosophers have drawn a very sharp line indeed between 'philosophical' questions (or conceptual analysis) and 'empirical' questions; between 'second order' and 'first order' statements about politics. By and large, the political scientists have been sensible enough to see that the drawing of this sharp boundary is hopelessly disabling for the study of social theory, and have ignored it. On the other hand, the philosophers who have imposed it

---

[3]See his review article on de Jouvenel's *Sovereignty* — "Political Theory: Truth and Consequences," *World Politics*, vol. xi, no. 1 (1958).

have been left in occupation of only a wafer-thin slice of the territory of politics—as *The Vocabulary of Politics* clearly demonstrates.

The philosophical impulse, in fact, is not the most important part of our inquiry; technical philosophy, after all, has only a limited influence; many of the most important political theorists of the last three centuries were not much influenced, or not influenced at all, by the technical philosophy of their own time. The philosophical impulse or influence is only one of those which have sustained political speculation; others have been equally or even more important. This brings me, then, to the 'ideological impulse' with which, in one way or another, the rest of this essay will be concerned.

III

The writers who have drawn attention to what they interpret as a languishing of philosophical thinking about politics have mainly in mind the political philosophy which has been an extension of moral theory—which inquires into the ends of the State and its morally right organization (What is the State that I should obey it?)—into the morally necessary or morally justifiable ordering of political society. The 'decline of political theory' is taken to be the decline of the moral interest in politics. 'On the one hand, there is a great deal of eagerness to deal with politics in moral terms; on the other, the insights of psychology, anthropology and of political observation have silenced the urge.'[4] It is this fact—if it is a fact—that is most in need of explanation.

Is it a fact that there has been a 'slackening' of the 'moral urge'? Once again it is not hard to construct a case against. There is, after all, a very large amount of contemporary discussion of the moral foundations and dimensions of politics; for instance, the many fashionable criticisms of secular or positivistic liberalism such as were examined by Frankel in his *Case for Modern Man*. Nor should we overlook the moral discussion to be found in the pages of sociologists who are interested in the *non*-political areas of social life. One striking (and perhaps strange) feature of recent American sociology has been the popularization of the notion of 'alienation'. This, together with the closely connected themes of anomie, de-personalization, the atomization allegedly inherent in large-scale industrial society, the supposed dissolution of 'community' and aggrandizement of the State and other depersonalized,

[4]Judith Shklar, *After Utopia* (Princeton, 1957), p. 272. J. P. Plamenatz's article "The Use of Political Theory," *Pol. Studies,* vol. viii, no. 1 (1960) and H. R. Greaves, "Political Theory Today," *Pol. Sc. Quarterly,* vol. lxxv, no. 1 (1960) are examples of this line of argument.

bureaucratized forms of organization, is surely one of the most widely-followed fashions of social thought at present. Perhaps there is a good reason for this; perhaps the social conditions and changes which appear to be morally most significant are not changes, or possible changes, in *political* arrangements or institutions, but those at other levels of society. The kind of lives people live in modern cities, the demands that industrial and other great organizations make upon them, the effects of commercialism, industrialization, and 'mass media' on popular culture—one could argue that it is in such contexts that the more important occasions for moral disquiet and reflection are to be found. In other words, if the moral interest in politics *has* declined, one reason could be that questions of political organization, of allocation of political rights and powers, &c., are not at present generally felt to be morally critical.[5]

IV

I want to develop this. There now prevails in England and the United States and in several other Western-type democracies a quite unusual degree of political relaxation and consensus. I shall not try to state carefully what this consensus embraces; but it obviously embraces the fundamental constitution of the liberal-democratic order. There is no significant social or intellectual movement which calls into question the broad structure of rights and powers understood to constitute or define a democratic policy. There are no new classes struggling to win a share in political power, none struggling for an enlargement of power in ways that would entail substantial modification of political foundations. In Western Europe since, let us say, the beginning of the seventeenth century, it is not often that this could have been said. One could point, of course, to important contemporary controversies about rights or liberties (e.g. controversies about limitations upon the freedom of action of trade unions), but such controversies tend less and less to raise issues of great generality, and generality has normally been taken to be the work of *philosophical* issue in politics.

Now, if this is roughly true, it is plausible to suppose that this consensus (and not technical changes in philosophy or the growth of empirical social science, or other developments of extremely circumscribed influence) is the main factor affecting the character of contemporary political theory. If classical political theory *has* died, perhaps it has been killed by the triumph of democracy. At any rate, this seems to me to be a very relevant consideration

[5]I am speaking of course of the Western democracies; the reader will immediately protest against this remark if it is applied to contemporary Africa.

which has not been sufficiently noticed by those who have written about the decay of political theory.[6]

In fact, the consensus appears to include more than the general system of powers and rights and the legally established institutions which give effect to them. It seems to embrace also objectives and justifications of policy. Is there not an all but universal acceptance of the belief that continuous technological and economic innovation, uninterrupted expansion of economic resources, a continuously rising standard of 'material welfare', are the main purposes of social life and political action, and also the main criteria for judging the success and validity of a social order? No doubt, there is in any of the societies I have referred to some public questioning and criticism of these objectives and criteria; nevertheless, these are the objectives and criteria which define the course of contemporary democratic politics. They are the 'built-in' criteria which render irrelevant and impotent any alternative social philosophy.[7]

[6]May we not suspect the influence of ideological consensus even in some of the arguments employed by recent English philosophers? The late Miss Margaret Macdonald, for example, in her well-known essay, *The Language of Political Theory*, argues that the orthodox question Why should I obey the State, or Why should I obey the law? is in principle unanswerable. I can give reasons why I should obey (or disobey) this particular law; but there is no answer to the general question Why should I obey the law (or the State)? Now, apart from the question whether this argument does justice to what such a philosopher as T. H. Green was really saying, we may ask whether the argument would in fact always hold. If we give the State a content (let us take it to be, for example, a secular political authority claiming ultimate or sovereign political power over all other institutions), have there not been obvious that the State, as distinct from other institutions, was entitled to claim final obedience? If there is, then, a real *general* issue, is it pointless to try to make a case in *general* terms for the supremacy of the State and its law, though we may admit that it is a general case only, and that there may quite well be conditions—as Green, along with other political philosophers, admitted—under which the case for the State's final authority does not hold? May not Miss Macdonald's argument derive some plausibility from the fact that the State and its legal supremacy are now so firmly established as a matter of historical fact that to ask in *general* Why should I obey the State? seems as sensible as to ask Why should I obey the laws of gravity?

[7]It is possible, of course, that the political and moral consensus may be more superficial than appears; and that there may be conflicts or frustrations growing in the deeper social soils that most of us are not sensitive enough to perceive. If the sociologists to whom I earlier referred are right in much of what they say about the psychological dissatisfactions and social dislocations of industrial society, then this may be so. At any rate, they have not yet become significant in practical politics, and, except for a few writers of the "new Left" in England and America, they have not provided material for new political formulations. In his *Beyond the Welfare State*, Myrdal tries to describe in more detail the consensus that exists in the stable democracies; he seems to have no doubt about the stability of the prevailing agreement upon the arrangements and objectives of the Welfare State.

To speak of unusual ideological consensus when it is popularly supposed that the world is divided by warring ideologies may seem paradoxical; but the career of communism in England, the U.S.A., and some other democracies reinforces the argument. Communism has had no important effect in these countries as an alternative political philosophy; in England, as Miss Iris Murdock has put it, communism has been left to the communists: one of the chief forces in creating and consolidating democratic consensus has been the repudiation of the consequences of communist revolutions. And one might document the growth of consensus in England by examining the history of socialist thought over the past three or four decades. There are now few socialist writers who advocate any systematic alternative to the basic *political* assumptions and arrangements of a liberal-democratic system. Most of the specifically socialist notions of extended democratic rights and institutions which had some currency earlier in the century—industrial democracy, workers' participation in management, guild socialism, and so on—are not much heard of now in serious politics. One of the most interesting points about such recent English works as Crosland's *The Future of Socialism* and Strachey's *Contemporary Capitalism* is that they disclose very plainly indeed how the standard institutions and procedures of liberal parliamentary democracy are now accepted as common ground.

V

But, further, there is the even more interesting and important fact that some of the most influential political theorists of the day have become consciously *anti*-ideological. A closer look at some of the arguments which have been brought to bear against ideological politics will help us to see more clearly what is happening in contemporary English and American political theory.

By and large, the ruling trend of contemporary theory has been reacting against the more optimistic philosophies or ideologies of the past two centuries; consciously or implicitly, it has set about deflating the larger ideas of human possibilities that recommended themselves to many thinkers in the past, and has engaged in the job of cutting down our notions of man's nature to size.

The argument against 'ideological politics' has taken a number of different lines. It may simply assert that ideological ways of formulating political attitudes and objectives have declined in the course of this century as a matter of fact. But most writers who have touched on this theme have intended to do more; they have produced an account of what they believe to be *rational* political action. One argument is that ideologically-dominated thinking has no relevance to the controlling facts of contemporary social structure and change. 'Grand alternatives' like capitalism and socialism are irrelevant, because our choice is not between all-inclusive and mutually exclusive alternatives; in any society, there may be an indefinite number of ways in which different institutions and social mechanisms may be arranged and administered. Sometimes, this point is connected with a wider point— that ideological thinking has usually been totalistic; that is, that it has assumed that every important characteristic of a society is connected with a single governing mechanism, and that the whole of human life can be transformed from a central point. Thus, it is suggested, ideological thinking tends to adopt global views of social structure and political action.[8]

Again, it has been argued that this totalistic illusion has been responsible, in those countries which have suffered ideologically-inspired revolution, for much of the barbarism of the twentieth-century upheavals. The attempt to transform society globally can never be successful, and demands the employment of force on a monstrous scale and in a never-ending process. The logic of the idea of total transformation leads to perpetual force, apart from the fact that ideological conviction is often associated with moral and political fanaticism.

Finally, I must mention the criticism of ideological politics that Edward Shils has developed, because it is theoretically the most penetrating and interesting. Shils's criticism connects with his theory of social groups and kinds of social cohesion. His argument is meant to suggest, I think, that those who have defined political action (or the change to be accomplished by political action) ideologically have erred by imposing upon civil society a character repugnant to it, one which rather characterizes other types of social grouping and adhesion. Civil society, according to Shils, is characterized by a plurality of groups, interests, and values, and the attachment of the members of civil society to the common set of values is normally moderate, lukewarm, sporadic, and intermittent. Thus, those who envisage a civil society as embodying a shared and intensely experienced set of common values are really imputing to civil society the emotional, psychological, or moral qualities that are characteristic of quite different types of social group, for instance, the sect or the community bound by 'primordial' ties of blood or propinquity. The attempt to create a civil society possessing a heightened emotionalism, and a

---

[8]This is suggested by the way in which some followers of Marx have talked about "the" revolution; as if there were one revolution that would transform society, and the eradication of all social evils waited upon "the" revolution.

more intense, inclusive, and continuous integration around a common 'centre', is thus bound to be destructive of liberty and other political values of civil society.[9]

For such reasons, much recent British and American political theory has been concerned with the devaluation of ideology and ideologies, with showing the importance of 'technique' as opposed to ideology, or with showing that 'incrementalism' (Dahl and Lindblom), or 'piecemeal engineering' (Popper), are the most rational methods of political change. Now, this quite considerable body of recent writing obviously raises some very important questions (the question of the nature and function of ideologies in politics has certainly not been exhausted); and it seems odd, therefore, that there should be so much talk about the decline or decay of political theory. Nor does this particular line of thought justify the suggestion that political theory has been entirely supplanted by factual or purely descriptive and explanatory political 'science'; for these writers are concerned with the justification of forms of political action and organization, just as political philosophers have always been. The method of justification is no doubt different; writers like Shils ground their conclusions on sociological premises rather than on more general philosophical ones. But this is but another illustration of the point already made that in twentieth-century political theory the discussion of the general issues is being detached from 'philosophy' and more and more closely linked with empirical social inquiry.

It could be argued, I think, that the thorough-going pluralism of present-day Anglo-American political theory has tended strongly to inhibit the formulation of general principles, values, or objectives of political life. It is the pervasive belief of current English and American political science that the 'essence' of democratic politics is a process of bargaining and of finding adjustments between competing demands, interests, values, ways of life— adjustments that will be more or less temporary and shifting as conditions change within and without society. In the more stable and affluent democracies this is the character that present political life has assumed. And this, surely, is enough to account for the relaxed atmosphere of modern

[9]The reference is primarily to the article, "Primordial, Personal, Sacred and Civil Ties," in *British Journal of Sociology*, vol. 8, no. 2. Some of the bearings of this view upon questions of political philosophy are suggested in *The Torment of Secrecy*. Many other lines of contemporary political thinking are allied to those I have summarized. For example, Talmon's studies of the history of political ideas, *Totalitarian Democracy* and *Political Messianism,* have a similar tendency; as have the various articles that have recently appeared discussing the positive functions of political apathy in democracies, for example, W. H. Morris Jones, "In Defence of Apathy," *Pol. Studies,* vol. iv, no. 6 (1954).

democratic politics, the absence of political ideas of general range and importance, and of comprehensive political doctrine. In general, the politics of
adjustment is one that directs itself to separate and limited issues, most of
which affect only limited sections of a community, and any one of which
engages rarely, and usually only marginally and casually, the interests or
passions of a large span of the public, and which are unlikely, therefore, to
generate political movements or coherent bodies of theory which aim to
articulate a whole cluster of issues. It is evident that this corresponds very
closely to Shils's account of the nature of 'civil society'.[10]

It would take me too far afield to try to examine in detail the now standard
arguments against 'ideological politics'; I shall make only one or two observations. One might argue, to begin with, that the writers to whom I am referring
are incautious in their acclaim of the passing of ideologies; that they are
generalizing too boldly from the special conditions that now happen to
obtain in a few societies. Again, it may even be misleading to say that in these
societies the function of ideology has vanished. It can be argued that the
politics of 'incrementalism', of bargaining and adjustment, of the pursuit of
limited objectives, can itself operate as it does only because of the strong and
wide ideological consensus that happens to rule in these societies. In his
Preface to Democratic Theory, Dahl makes the point that the processes of
bargaining and adjustment of claims involve agreed values and principles
which keep political conflicts within bounds, limit the demands which
minorities will seek to have granted, define the range within which acceptable
solutions are known to lie, and so on. But this is a point of general importance. Recent political theorists have been apt to under-emphasize the extent
to which all the elements which enter into the consensus operate as a necessary condition of effective political bargaining and compromise. Ideology
may be no less an important element in a political and social system because
it lies below the level of general political controversy.

Again, just because of the special circumstances of our time, we may be too
ready to conclude that ideology is a false, irrational, and even disastrous guide

[10]It is not only in political thinking that particularism or piecemealism is the prevailing
habit of thought. C. Wright Mills' recent book, *The Sociological Imagination,* may be
read as a protest against this habit of thought in a wider context. If I follow him correctly, when he advocates the "sociological imagination," he is protesting against the
practice of many sociologists—the "abstracted empiricists"—of concentrating upon the
separate and circumscribed social phenomenon or problem. He still believes that one can
explore the structure of society as a whole; that there are controlling areas (or at least
especially strategic areas) through which a wide range of social life can be affected; and
that contemporary social theorists fail to attend to those strategic areas within the social
system which have the widest influence on freedom and other values of democratic society.

to political *action*. We look back over recent history, and we see that the aspirations and expectations of ideological and utopian thinkers or agitators differ ludicrously from the states of affairs that actually came to be: such highly-charged ideas as equality, fraternity, 'positive' freedom in the sense of general participation in the control of social affairs, and notions about a class-less society, common ownership and the like, seem to have come to very little. And these large moral intimations have apparently not only been held to be irrelevant to the actual course of events: it is often argued that they have been pernicious in their effects: they have encouraged colossal blundering, they have blinded men to the understanding of their own limitations, to the reality of original sin (Reinhold Niebuhr's account of the human situation accords with many of the other fashionable currents of present-day social thought); they have provided facile justifications for ruthlessness and terror. Michael Polanyi has somewhere argued that the revolutionary excesses of this century have resulted partly from 'the excess of theoretical aspiration over practical wisdom'. Consequently, it is not hard to find grounds for arguing, as Popper does in effect in *The Open Society and its Enemies,* that gradual, piecemeal, 'experimental' attack on limited and particular problems, the pragmatic alleviation of particular evils, is the only rational method of political change.

In a sense, this sort of argument is incontrovertible. Political ideology has often been mainly faith, myth, superstition, political and moral dogmatism and fanaticism; when at full flood it has sometimes produced the most appalling destruction of existing institutions, traditions, and values. It would indeed be difficult to hold that there was anything rational about such ideology-impregnated social upheavals: to say that they are a 'rational' way of bringing about desired social change would be as strange as to say that an earthquake is a good way of producing a lake.

Yet it seems to me that none of these arguments suffices to dismiss 'ideological politics' as an obsolete and irrational method of social change. They cannot be 'justified'; but they may be inevitable in some circumstances; and we may also be able to argue—with the wisdom of hindsight and from the point of view of historical determinism—that they were the necessary condition for the production of certain social changes now accepted as desirable. 'Justification' and 'rationality' are categories applicable only within spheres of social action and change where calculated choice can be made; they apply only within the means-end model of social change and explanation. But could we not argue that there are certain types of social change which are (or were) desirable changes, but which could not have come about as a result of rational calculation and piecemeal adjustment, but only as the short- or long-term consequences of widespread ideological and even utopian upsurge and agitation?

I am aware that in these very swift remarks I have run together with nothing like sufficiently careful definition and discrimination some exceedingly hard questions of political analysis and theory. And I confess that I do not know how to prove that phases or periods of intense ideological activity (such as the activity of the Levellers and the Diggers in the English civil war, or the ideological ferment that preceded and accompanied the French Revolution, or the swell of socialist myth-making, moralizing, and social criticism that grew throughout the nineteenth century) are a necessary lever of political change, even though they never succeed in bringing about the results that ideologists believe they are bringing about. But one can argue negatively. One can argue that the 'unideological' politics of adjustment and piecemeal change must necessarily accept limited goals and types of social change, or again, that the many built-in pressures that support order and stability, the natural need and desire to go on living the daily life, operate to sift and narrow the objectives that are likely to be put on the agenda of responsible politics. (This, in fact, was one of the stock Marxist arguments against the politics of gradualism and reform—that the policy of incrementalism or rational calculation will involve us in accepting as constants certain structural features of the existing system, and certain moral or ideological elements that are embedded in that structure.)

To put this in another way—in any given state of society there will be well-established institutions and habits of moral thinking, which are central in the sense that they protect important elements, and which operate to limit the objectives, methods, and types of change which are accepted as matters for political policy and governmental action, so that at any given time that part of the social structure that is at all generally *recognized* as subject to political action and change is always comparatively small. But it is in relation to what must be called the institutional and ideological *infrastructure* that ideological ferment and ideological politics have a very important function. They have their important effects below the level of 'rational' or programmatic political action, in eroding or loosening established moral and ideological habits and certainties, in producing the climate of opinion in which it is ultimately possible for new sorts of political or social objectives, new forms of social control and organization, new techniques of social action, to be accepted as parts of the ordinary programmes of political parties.[11]

---

[11] The only support that one could give to this assertion would be in the form of extended historical analysis. One would have to show how prolonged periods of ideological ferment,

However, it is not my intention in this article to embark upon a thorough examination of this question. My comments are simply meant to illustrate two main points: (*a*) That recent political scientists have in fact been raising interesting and important problems of political theory and their discussion is a continuation of discussions that have been going on in Western political theory for centuries. (It is evident that some of the issues raised are very close to those raised by Burke about the French Revolution or by Marxists in their controversies with 'gradualists' and reformers.) (*b*) Yet, at the same time, this example does illustrate an important shift of interest in recent political speculation. In the democratic countries practical politics are mainly concerned for the time being with limited objectives and adjustments: many political scientists have come to accept this style of politics as the rational norm for all political activity: the discounting of ideology has been accompanied by a scepticism concerning general speculation about the moral issues of politics, a disposition to assume that thinking about 'techniques' alone qualifies as really rational or practical political thinking.

VI

Let me take two other examples. The anti-ideological trend of so much recent political theory ('anti-ideological' both in the sense of discounting the importance of ideologies in politics, and in the sense of attacking and debunking political ideologies that have been very influential) is very plain in much of what is now being said about the nature of democracy and about the working of democratic institutions, especially political parties.

I will start with Schumpeter's brilliant discussion in *Capitalism, Socialism and Democracy* which expresses a line of thought and an emphasis which reappears substantially in later books.[12] Schumpeter begins, it will be remembered, by rejecting 'The Classical Theory of Democracy' which he formulates in this way: 'The democratic method is that institutional arrangement for arriving at political decisions which realizes the common good by making the people itself decide issues through the election of individuals who are to assemble in order to carry out its will.' He rejects this view because it involves assumptions and concepts about non-existents—a common

no matter how "utopian" the ideologies might have been, ultimately produced important political results in the form of quite common-place programmes and policies. Examples are the revolutionary current in France from the late eighteenth century to the end of the nineteenth, or the nineteenth-century British movement of utopian socialism. A more extreme, and large-scale, example would be the rise, spread and ultimate political effects of the great world religions. There are some interesting remarks about some of the topics I have touched on in the last few paragraphs in Howard Horsburgh's article, "The Relevance of the Utopian," *Ethics,* vol. lxvii, no. 2.

12 For example, Dahl's *Preface to Democratic Theory* and Down's *An Economic Theory of Government Decision-Making in a Democracy.*

good, a popular will, &c. He goes on to expound and defend 'Another Theory of Democracy' of which the formula is: 'The democratic method is that institutional way for arriving at political decisions in which individuals acquire the power to decide by means of a competitive struggle for the people's vote.'

Obviously, this involves a very different notion of the functions of the 'elements' in a democratic system and the relations between them. The leaders of the political parties decide, not 'the people'. It is the more or less organized groups of men competing for power who have the initiative and supply the political drive: 'so far as there are genuine group-wise volitions at all . . . [they] do not assert themselves directly . . . [but] remain latent, often for decades, until they are called to life by some political leader who turns them into political factors' (p. 270, 2nd edition). Policies and programmes are to be viewed as weapons employed in the competition for office, taken up or discarded according as they help or prejudice the party's competitive position; some question will become an 'issue' in politics when a leader or party judges it to be 'a good horse to back'. And a political party 'is a group whose members propose to act in concert in the competitive struggle for political power' (p. 283).[13]

A model like Schumpeter's is not to be criticized for being unrealistic. Any model involves selection and simplification: it is to be judged by its capacity to explain (and perhaps predict) the facts it is intended to explain. No doubt we could explain within the limits of Schumpeter's assumptions a great many of the political events of a democratic state. Nevertheless, I want to comment on a couple of the interesting features of his simplification.

In the first place, his model places heavy emphasis on manipulation and leadership—on the making and propagating of policy—and its tendency is to draw attention away from the 'infrastructure'. I do not intend to imply that he would deny the importance of the infrastructure; nevertheless, it is important to be quite explicit that this special emphasis is there.

Now, if we like, we may apply the word 'politics' to one level of activity only—to the level where policy operates, where individuals and groups more or less explicitly and deliberately seek adjustments and arrangements of their particular interests and activities. But, if we define the political in this way, it

---

[13]So also Downs, on *Economic Theory and Democracy*, p. 28: "parties formulate policies in order to win elections, rather than win elections in order to formulate policies." This is described as "the fundamental hypothesis of our model."

is very important to remember that the range of the political is always oscillating, and may at times oscillate somewhat violently.[14] And for Schumpeter to say that 'so far as there are genuine group-wise volitions at all . . . they do not assert themselves directly . . . but remain latent often for decades until they are called to life by some political leader who turns them into political factors' is to be guilty of a very considerable over-simplification. It is true, of course, that this is how things often happen; political leaders formulate policies which are not formulated by other social groups; they crystallize or focus attitudes or demands that would otherwise remain uncrystallized; they may propose solutions that no one else has proposed. But to leave the matter there would be to postulate a gap between the politician (and the political party) and other social organizations which may be wider in some societies than in others, but which is not an invariable feature of all democracies. The party politician who appears in the political theory of Schumpeter and many other present-day political theorists is an abstraction. In 'real life' not all politicians are members only of a political party, or committed only to the success of a party (as 'success' is defined in the sort of model I am discussing). They are often also members of other social organizations; and very often they may be said to belong to a *movement*—and a movement is a social as well as a political phenomenon, and something it would be difficult to define except (at least partly) by reference to doctrine.

Now it is a matter of common observation that politicians are very often in the grip of a conflict between the beliefs or interest of their organizations or movements and of their party. And how they act in the end will not always be explicable solely by reference to the conditions of party success in the competition for power. Moreover, democratic societies differ from one another as regards the latitude for manoeuvre that parties enjoy. Within the one society there is an oscillation over time: the relations between parties and 'society' change, and there are occasions when the impact of demands, or of more general social and political ideas generated within social movements or organizations, upon the life and actions of parties is much greater than at

---

[14]It seems to me that recent political science has suffered from concentrating so heavily on the study of short-term political events (e.g. the study of the single election), on the act of "decision-making," on "bargaining models" and so on. This may have had advantages from the point of view of concreteness, empirical exactness and rigour. But it has brought about a very drastic abstraction from a great deal of political reality. Rostow, it will be remembered, in his *British Economy in the Nineteenth Century,* suggests an outline of the relations between economic change and political action. His schema involves two interrelated tripartite divisions: one between long-term, trend or medium term, and short-term economic processes, the other a division between economy, society and politics. His suggestions concerning the different ways in which the three types of economic change operate at the political level could be profitably explored further by political theorists.

others.[15] This being so, the model of democratic politics which Schumpeter proposes will be helpful for explanation only in certain cases. And, even with this limitation, it is more likely to be helpful in the understanding of *short-term* runs of political decisions than in the understanding of a long-term direction of political change.

This, then, is the kind of emphasis and selection which the now fashionable Schumpeterian model of democracy contains. It is relatively uninterested in the important Marxian notion of 'shifts in the foundation' or infrastructure and their long-run political effects; or, if we may use a different image, it largely ignores the series of concentric circles within which, in some societies and at some times, the generation of social attitudes, ideas, and ideologies takes place. Perhaps the most important point I want to make is that these circles oscillate as conditions change: they grow wider or narrower, as regards both the range of social institutions or conditions which become subject of social questioning and idea-making, and the numbers of those who are to some degree caught up in social criticism.[16]

One thing that may be said about Schumpeter's account is that it tends to stress the specialized and professional character of political activity; that its intention and effect is one of ideological deflation. And this brings me to the other comment I wish to make about his theory. Most of the so-called theories of democracy in the history of political thought have been primarily normative or prescriptive. One important strain of democratic thought has connected democracy with the enlargement and greater equalization of

[15] And sometimes a difference regarding the current "issues" of politics: regarding some issues, a party may have no alternative but to obey pressure "from below"; regarding others, it may be able to play the electoral market in the manner Schumpeter describes.

[16] In his review of de Jouvenel's *Sovereignty in World Politics* to which I have already referred, Dahl employs this concept of oscillation in speculating about the nature of democratic "consensus." His point, of course, is very closely related to mine. It would be a legitimate comment that Schumpeter does not pretend to be providing a model of *any* political system but only of democratic systems. And he might argue—indeed, there are plain indications that he would argue—that a democratic system will operate successfully (in the sense of maintaining over a long period its character and structure) only if conditions are as I have described them—in particular, only if the range of matters that come up for political decision and action remains narrow. This is now, of course, a widely-held view; one aspect of the reaction against socialist ideologies, or against notions of "holistic" planning, is the argument that democracy is a method and system of government which requires as a condition that "the effective range of political decision should not be extended too far" (Schumpeter). It is dubious whether this particular hypothesis can be given any hard meaning; what I have already said about the way in which consensus oscillates suggests that how much a government can do and get away with—or a party propose and get away with—will be affected by many different conditions which are far from being stable. However, it will be clear that this particular theory about democracy is closely allied with Shils's account of the nature of "civil society" to which I referred earlier.

opportunities for participating in the control or management of common affairs for sharing effective social responsibility. On this view, part of the task of a theory of democracy would be to investigate the means by which self–government or participation in the direction of affairs could be more widely extended. Mill puts very succinctly what has been a pretty constant problem and theme in the growth of democratic theory: 'A democratic constitution not supported by democratic institutions in detail, but confined to the central government, not only is not political freedom, but often creates a spirit precisely the reverse, carrying down to the lowest grade in society the desire and ambition of political domination.' This is not only succinct, but also perceptive—as the post-Millian growth of party discipline and party machines, of political bosses, and of publicity agents and carefully managed publicity campaigns remind us.

Perhaps there is no logical incompatibility between this and the Schumpeterian model; one might, for instance, say that Schumpeter is specifying the minimum conditions of democracy at the level of central government, and that his specification is not affected by how much or how little decentralization and diversification of control there might be down below. But I doubt it. I suspect that the more the two positions were developed, the more theoretical conflict would become apparent. On Schumpeter's view, it is *the* function of political parties to compete for votes by raising issues and proposing policies; it is *the* function of the public to express a preference between competing leaders and would-be governments. He appears to be saying that so far as democracy is concerned, this is not merely how democratic systems happen to work now, but that it is *the most that can be expected*. In effect, his model has a normative or prescriptive ring about it; and this is the more so when it is examined in the context in which he places it, viz. the rejection of the 'classical theory of democracy' with its very different conception of the meaning of self-government and of individual political participation and responsibility.

My second example is Dahl's model in *Preface to Democratic Theory*. This differs a little from Schumpeter's in that Dahl assigns a less prominent place to parties and the electoral competition and a more prominent place to organized minorities and pressure groups. He warns us against attributing too rich a function to elections; in his view, the main function of elections in the democratic system is that they extend the range of the minorities which exert an influence on governmental decisions. According to Dahl, democracy is neither rule by the majority nor rule by a minority, but rule by *minorities*. 'Thus the making of governmental decisions is not a majestic march of great majorities united on certain matters of basic policy. It is the steady appeasement of relatively small groups' (p. 146). (Dahl at least has it in common with Schumpeter that he rejects the majority and anything that smacks of the notion of the general will.)

One might say that Dahl's assertion is just not true as a universal proposition; that there are not a few occasions and issues on which a majority does form and exert its influence. Recent political theory has no doubt gained in getting rid of loose and muddled concepts like 'the general will' and the 'common good', and uncriticized, question-begging ones like 'the majority'; but it is another matter whether it is fortunate in what it has substituted. In Dahl (and in the whole tribe of 'pressure group' analysts) the emphasis falls heavily on the notion of the determinate, relatively 'given', or impermeable, minority or group, possessing its own clear and determinate interests which have to be attended to by parties and governments. This, no one will want to deny, is *one sub-system* within the very complex system of democratic politics; but it exists in interplay with other sub-systems, including the interaction of interests, institutions, movements, ways of life within a process of general influence, and 'discussion' (if I may fall back on one of the governing conceptions of older theorists of democracy), and the resulting slow spread of general attitudes or bodies of belief which certainly affect the course of politics in the long run. In rejecting the categories and assumptions of the older philosophical idealists and monists, some of the more recent school of pluralists have tended to play down the social processes by means of which some sort of common denominator of sentiment and idea is created within a society, processes which are undoubtedly important for politics, and which their idealist predecessors rightly took to be pretty central for political theory, even if they misrepresented or unduly magnified them.

In an earlier section I illustrated the general reaction against ideology which has marked recent political and sociological thought. Correspondingly, then, in some recent democratic theory there has been an undermining of versions of *democratic* ideology which have been very prominent until quite recently.

VII

I have already explained that it is not my object to examine the theoretical strength of the views I have been considering. My main object has been to draw attention to some very common characteristics of recent political thought with a view to explaining the widely shared impression that political theory or political philosophy has lost its inspiration. If we take the work of such writers as Schumpeter and Dahl, it is absurd to say that the energy or the rigour of political theorizing have declined; on the contrary, it has acquired an analytical thoroughness and sharpness, a closeness in argument, that is pretty new. But what this more recent work does show is a narrowing of moral interests and expectations, a dismissal of wider notions of equality, freedom, participation, &c.,[17] and, accompanying this, the tendency to be most interested in the existing machinery of democratic systems. This is not simply a matter of science replacing the more philosophical interest in principles, values, or objectives. The ambition to lay the foundations of an empirical science of politics is no doubt a very important intellectual influence; but the present trend is also critical: it expresses an ideological or philosophical standpoint of its own, an inclination to accept as inevitable, or at least as more rational than any alternative, the broad types of organization, the distribution of rights and roles, the methods of adjusting existing interests, which have by now come to *define* democracy in the Anglo-Saxon democracies. In short, as I have said before, the current feeling that there is no very persuasive alternative to the prevailing methods and orthodoxies of Anglo-American democracy is at least one of the reasons for the shortcomings (if shortcomings they are) of contemporary political theory.

[17]Instead of illustrating my general thesis by dealing with recent theories of democracy, I might have taken recent writing about liberty, one striking feature of which has been an emphasis on the value or importance of "negative freedom" and the distrust of notions of "positive freedom." Berlin's *Two Concepts of Liberty* is quite typical in this respect. Berlin's way of reviewing somewhat indiscriminately many different concepts of "positive freedom," ranging from the special views of Hegel to much more prosaic attempts to connect liberty with the exercise of political initiative, is surprising and questionable; all the same, in his sensitiveness to the possibly illusory and dangerous character of ideas of "positive freedom," he is very much in tune with his time. On a different point: the trend of thought I describe in the text is not of course entirely novel, as readers of Michels's *Political Parties* will be well aware; the argument between the supporters of a radical democratic ideology and those who insist upon the hard logic of social organization has been going on for some time. What is perhaps characteristic of more recent years is the unusual weakness of the strain of moral criticism and speculation.

Chapter Five

**A Debate on the End of Ideology:
The Philosopher versus the
Sociologist**

In the previous chapter, the alleged end of ideology was touched on in several places. But in the articles in this chapter that problem is addressed in detail, from two different points of view. The debate first appeared in the influential intellectual journal *Commentary*. Henry David Aiken, a professor of philosophy, surveys the arguments for the end of ideology, and evaluates the effects of these arguments on political theory and on the prospects of developing objective principles to guide political action. Professor Aiken's opponent is Daniel Bell, a professor of sociology. His critical reply to Professor Aiken's analysis raises a number of difficulties, such as the many ambiguities of the term ideology, the distinction between moral and moralistic discourse, and the means of evaluating political principles. Finally, Professor Aiken's rebuttal attempts to clarify certain points of his original statement, and to answer some of Professor Bell's critical barbs.

The Revolt against Ideology*

Henry David Aiken

Can it any longer be doubted that, on all sides of the Iron Curtain, the age of Leviathan is upon us? And for serious men does there remain any significant form of activity that is politically indifferent? We still profess loyalty to the ideal of "free inquiry," but the fact is that, directly or indirectly, governments supply the major resources, and politics most of the incentives, for our scientific research. And if some fortunate scientists of eminence are still encouraged to do "pure" or "basic" research, according to their interest, the primary reason is not that such studies exemplify one of man's essential intrinsic goods, but that the state cannot survive without them. Indeed, our universities and governments, along with our great industrial complexes, look increasingly like the interlocking arms of a great, if also headless, political establishment. Free enterprise (who doubts it?) is everywhere a dead issue save in the mythology of fundamentalist Republicanism, and whether our political leaders favor state capitalism or corporate socialism, the welfare state is accepted by all as an irremovable reality. Politics provide the primary themes of our literature, and when the critics charge a novelist or poet with "retreating from life," what they mean by "life" does not need to be construed. "Aesthetics" signifies merely enfeeblement and irrelevance; the "pure" artist, like the pure scientist, is a dying species, and none will mourn him save perhaps a few old "new critics" who, be it added, well understood the political meaning of their own dandified aestheticism. Our most exigent moral perplexities are overwhelmingly political, and our gods, such as they are, seem wholly preoccupied with affairs of state.

I must admit, however, that there still exists one quiet place where a man may go if he is nauseated by problems of politics and hence of power, and one course of study which he may still pursue without fear of political encroachment: he may go, that is, to the graduate school of any great university and take up the subject known there as "philosophy." Among the intellectuals, to my knowledge, we philosophers alone are politically inert. The meaning of the concept of political obligation fascinates some few of my colleagues, but I have rarely heard them, in congress assembled, discuss their political obligations. And if any were asked to offer their opinions concerning

*Henry David Aiken, "The Revolt against Ideology," *Commentary*, 38 (April 1964), 29-39. Reprinted from *Commentary* by permission; Copyright ©1964 by the American Jewish Committee.

the ends, or limits, of government they would probably either decline to answer or regard the question as philosophically improper.

In order to prove the rule, there remain a few notorious exceptions such as Bertrand Russell, Jean-Paul Sartre, and Professor Sidney Hook. But we have Russell's own word for it that his politics, like his ethics, and his philosophy have nothing in common except that both were hatched under the same head of hair, and both Sartre and Hook are frequently dismissed by their more academic colleagues as publicists who have deserted philosophy for careers as ideologists and politicians. Recalling the greatest names in the history of philosophy from Socrates to Aquinas and from Hobbes to Mill, one may wonder momentarily how such a state of affairs could have come to pass. But when one remembers what men have done, and in many parts of the world are still prepared to do, in the name of a political philosophy, the answer seems evident: from a "pragmatic" point of view, political philosophy is a monster, and wherever it has been taken seriously, the consequence, almost invariably, has been revolution, war, and eventually, the police state. Russell himself once wrote an essay entitled, "The Harm that Good Men Do." Many would regard this as an appropriate subtitle for any honest and realistic history of political philosophy. With Socrates, political philosophy became a gadfly; in Plato, a monstrous dream; in Rousseau, Fichte, Hegel, Marx, and the rest, it has become a scourge and an obscenity.

Such is the prevailing view. And if Peter Laslett, the editor of a recent volume of essays on political philosophy, is correct in saying that "for the moment, anyway, political philosophy is dead," then none mourn its passing less than the philosophers themselves. Those few who, as philosophers, still suppose that they have a useful political role to play, discover it to be only that of unmasking the pretensions of other political philosophers.

Just what is wrong with political philosophy as a genre nonetheless remains obscure. Of course many political philosophies from Plato to Aquinas, and from Hobbes and Rousseau to Hegel and Marx, have been tied to the kites of theological or metaphysical systems. And for some, no doubt, this fact suffices to put them beyond the pale. But roundhouse objections to "metaphysics" are less fashionable than they were some years ago. In fact, under pressure from the philosophers of ordinary language, philosophical analysts are increasingly reluctant to proscribe as meaningless any established form of discourse on principle, as the positivists used to do with the propositions, not only of metaphysics and theology, but also of ethics. In this respect, recent analytical philosophy has steadily moved in the direction of pragmatism or, I had better say, the direction in which pragmatism has tended to move since the days of William James. Any form of utterance, so it is now argued, is to be interpreted and judged only in the light of its own characteristic "practical bearings." Thus, for example, if political philosophers in their own terms are given to general moral evaluations of political activities and institutions, the question is only whether such appraisals, all things considered, are acceptable as value judgments: that is to say, do they express commitments to which, on sober second thought and in view of the historical record, we should be ready to give our own conscientious assent? Do the lines of social action which they commend appear on the whole to be worth the trouble it would take to realize them? Above all, would we in conscience be able to give our blessings to the sort of "representative man" who might emerge if such lines of action were resolutely pursued?

Questions of this sort, which I take more seriously, have produced another round of objections which, although they do not rule out political philosophy on supposedly semantical or logical grounds, do nonetheless seem to condemn it virtually as a genre. These objections are all the more telling and all the more significant since they come from a quarter in which there has been no general animus against metaphysics and no self-denying ordinance which would exclude from the purview of philosophy any problem that is not purely a conceptual problem about the "logic" of expressions.

To my knowledge the most powerful attack upon political philosophy from this quarter (which for convenience may be called "existentialist") is to be found in Albert Camus's arresting work, *The Rebel.* Camus's indictment is easily misunderstood. To be sure, it is profoundly anti-rationalistic, but it is by no means based upon a romantic or nihilistic disillusionment with human reason or with the value of its exercise. Quite the contrary, reasonableness, in the more classical sense of the term, is Camus's forte. What he condemns, rather, are the crimes incited by the political philosophers in the name of Reason or of Reason's God. All men, say the philosophers, are created equal; *ergo,* let them be restored at once to their pristine estate, whatever the cost. All men are by nature free, yet everywhere they are in chains; *ergo,* Reason demands that they immediately be released, though ten thousand jailers perish in the process. Man is, above all, the rational animal, but because of the blinders which the ancient regime places before his mind, he cannot freely exercise his reason; then destroy the regime, let reason, or its self-appointed representatives, reign, and the devil take those who stand in the way. No doubt the political philosophers never meant to be quite so simple or so brutal as these caricatures suggest. But what of their followers, those who take them, or try to take them, at their word? Can the political philosophers altogether disclaim responsibility for their crimes? Is there not an ingrained metaphysical or moral pride, a fatal lack of continence in the very attempt of political philosophers to set forth, whether in the name of reason or of nature or of humanity, the absolute ends of government and the supposedly invariant forms of the just society?

But Camus's criticisms are by no means directed exclusively to the 18th-century *philosophes* and their descendants. They are extended also to the Hegelians and the Marxists who attempt to formulate a universal law, or dialectic, of historical development which is then made to double in brass as an immanent principle of justification for their own incitive prophecies about man's social destiny. Whether such prophecies proclaim a future of unlimited freedom, of absolute justice and equality, or of perpetual peace, in each case they too represent that criminal pride of reason which destroys the sense of limitation which for Camus is the beginning of political, as of every other form of, wisdom.

From these remarks it would be easy enough to conclude that Camus's indictment of traditional political philosophy is actually an indictment of philosophy itself. And so in a way it is, at least as philosophy has been conceived and executed in the dominant Western tradition. Yet Camus is not just another literary counter-philosopher. Nor is his indictment of rationalistic political philosophy a condemnation of political philosophy *per se.* For it is plain that, as Sir Herbert Read points out in his discerning preface to the English translation of *The Rebel,* Camus himself has a philosophy of politics. But it is, at any rate, a philosophy of politics radically different from those of his predecessors. For Camus makes no attempt to define *the* function or the end of government or to state *the* rightful basis of political authority. Nor does he propose any universal principle of political action save one of self-limitation or restraint. It is also characteristic of Camus that although he repudiates any and all forms of unlimited revolution, he accepts the necessity, on occasion, of rebellion or civil disobedience.

Despite many differences both in philosophical background and in literary style, there are striking parallels between Camus's existentialist critique of modern political philosophy and those to be found in the writings of the pragmatist, John Dewey. In Dewey one finds the same hatred of essentialism and apriorism, the same antipathy to utopianism, and the same distrust both of radical individualism and of radical collectivism. There is a similar emphasis upon the concrete "problematic situations" (as Dewey calls them) which alone he takes it to be the business of "creative intelligence" to resolve. And there is the same underlying humanism which opposes the sacrifice of living men to principles and to ideals realizable, if at all, only in an abstract and

indefinite future. For obvious reasons, Dewey was more confident than
Camus of the efficacy of democratic procedures, at least in "developed"
societies. Yet he was by no means prepared to demand the immediate institution of such procedures in all countries and circumstances; nor did he, like
more romantic majoritarians, regard the will of the many as an absolute
source of rightful political authority. Democracy for Dewey is a method
rather than an end. Or if, in certain writings, democracy also tends to become
an end, then it is in a looser sense of the term which now begins to take on
meanings more strictly associated with the concepts of community, fraternity, and social equality.

Dewey's pragmatic criticisms of earlier political philosophy are usually
regarded as methodological rather than moral—although in his case, as in that
of all pragmatists, it is always a question where problems of method leave off
and problems of ethics (and politics) begin. Thus, whereas Camus ascribes the
primordial fault of the political philosophers to their incontinent passion for
absolute transcendence of the finite conditions of man's historical social
existence, Dewey ascribes it to the illusory "quest for certainty" which,
according to his reading, dominated virtually the whole history of philosophy
before the 20th century. Yet in Dewey's case also, one senses that the more
radical evil lies not in the illusion itself but in its attendant waste and destruc-
tiveness. The quest for certainty begins in hope and ends in skepticism and
despair. In promising us an unlimited intellectual and moral security, it brings
us by stages to the war of all against all. Dewey's more unfriendly critics have
often charged him with advocacy of the gospel of human perfectibility. No
criticism could be more perverse. Man, as Dewey conceives him, is, once for
all, a mortal creature who lives and has his being within the orders of nature
and of history. Indeed, this is the governing metaphysical principle underlying
his logic, his theory of knowledge, and his moral philosophy. Uncertainty,
and hence imperfection, are ingrained in the very texture of human existence.
And no method, including the methods of science, can extricate us from
them.

In other spheres, philosophical forgetfulness of this fact has been unfortunate; in politics, as in ethics, it has proved a calamity. This is not to deny that
Dewey has a philosophy of politics, but like Camus's it is of a sort quite
different from the major political philosophies of the tradition. He is sometimes criticized for offering us no explicit general theory of governmental
authority, no principled statement of the grounds or proper limits of political
obligation—above all, no settled position toward the most vexatious of
modern political problems, namely, revolution. But Dewey's vagueness on

these scores is quite intentional. In politics as in ethics, Dewey repudiates any and all fixed principles for the institution of the good society or for the establishment and maintenance of good government. His preoccupation as a political philosopher is solely with the controlling attitudes which men bring to their political deliberations.

Marxism and Ideology: The First Revolt

Impressive as they are, the foregoing criticisms of political philosophy are largely matters of individual judgment. And if the professional philosophers now decline to do political philosophy, it may be argued that this is owing to their own disillusionment with the achievements of their predecessors rather than to any inherent fault in political philosophy as a genre. It remains to ask whether there may be, after all, some deep-lying confusion of mind, some pervasive logical fault or category mistake, which really does afflict political philosophy as a form of discourse.

As a way of confronting this question, it may prove useful to examine certain aspects of the widespread attack against the modern offspring of and successor to political philosophy, namely, ideology. Most of the "anti-ideologists," as I shall call them, share certain attitudes in common with the existentialists; indeed, it is my impression that some of them owe more to the latter, and particularly to Camus, than they have as yet acknowledged. They owe something also to the pragmatists; in fact, most American anti-ideologists fancy their own point of view as essentially "pragmatic." But (generally speaking) they go beyond the existentialists and the pragmatists in contending that ideological thinking is the function of certain features of the social situation in which intellectuals as a group find themselves in an era of exact science, advanced technology, and the welfare state. In predicting the end of ideology, they thus imply that the social and intellectual conditions which have been conducive to ideological thinking are now disappearing. Their own role, in effect, is to make certain that the prediction will come true.

Now the primary target of our contemporary Western anti-ideologists is, of course, Marxism. And in prophesying the end of ideology, it is the end of Marxism of which they mainly dream. It is worth remembering, therefore, that: (a) Marx was the first great critic of political philosophy; and (b) he was also the first great prophet of the end of the ideological age.

According to Marx, ideology always involves a conception of reality which systematically "inverts" the whole relation of thought to being.[1] As a form

[1] In this section I have been aided by Stanley W. Moore's *The Critique of Capitalist Democracy, An Introduction to the Theory of the State in Marx, Engels and Lenin*

of thought, therefore, ideology is inherently confused; it stands to science, in Marx's words, as an inverted image in a "camera obscura" stands to a veridical perception. This inversion, of which Hegel's "objective" idealism is a prime philosophical example, results directly or indirectly from that process of "alienation" whereby human artifacts, including "ideas," are invested with a power and a reality that are supposedly independent both of their producers and of the material conditions and operations involved in their production. Such an investment, which philosophers call "reification," is also necessarily accompanied by "mystification," i.e., by an obscuring of the interests and relationships that actually determine social behavior. For example, in imputing an independent reality and power to their reified ideas and principles, their rights and duties, their ends and "reasons," men thereby conceal from themselves the fact that it is they, the creators of such entities, whose underlying actions and whose work alone give them whatever significance they may have.

Except for genuinely empirical science, the whole cultural "superstructure" of hitherto existing societies is permeated by the same process of alienation and ideological inversion. For this reason it would be a radical mistake to conceive of ideology as limited to political philosophy; on the contrary, ideology also includes, among other things, religion, ethics, art, metaphysics, and the "dismal science" of economics. Properly understood, political philosophies are merely special applications of far-flung ideological patterns that invest them with their own magical "authority" and "justification." Furthermore, since alienation is a social process, ideologies, whether as wholes or as parts, are to be understood as expressions, not of the interests of isolated individuals, but of the conflicting concerns—or better, tendencies—of social classes. It is thus only by relating political ideologies to their objective social conditions and causes that we can begin to interpret their true objective meaning (i.e., what they signify or portend within the order of nature), and hence, by stages, to correct the inverted images of reality which they present to the ideologists themselves. One of the primary functions of Marxism, in fact, is precisely to provide the intellectual, including the social-theoretical, tools for such interpretations and corrections, and thus for the first time to enable us, in principle, to demythologize ideology.

(Paine-Whitman Publishers, New York, 1957). Moore's fourth chapter, "Ideology and Alienation," pp. 114-137, is highly compressed and schematic, but I know of no other discussion of the subject which, within its limits, is so clear and so accurate. I have also benefited from Norman Birnbaum's *The Sociological Study of Ideology (1940-60)*, *Current Sociology*, Vol. IX, No. 2 (1960), Basil Blackwell, Oxford, England. Birnbaum's essay, which he subtitles "A Trend Report," is a masterly survey of current literature on the subject of ideology, including Marxist ideology theory. It also contains an invaluable critical bibliography.

But it is one thing to explain ideology and another to overcome it. Mankind as a whole can permanently overcome ideological thought (and action) not by any process of purely conceptual analysis on the part of individual philosophers, but only by removing the material causes of alienation which, according to Marx, are rooted in the institution of private property. And it is for this reason, and this reason alone, that Marx's historical prophecy of the coming of world socialism amounts at the same time to a prophecy of the end of the ideological ages.

Disillusionment in the West: The Second Revolt against Ideology

Marx's view of ideology underlies the thinking of most of our own anti-ideologists. However, they go beyond Marx in extending the pejorative associations of the term to the role of ideology in ordering human attitudes. Thus, they not only regard ideological doctrines as wrong-headed; they also object to their employment as vehicles for the formation, guidance, and control of social behavior. But they go Marx one better in another way, for they also regard Marxism itself as a prime example of ideology.

The first non-Marxist writer, so far as I know, explicitly to inquire whether we might be approaching the end of the ideological age was Raymond Aron in his book, *The Opium of the Intellectuals.* The prevailing temper of Aron's book is not unlike that of Camus's *The Rebel.* There are also a number of striking parallels between Aron's point of view and that of Karl Popper, as developed in the latter's *The Open Society and its Enemies.* For example, there is the same constitutional distrust of large-scale social planning, the same insistence upon the impossibility of large-scale historical predictions of social behavior, and the same celebration of the virtues of "the open society." Above all, there is the same castigation of any attempt to determine the drift and meaning of human history as a whole and hence of the attempt to formulate universal and necessary laws of historical development.

"The last great ideology," says Aron, "was born of the combination of three elements: the vision of a future consistent with human aspiration, the link between this future and a particular social class, and trust in human values above and beyond the victory of the working class, thanks to planning and collective ownership." Aron believes that at the present time the hope aroused by that ideology is gone beyond peradventure. One main reason for this disillusionment, so he argues, is that "Confidence in the virtues of a socio-technique has begun to wane." Furthermore, on this side of the Iron Curtain, no one believes any longer in the reality of a social class that will carry us, under the leadership of the socio-economic engineers, to the frontiers of the classless society. Like Camus and Popper, Aron cannot bring himself flatly to renounce the values of the Enlightenment; but in practice he is no more able than they to take them with absolute seriousness as governing ideals for the reconstruction of society in the 20th century. In his own terms, he no longer fully believes in the vision of a future consistent with "human aspirations." And it is this fact perhaps that accounts for the vein of pessimism and the self-division which run through his writing.

In any case, it is plain that for Aron the approaching end of the age of ideology represents also a crisis of faith and of hope for mankind. On the penultimate page of his book, Aron asks, "Does the rejection of fanaticism encourage a reasonable faith, or merely skepticism?" His analogical answer is that "one does not cease to love God when one gives up converting pagans or the Jews and no longer reiterates 'No salvation outside the Church.' " Coming as late as it does in Aron's book, this has something like the effect of an unprepared major cadence at the end of a funeral march. What is its basis? No matter how personal one's religion may be, it is hard to see how it could fail to be attenuated by a radical renunciation of one's belief that it should prevail. If one really gives up trying to convert the "pagans," does this not entail reservations about the value as well as the possibility of converting them? If so, does this not also suggest that one has ceased completely to love God or else that only a gesture toward the love of Him remains? Making due allowance for the analogy, I cannot, as a pragmatist, see how one can be said actively to seek a less cruel lot for humanity if one can trust no technique and no plan for its amelioration. To will the end is to will the means, and to reject the means is, in practice, to renounce the end. Like Peirce in another connection, one is minded to say to the political as well as to the epistemological moralists: "Dismiss make-believe!" This means also, so far as I can see, "Dismiss professions of 'reasonable faith' if you do not believe in the *power* of reason; and do not talk about abolishing 'fanaticism,' unless you believe that there is a way (or 'technique') of abolishing it." Like all anti-ideologists, Aron is opposed to the expectation of "miraculous changes" either from a revolution or an economic plan. Very well. The question is whether he gives us any reason to expect unmiraculous changes from any sort of concerted human action. "If tolerance is born of doubt, let us teach everyone to doubt all the models and utopias, to challenge all the prophets of redemption and the heralds of catastrophe." And, "If they alone can abolish fanaticism, let us pray for the advent of the skeptics." The rhetoric is appealing. But it smacks of ideology, in Aron's own sense. For toleration is also a principle and a method. And it too has its dangers.

These comments are not made in a spirit of mockery. My purpose is rather to make clear what may be implied in the prophecy that we are living at the end of the ideological age, the age, in Mr. Aron's own apt words, in which men still actively search "for a purpose, for communion with the people, for something controlled by *an idea and a will*" (my italics). As he points out, we Westerners have suffered an increasing fragmentation of our universe; our poetry becomes more and more obscure and diffuse, and our poets are isolated from one another as well as from "the big public" which "in their heart of hearts, they long to serve"; our scientists have ideas aplenty but no control over their use or indeed any consistent belief in the possibility of their control; our scholars control limited areas of specialized knowledge, but present-day science "seems to leave . . . . [them] as ignorant of the answers to the ultimate questions as a child awakening to consciousness"; and our economists and sociologists, for all their facts and statistics, their jargon and their lore, have not the vaguest notion whether "humanity is progressing toward an atomic holocaust or Utopian peace." This process of fragmentation and dissociation, moreover, is not new; it has been going on at an ever more rapid pace, at least since the Renaissance. But here precisely, as Aron admits, "is where ideology comes in. . . ." For ideology represents the insistent demand for a coherent *way* of individual and social life, an orientation toward the world and toward the human predicament, controlled as he says both by an idea and by a will, or, rather, by a will infused with an idea and an idea animated by will. Ideology, as Aron tacitly acknowledges, is a creature of alienation; but it represents also a passion to reduce alienation, to bring it down to bearable human proportions. It also represents the belief that alienation may be reduced through collective human endeavors. Thus, by his own account, an end to the age of ideology would amount to this extent to a virtual skepticism about the possibility of reducing alienation through corporate planning and action (ideas infused with will). And this means that man has no choice but to live with alienation. Here, however, one faces precisely one of those metaphysical and historical "necessities" against which the anti-ideologists themselves rail when they find them in the writings of other ideologists. Here, too, it seems, we are faced with a "simplified" idea of man's fate which, as in the case of the Stoicism it is plainly a variant of, forms the basis of still another ideology, an idea that in this instance is, if I may say so, fused with inaction.

The Sociological Critique of Ideology

Aron's analysis of ideology, although suggestive, does not take us very far. Let us therefore cross the ocean to the heartland of contemporary anti-ideology. In the United States perhaps the leading anti-ideologist is the sociologist and social critic, Professor Daniel Bell. Bell, who knows his Marx, is also a good strategist. Already in the introduction to his book, *The End of Ideology,* he moves beyond Aron, for, unlike the latter, he proposes to make a positive virtue of alienation. "Alienation," he tells us flatly, "is not nihilism but a positive role, a detachment, which guards one against being submerged in any cause, or accepting any particular embodiment of community as final. Nor is alienation deracination, a denial of one's roots or country." This persuasive definition has its points. It is also an interesting instance of the notion of an idea fused with will which Bell, like Aron, tends to identify with ideology.

As befits a sociologist, Bell is concerned not just with the content of ideas but with their social origins, causes, and roles. Thus, in an attempt to locate the sources of ideological thinking, he begins his analysis with a characterological division of the intelligentsia into two main types: (a) the "scholars"; and (b) the "intellectuals." The scholar, as Bell conceives him, "has a bounded field of knowledge, a tradition, and seeks to find his place in it, adding to the accumulated, tested knowledge of the past as to a mosaic." He is, so to say, a "pro" for whom "the show must go on," however and whatever he himself may feel about it. Accepting the scholarly tradition within which he has found a place, he is able to judge himself, or at least his scholarly performance, by impersonal and objective standards. And if he performs with a modicum of efficiency and does not stray beyond the limits of his scholarly "competence," he is entitled to a modicum of self-respect. Indeed, his self-respect, like his role-governed conception of himself, is a function of his assurance of the respect of his peers and, more indirectly, of the society of which his discipline is an established part.

The intellectual, on the other hand, has no such responsibility or security. Lacking a scholarly discipline, perhaps lacking the talent for achievement within such a discipline, which can hold him continuously responsible to "objective" methods and to "facts" wholly independent of himself, his only recourse is an endless dialectic and critique of general ideas. And because he is without a legitimate social role to play within society, he perforce finds himself alienated from its institutions and is left to manipulate his "ideas" in a mood of unrequited and unfocused resentment. He doesn't so much think with his ideas as feel through them. In the discourses of an intellectual, therefore, the thing to look to is not his argument, which, where it exists, is merely a vehicle for his resentments, but rather to the effect which it is meant to induce. He presents his readers not with information but with a goad and with an outlet for their own repressed emotions of estrangement or violence. He may, in the process, tell them something, but it is doing something to them that is his real, if unavowed, aim. For him, the beginning and end of a process of reflection is not a specific problem about objective processes and events; as Professor Bell charges, he begins always with "*his* experience, *his* perceptions of the world, *his* privileges and deprivations, and judges the world by these sensibilities." For him, the "world" is not a thing in itself, but rather his will and his idea, and if there is something *there*, in itself, then he acknowledges it only as something which he is up against and which exists only in so far as he is up against it. His business, in Marx's words, is not to understand the world, but to change, or better, to overcome it. And if he can't change it in any other way, he may at least reject it, and thus, by an obvious inversion, still show his superiority to it.

In this way, every statement and every discussion becomes for the intellectual an implicitly political move in an endless game of power. Of course he fancies his own moves really to be in the interest *(n. b.)* of "justice" or "freedom," while those of his "opponents," whether they invoke the names of "legitimacy" or of "law and order," are actually made in the interest of business as usual which it is the function of the established order to protect and to promote. The sad fact remains, however, that the intellectual's power *is* severely limited by the existing system. Hence, in order to maintain the illusion of his freedom or of his power to realize it, he is obliged, as Bell puts it, to embark "upon what William James called 'the faith ladder,' which in its vision of the future cannot distinguish possibilities from probabilities, and converts the latter into certainties."

What is the nature of the conceptual tools with which the "free-floating" and unscholarly intellectual does his work? In order to answer this question, Bell is obliged to move from sociology to logic and semantics. Thus he speaks repeatedly, in terms which I find merely more explicit than Aron's, of ideology as being somehow a "fusion" of thought with emotion or passion which at one and the same time does the trick of "simplify[ing] ideas, establish[ing] a claim to truth, and, in the union of the two, demand[ing] a commitment to action." The result—and it is this which Bell most seriously objects to—is not just a "transformation" of ideas, but also a transformation of people. The typical effect of any ideological argument is, then, a kind of conversion. The road by which the ideologist comes to Damascus doesn't matter; what matters is that he is made to see the light. Says Bell: "Ideology is the conversion of ideas into social levers. Without irony, Max Lerner once entitled a book 'Ideas Are Weapons.' This is the language of ideology. It is the commitment to the consequences of ideas."

Bell is rarely more analytical than this, but toward the end of his study he does say one further thing which is at least symptomatic of the point of view which he represents: "If the end of ideology has any meaning, it [sic] is to ask for the end of rhetoric, and rhetoricians, of 'revolution,' of the day when the young French anarchist Vaillant tossed a bomb into the Chamber of Deputies, and the literary critic Laurent Tailhade declared in his defense: 'What do a few human lives matter; it was a *beau geste.*' " The general idea that concerns us here is not the tacit identification of ideology with revolutionary activity, especially of the more bizarre and feckless sort, but rather its identification with rhetoric.

If by "rhetoric" Bell means the use of language in order to persuade or influence others—and many things he says suggest that this is his meaning—then his vision of the end of ideology as an end to rhetoric is a utopian fantasy. Worse, it is an evil fantasy, for it implies a conception of human relations which would deprive us of the right to address one another except for the purpose of comparing notes about matters of fact. Consider what would happen were such a fantasy to come true. In any ordinary sense, it would mean a virtual end to discourse, to communication, and to argument. For it would mean an end to any speech-act addressed to others with a view to their guidance, their instruction, their edification, or their pleasure, with a view, in short, to changing their minds. Indeed, the image of man implicit in Bell's dream of the end of ideology is precisely one of an academic grind or functionary to which he himself, as a counter-ideologist and counter-rhetorician, is fortunately unable to conform.[2]

[2]What Bell does not sufficiently emphasize is that the intellectuals' "faith ladders" have indeed converted possibilities into certainties. Otherwise it is hard to see why he and his fellow anti-ideologists make such a hullabaloo about ideology and why they are enthralled with the thought that we have reached the end of the age of ideology. The simple fact is that ever since the French Revolution the intellectuals, with the help of their ideologies, have been moving mountains. And if *their* ideologies are exhausted, as Bell contends, this does not necessarily entail the end of ideology as such. No doubt the old ideologies of the right and the left have lost much of their power to persuade, and no doubt, all over the world, radicalism and intellectualism in our time must inevitably take new forms. But they will persist, by Bell's own analysis, until every intellectual has become a scholar (or worker) and until every scholar becomes a scholar (or worker) merely; that is, until there are no full- or part-time "out-groups" (to employ a fashionable term of sociological analysis) and no general ideas for them to think with. At this point one begins to have visions of an academic utopia within which there are no "free-floating" intellectuals, no alienated, critical minds, such as Professor Bell's, that are not wholly committed to their vocations and that possess an over-plus of energy and passions that is not expended in the conduct of their own "researches." In such a utopia (if I may speak metaphorically) there would be no New York and no Concord, but only a series of semi-urban centers for semi-advanced study for semi-advanced scholars who would sternly deny themselves the use of any concept or the affirmation of any statement

The American anti-ideologists, Bell included, regard themselves as pragmatists. However, we should remind ourselves that it is the great pragmatists who have insisted, time out of mind, that ideas have consequences and that, indeed, their operative meaning can only be construed in consequential terms. Rhetoric, from this point of view, is not necessarily a bad or degenerate form of expression; rather it is a dimension of any form of speech which is addressed to others. Furthermore, pragmatism is also a normative theory which asks us to evaluate any form of speech, and hence of rhetoric, in terms of its consequences. The question, therefore, is not whether a discourse persuades or influences other minds and other hearts, but how it does so and with what effect. Not every rhetorician is a demagogue. Plato's Socrates professed to despise the Sophists because they were rhetoricians, and this Socrates, I surmise, is the grandfather of all the countless anti-rhetoricians and anti-ideologists from his day to Bell's. But it should not be forgotten that Socrates himself was a master rhetorician and that his admirers ignore the fact because they believe his cause was just. Moreover, Socrates was not only a lover of truth; he was also, politically, a reactionary whose hatred of the Sophists was directed not only to their rhetoric but also to their liberal, democratic, and plebeian political and social attitudes. In saying this, I do not mean to attack our latter-day anti-ideologists by innuendo. I do mean to say that the plain effect of *their* rhetoric is to reinforce acceptance of our own institutional status quo and to declass those "intellectuals" who seek to modify in any radical way the fundamental structures of "Western" political life.

There remains a secondary sense of the term "rhetoric" which Bell may also have in mind. In this sense, rhetoric means eloquence. So conceived, the demand for an end to rhetoric is tantamount to a request for plain talk and, so to say, for an age of prose. So far so good. But there may be more to it than this. Elsewhere Bell harps upon the theme that "Throughout their history, Americans have had an extraordinary talent for compromise in politics and extremism in morality." It is plain that Bell is repelled by "this moralism," though, I gather, not so much because it is hypocritical but rather because, as moral, it is uncompromising. "The saving grace, so to speak, of American politics, was that all sorts of groups were tolerated, and the system of the 'deal' became the pragmatic counterpart of the philosophic principle of toleration. But in matters of manners, morals, and conduct—particularly in

whose "practical bearings" cannot be shown to lie wholly within the range of their legitimate scholarly activity or work. Such a utopia, I fancy, would have no place even for counter-ideologists like Professor Bell whose own "restless vanity" (the phrase is his) is evidently not sated by the rewards that accrue from the performance of his scholarly labors.

the small towns—there has been a ferocity of blue-nosed attitudes unmatched by other countries." And again, "It has been one of the glories of the United States that politics has always been a pragmatic give-and-take rather than a series of wars-to-the-death." Of course this last is *not* true. Among our national "glories" have been a war for independence and a civil war, both of them (among other things) wars of principle. Our periods of "give-and-take" have usually also been periods of drift and complacency which have ended in orgies of political corruption and degradation. In one domain, however, Bell believes that our underlying political "postures" have not been "pragmatic." "One of the unique aspects of American politics is that . . . foreign policy has always been phrased in moralistic terms. Perhaps the very nature of our emergence as an independent country forced us to constantly adopt a moral posture in regard to the rest of the world; perhaps being distant from the real centers of interest conflict allowed us to employ pieties, rather than face realities. But since foreign policy has usually been within the frame of moral rather than pragmatic discourse, the debate in the fifties became centered in moral terms."

These passages are typical. In asking for an end to rhetoric, what Bell appears to be calling for is, among other things, an end to *moral* discourse and a beginning of consistent "pragmatic discourse" in every sphere of political life. What does this mean? So far as I can make out, it means an end to judgment and to principle, to praise and to blame, in the political domain and a beginning of plain, unvarnished "politicking" in the name of our "realistic" national, social, or individual "interests." It means, in effect, that in political discourse two and only *two* forms of expression are to be regarded as legitimate: (a) realistic, verifiable statements of fact; and (b) bald, undisguised expressions of first-personal (singular or plural) interest. On such a view, one would be permitted to say, "I don't like segregation and I will try—without, however, upsetting the apple cart—to do what I can to limit segregationalist practices," but not "Segregation is an affront to the humanity of the Negro people," or, "Those who practice segregation are unfair and unjust." What is wrong with moral, as distinct from "pragmatic," discourse? It is not to be doubted that moral discourse is more eloquent and more incitive, and in this sense more rhetorical, than the "pragmatic" forms of speech which Bell prefers. But what is wrong with eloquence *per se*? No doubt it should not be used to cloud an issue, to obscure relevant facts, or to promote unreason. But this is no more a necessary consequence of moral discourse than of any other form of eloquence. Without eloquence, especially in times of crisis, few great political movements would succeed. In fact, eloquence, including the eloquence of moral judgment, is native to the language of politics, and particularly so, as Bell himself admits, in democratic societies where persuasion of the great masses is a condition of success. Thus to put an end to eloquence would be to put an end, not only to "moralism" (which is usually nothing more than the morality of those with whom we disagree) and to "ideology," but also to any form of politics in which great issues are stated or argued in terms of human rights and responsibilities and in which it is essential to gain the approval of the people, or their representatives, before any fundamental change in governmental policy is made. Perhaps a tightly knit, self-interested, and all-powerful elite might get along (among its members) with "pragmatic discourse" alone. But despite Bell, democratic politics does not just mean "bargaining between legitimate groups and the search for consensus." It means also a form of politics in which men are governed by, and hence with reference to, principles and ideals—in a word, to morals and to ideology.

But now a word of caution: It is no part of my intention to suggest, much less admit, that ideology and morality *are* rhetoric; the equation is Bell's, not mine. I contend only that if, as is true, ideological discourses are full of rhetoric (in the above senses), there is no reason to deplore the fact. Quite the contrary.

Webster also mentions a third sense (or senses) of "rhetoric" which for our purposes is perhaps the most interesting of all. In this sense, "rhetoric" means "ostentatious or artificial speech." That some ideologists and moralists are ostentatious need not be denied. My own impression, however, is that academic scholars, particularly in some of the more immature sciences of man, are at least as prone to ostentatious speech (and thought) as other intellectuals. Sociology, indeed, might almost be defined as the ostentatious science. But except in beautiful women, ostentation is surely a minor vice, and only a fool would write off a whole field of study or an entire form of expression because some of its practitioners, like Molière's learned ladies, tend to give themselves airs.

Artificiality is another matter, which will repay closer scrutiny. Now "artificiality" often connotes a way of doing things which, although not necessarily ostentatious, is mannered, contrived, studied, and "unnatural." On occasion, a rhetoric which is artificial in this sense can be very powerful, as for example, in the poetry of Milton or in the prose of Burke and Macaulay. Among moralists and men of letters one associates it with the conservative wits of the 18th century and with the elaborate courtesy and the elegant banter of Matthew Arnold and his disciples. For obvious reasons, it is not a rhetoric characteristic of revolutionary ideologists. In our own time one runs into it only occasionally among writers of the right or the right-center. In England, Michael Oakeshott employs it with some effect, as (in another way) do T. S. Eliot and his followers. In this country, some of the so-called southern agrarians, such as Allen Tate, are minor masters of this rhetoric. But I fancy that Tate, at least, is well aware that he is fighting in a lost cause, and his style, like a ruffled cuff, is intended to give us a heightened sense of the fact. To my unaccustomed ears, the Encyclicals of Leo XIII, which are among the modern masterpieces of Catholic ideology, are also effective examples of a rhetoric of this sort. Indeed, it is precisely the impervious, anachronistic artificiality of Leo's prose which makes one realize how remote, for better or worse, is the concessive modernity of his social thought from the radical liberalism of a Bentham or a Mill.

But "artificiality" has another connotation in this context that is more central to our theme. In this sense, I take it, rhetoric is to be contrasted with literal statement. Here I must limit my remarks mainly to political ideology, but what will be said holds also of all ideologies, including those we normally think of as religious or metaphysical. Now political ideology is nothing but political discourse (as distinct from political science) on its most general formative level. It is, that is to say, political discourse insofar as the latter addresses itself, not just to specific, piecemeal reforms, but to the guiding principles, practices, and aspirations by which politically organized societies, absolutely or else in certain typical situations, ought to be governed. This being so, political ideologies inevitably include, among their leading articles, statements of general principle or method and expressions of basic attitude, orientation, and concern which, as they stand, are so highly abstract as to appear to many minds preoccupied with day-to-day problems of "practical politics" virtually meaningless. Such statements are of course habitually formulated in terms like "general welfare," "common good," "justice," "equality," "democracy," "security," and the rest.

But these very terms, so natural or even essential, when one is defining and appraising political practices or systems, also tend through over-use to become mere counters which elicit from us the tired, stock response that leaves us, and hence the practices themselves, unchanged. Or worse, because our responses are dull and routine, and hence *practically* of no political importance, we may conclude that all general philosophical discussions of politics are pointless and that one political ideology is just as good—or bad—as any other. What does matter, so we feel, is not what we say or think about "the system," but only what we do within it. And so, by stages, we are led to the conservative conclusion that political manifestoes, declarations of

independence, and constitutions (with their embarrassing ideological pre-
ambles) make no difference to society as a going concern. In short, so far as
we are concerned, ideology is useless verbiage. On the other side, unfortunately, we discover to our dismay that other peoples, politically and intellectually less "advanced" than ourselves, are enflamed, sometimes to the
point of revolution, by ideological discourses, fresher and more affecting, in
part because less literal and less abstract, than those to which we are accustomed. And to our contempt for our own ineffectual ideological abstractions
we now add a positive hatred (or fear) of an ideological rhetoric which
suddenly endows those same abstractions with a new life that disturbs
our own.

It should be observed, however, that our very hatred is itself a backhanded
tribute to the power of ideology. And if, out of a misplaced loyalty to "reason," we merely limit ourselves to "exposing" it, we stand in danger of losing
our world. Most of us, realizing that the world is *never* well lost, find ourselves drawn back inescapably into the ideological struggle which, if we are to
win it for ends that are right and just, requires that we produce a counter-
rhetoric more imaginative, more distinguished, and more durable than that of
our opponents. But if, as literalists of the imagination, we still decline to go
the whole hog, resorting now only to formal reaffirmation of the old abstract
"principles" which no later than yesterday we professed to find meaningless,
who will believe us? Why should they? They have heard the same golden
words mouthed a thousand times on the party platforms by hacks who have
no notion of their meaning. And, if it comes to that, what *do* they mean?

In science it normally suffices to state a fact, and one man may do this as well
and as accurately as another. But in the sphere of conduct much more is
involved. For here we have to do with matters of attitude and intention and
with problems of authenticity, legitimacy, and authority. Here words must
not only predict what will be but determine what shall be; they must not
only inform but also prepare and initiate lines of action. And what *is* it that is
being determined, prepared, and initiated? This, so I contend, can be fully
revealed only through the "poetry" which the ideologist may afford us.

Since Plato, rationalists have ever been afraid of poetry. And even those who
profess not to be so worry lest "the people" confuse the true poet with the
counterfeit. But just as true poetry, known and loved, is the only real protection against the malefactions of pseudo-poets, so also its ideological analogue
is the only guarantee against the factitious "myths" of a Rosenberg, a Hitler,
or a Mussolini. Our worry, in America, should be not that the false rhetoric of

"foreign" ideologies may divert our people from their loyalties to our establishment, but that we do so little to replenish the fund of ideological poetry
with which the founding fathers, along with Lincoln and a few others, have
provided us. Our contemporary ideology is, or seems to be, all ghost-written.
The voice sounds as reedy and hollow as are the men who contrive it. But if
we should lose the power both to create and passionately to respond to a
great ideological rhetoric, we would also lose the power to tell the difference
between the phony and the real thing.

Further, figurative and hence rhetorical language enables, or compels, men to
perform in advance of experience those crucial symbolic actions and imaginative experiments upon which, as Dewey has persuasively argued, genuinely
rational judgments of practice and of value entirely depend. Know the truth,
and the truth will set you free: how dangerous and how misleading is this
half-truth. How, in a moral and practical sense, *are* we to know it? I can
assent to the proposition that on the first day of an atomic war every major
city in the United States would be destroyed, without in the least *realizing*, in
human terms, what the statement really means. In order that I may even
remotely grasp such an idea, in absence of the event, I must somehow try
symbolically to live through the horror and the agony of such a calamity. But
this is precisely what the cold, literal, objective statement of fact does not
require me to do. To this end, therefore, it is essential that I find a way of
thinking and talking about the fact which will make me realize from a practical, and even, if you please, from a metaphysical point of view, what it comes
to. For most of us, this can be done only through the artificial linguistic
devices, known to every reader of fiction and of poetry, which enable us to
perform "in imagination," as we say, those symbolic actions in which alone
the "reality" of *literary* art exists. To disdain "rhetoric," therefore, is to disdain the very condition through which full practical understanding and judgment is possible. And to deny oneself its use is not to guarantee the
preservation of scientific "objectivity" but to preclude the possibility of
really being objective in trying to decide, in political terms, what one's way of
life is to be.

It remains to say a word about "simplism," that final bogey of the anti-
ideological mentality. Through rhetoric, according to Bell, ideology infuses
ideas with passion, thus, as might be expected, winning friends and influenc-
ing people. But the principal underhanded intellectual (or is it, too, rhetorical?) trick of the ideologists is to "simplify ideas." It therefore seems
necessary to remind the anti-ideologist that simplification, so far from being a
fault peculiar to ideology, is, as William James well knew, a large part of the

saving virtue of rationality itself. To oppose simplism on principle, in politics
as in every other sphere of activity, is not to make a legitimate demand for
recognition of the complexities and diversities of political life, but, in effect,
to ask for an abandonment of policy and a fatal acquiescence in the drift of
events. For simplification is an essential feature of any rational initiation of
action. To refuse to simplify when one confronts a problem is in effect to
reject the obligation to reach a solution; it is to make a game of possibilities
and hence to move automatically outside the context of agency and choice.
Every procedure that helps us to make decisions does so precisely by reducing
the range of possibilities which we may reasonably be expected to consider.
And every method, in setting a limit to the considerations that ought to be
taken into account, thereby secures our deliberations against an endless
spread of doubts.

On this score particularly, Professor Bell seems merely disingenuous when he
tells us—incidentally letting a fair-sized ideological cat out of his own elastic
bag—that although "There is now more than ever some need for utopia, in the
sense that men need—as they have always needed—some vision of their potential, some manner of fusing passion with intelligence. . . . The ladder to the
City of Heaven can no longer be a 'faith ladder,' but an empirical one; a
utopia has to specify *where* one wants to go, *how* to get there, the costs of
the enterprise, and some realization of, and justification for the determination of *who* is to pay." There is a rather terrible irony in the fact that Bell,
who in other contexts is so prone to rail against those who think in terms of
all or none, should find it so hard at this point to think in terms of degree.
Were one seriously to try, in detail and at the outset, to meet all his requirements for a "good" utopia, the magnitude and complexity of the task would
paralyze thought. The "good" utopian, like the unholy ideologist, must settle
for considerably less if he is ever to bring his deliberations to a conclusion.
And if he eventually does reach a conclusion, then no matter how long he
reflects and however precise his calculations, it will have been conceived in
sin. For it will always reflect a radical simplification of the possibilities and
the alternatives which a more scrupulous utopian would think it obligatory to
consider.

But Bell's advocacy of even his "good" utopias is, at best, half-hearted. For
he really has no faith in any long-range scheme aimed at the amelioration of
society as a whole. "Ideology," he tells us, "makes it unnecessary for people
to confront individual issues on their individual merits." But in one sense this
is true of any rule, any procedure, and any plan, including the plans of piecemeal social engineers like Bell and Popper. What would be the point of any

such scheme, however limited in its scope, unless it relieved us of the necessity of confronting every blessed individual issue on its (otherwise) individual merits? And if it comes to that, what is an "individual issue," and what is it to confront one on its "individual merits"? Is the issue of desegregation, for example, one such issue or is it many? Indeed, is the issue of desegregating one individual classroom in one individual school in one God-forsaken county of the state of Mississippi an individual issue? And if it is, what, pray, are *its* individual merits? How far do these extend?

One of the overwhelming advantages of a bill of human rights (which is nothing but a schedule of enforced ideological commitments), is that it drastically reduces the number of "issues" over which men in societies must continue to quarrel. In this way it reduces the terrible wear and tear of political life which, even in the best-run societies, is nearly unendurable. Bell and his allies, following Popper (and at a distance Bergson), are admirers of the "open society." But of course a completely open society, if such ever existed, would be not a society, but a chaos. If an "open society" is one in which each individual issue is decided, *ad hoc*, on its own peculiar merits, then who wants an "open society"? And if a "closed society" is one in which, owing to the presence of a prevailing ideology (or constitution), many issues are, in any practical sense, dead issues, why then let us by all means continue to have a closed society. Were we Americans seriously to invoke the principle that individual cases should be settled exclusively on their (otherwise) individual merits, we would have to repudiate our Declaration of Independence and to dismantle our whole constitutional system and the characteristic rule of law which it provides.

Is this what the anti-ideologists want? The question is by no means merely "rhetorical." Consider, for example, what the most determined and most consistent of anti-ideologists, Professor Michael Oakeshott, has to say about the Declaration of Independence. It is, he tells us, "A characteristic product of the *saeculum rationalisticum*. It represents the politics of the felt need interpreted with the aid of an ideology. And it is not surprising that it should have become one of the sacred documents of the politics of Rationalism, and, together with the similar documents of the French Revolution, the inspiration and pattern of many later adventures in the rationalistic reconstruction of Society." Whatever else may be true of Professor Oakeshott, he at least knows an ideology when he sees one and is candid enough to say so. It would clear the air if his fellow anti-ideologists on this side of the Atlantic would speak as clearly and unequivocally.

Let us no longer mince words. Our own anti-ideological foxes are no more "empirical" and no less rhetorical than their leonine opponents; they are, on broad issues, merely more indecisive and more eclectic. As it stands, their point of view is so lacking both in consistency and in clarity that, as I have discovered at some cost, it is virtually impossible to argue with them without fear of doing them some frightful injustice. Still, out of a sophisticated but paralyzing fear of over-simplification, they have managed to fashion a kind of counter-ideology, or fetish, of complexity, difficulty, and uniqueness. They tell us that "the present belongs to the living" and that we should lift from our shoulders "the heavy hand of the future" as well as "the dead hand of the past." Yet they evidently have not the courage to say that the preamble to the American Constitution, which speaks among other things of securing the "Blessings of Liberty to ourselves *and our Posterity*," is so much wicked ideological flourish and moonshine. Their "pluralism" has become a kind of mania which, when pressed to its own counter-ideological extremes, leads inescapably (as William James long ago perceived) to anarchism and, at last, to nihilism. Were their political and social attitudes generally to prevail in the West—and it is primarily of the West that they speak in talking of the end of ideology—the result would be a pessimistic *carpe diem* philosophy which would render us helpless in the world struggle against the ideology of Communism. At home, in the political parties, in the Congress, and in the courts, it continually weakens what remains of our national commitment to the ideological principles that animate our constitutional system; in the Presidency, it provides merely the covering excuses for a spate of uncorrelated, "piecemeal" moves which, however admirable from a tactical point of view and however skillful as "pragmatic" politics, result in an ever increasing loss of basic political control and social direction. Curiously, the over-all picture is one of Hegelian "gray on gray." The only difference is that unlike our anti-ideologists Hegel knew that gray on gray is the color of barrenness, of late autumn and approaching winter.

Ideology—A Debate*

Daniel Bell and
Henry David Aiken

Daniel Bell

Define your terms, the philosophers enjoin us. One of the difficulties with
Henry David Aiken's essay, "The Revolt Against Ideology," is the
multiplicity of senses in which he uses the word "ideology," as well as the
ambiguity of his prescriptions. He begins by citing with approval the Marxian
conception that ideologies are "inverted images of reality"—ideas falsely
divorced from the material conditions that produce them—and that the function of social analysis is to "demythologize ideology"; and he concludes—no
longer mincing words!—by saying that persons like myself, who talk of the
"end of ideology," would "render us helpless in the world struggle against the
ideology of Communism" and weaken "what remains of our national commitment to the ideological principles that animate our constitutional
system."

Now, since I accept a Marxian conception of ideology as the starting point for
analysis, and since I call myself a pragmatist (as does Mr. Aiken), I am puzzled by the transitions through which I end up as subversive of my own
ideals, if not of my country's. Let me therefore indicate what I mean by the
"end of ideology," and later confront Mr. Aiken himself directly.

The Marxian discussion of ideology flows from the concern with alienation.
But the context is as broad as the "human condition" itself. The root of it all
is in man's unhappy awareness of a divided consciousness, and his yearning or
search for an Absolute. In Christian terms, man is separated from God and
searches for re-unification through the figure of Christ. For Hegel, religious
alienation is but one aspect of a cosmic drama in which everything is rent by
duality—spirit and matter, nature and history, God and man—and the "realization," or the "end of philosophy," will occur when all dualities are overcome, when man no longer is both subject and object, or lives between
society and State.

*Daniel Bell and Henry David Aiken, "Ideology—A Debate," *Commentary,* 38 (October
1964), 69-76. Reprinted from *Commentary* by permission; copyright © 1964 by the
American Jewish Committee.

Marx's great vision provided a naturalistic foundation for the Hegelian drama. The source of man's duality, he said, lay not in thought but in the division of labor and in the social classes. The "realization" of philosophy, in other words, lay in economics, and the agency of human fulfillment was not the Idea but the Proletariat. The unity of "thought and being," the union of appearance and reality, and the end of all ideology (a phrase, as Lewis Feuer reminds us, that was first used by Engels in his essay on Feuerbach) would come, said Marx, when man finally conquered material necessity and began living in a purposeful, self-directed community.

Marxism itself, however, became an ideology with the assumption, to be found in Marx's later work as well as in the vulgarization of his thought by Engels, that there was a single key to the "realization" of philosophy—the abolition of private property. Abolish private property, and all exploitation would disappear. As Communist apologists later put it, there could be no classes and exploitation in the Soviet Union because there was no private property in Soviet society.

It is necessary to emphasize some distinctions in order to focus the questions that divide us. Originally, "ideology" simply meant sense impressions; in opposition to the rationalists, the ideologues sought to "purify" ideas by accepting only those which come through the senses. For Marx, "ideology" referred to beliefs which masked private interests; thus, such doctrines as natural rights, with their claim to a universal transcendental validity, were really constructed to justify the needs of the bourgeoisie. Among the specific examples of ideology that Marx gives (in the essays on *The Jewish Question*) are the guarantees of property rights and civil rights in the various state constitutions of the United States. In the 20th century, "ideology" acquired a broader and more impassioned meaning. As the political struggles of the age took on the intensity of the earlier religious wars, the word came to denote in politics what the terms "creed" or "faith" had meant in religion.

During its crusading Bolshevik phase, Marxism became a *total* ideology. As I used the term:

A *total* ideology is an all-inclusive system of comprehensive reality, it is a set of beliefs, infused with passion, and seeks to transform the whole of a way of life. This commitment to ideology—the yearning for a "cause" or the satisfaction of deep moral feelings—is *not* necessarily the reflection of interests in the shape of ideas. Ideology . . . in the sense used here is a secular religion.

Those of us who speak of the "end of ideology" mainly mean to reject this mode of commitment, which had such a disastrous effect on the thought and politics of the radical and utopian movements of the past two generations. As developed by such writers as Raymond Aron, Edward Shils, C. A. R. Crosland, and S. M. Lipset, the theme of the "end of ideology" has become a call for an end to apocalyptic beliefs that refuse to specify the costs and consequences of the changes they envision. The "end-of-ideology" school (if a school it is) is skeptical of rationalistic schemes that assume they can blueprint the entire life of a society; it argues that the existing political tags "conservative" and "liberal" have lost their intellectual clarity; it is critical of existing institutions, but it does not accept the assumption that social change is *necessarily* an improvement. In short, it is pragmatic in the triple sense in which Dewey used the term: it defines the consequence of an action as a constitutive element of the truth of a proposition; it assumes the inextricable relation of ends and means; and it believes that values, like any empirical proposition, can be tested on the basis of their claims.

Now the curious thing is that none of this history—either of the term "ideology" or of the background of radicalism—is reflected in Mr. Aiken's discussion of ideology. He does not say whether these judgments on the past were wrong or right. He treats the word "ideology" only as a formal problem for analysis. The reason, perhaps, is that he is out to make a case—a lawyer's case, not a philosopher's case—and he goes at it in the best lawyer's manner.

The central point in his discussion of my own contribution to the theme is his analysis of the word "rhetoric." I wrote:

If the "end of ideology" has any meaning, it is to ask for the end of rhetoric, and rhetoricians, of "revolution," of the day when the young French anarchist Vaillant tossed a bomb into the Chamber of Deputies and the literary critic Laurent Tailhade declared in his defense: "What do a few human lives matter; it was a *beau geste!*"

After quoting this passage, Mr. Aiken comments:

If by "rhetoric" Bell means the use of language in order to persuade or influence others— and many things suggest that this is his meaning—then his vision of the end of ideology as an end to rhetoric is a utopian fantasy. Worse, it is an evil fantasy, for it implies a conception of human relations which would deprive us of the right to address one another except for the purposes of comparing notes about matters of fact.

I submit that the two paragraphs have nothing to do with each other. I was calling attention to the *distortion* of the discourse of persuasion—after all, what is a bomb?—rather than its classical use. The "end of rhetoric," in the context I gave it, plainly means an end to a way of thinking and acting which substitutes the worship of the Word—the verbal fetish of Revolution—for a moral analysis of consequences. If the fetishism of commodities is the "secret" of capitalism, is not the fetishism of rhetoric—the reliance on political slogans—the "secret" of radicalism?[1]

Next: I wrote that American life has suffered from an excess of "moralism." My examples were the small-town fundamentalist restrictions on personal conduct; McCarthyism—an extension of such moralizing in politics; and the formulation of foreign policy from one administration to the next in moralistic terms. (And, one can now say, the political rhetoric of Barry Goldwater.)

Writes Mr. Aiken:

> In asking for an end to rhetoric, what Bell appears to be calling for is, among other things, an end to *moral* discourse and a beginning of consistent "pragmatic discourse" in every sphere of political life. What does this mean? So far as I can make out, it means *an end to judgment and to principle* [my italics], to praise and to blame, in the political domain and a beginning of plain, unvarnished "politicking" in the name of our "realistic" national, social, or individual "interests."

Again I call foul, this time at the shift from *moralistic* to *moral*. Moralizing, or being moralistic, is a distortion of the moral mode. It is the "ideological" use of morality for the sake of a hidden purpose.

As it happens, I do believe in "pragmatic discourse"; but is pragmatic discourse without principle? Isn't Locke's *Letter on Toleration* a form of pragmatic discourse? Isn't Kant's distinction between public and private—one the realm of agreed-upon procedure, the other the realm of conscience—a pragmatic one in its context? Pragmatic discourse in politics emphasizes the search for a reasoned consensus, rather than treating political issues as a war-to-the-death. It involves an "ethic of responsibility," but as Richard McKeon has pointed out, "responsibility is determined by the reciprocities in the actions of men." Where there is no reciprocity, conflict may—and at times should—develop. Between a racist and myself there is no reciprocity; between a Nazi and myself there is no reciprocity; between a Communist and myself there is no reciprocity. But where there is, or can be, an acceptance of the rules of the game—of the process of open discourse and reciprocity—there *should be* social compromise. Is this not judgment—and principle?

What is the lawyer's case that Mr. Aiken is seeking to make? On the one hand, it is a cumbersome theoretical formulation; on the other, a simplified political point.

---

[1]Even sillier is Mr. Aiken's next comment: "There remains a second sense of the term 'rhetoric' which Bell *may also have in mind*. [Italics mine.] In this sense, rhetoric means eloquence. So conceived, the demand for an end to rhetoric is tantamount to a request for plain talk, and, so to say, for the age of prose." Now really!

Mr. Aiken writes:

Now political ideology is nothing but political discourse . . . on its most general formative level. It is, that is to say, political discourse insofar as the latter addresses itself, not just to specific, piecemeal reforms, but to the guiding principles, practices, and aspirations by which politically organized societies, absolutely or else in certain typical situations, ought to be governed. . . . Here words must not only predict what will be but determine what shall be; they must not only inform but also prepare and initiate lines of action. And what *is* it that is being determined, prepared, and initiated? This, so I contend, can be fully revealed only through the "poetry" which the ideologist may afford us.

Here Mr. Aiken completely muddies the waters. For he has simply taken an old-fashioned definition of *political philosophy* and arbitrarily called it— despite the tortuous history of the word—*political ideology*. In fact a number of writers today—usually conservative ones who ask for a return to first principles—have decried the absence of political philosophy in the schools, charging modern political theory with "scientism." By calling for political ideology, Mr. Aiken has given us a stylish way of posing the problem. But otherwise the only gain is in confusion.

His political barb is more pointed:

I do not mean to attack our latter-day anti-ideologists by innuendo. I do mean to say that the plain effect of *their* rhetoric is to reinforce acceptance of our institutional status quo and to declass those "intellectuals" who seek to modify in any radical way the fundamental structures of "Western" political life.

If you set up a straw man, it will burn brightly when you put a match to it. As in so much of Mr. Aiken's essay, there is a fine resonance but an astonishing lack of specificity in these statements. I don't know what Mr. Aiken regards as the "fundamental structures of 'Western' political life." To my mind, the fundamental structure is the democratic process, and this I do not want to change. To speak further for myself, since the question of political identification is at issue, I am a democratic socialist, and have been for almost all of my politically conscious years. As such, I wish to see a change in the fundamental structures of our economic life. I deplore the social and economic power of the corporation. I detest the cult of efficiency which sacrifices the worker to the norms of productivity. I favor national planning in the economy. I want to see more public enterprise. And I want to introduce other criteria than those of the market or the private profit motive as means of allocating resources in the society. I have guiding general principles, rooted in conceptions about the nature of work and community, which shape these views. But I also have a test which guides the introduction of these changes; and I think the differences between Mr. Aiken and me on this question are the nub of the issue.

I wrote:

There is now more than ever some need for utopia, in the sense that men need—as they have always needed—some vision of their potential, some manner of fusing passion with intelligence. . . . The ladder to the City of Heaven can no longer be a "faith ladder," but an empirical one; a utopia has to specify *where* one wants to go, *how* to get there, the costs of the enterprise, and some realization of, and justification for, the determination of *who* is to pay.

To this, Mr. Aiken retorts:

Were one seriously to try, in detail and at the outset, to meet all his requirements for a "good" utopia, the magnitude and complexity of the task would paralyze thought.

I find it hard to understand these remarks. The context of my discussion was quite clear. I pointed out that Lenin instigated the Russian Revolution with no idea at all of the meaning of planning or socialization (other than the simple-minded notion, expressed in *State and Revolution*, that the entire economy would be run like a single enterprise), and that the lives of millions of people were thus committed on the basis of an abstract promise. Or, to take another example: when Stalin decided in 1929 on the ruthless collectivization of agriculture in line with the ideological premise that individual peasant property should be eliminated, was not the question of costs and consequences relevant? Or again, to bring the issue closer to home: if an urban renewal program bulldozes a neighborhood in response to the liberals' ideological image of "slum clearance," should one not apply tests of the consequence of this action for community life?

Does Mr. Aiken want to build a bridge to the future without any tests of costs and consequences? His fear is that such a demand would inhibit all change. But why? Is it really so difficult? Have we no resources at all in sociological and economic knowledge to assess the social costs of change? Surely we know enough by now about the effects of social change—the devastation in the depressed areas, the school dropouts, the manifold impact of automation—to understand what our *failure* to plan has cost.

But all this is bootless, for I am asking Mr. Aiken to be concrete, and he is relentlessly abstract. Yet if the debate is to have any meaning, if Mr. Aiken wants to be radical, let him state in detail what he wants to be radical about. Then we can argue whether it is desirable or not, and what criteria we should use. But is it not the mark of the ideologue that he is usually so general and vague?

From past experience as well as from this exchange, I feel that what is really involved here is not a conflict of intellectual positions but a conflict of contrasting temperaments. Once upon a time there was a primary and meaningful tension between the orthodox and the antinomians. The orthodox, whether priests, clerks, or scholars, believed in a ritual or a tradition, a set of "right" beliefs, which were enforced in varying degrees on the society. The antinomians—gnostics, vagabonds, bohemians, rebels—resisted institutional authority, were defiant of tradition, law, and system, and sought to guide their lives by esoteric standards of conduct.

Such divisions used to be clear. But the history of the past several hundred years has seen the absorption, or containment, of heresy. Religious antinomianism and "enthusiastic" movements became orthodoxies after the Reformation. The aesthetic Rebellion that emerged after 1885 was largely drained into politics in the 1920's and 1930's, as seen most markedly in the movement of the Dadaist leaders—Aragon, Tzara, and Eluard—into the Communist party. And the most subterranean of traditions, which runs from de Sade through Lautréamont to Genet and Burroughs, is today publicly acclaimed by the chic avant-garde and its camp-followers.

The point of all this is that the currently fashionable talk about Establishments and anti-Establishments, of cultural radicalism and the official academy, is substantially meaningless. What is one to make of the state of cultural criticism when Harold Rosenberg attacks F. R. Leavis as a cultural fascist in the columns of the *New Yorker* and Richard Poirier defends Leavis in the pages of *The New York Review of Books*? In *Playboy* sexual radicalism is "philosophically" intertwined with economic free enterprise; in the *Herald Tribune*, Leslie Fiedler explains the avant-garde to the stockbrokers. The notion that Mr. Aiken is a critic of society and that I am not, that Norman Podhoretz is a radical and Lionel Trilling a "revisionist liberal," makes no sense. Today our entire society is committed to change, and in a direction which was first pointed out by the Left. In the realm of "culture" the ramparts have been manned, and each is at the station perhaps appropriate to his distinction: Harold Rosenberg is at the *New Yorker*, Norman Mailer and Dwight Macdonald at *Esquire*, Alfred Chester at *Book Week*, Seymour Krim at *Nugget*, Nicholas Calas at the *Village Voice*; and Paul Goodman is almost in the academy. Everyone is happily playing the heretic in the fields of official clover and busily exposing the nakedness of everyone else.

The shock of change, though, is real enough: the realization that escapes no one is that the egalitarian and socially mobile society which the "free-floating intellectuals" associated with the Marxist tradition have been calling for during the last hundred years has finally emerged in the form of our cumbersome, bureaucratic mass society, and has in turn engulfed the heretics. With this realization begins the process of disengagement. But it is not generally a process of responsible social thought and self-scrutiny, not an attempt to find out what kind of institutional structures in a large-scale society will best accommodate the older visions of community and individual freedom and self-determination. One simply labels oneself a radical, calls for (but rarely produces) utopian thought, and argues that the great need is to be "critical." Such disengagement is, quite simply, an escape from intellectual responsibility. Mr. Aiken's essay, with its abstract talk of moral discourse, provides a lovely cover for such an escape.

But if the old division of political temperaments into orthodox and antinomian has apparently broken down, there is still perhaps some usefulness in a three-part classification: the ideologues, the moralists, and the skeptics.

Ideologies, as organized systems of belief with ready formulas for the manipulation of the masses, are, in effect, new orthodoxies. The yearning for an ideology, the hunger for a cause, the craving for belief often mask the conformist's desire for power or the rebel's unconscious need to submit to authority. Such a reductive analysis, of course, risks the traducing of individuals who may be genuinely motivated to serve mankind selflessly or to search for new means of implementing their ideals. However, the judgment itself is not of persons but of the nature of ideologies, and of the way in which the "functional necessities" of organizing and implementing ideologies traduce all idealism.

To go back to Marx's original sense of the term, an ideology is an illusion, a false consciousness. Or, as Philip Rieff has recently remarked, "Only an illusory history, or an illusory religion, or an illusory politics, could lead humans to the therapy of commitment." The yearning for a cause, for some transcendent purpose, is, of course, one of the deepest impulses of the sentient human being. The danger, always, is that this impulse will be manipulated in ways that betray its idealism. Such seductions are rarely overt or crude. It is usually the apocalyptic element, the call for a last act of violence in order to end violence, of a final deed of murder to eliminate murder, which is the agency of the ideologue's betrayal. In the dialectic of betrayal, means become ends and justifications of themselves.

Then there are those often lonely protestants who have stood outside the corridors of ideology or the pathways of power, and have spoken as moralists. In the tradition of prophecy, the moralists, on the basis of conscience, call

injustice to account. In his tone and in his wrath, Mr. Aiken strikes me as a
quondam moralist—which makes me all the more puzzled by his present
effort to patch shreds of ideology into an intellectual argument. He does so,
as I have pointed out, only be tearing the word "ideology" from its historical
and sociological context, and by arbitrarily identifying it with political philosophy and moral discourse.

But why not speak directly in the language of morals and ethics? I can
account for this failure only by the fact that the religious tradition—which
has been the foundation of prophecy—has itself been undermined, and that
the moralist has consequently lost much of his basis of judgment. Jeremiah
and Deutero-Isaiah could call for a return to tradition, a departure from the
merely ritualistic observance of the law; but what can Mr. Aiken ask us to
return to? The modern moralist can become either an existentialist or an
ideologue, and the option now seems to be running in the latter direction.

Most skeptics, I suppose, are lapsed ideologues. This, in turn, may explain
why the theme of the "end of ideology" has so often had a negative side. It
began as a recoil from the easy optimism of "illusory politics" and found its
texts in such documents of disillusionment as John Milton's *Ready and Easy
Way* and Alexander Herzen's *Letters from the Other Shore*. Skepticism does
have its dangers—it can lead to cynicism, quietism, or despair.

Where the theme of the "end of ideology" is currently most relevant is in
Eastern Europe, among the intellectuals who have experienced at first hand
the deadening effects of an official ideology, and among the young generation
for whom ideology is simply flatulent rhetoric. (It is curious that Mr. Aiken
seems to assume that ideology is always nascent and passionate, and neglects
its more pervasive role as a coercive, official force.) In a recent issue of
Survey, a Czech writer describes the calloused attitude to politics of those
who have grown up in an ideological regime:

A strange, frightening breed, this new generation, these men and women born during the
last war or even later, who never knew any other social order and who are the products
of our society. Purposeful, tough, smart, resourceful in handling their own affairs,
down-to-earth, uncommunicative outside their own group, full of obvious pity for their
fathers and their ridiculous manoeuvers, full of energy to get the best out of life now and
for themselves.

To them, ideology and politics and, indeed, any form of public activity are a lot of bunk,
just hollow words with little relation to reality. Not that they are anti-Communists,
a meaningless term in their ears: they just could not care less. They were born into
socialism and they live in socialism and what they see around *is* socialism. Pretty dull
and shabby, and certainly nothing much to write home about. . . .

If there is still to come the final ignominy of a burial of Marxism-Leninism as we understand it today, it will be effortlessly carried out by these generations already born into socialism. And so it should be! For I believe that these young people, these young socialists will at last realize, because of what we did, that there is no socialism without freedom and that life is far more important than ideology.

The intention, then, of the "revolt against ideology" is not to make one insensitive to injustice or to the need for a transcendent moral vision. It is, rather, to make one wary of the easy solution and to deny that any embodiment of community is final. I once wrote that one of the tragedies of Marxism was that Marx, having provided a naturalistic explanation of the meaning of alienation, then narrowed the concept by locating its source entirely in the rule of private property. As we know now, to our sorrow, there are other, more debasing forms of degradation and dehumanization—the systems of totalitarianism—than economic exploitation.

However, the thinking connected with the "end of ideology" is not directed against Marxism or any other radical creed; nor does it involve a quarrel with utopianism and its visions. What it does is give us a perspective on modern history which emphasizes that the achievement of freedom and the defense of the individual constitute a permanent revolution; and it tells us that this revolution resists any final definition. It is for the sake of individual freedom that the claims of doubt must always take precedence over the claims of faith, and that the commitment to action must proceed from the ethic of responsibility.

Henry David Aiken

On the whole Mr. Bell's reply confirms my earlier impression of the essential intellectual and spiritual confusion of the anti-ideology movement, the poverty of its ideas, and its total lack of a coherent, substantive social and political philosophy that goes a step beyond reaffirmation of shibboleths about which both of our major political parties (at least until Goldwater's ascendancy) have been in all-too-complete agreement for a generation.

There is, to be sure, one small part that doesn't quite jibe with this impression, but it is so curiously, almost touchingly, inconsistent with the remainder that I can only wonder about the degree of Mr. Bell's self-awareness in mentioning it. Specifically, he says that he has been a "democratic socialist for almost all of [his] . . . politically conscious years." Can he be serious? In other writings, including *The End of Ideology*, he has opted emphatically and without qualification for "the mixed economy"—which, of course, no socialist could accept save as a temporary stop-gap.

Socialism, I take it, is above all the position that at least the control and operation of the means of production, distribution, and exchange should be in the hands of society as a whole rather than of private individuals, groups, or corporations. Actively to take steps to bring about socialism in the United States would at once involve Mr. Bell (or anyone else) in a very sharp and deep disensus, both politically and ideologically, with the great majority of the American people, including virtually the whole industrial-business-governmental-scholarly establishment. In this country the existing democracy, or republic, is for practical purposes incompatible with socialism. And just for that reason, as S. M. Lipset, Mr. Bell's ally, has pointed out, socialism is here politically and ideologically a dead issue. Mr. Bell knows this. He must realize therefore that being a socialist in America is, for most men, rather like being a Christian: it is entirely safe to be one because socialism, for all but a revolutionary few, is outside the bounds of political possibility. In short, Mr. Bell's "socialism," the wishful and wistful sincerity of which we need not question, is, in Marx's sense, entirely utopian, and hence practically and functionally meaningless. Mr. Bell often has written perceptively and relevantly about sources of alienation among American workers. But what has he to offer, as a *socialist*, toward its drastic alleviation? I submit: nothing, or next to nothing. Here is precisely the sort of ideological schizophrenia which, in part, my essay was designed to expose.

But let me at once remove a possible source of misconception. Mr. Bell has spoken for himself; as for me, I am not a Marxist, vestigial, revisionist, or otherwise. My fundamental intellectual and moral antecedents are British, American, and Jewish. And although I mean always to speak of Marx *and* Engels with respect, I find it hard to understand how Mr. Bell could have gained the impression that my "citing" [*sic*] of the Marxist conception of ideology as "inverted images of reality" was meant to be approving.

However this may be, let me say for the record that I consider the Marxist (and hence Bellean) theory of ideology itself as at once vague, confused, programmatic, and useful nowadays only for purposes of popular polemicizing. On this score, Lenin's theory of ideology is surprisingly better, since it freely acknowledges Marxism to be an ideology, and since it perceives that, in general, ideology can be properly conceived, not in aprioristic, metaphysically pejorative terms, but functionally and dynamically as a form of thought which, for better or for worse, is meant to focus, guide, and energize the minds (and bodies) of men in society. As Lenin saw, it is the role, not the content, which determines whether a theory or doctrine is working ideologically. Thus, in the context of social action, scientific theories, philosophical doctrines, religious creeds, and even sociological statistics, may all serve an ideological role, just as well, or better, than ideas that are, or are supposed to be, "inverted images of reality." And let me add, finally, lest again I be misunderstood, that I am not remotely a Leninist either—although, in justice, I am bound to say that, after Marx himself, Lenin remains the most interesting and suggestive among Marxist thinkers. Lenin is, above all, an institutionalist in his approach to the problems and tasks of socialism, which is precisely what Bell is not. Alas, it was my reading of Lenin that, ironically, convinced me that world socialism is probably a utopian dream.

Mr. Bell's own variations on a theme by Marx are, from my point of view, conceptually and historically regressive, polemically misleading, and ultimately (when taken seriously) debilitating so far as the causes of the alienated, the disenfranchised, and the disinherited are concerned. Moreover, they leave our "confrontation," as Mr. Bell calls it, quite unaffected—except insofar as they inadvertently help to show (what I myself earlier pointed out) that the anti-ideologists, and especially Mr. Bell, are in effect merely quasi-Marxian conservatives who have done little or nothing to advance the master's theory of ideology, but on the contrary have merely applied his ideas rather mechanically and obviously to Communism itself in defense of the primary political and social status quo in the "free world." My contention was—and is—that the anti-ideologists leave us at once morally, intellectually, and, if I may say so, metaphysically helpless in "our" confrontation not only with the Communist world, but also with the great "neutralist" movements that are emerging all over the globe, and especially in the ex-colonial areas where neither socialism nor (political) democracy appears to stand a chance of realization. Now is a time, if there ever was one, for creative and constructive social and political thought. In such a situation what are the anti-ideologists doing, really, but warning us against the dangers of the faith ladder? Well, maybe we just do need a bit of faith in the future of humanity.

Mr. Bell says that pragmatism, at least in Dewey's version, defines "the consequences of an action as a constitutive element of the truth of a proposition." This, I would say, is rather the way Dewey must look under water. I myself think that Dewey's doctrine of the continuum of means and ends is a notable contribution to moral philosophy. But Mr. Bell makes no genuine use of it; he merely *says* he does. Marx, I may add, was implicitly employing this methodological principle in his own attacks upon utopianism, and especially utopian socialism. Mr. Bell and his "socialist" friends do not employ it; quite the contrary, theirs is a merely ideal, sentimental socialism, untouched by the slightest hesitation about what socialist aspirations can mean in a historical context in which no determinate program exists for realizing it. As for the thesis that "values, like any empirical proposition [*sic*], can be tested on the basis of their claims," it is one of the weirdest attempts at redaction of the Dewey-Hook theory regarding the empirical, or even scientific, verifiability of value judgments that I have yet seen.[2]

Mr. Bell claims that I treat the word "ideology" only as a formal problem for analysis, and that the reason for this is that I am out to make a lawyer's rather than a philosopher's case. How odd. Well, I did mean to make a case, the best I knew how to make. And it is all the same to me how Mr. Bell chooses to classify it, so long as it is, as he allows, "the best" of its kind. As a means to a moral and ideological end, I was and am interested in the "formal" problem which the word "ideology" presents to the logical analyst, although Mr. Bell at the outset appears to deny this when he complains that I do not "define" ideology. It was not my purpose to define it, but to study and to characterize what other people, including Mr. Bell, seem to think about it. I tried to determine what Mr. Bell might be taken to mean and then to show that, once *his* rhetoric was stripped to its fighting weight, even his notions of ideology did not commit him, or us, to an across-the-board attack upon ideology as such. Again, I suggested that all ideologies should be judged, not *en bloc*, but in the light of their own respective practices and envisageable consequences. And it was precisely in these terms that I attempted to appraise the merits of Mr. Bell's own anti-ideological ideology. He doesn't reply to my specific contentions—including in particular the charge that the anti-ideological school has fallen into a weary, disillusioned *carpe diem* philosophy which may be suitable for self-centered valetudinarians but is certainly unsuitable for determined, untired, radical liberals who believe that the free world has a real future if it moves boldly and creatively and immediately on its own terrible problems of poverty, inequality, prejudice, and fear. In short, my aim has been to employ the study of a word in use, in order to expose, and if possible transcend, a point of view which in the past I myself have found all too tempting.

Eventually, Mr. Bell gets around to quoting a passage from my essay in which, after the preparation I thought I needed, I state what in my judgment a political ideology, if not a total ideology, really comes to. By extrapolation it would be easy to derive from this my views about "total ideology," were these not already available in my little book, *The Age of Ideology*. So the

[2]Anyone interested in why I consider this theory indefensible can find the reason in my essays on Hook and Dewey, *Commentary*, February and October, 1962. An earlier, more detailed version of the same position may be found in my book, *Reason and Conduct*.

charge that I don't provide a "definition" of political ideology (at the outset?) strikes me as somewhat perverse. As for the point that the "definition" of political ideology which I offer is merely a misleading definition of political philosophy, let me reply that if Mr. Bell can bring himself to take another look at my essay, he will find that I myself actually lead off by asking why so many people declare political philosophy to be dead. I turn later to a consideration of ideology precisely in order to find an answer to that question. And in fact I was led in the first instance into a discussion of the end-of-ideology school through an attempt to discover what, at bottom, people now object to in political philosophy. If my "definition" of political ideology turns out to be nothing but a "stylish" redaction of "the old-fashioned definition of political philosophy," so be it. For then in refurbishing ideology, I shall have done, as I meant to do, two jobs at once.

On this score, there remains only to be added that in my opinion the ideologists often have treated the problems of political philosophy more imaginatively and in greater depth than their more classical predecessors. And the reason for this is that they nearly always see the necessity of viewing a political philosophy (or ideology) not only in the perspective of a system of moral principles, but also within the context of a philosophy of history, a metaphysical *Weltanschauung*, and, if one can be found, a theology. It is this context, largely lacking except in negative terms in the works of the anti-ideologists, which gives depth and range and power to a political ideology. And, indeed, if one knows where to look for it, the greatest classical political philosophies, such as Plato's and Aquinas's, have always provided it.

Mr. Bell's cry of "foul" in response to my charge, or informed guess, that the anti-ideologists are not only anti-moralistic but also anti-moralists who really mean to go altogether beyond "good and evil," is premature. My advice to him here is to re-read, not my words, but his own. In the passage about total ideology which he quotes from his own book, there is this sentence: "This commitment to ideology—the yearning for a cause, the satisfaction of deep *moral* feelings—is not . . . " etc. (my italics). Here, plainly, is not the obvious pejorative adjective "moralistic" but the now pejorated adjective "moral" itself. There are other analogous passages in Mr. Bell's writings, as well as a good many that might be quoted to advantage from the writings of his allies. I stand my ground: Mr. Bell's attack is not directed merely against "moralism"—which, of course, is nothing but the other chap's morals—but against morality as a form of discourse, a form of policy, a way of deciding what is to be done (and said).

Mr. Bell asks me, as I hoped he might, to be concrete. Very well (although it should be emphasized that there is nothing wrong with being abstract when the problems at issue are abstract and general, as they are to a degree in the present context). I believe in the necessity of constant, incessant pressure from the Left upon the Establishment and the status quo in order to rectify grave social wrongs: injustices, inequalities, and other miseries that are removable through collective social action. I believe, furthermore, in a never-ending "resistance" and spiritual rebelliousness. In our time, I think that the first order of business is a continuing, stop-at-nothing effort to obtain, not merely a nuclear test ban, but a progressive, ultimately total, dismantling of our entire machinery for nuclear warfare, lest some benighted Goldwater, unacquainted with the theory of games, should not merely threaten to use it, but use it. I believe in the necessity of a foreign policy for America which is predicated on the principle that any sort of brinksmanship, in whatever cause, is deeply immoral, a test not of courage but of inhumanity or madness or both. I seek, further, an approach to the problems of "underdeveloped" regions and nations which is radically non-military and which is completely indifferent to questions of ideology, race, color, or previous condition of servitude. I want us to pursue a realistic policy in regard to China, one which recognizes that China is a permanent, or semi-permanent, political and social reality which cannot be dealt with by the methods employed by the American government during the past decade. Whether we "like" the Chinese government is quite irrelevant. It belongs in the UN if Spain and Russia and Egypt belong. But this is merely emblematic. It is the "either-or" mentality exemplified by the anti-ideologists in their thinking about the confrontation between the Communist worlds and the "free" worlds which seems to me so inhuman, so dangerous, so suicidal.

Domestically, I applaud a hard, tough, *uncompromising* effort to bring the Negro people up to scratch, legally, politically, economically, humanly. People deplore the riots. What they should deplore are the causes of the riots; and what they should do about them is to remove those causes. *This can be done*, particularly if we divert a third or a half of the money and effort spent on building the military establishment, moon shots and all the rest of it, into imaginative public-works projects, educational developments, medical programs, and humanistic social activities in which all classes and colors of Americans participate together. Harlem (and "Harlem" works a bit like "Goldwater," as a type-word) is a national, not a regional, problem, and it can't wait a generation for a solution. There is also the immense aesthetic and even religious problem of saving America and the world from total permanent disfigurement. Much of New York, for example, is now so hideous that one wonders how human beings can endure it. But it is a dream city by comparison with Detroit and Chicago. The countryside is in ruins. The air stinks. The water, what there is of it, is undrinkable. And so on. A world as ugly, as fearful, as uncertain of itself as ours needs sympathy, but it needs continual action—bold, determined, and radical. Nothing else will suffice.

In part the differences between Mr. Bell's party and my own are doctrinal. But there are indeed basic differences of attitude or posture toward the whole conduct of life of men in societies. This becomes apparent in our respective conceptions of the democratic process itself. For Mr. Bell, it seems, democracy virtually means compromise. For me, compromise is as compromise does: some compromises are desirable; some necessary; others are dishonorable. Where questions of civil liberty, economic equality, and social justice are concerned, I consider compromise with the "interests," with prejudice, with indifference to be dishonorable, and I do not commend it. All too often, even in a democracy, compromise suggests, not sweet reasonableness and good will, but inaction, vacillation, collaboration, timidity. For me democracy is, minimally, a device for checking the accumulation of political power; maximally, it is a mode of participation in the communal life and a sharing of fundamental responsibilities toward the common good. What lies between seems to me, often, less admirable.

More broadly still, for Mr. Bell it appears that problems of politics generally are to be viewed, first, as problems of calculation and, secondly, as problems of adjustment (or compromise). For me, they involve much more, as is evident in my views about the role of rhetoric in political thought and discourse. To my mind, therefore, the end of ideology is, in a sense, almost tantamount to the end of politics itself. Beneath all, the anti-ideologists are men of doubt; their temperament, in the language of William James, is that of the "tough-minded." All too often, sadly, the same is true of me, but I do not glory in the fact. Pessimism is a fact of life; optimism, in our time at least, almost a matter of grace. Thought, analysis, inquiry—and the itch of doubt which animates inquiry—are *of course* indispensable conditions of rational life. But aspiration, passion, hope, volition, and choice also belong inalienably to the life of the mind and the spirit. Without them, in the heat of the day, we languish, we perish. We must not allow ourselves to be paralyzed by thought; rather we must *use* it. We must not let it divert us from the necessity of action. We *dare* not forever stand and wait; we *dare* not continue to temporize. It is late, and there is a world at stake.

Chapter Six

Ideology versus Existential
Moderation:
Camus and the Tradition

Professor Aiken argues, in "The Revolt Against Ideology," that one of the
attacks against traditional political theory has come from the existential
position. He singles out Albert Camus' *The Rebel* as the most significant
example. Aiken says that Camus has a philosophy of politics that is radically
different from that of his predecessors. He contends that Camus' indictment
of traditional political philosophy may be "profoundly anti-rationalistic," but
is not based on a disillusionment with human reason: "Quite the contrary,
reasonableness, in the more classical sense of the term, is Camus's forte."

I agree with Professor Aiken that one important attack on traditional political
philosophy is leveled by those contemporary writers described as "existentialist." But I find agreement with his interpretation of Camus' alternative
more difficult, for reasons stated below in my critique of Camus' key concept
in *The Rebel*.[1]

[1] The statement of Camus' position which follows is adapted from the first part of my
essay on Camus, a long section of which follows the selection from *The Rebel.*

Like many other men of his time, Camus was appalled by the use of contemporary ideologies—especially those of the Communists and the Fascists—to justify what he calls "crimes of logic"—mass murder, concentration camps, brainwashing, and genocide. More appalling than the actions themselves, in some respects, is the fact that they are justified by an appeal to philosophy. Camus singles out as the most pervasive and pernicious of all contemporary ideologies the doctrine of "historicism." By this he means the political doctrine, derived from philosophical arguments, that man has no given or essential nature, thus making any kind of action permissible.

Camus' own position is essentially an attempt to reconcile the idea that man is necessarily involved in history with the idea that he also is capable of resisting history by a measured revolt against it. The first idea underlies the way in which Camus approaches the problem of ideology. His premise is that there are no permanent starting points in the posing of questions, nor any permanent answers to determine the direction and substance of human action; stated more positively, the questions or problems are always a function of the specific historical era. Thus the nineteenth century, Camus says, was a time of negation, in which the supreme question was whether one was justified in committing suicide. And the twentieth century is a time of ideologies, in which the supreme question is whether murder authorized by philosophy is justified.

Camus' argument that these questions have dominated man's existence in the past century and a half rests on the conviction that nineteenth-century philosophy—above all that of Hegel and Nietzsche—revealed the truth that there are no transcendent, permanently valid principles or meanings. The conclusion drawn from the resulting existential position is that man lives in an absurd condition in an absurd universe. It is a universe in which there is no reasonable explanation of injustice, evil, or that greatest of human scourges, death. Nor is there any reasonable explanation of man's own alleged reason.

The other side of Camus' argument is his attempt to show that, to the extent that man has a nature, it exists in the form of his ability to rebel or revolt against the sense of absurdity. The title of his book, *The Rebel*, tersely communicates Camus' conception of man as the being who defines himself by a revolt against his condition.

In the light of this conception, Camus tries to understand the genesis and nature of modern European ideologies that are at the root of ideological politics. He dates such politics from the French Revolution. But he believes a climax or even a crisis is reached in the totalitarianism of the twentieth century. Camus sees us standing at the threshold either of a renaissance of man or of an endless vista of terror and death created by the relentless application of armed doctrines. But he believes in the reality of man's ability to revolt against and go beyond contemporary ideologies. To accomplish this, however, men must return to the original meaning of revolt, which Camus claims to have re-discovered in classical Greece. Revolt must, as it was with the Greeks, be guided by a sense of moderation—of *mesure*. The selection from *The Rebel* juxtaposes true or creative revolt with metaphysical revolt— one form of revolt gone to extremes.

Many critics have singled out Camus' conception of man as defined by creative, "moderate" revolt as *The Rebel*'s most original and hopeful insight. Because of it, Sir Herbert Read says, we may once again have "confidence . . . in man and the future" after "an age of anxiety, despair, and nihilism."[2] R. W. B. Lewis calls Camus "the apostle of *mesure*," and praises his "ideal of well-balanced rebellion."[3] Henri Peyre declares that Camus' "true spiritual motherland was classical Greece," citing as evidence his "preference for Hellenic over Christian values."[4] Leon Roth says that "The discovery of the universal significance of revolt makes [*The Rebel*] so remarkable an achievement. . . ."[5] These appraisals indicate that Camus' interpretation of ideology, the core of which is his idea of revolt gone to extremes, is generally accepted on its own terms. I will question that acceptance in my essay and sketch the reason I consider Camus' own interpretation to be problematic at its core.

[2] Albert Camus, *The Rebel*, Anthony Bower, trans. (New York: Alfred A. Knopf, Vintage Books, 1956), p. vii.

[3] R. W. B. Lewis, "Caligula: Or the Realm of the Impossible," *Yale French Studies*, No. 25, pp. 52-54.

[4] Henri Peyre, "Camus the Pagan," *Yale French Studies, loc. cit.*, p. 22.

[5] Leon Roth, "A Contemporary Moralist: Albert Camus," *Philosophy* (October 1955), p. 299.

From *The Rebel**

Albert Camus

. . . Man's solidarity is founded upon rebellion, and rebellion, in its turn, can only find its justification in this solidarity. We have, then, the right to say that any rebellion which claims the right to deny or destroy this solidarity loses simultaneously its right to be called rebellion and becomes in reality an acquiescence in murder. In the same way, this solidarity, except in so far as religion is concerned, comes to life only on the level of rebellion. And so the real drama of revolutionary thought is announced. In order to exist, man must rebel, but rebellion must respect the limit it discovers in itself—a limit where minds meet and, in meeting, begin to exist. Rebellious thought, therefore, cannot dispense with memory: it is a perpetual state of tension. In studying its actions and its results, we shall have to say, each time, whether it remains faithful to its first noble promise or if, through indolence or folly, it forgets its original purpose and plunges into a mire of tyranny or servitude.

Meanwhile, we can sum up the initial progress that the spirit of rebellion provokes in a mind that is originally imbued with the absurdity and apparent sterility of the world. In absurdist experience, suffering is individual. But from the moment when a movement of rebellion begins, suffering is seen as a collective experience. Therefore the first progressive step for a mind overwhelmed by the strangeness of things is to realize that this feeling of strangeness is shared with all men and that human reality, in its entirety, suffers from the distance which separates it from the rest of the universe. The malady experienced by a single man becomes a mass plague. In our daily trials rebellion plays the same role as does the *"cogito"* in the realm of thought: it is the first piece of evidence. But this evidence lures the individual from his solitude. It founds its first value on the whole human race. I rebel—therefore we exist.

Metaphysical rebellion is the movement by which man protests against his condition and against the whole of creation. It is metaphysical because it contests the ends of man and of creation. The slave protests against the condition in which he finds himself within his state of slavery; the metaphysical rebel protests against the condition in which he finds himself as a man. The rebel slave affirms that there is something in him that will not tolerate the manner in which his master treats him; the metaphysical rebel declares that he is frustrated by the universe. For both of them, it is not only a question of pure and simple negation. In both cases, in fact, we find a value judgment in the name of which the rebel refuses to approve the condition in which he finds himself.

The slave who opposes his master is not concerned, let us note, with repudiating his master as a human being. He repudiates him as a master. He denies that he has the right to deny him, a slave, on grounds of necessity. The master is discredited to the exact extent that he fails to respond to a demand which he ignores. If men cannot refer to a common value, recognized by all as existing in each one, then man is incomprehensible to man. The rebel demands that this value should be clearly recognized in himself because he knows or suspects that, without this principle, crime and disorder would reign throughout the world. An act of rebellion on his part seems like a demand for clarity and unity. The most elementary form of rebellion, paradoxically, expresses an aspiration to order.

This description can be applied, word for word, to the metaphysical rebel. He attacks a shattered world in order to demand unity from it. He opposes the principle of justice which he finds in himself to the principle of injustice which he sees being applied in the world. Thus all he wants, originally, is to resolve this contradiction and establish the unitarian reign of justice, if he can, or of injustice, if he is driven to extremes. Meanwhile, he denounces the contradiction. Metaphysical rebellion is a claim, motivated by the concept of a complete unity, against the suffering of life and death and a protest against the human condition both for its incompleteness, thanks to death, and its wastefulness, thanks to evil. If a mass death sentence defines the human condition, then rebellion, in one sense, is its contemporary. At the same time that he rejects his mortality, the rebel refuses to recognize the power that compels him to live in this condition. The metaphysical rebel is therefore not definitely an atheist, as one might think him, but he is inevitably a blasphemer. Quite simply, he blasphemes primarily in the name of order, denouncing God as the father of death and as the supreme outrage.

The rebel slave will help us to throw light on this point. He established, by his protest, the existence of the master against whom he rebelled. But at the same time he demonstrated that his master's power was dependent on his own subordination and he affirmed his own power: the power of continually questioning the superiority of his master. In this respect master and slave are really in the same boat: the temporary sway of the former is as relative as the submission of the latter. The two forces assert themselves alternately at the moment of rebellion until they confront each other for a fight to the death, and one or the other temporarily disappears.

In the same way, if the metaphysical rebel ranges himself against a power whose existence he simultaneously affirms, he only admits the existence of this power at the very instant that he calls it into question. Then he involves this superior being in the same humiliating adventure as mankind's, its ineffectual power being the equivalent of our ineffectual condition. He subjects it to our power of refusal, bends it to the unbending part of human nature, forcibly integrates it into an existence that we render absurd, and finally drags it from its refuge outside time and involves it in history, very far from the eternal stability that it can find only in the unanimous submission of all men. Thus rebellion affirms that, on its own level, any concept of superior existence is contradictory, to say the least.

And so the history of metaphysical rebellion cannot be confused with that of atheism. From a certain point of view it is even confused with the contemporary history of religious sentiment. The rebel defies more than he denies. Originally, at least, he does not suppress God; he merely talks to Him as an equal. But it is not a polite dialogue. It is a polemic animated by the desire to conquer. The slave begins by demanding justice and ends by wanting to wear a crown. He must dominate in his turn. His insurrection against his condition becomes an unlimited campaign against the heavens for the purpose of bringing back a captive king who will first be dethroned and finally condemned to death. Human rebellion ends in metaphysical revolution. It progresses from appearances to acts, from the dandy to the revolutionary. When the throne of God is overturned, the rebel realizes that it is now his own responsibility to create the justice, order, and unity that he sought in vain within his own condition, and in this way to justify the fall of God. Then begins the desperate effort to create, at the price of crime and murder if necessary, the dominion of man. This will not come about without terrible consequences, of which we are so far only aware of a few. But these consequences are in no way due to rebellion itself, or at least they only occur to the extent that the rebel forgets his original purpose, tires of the tremendous tension created by refusing to give a positive or negative answer, and finally abandons himself to complete negation or total submission. Metaphysical insurrection, in its first stages, offers us the same positive content as the slave's rebellion. Our task will be to examine what becomes of this positive content of rebellion in the actions that claim to originate from it and to explain where the fidelity or infidelity of the rebel to the origins of his revolt finally leads him.

Metaphysical rebellion, in the real sense of the term, does not appear, in coherent form, in the history of ideas until the end of the eighteenth century —when modern times begin to the accompaniment of the crash of falling ramparts. But from then on, its consequences develop uninterruptedly and it is no exaggeration to say that they have shaped the history of our times. Does this mean that metaphysical rebellion had no significance previous to this date? In any event, its origins must belong to the remote past, in that we like to believe that we live in Promethean times. But is this really a Promethean age?

The first mythologies describe Prometheus as an eternal martyr, chained to a pillar, at the ends of the earth, condemned forever because he refuses to ask forgiveness. Aeschylus adds still further to his stature, endows him with lucidity ("no misfortune can fall upon me that I have not myself already foreseen"), makes him cry out his hatred of all the gods, and, plunging him into "a stormy sea of mortal despair," finally abandons him to thunder and lightning: "Ah! see the injustice I endure!"

It cannot be said, therefore, that the ancients were unaware of metaphysical rebellion. Long before Satan, they created a touching and noble image of the Rebel and gave us the most perfect myth of the intelligence in revolt. The inexhaustible genius of the Greeks, which gave such a prominent place to myths of unity and simplicity, was still able to formulate the concept of insurrection. Beyond a doubt, certain characteristics of the Promethean myth still survive in the history of rebellion as we are living it: the fight against death ("I have delivered men from being obsessed by death"), Messianism ("I have instilled blind hopes into men's minds"), philanthropy ("Enemy of Zeus . . . for having loved mankind too much").

But we must not forget that *Prometheus the Firebringer*, the last drama of Aeschylus' trilogy, proclaimed the reign of the pardoned rebel. The Greeks are never vindictive. In their most audacious flights they always remain faithful to the idea of moderation, a concept they deified. Their rebel does not range himself against all creation, but against Zeus, who is never anything more than one god among many and who himself was mortal. Prometheus himself is a demigod. It is a question of settling a particular account, of a dispute about what is good, and not of a universal struggle between good and evil.

The ancients, even though they believed in destiny, believed primarily in nature, in which they participated wholeheartedly. To rebel against nature amounted to rebelling against oneself. It was butting one's head against a wall. Therefore the only coherent act of rebellion was to commit suicide. Destiny, for the Greeks, was a blind force to which one submitted, just as one submitted to the forces of nature. The acme of excess to the Greek mind was to beat the sea with rods—an act of insanity worthy only of barbarians. Of course, the Greeks described excess, since it exists, but they gave it its proper place and, by doing so, also defined its limits. Achilles' defiance after the death of Patroclus, the imprecations of the Greek tragic heroes cursing their fate, do not imply complete condemnation. Oedipus knows that he is not innocent. He is guilty in spite of himself; he is also part of destiny. He complains, but he says nothing irreparable. Antigone rebels, but she does so in the name of tradition, in order that her brothers may find rest in the tomb and that the appropriate rites may be observed. In her case, rebellion is, in one sense, reactionary. The Greek mind has two aspects and in its meditations almost always re-echoes, as counterpoint to its most tragic melodies, the eternal words of Oedipus, who, blind and desperate, recognizes that all is for the best. Affirmation counterbalances negation. Even when Plato anticipates, with Callicles, the most common type of Nietzschean, even when the latter exclaims: "But when a man appears who has the necessary character . . . he will escape, he will trample on our formulas, our magic spells, our incantations, and the laws, which are all, without exception, contrary to nature. Our slave has rebelled and has shown himself to be the master"—even then, though he rejects law, he speaks in the name of nature.

Metaphysical rebellion presupposes a simplified view of creation—which was inconceivable to the Greeks. In their minds, there were not gods on one side and men on the other, but a series of stages leading from one to the other. The idea of innocence opposed to guilt, the concept of all of history summed up in the struggle between good and evil, was foreign to them. In their universe there were more mistakes than crimes, and the only definitive crime was excess. In a world entirely dominated by history, which ours threatens to become, there are no longer any mistakes, but only crimes, of which the greatest is moderation. This explains the curious mixture of ferocity and forbearance which we find in Greek mythology. The Greeks never made the human mind into an armed camp, and in this respect we are inferior to them. Rebellion, after all, can only be imagined in terms of opposition to someone. The only thing that gives meaning to human protest is the idea of a personal god who has created, and is therefore responsible for, everything. . . .

Ideology, Political Philosophy, and History*

Richard Cox

I

There are . . . two aspects of Camus' interpretation of ideology. The first aspect is the delineation of revolt as the ultimately defining form of conscious human activity. The second aspect is a history of revolt. But the two aspects are by no means independent. The historical material is used to build up the definition of revolt; and the definition of revolt is used to build up a criticism of historical instances of revolt gone to extremes. Nor is this interdependence accidental. On the contrary, it derives from the fact that "history" is, for Camus, both the central problem of our times and the vehicle by which his own consciousness of the essential character of revolt has come into being. It is, then, his "historical" consciousness which provides both the key to Camus' interpretation and the source of the central difficulty in that interpretation. In order to demonstrate that this is the case, I shall now turn to an analysis of the kinds of evidence Camus uses in his attempt to show that ideology is revolt gone to extremes.

The evidence appears, at first glance, to be both analytical and historical. Thus when Camus begins his substantive treatment of revolt, he chooses as the crucial example the revolt of the slave against the master, about which he argues as follows: At first, the slave is mute, obedient, and lacks judgment and self-consciousness. But suddenly one day, when he finally is struck by the absurdity of his condition, he turns and takes a stand. By his revolt he simultaneously says "no" to the master's command and "yes" to the existence of a "limit" beyond which the master may no longer go. Thus by his revolt he brings into existence that which previously was non-existent: a still-confused, yet fundamental "value" common to himself and the master. More fundamental still, by his revolt he actually "established" the "existence" of himself and his master as human beings; for in becoming conscious of his power to "deny" the master, he also "recognizes" the master as having an "existence" and, conversely, forces the master to recognize him as a self-conscious being.

*Richard H. Cox, "Ideology, History and Political Philosophy: Camus' *L'Homme Révolté*," *Social Research*, 32 (Spring 1965), 79-90, 95-97. Reprinted by permission.

The value contained in revolt is, however, still confused and lacking in any very precise content at this primeval stage. It acquires content as those who revolt become more and more conscious of the persistent themes which are to be discovered in their own "works." The themes . . . are . . . the protest against death, the demand for unity, and the attempt to establish order and justice. They are said to appear at the very beginning of western thought, in the form of "metaphysical" revolt—that is, the protest against not only man's specific condition, but also against the very "ends" of man and of creation. The crucial part of this argument is the analysis of the myth of Prometheus. . . . Thus historical evidence is brought to bear to buttress the argument developed first on analytical grounds.

Prometheus' revolt is the original model, according to Camus, because it partakes of the Greek genius for *pensée aux deux visages*—the equilibration of the "yes" and the "no." It is thus guided by the idea of *mesure*, which, according to Camus, the Greeks had "deified." He says, contrasting the Greeks to us:

In their universe there were more mistakes than crimes, and the only definitive crime was excess. In a world entirely dominated by history, which ours threatens to become, there are no longer any mistakes, but only crimes, of which the greatest is moderation.

Thus, in Camus' interpretation, Prometheus revolts against Zeus, a personal God, but not against the whole of creation. He revolts against a particular evil, but does not consider his action to be part of a universal struggle between absolute evil and absolute good. He protests against death, but he does not thereby deny nature; on the contrary, he shares the Greek belief that man participates in nature, and that therefore to revolt against nature is to revolt against oneself: "It was butting one's head against a wall." He denies the right of Zeus to punish, but he does not deny personal guilt as a reality. He accuses Zeus of tyranny, but he does not deny the need for political rule.

These same conceptions of limited revolt are present, according to Camus, in the examples of Achilles, Oedipus, Antigone and Plato's Callicles.[1] For the Greeks, it seems, were incapable of "a simplified view of creation." And as for the uses of thought, "The Greeks never made the human mind into an armed camp, and in this respect we are inferior to them." In short, revolt at its origins in western thought had attained to a profound sense of the tension which is characteristic of true revolt. It therefore was incapable of the extremes which are characteristic of "ideology."

[1] This choice of examples reveals the "artistic" tendency of Camus' analysis. Striking by its omission, here and elsewhere, is reference to Greek philosophic thought.

These insights into Greek thought provide the criteria by which Camus subsequently passes judgment on modern fanaticism. To the extent they strike at
the heart of that problem—the *démesure* characteristic of modern ideologies—
they are powerfully suggestive. But it must also be said that, because they are
essentially problematic in their historical accuracy, they help to obscure the
issue as well as to throw light upon it. The problematic character of the
insights is a function of a basic tension concerning the problem of history and
its relation to human action. On the one hand, Camus denies that man's
nature is totally historical. Here, he turns for support to the Greeks. On the
other hand, he also denies the possibility of transcendent knowledge and
affirms that man's *reality* is essentially historical. Here, he turns to Hegel and
Nietzsche.[2] His treatment of the revolt of slave against master, for example, is
almost a copy of his interpretation of Hegel's treatment of that same theme
in the *Phenomenology of the Mind*: the very abstractness of the analysis, the
idea that "existence" depends upon "revolt" and upon the generation of
"self-consciousness" with respect to the "other," and the central place occupied by the idea of "rights" and "liberty" indicate only too clearly the source
of his inspiration. . . . Nietzsche then becomes, in one sense, the real hero, for
it is he, according to Camus, who has most courageously faced up to the
problem of nihilism which results from the destruction of all vertical
transcendence. . . .

It is not necessary, for my present purposes, to enter into the question
whether Camus accurately interprets Hegel and Nietzsche in all details. It is
sufficient simply to notice two points. First, he considers the crisis engendered by their philosophies to be the supreme reality of our time. Second, his
own method, framework, and mode of discourse profoundly reflect certain
main themes which they had developed. Thus his central concept of revolt is
permeated with the idea that the history of the western mind is essentially
the true but tragic record of man's realization of the absurdity of his condition. My main conclusion is that Camus' interpretation of the genesis and
nature of ideologies is then a product, in the most profound sense, of that
very *historisme* against which he claims to be in revolt.

To show concretely that this is the case, I propose now to reconsider Camus'
own key historical example, the myth of Prometheus. The myth is, as Camus
acknowledges, part of early Greek theogony. Since the primary literary
source for his argument is the *Prometheus Bound* of Aeschylus, the issue
narrows to his interpretation of a Greek tragic poet. That issue has two
aspects. First, is Aeschylus' "poetic" treatment of myth equivalent to Camus'

[2]See *The Rebel*, pp. 66-68, 142.

"artistic" treatment? Second, and more crucial for our present problem, does Aeschylus in fact understand Prometheus' revolt as arising out of consciousness of the absurdity of existence?

The answer to both questions must be in the negative. For the fact is that Camus, instead of trying to understand the Greek poet's treatment of the myth in its own terms, starts from the presupposition that the Greek mind is the first example of "revolt" in Western thought. He thus imposes a framework on the evidence, then turns around to use that evidence to prove the validity of the framework. In doing so, however, he in effect proves only that his particular conception of revolt may be read into the historical evidence, not that revolt is one of the two universes in which man necessarily lives.[3]

The difference between Aeschylus' and Camus' interpretations of the myth of Prometheus is the difference, as I now wish to establish, between two fundamentally different conceptions of the status of human action. The interpretation of Aeschylus is a poetic view which precedes or is coeval with the emergence of philosophy in the West and which is rooted in the conception that man is an intelligent part of a natural order, the *cosmos*. The interpretation of Camus is an artistic view which is the result of a profound transformation of the poetic understanding by modern philosophy and which is rooted in the conception that man is an absurd element in an alien, disordered environment. This contrast may be made evident by examining more closely Aeschylus' treatment of the Prometheus myth and then comparing it to Camus' treatment.[4]

The themes and the structure of the *Prometheus Bound* are beautifully complex; they imitate the reality which Aeschylus poetically portrays. The simple dramatic theme is, of course, the punishment of Prometheus by Zeus for stealing fire and giving it to man. The complex symbolic themes imbedded in this drama are first, the relations of the gods to one another and to the elemental forces of the *cosmos* and second, the relation of the gods to man, including particularly the divine origin of the human arts.

These themes are expressed both directly and through the structure of the play. In the first place, the four elements of the *cosmos* are woven into the very texture of the play, with respect both to the gods and to men.[5] To take

[3]Cf. Eric Voegelin, *The World of the Polis* (Baton Rouge: Lousiana State University Press, 1957), p. 253 ff.

[4]I have used George Thomson's edition of the *Prometheus Bound* (Cambridge: The University Press, 1932).

[5]See especially S. M. Adams, "The Four Elements in the *Prometheus Vinctus*," *Classical Philosophy* (April 1933), pp. 97-103.

first the gods, we find that Prometheus' first utterance is an appeal to ether, water, earth and sun to witness the injustice of his punishment. He does not appeal directly to the fourth element, fire, apparently because his theft of that element has caused him to forfeit any right to call on it. But fire, nonetheless, plays a crucial part; in the form of the blacksmith's art it is, ironically, the means by which he is bound to his lonely peak. The three other elements are also involved throughout the action: Prometheus' appeal is answered by water in the person of Okeanos and the Okeanides; he has the natural support of earth because his mother, Thetis, is identified with Gaia or earth; and the ether is the medium through which the winged gods come and go. At the very end of the action, he again appeals to earth and ether, but is silent about water, apparently because it has already played its part.

As for man and his relation to the elements, the outstanding fact is that it is fire, the stolen element, which forms the basis of the arts and thereby provides man with the ability to exercise a certain kind of power with respect to nature. *Techne* or art is said not to have existed in any form among men prior to the gift of Prometheus. Furthermore, Prometheus says that originally man confused everything, which is to say that the very *idea* of the nature of things was wanting.[6] It is Prometheus, a god, who thus supplies not only the arts, but also the knowledge of the nature of things, upon which the efficacy of the use of the arts depends. And yet he, though a god, is also bound by the nature of things: he cannot overcome the bonds inflicted upon him, ironically, by that very art which he stole to give to man. The implication is that both gods and men are limited by the nature of things; and that man's *techne*, even though it is a gift of the gods, can be successful only to the extent that it recognizes such limits. But that recognition depends upon human understanding of man's place in the whole; it depends upon knowledge. At bottom, then, it is knowledge of the order of nature which is meant to guide human action; but such knowledge links man to the gods, both in the sense that it is godlike and in the sense that it derives from the action of a particular god, whose very name means "forethought."

The grandeur of Aeschylus' conception is also revealed most vividly by his architectonic treatment of the theme of knowledge of past, present, and future, at the level of both gods and men.[7] The dramatic action begins at the precise moment Prometheus is bound to a wild peak. But this dramatic present is in fact, from the viewpoint of Aeschylus and his audience, the remote past. The inquiry into the even more remote past—indeed, into the

---

[6]*Prometheus Bound*, lines 463-470.

[7]See Thomson's Introduction to *Prometheus Bound*, pp. 13-17, for a more elaborate analysis of the intricate quality of this aspect of the play.

very origins—proceeds by means of the speeches in which Prometheus describes the time when the gods first existed, the primeval situation of man, and the bringing of the arts to man. On the other hand, Prometheus also, as befits his name, speaks prophetically. He describes what is to happen to Io, a mortal, and to himself and Zeus, who are gods. The complex relationship of the future of the gods and of men is indicated by the fact that it is a future descendant of Io's who will eventually free Prometheus, thus in a sense repaying him for his help to man, and by the fact that the eventual reconciliation of Zeus and Prometheus will end the tyrannical actions of Zeus both towards men and towards gods. Prometheus thus exhibits foreknowledge of both gods and men, the kind of knowledge which originally belongs to divinity and which is possessed by man only to the extent that he shares in the divine attribute. It is hardly accidental, then, that in the catalogue of the arts he gave to man, Prometheus speaks at greatest length and in most elaborate detail of the *mantike techne*, the art of prophecy.[8]

The link between gods and men is revealed, in the third place, by the fact that Zeus' tyrannical will is directed both at a particular god and a particular mortal. In each case, the action which arouses Zeus' wrath and the punishment decreed are appropriate to god and man respectively. Yet there is common ground for a sense of outrage and injustice and a common realization of the nature of punishment. Thus Prometheus gave an *arche* or power belonging to the gods to mortals. He is punished by being chained by other gods to a dark and lonely peak beyond the boundaries of the civilized world. He is thus deprived of the divine ability to move everywhere in heaven and on earth, and is subject to the ridicule and contempt of the other gods for being in so ungodlike a situation. Io, by contrast, refused to yield to the importunities and lust of Zeus. She is punished by being compelled to leave family and city, and to wander over the earth under the persecuting eyes of Argus. In both cases, however, eventual mitigation of the punishment is adumbrated through the future reconciliation of Zeus and Prometheus.

It is in the context of the entire poetic drama, which is to say in the context of such conceptions and themes as have been sketched in the preceding paragraphs, that the "revolt" of Prometheus must be understood. His action is simultaneously philanthropic and political. It is philanthropic in the sense that he brings about that salvation only by disobeying the god-tyrant. But his philanthropy is, very curiously, limited in one decisive respect. Although he repeatedly claims to have given *all* the arts to man, an examination of the list of arts he specifically refers to reveals a striking omission: he never mentions or even alludes to the political art.[9] The crucial importance of that omission

---

[8]*Prometheus Bound,* lines 500-515.

[9]Specific references to *techne* occur several times in the first half of the play; see lines 7, 47, 87, 110, 270, 493, 514, 530. The list of arts falls into two parts; see lines 470-522.

is emphasized, subsequently, in the *Protagoras* of Plato. He makes his
Protagoras tell a myth in which the political art is explicitly distinguished
from the other arts. It is said to be the condition of men's living together and
of the right use of all the other arts, and it was given to man not by Prometheus but by Zeus. And in his *Second Epistle*, Plato interprets the Prometheus myth to mean the primordial attraction and joining together of
wisdom and great power. Now whether Aeschylus' Promethean trilogy was
the source of such Platonic notions we cannot say. But what we can say is
that the *Prometheus Bound* contains the repeated theme of a future reconciliation between the two gods. The question is what the significance of that
reconciliation may be.

The clue to the significance lies, I believe, in the political aspect of the revolt.
Zeus' tyrannical rule, one aspect of which is the arbitrary assignment of
powers to the gods and another the arbitrary decision to destroy mankind, is
the immediate cause of Prometheus' defiance. But Prometheus himself suffers
from a grave fault. Kratos and Hermes, who are in the service of Zeus, and the
Okeanides and Okeanos, who are friendly to Prometheus, all charge him with
grossly intemperate accusations and denunciations of Zeus. Each of the pro-
tagonists is therefore said to suffer from *nosema*, or disease.[10] Each lacks
sophrosyne, or temperance. The future reconciliation of the two gods depends on each learning *sophrosyne* through suffering (Zeus suffers from the
torment of not knowing Prometheus' secret concerning the future rebellion
against the god-tyrant; Prometheus suffers from the increasingly cruel punish-
ments inflicted by Zeus at the end of the *Prometheus Bound*). *Sophrosyne*
transforms opposing principles of justice through reconciliation.

We may now bring together the two different but closely related treatments
of the political problem. The absence of the political art among men is parallel to the absence of *sophrosyne* in the political conduct of the gods. The
implication of the latter absence is that if *sophrosyne* is not learned, there
will continue to be a series of terrible tyrannies ended by fearsome rebellions.
The implication of the former absence is more difficult to specify from the
text of the extant play. But if men possess none of the political virtues because of the absence of the political art, it is problematic at best whether the
Promethean gift of the other arts can, by itself, suffice to guarantee the right
use of those arts. The implication is, then, that Prometheus' philanthropy is
problematic; it may even be intemperate, for it is not accompanied by the
political art, by which all the other arts would be controlled. Philanthropy
without *sophrosyne* may be as dangerous for justice as is the tyrannical rule

[10]See Thomson's Introduction, pp. 11-12.

of Zeus; but if this is true for the gods, it must be even more true for men, who are below the gods.

The contrast between Aeschylus' and Camus' interpretations of the Prometheus myth is fundamental. To Aeschylus, as the preceding paragraphs indicate, the revolt must ultimately be understood in reference to an objective order of things—of which man is a part and of which he may, but does not necessarily, achieve knowledge; but whether he achieves it or not, it is that knowledge which provides the guide for action. To Camus, on the other hand, the revolt has reference to the *absence* of an objective order of things and is motivated by the absurdity of a situation in which a god may behave tyrannically. Its aim is to force the pretended divinity out of its privileged position in eternity into the position of man, which is to say into the historical condition, where there is no possibility of taking refuge in an objective order of things as a guide to action. The emphasis thus shifts decisively from the timelessness of the problems, as understood by Aeschylus, to the relationship of man to his own temporal doings, as understood by Camus.

In this, Camus shares in the profound and larger shift in modern thought by which the original or classical opposition of nature and art is replaced by the opposition of history and art.[11] To Aeschylus, the proper use of art or *techne* is dependent upon knowledge of the nature of things. In this case history, or human activity, is strictly subordinate in its importance to the question of the *logos* of the *cosmos*. To Camus, by contrast, art is the power of man to create, through acceptance of the knowledge that there is no knowable and meaningful nature of things. In this case history, or human activity, becomes both the problem for and the potential source of human creativity.

This conception of art is the basis of Camus' interpretation of political action. For although he denies that the artist as such can or should directly guide political life, in the final analysis he judges political action by the criteria of art in his sense of *révolte à la mesure*.[12] The problem remains whether such a conception of politics is adequate. To answer that question comprehensively would of course lead far beyond this essay. It would demand, for example, nothing less than a comprehensive judgement upon the validity of Camus' premises that absurdity is the starting point for all truly human action, that

[11]For an extended treatment of this shift, see Karl Löwith, "Nature, History and Existentialism," *Social Research* (March 1952), pp. 79-94.

[12]Camus' essay is prefaced by a quotation from Hölderlin which expresses the love of the poet for the earth. It ends with Camus' own prose-poetic statement of the same theme. In between, the argument of the whole work builds toward and culminates in the section which Camus titles "Rebellion and Art."

all human action is self-dependent, and that *mesure*—in his sense—is the guiding principle for human action. Failing that, I shall confine my remaining remarks to showing that, although Camus claims to return to the classical concept of *mesure*, he in fact reads into classical thought a conception as alien to *sophrosyne* as his interpretation of Prometheus' revolt is alien to Aeschylus' understanding. In each case, the difficulty is that of reconciling an idea which is rooted in the premise that history is the central problem with an idea which is rooted in the premise that the *cosmos* and man's relation to it is the central problem.

There are two difficulties with Camus' claim to have returned to the Greek concept of *mesure* as the proper guide to political action. First, the claim is based on astonishingly sparse historical evidence, as well as faulty argument. It is true that he cites a number of poetic instances of Greek *mesure* in *révolte*; but of these, he gives an analysis only of Prometheus; and as I have argued above, that analysis is based on modern principles. What is more, Camus barely refers to Greek political philosophy as such. One would have expected, for example, at least an analysis of the philosophic use of the Prometheus myth in Plato's *Protagoras* and of the philosophic reflection upon *sophrosyne* in Plato's *Charmides*. By his silence with respect to these crucial historical sources, as well as the more prosaic treatments of Aristotle, Xenophon, or Plutarch, Camus tacitly indicates the subordination of political philosophy to artistic interpretation and cuts his argument off from the substantive sense of the Greek *sophrosyne*.

A second difficulty with Camus' claim is that his concept *mesure* is abstract and formal, whereas the Greek concept *sophrosyne* is concrete and substantive in its application. This difference derives, in turn, from the fact that for Camus the content of *mesure* is set essentially by the extremes of any given historical situation; but for the Greeks the content of *sophrosyne* is set both by historical circumstances and by an analysis of the intrinsic limits of proper human action within the whole of which man is a part. . . .

The Greeks understand human action not as supreme, but as directed toward and completed by *theoria* or contemplation of the whole or *cosmos* within which that action takes place. By contrast, Camus' principle par excellence of *révolte à la mesure* is abstract and formal, for it is necessarily defined in terms of the given historical situation, and that situation necessarily changes. It replaces the idea of the political art with the idea of the artistic political act. It tacitly denies the possibility of the dependence of political acts upon an order of nature because it originates in the "experience" of absurdity. Its conception of the limits of human action is derived, therefore, from the need to define human action in purely human terms, and yet to prevent the accumulated mass of human actions—history—from simply engulfing the individual actor. The solution of creativity in the form of revolt achieves this result, for it is a purely human product set against other human products. The solution of *mesure*, as the limit set to revolt, is equally human in that it derives from the human recognition of the humanity of others, and not from any extrinsic source, such as the order of nature or of God.

II

The problem of the genesis and development of ideologies is an historical problem. It is the problem of when and how ideologies have appeared and what their worldly fortunes have been. But the more fundamental problem is to define an ideology so as to distinguish it from other forms of thought. To do this, however, it is necessary to render a judgment on the nature and status of human thought and action in their relation to the nature of the world within which all thought and action take place. Camus has provided answers to both these questions. I have tried to show that those answers derive from his basic conviction that the condition of man is essentially an historical condition and that, paradoxically, this is the guarantee of human freedom: even when man revolts, and when he observes *mesure* in doing so, these are historical actions, guided by no extrinsic order but by man's own creation. But it is precisely because of this reduction of the criteria of judgment to human acts that it is impossible to accept Camus' claim to have returned to the classical concept of *mesure*, let alone his claim to have discovered the beginnings of metaphysical revolt in Aeschylus. The paradox and the irony are that Camus himself points to the fact that for the classical Greeks the world is not simply an historical world. And yet, his mistake is to suppose that it is an historical world at all in the modern sense of that term. His attempt to force the Greek concept of *sophrosyne* into the mold of *mesure* can only produce a false sense of being true to our "tradition," not a real return to it.[13] *Sophrosyne* is a reflection of a cosmic philosophy, *mesure* of a humanistic philosophy. The first is the result of being guided by the order of nature which is the ground of human action, the second is the result of being guided by the "experience" of the absurdity of the human condition. The first is profoundly political; the latter is artistic.

Camus' distortion of the classical view would be no great matter if it were merely a question of an isolated example of his historical method. In fact, however, this distortion exemplifies the problematic character of the method,

[13]Whether such a return is possible and desirable is a larger question which cannot be answered here.

and therefore of the interpretation of the nature of ideology. For if it is true that ideology is revolt gone to extremes, or the "divinisation" of human thought, then the question of what is divine as opposed to what is human must somehow be answered. Camus' way of answering the question is to rely upon the categories of that philosophy which reduces philosophy to history and man to historical man. The difficulty is that in the process, the initial *articulation* of the question of what is divine as opposed to what is human is lost. This difficulty, however, no longer appears as a difficulty but as a proof of the growing awareness of man's true condition. In *L'Homme Révolté*, the conviction of such a growth takes the form of the assertion that we can no longer choose our problems, they choose us. That assertion, based as it is on the denial of the existence of permanent problems, contains the root of the difficulty. For by its insistence that the problem of ideology must be understood in terms of a consciousness of the radically historical character of the human condition, it undermines and then consigns to oblivion that form of inquiry for which "revolt" is one form of contemporary replacement: political philosophy in the original sense of an inquiry into the nature of political life and its place in the whole or *cosmos*.

Part Three

Ideology and Politics

Contemporary conceptions of the role that ideology plays in actual politics both reflect and influence our present ideological climate of thought. The materials in Parts One and Two indicated the sources and the nature of the theoretical concepts of ideology which have been most influential in shaping that climate of thought. We will now look more closely at the political developments which contributed to it—first in Europe and then in more detail, the development in America.

The Development in Europe

My thesis is that the ideological style of modern politics is closely connected to, indeed profoundly reflects, the appearance of doctrinally-inspired revolutions in Europe. More specifically, my thesis is that two of these revolutions, the French and the Russian, were both paradigms of doctrinally-inspired political movements, and that as a major consequence of them, a pattern of doctrinal politics has been established. It is impossible to fully elaborate, qualify, and document this thesis in an introductory essay, but a highly condensed amplification of its main points follows.

Politically, the French Revolution was a conflict between those who supported the monarchical government and those who wanted to replace it—by violence if necessary—with a republican government. Political conflict concerning the form of government is very ancient as is theoretical discussion of the relative merits of the different forms. Thus both Athens' and Rome's political histories record many such conflicts; and the political theories of Plato and Aristotle in Athens and of Cicero and Polybius in Rome contain subtle analyses of the merits of the different forms. But the theoretical discussions of the classical theorists were rarely related to actual political conflicts. To state exactly why this was so would require a lengthy analysis. Here, it is sufficient to say that classical theory resisted being reduced to doctrinaire principles because prudence, or practical wisdom, was considered indispensable in the application of principles to actual situations.

By the latter part of the eighteenth century classical political theories had been subjected to intense critical scrutiny for over a century. One consequence of that criticism was that eminent figures—including David Hume, Edmund Burke and Alexis de Tocqueville—observed a growing tendency for political conflicts to become fused, in a radical and novel way, with modern speculative theories concerning man and politics.[1] And as the selections from the works of Destutt de Tracy and Antoine Rivarol have shown, the sense of radical theoretical innovation was joined during the French Revolution with unprecedented opportunities to apply such theory directly.

The French Revolution epitomized this explosive fusion of political and doctrinal conflict.[2] The republicans derived their principles from the theoretical conception that men have a natural and inalienable right to choose their rulers. The monarchists derived theirs from a combination of ancient prescriptive right, religious dogma, and the theory of the divine right of kings.

Once the enormous potentialities of revolution were realized, its possibility came to dominate European political life. Politically, the domination initially took the form of a greatly heightened consciousness of the conflict concerning the form of the regime—that is, conflict between doctrinally-based republican and monarchical factions. This is nowhere more evident than in France itself. During the nineteenth century in France there was an irregular oscillation between monarchical and republican regimes—an oscillation which took place against the backdrop of and on the basis of a deep awareness of the example supplied by the great Revolution and the various stages of reaction to it. More generally, this political-doctrinal conflict between

[1]See the following: David Hume, "Of Parties in General," *Works,* Vol. III; Edmund Burke, *Thoughts on French Affairs* and *Reflections on the Revolution in France;* Alexis de Tocqueville, *L'Ancien Régime et la Révolution.*

[2]See Edmund Burke, *An Appeal from the New to the Old Whigs.*

republicans and monarchists remained dominant in Europe into the early part of the twentieth century. But since the Russian Revolution, it has been absorbed into a newer and now dominant form of political-doctrinal conflict.

The Russian Revolution began, and was understood in Western Europe for some time as merely a new installment in the century-old conflict between republican and monarchical principles. Gradually, however, it became clear that much more was involved. First, the ascendant anti-monarchical parties —and especially the Bolsheviks—proved to be guided far less by the century-old principles of doctrinal republicanism than by the more recent and demanding principles of scientific socialism, as developed by Marx. At issue was not just a revolution in the form of government but a revolution in virtually every aspect of human social existence. Second, the bitter conflict among the various anti-monarchical parties reflected a profound disagreement over which party was most entitled to represent the will of the people. The bitterest conflict of all took place, significantly, among the socialist parties. The result of both these developments was to transform the older conflict between doctrinal republican and monarchical factions into one between different doctrinal parties claiming the exclusive right to represent the people in the revolutionizing of the entire society.

This transformation—indeed, *radicalization*—of the political-doctrinal conflict of the nineteenth century is the basis of the newer ideological style of politics revealed in Europe in the 1930s. The Bolsheviks challenged the legitimacy of the constitutional republican regimes in the West in as compelling a fashion as it did the remaining monarchical regimes. In posing this challenge—which became really threatening, it should be noted, only as the Bolshevik regime established itself in effective power—the Russian Revolution, as George F. Kennan has recently argued, had the profound effect of polarizing the European political spectrum.[3] The Italian Fascist and German Nazi parties were, of course, profoundly opposed to Communism. Yet they were, ironically, a testimony to the power of its example. For they, too, challenged all other parties in their claims to represent the true desires, aims and spirit of their peoples. They carried on the competition by savagely attacking the doctrines of both liberal republicanism and Communism with an arsenal of opposing doctrines.

But the full power and effect of this reaction was not clear until the Nazis themselves came to power. Then it immediately became evident that they

[3]George F. Kennan, "The Russian Revolution—Fifty Years After: Its Nature and Consequences," *Foreign Affairs,* 46 (October 1967), 1-21.

(even more than the Italian Fascists), were determined to revolutionize the entire society, and to carry on not only political but military warfare against all other regimes. In this case, as with the French and Russian Revolutions, Fascism and Nazism were perceived as grave threats only after they became the basis of the policies of large and powerful states.

Today, given the ideological climate of thought, the fierce ideological conflicts of the 1930s may appear to be only an acute form of the typical pattern of politics. But one finds quite another perspective on the matter in political analyses written in the 1930s by informed observers in Western European democracies. First of all, such observers generally are surprised, perplexed, and apprehensive. In March, 1937, Professor Ernest Barker, one of England's leading scholars of political theory and comparative government, gave an address in which he observed that ideology is "a barbarous term, popularized of late by our Foreign Minister." He goes on to call the term "a boundless, formless horrendous monster without any light," and argues that it has "flowed from the peculiar vocabulary of Marxism into the peculiar vocabulary of statesmen and publicists." He adds that the "comprehensive" character of the ideas referred to by the term reflects the fact that Marxism had succeeded in compelling most political leaders to subscribe to the principle that political conflict *typically* is to be understood as a conflict about both the aims and methods of politics, about economics, and even about the "whole of social life."

Barker next argues that there were ideologies and conflicts of ideologies before the twentieth century and that many past issues survive into the 1930s. Yet he concludes that "we are now face to face with a war which primarily and originally seems to be of a different order." It is different in two respects. First, it is a war concerning the "social-economic basis" and "complexion" of the community. Second, it "actuates and energizes, on a new scale and with a new grandeur, the whole of the population." It is, in short, a war in which "mass philosophies are engaged in struggle with mass philosophies."[4]

Sir Alfred Zimmern, another English scholar, also observed the novelty of the emergent ideological politics. In the introduction to his book, *Modern Political Doctrines*, published in 1939, Zimmern notes that a very important change has taken place in Europe within a single generation. That change consists of the movement of the discussion of political ideas and doctrines from "behind closed doors, in the class-room or the country house" to the

[4]Ernest Barker, "The Conflict of Ideologies," *International Affairs,* 16 (1937), 341-354.

"house-tops, with the aid of loud-speakers to convey [the ideas] across the
frontiers of states and the boundaries of continents."
In explaining his inclusion of different kinds of writings, Zimmern feels
obliged to meet the possible criticism that he has improperly mingled the
ideas of "pure thinkers" with those of "men, who, though primarily thinkers,
played a prominent part in public affairs," and "men, prominent in public
affairs who, in spite of their pronounced opinions on questions of political
theory, have no claim to be classed as thinkers at all." Zimmern justifies the
inclusion of the ideas of the latter two classes of men on the grounds that
their representatives now dominate politics. He refers to Hitler and Mussolini
as belonging to the last of the three classes, and as being important because
their works "reveal to us how, in this age of catchwords and propaganda, men
of action can appropriate and vulgarize, for their own purposes, ideas that
have long been in the air." Lenin, he feels, belongs to the second class, and is
important both because he occupies a "large place" in the "history of
Socialist thought," and because he was "primarily a man of action for whom
ideas were swords."[5]

An important effect of the unexpected doctrinal-political battle between
Fascism and Communism was the way in which it progressively affected the
perception of the principles of liberal or constitutional democracy. During
the early phase of this conflict, political and scholarly supporters of liberal
democracy in Europe characterized it as an ideological conflict, but excluded
liberal democracy on the grounds that its principles were not an ideology, and
therefore it could not indulge in ideological warfare.

In the 1930s it became increasingly obvious that liberal democracy itself was
under assault from two different kinds of ideological regimes. The Fascist
regimes, like the Russian Communist regime, sought to justify their policies
by mobilizing massive public support. To liberal democratic observers, this
was a manipulation that made a mockery of democracy. Thus Zimmern
observed:

. . . we are face to face with systems whose rulers plume themselves on being democratic
and make play with the apparatus of elected assemblies and popular votes. . . . [6]

But such criticisms were ineffective; this claim to popular—hence
"democratic"—support, had a profound effect in the West. Above all, it
challenged liberal democracy's basic claim to represent the will of the
people.

[5]Alfred Zimmern, editor, *Modern Political Doctrines* (London: Oxford University
Press, 1939), pp. ix-xiv.

[6]*Ibid.,* p. xvii.

Under these circumstances, the initial resistance to categorizing the principles of liberal democracy as an ideology gave way to a qualified acceptance of the term. This is illustrated, once again, in Barker's 1937 lecture. He recognized the novelty of the situation by explicitly asking whether it was "right to speak of an ideology of Liberal-Democratic states." His answer was that it is both right and wrong to do so. It is right in the sense that on the "essential issue" of the method and process of government, liberal democracy has a doctrine—the necessity for discussion. But it is wrong in the sense that unlike an ideology, liberal democracy has no doctrine of a single end; the common ends or aims of the community are determined by discussing a "plurality of ideas." Barker concludes that there is as great a "mental fight" between the "States of discussion and the States of the single party" as that between the Fascists and the Communists.[7]

In his comments on Barker's lecture, Professor A. D. Lindsay, another political theorist from Oxford, went even further in denying that liberal democracy has an ideology. He argues on one hand that "doctrines which you can reason and think out honestly and with no ulterior motives" are not "properly called ideologies." On the other hand, it is equally obvious that Fascism and Communism are "nonsense" from the "intellectual" point of view—above all from the intellectual point of view as contained in political theory. Their ideologies, says Lindsay, "do not bear thinking out." They are "irrational" doctrines, meant only to "make everyone frightfully excited." They reflect the need to "fuse disintegrated peoples," a task that cannot be done by truth, only by slogans.[8]

These arguments and observations are worth recalling and pondering today, for two reasons. First, they reveal that as late as the end of the 1930s, informed observers in Western Europe felt that it was politically important to make a theoretical as well as a practical distinction between ideologies and principles of liberal democracy. Second, they direct attention to the powerful forces which were operating to draw those principles into the vortex of the ideological conflict. For the fact is that by the early 1940s, it had become common practice for the principles of liberal democracy to be called an ideology, whereas only a decade earlier such a practice was rare.

This absorption of liberal democratic principles into ideological politics makes the decade of the 1930s decisive in the evolution of the contemporary

[7]Barker, *op. cit.*, passim.

[8]Barker, *op. cit.*, "Summary of Discussion," pp. 354-356.

ideological climate of thought. That absorption revealed, perhaps even more than had the earlier European reactions in the form of the rise of the Fascist regimes, the profound and complex impact of the challenge posed by the Russian Revolution. It set the stage for the agonized indecision of Western democratic leaders concerning how to oppose one ideological enemy without aiding the other. It prepared the way for the joint policy of "unconditional surrender" in World War II, which helped bring one of those enemies into the heart of old Europe. It thus prepared the way for the immediate post-war polarization of the ideological conflict into one between the two regimes which had shared in the military victory over Fascism. In short, it foreshadowed the Cold War, the dominant political pattern of the contemporary age.

The Development in America
The development of the ideological climate of thought in America is derivative of its development in Europe. But the manner and pace of its development reflect distinctive features of American politics and history.

The character of American republicanism has been different from that in Europe. The American republic was founded in explicit opposition to the monarchical government of Great Britain. And the Declaration of Independence stated the American claim of the natural right of men to be governed by rulers of their own choice. But this justification was closely joined to and somewhat overshadowed by justifications based on traditional English legal rights and political practice.

Edmund Burke made a basic distinction between America's break with England, which he believed to be generally consistent with the fundamental principles of the English constitution, and the French Revolution's attack on the Bourbon monarchy, which he called a radical innovation in politics. The latter was a revolution in the true, modern sense—a project to destroy the ancient French regime and to replace it with a republic dedicated to doctrinal and physical warfare on all monarchical regimes.

The American republic was also distinguished from its French counterpart by the fact that it was established by the overthrow of a distant European monarchy, not one indigenous to America. Professor Louis Hartz has argued that this fact has been of decisive importance in determining the character of the regime in America. He argues that the absence of an indigenous ancient regime made unnecessary both a radical, doctrinally-based revolution of the French kind and the consequent attempts at counter-revolution. The

American republic, isolated from the whole network of ancient monarchies in Europe, was at once united in its principles and relieved of the necessity to be "messianic" in character. Furthermore, according to Hartz, the unique circumstances of the creation of a new constitutional order in the wilderness of North America lent force to a peculiarly American sense that the republic's guiding principles were self-evident and absolute. This happened, he argues, because the establishment of the constitution was viewed as simply a case of putting into practice John Locke's theory that men have a natural right to form a government by mutual compact, and because the accomplishment of this in a wilderness was understood as a confirmation of the truth of the theory.[9]

Thus American republicanism was distinguished, during the nineteenth century, from the European pattern of doctrinal republicanism versus doctrinal monarchism. James Fenimore Cooper wrote in the Jacksonian period: "Every other enlightened nation of the earth is at this moment divided between great opposing principles; where here, if we accept the trifling collisions of pecuniary interests, everybody is of the same mind except as to the ordinary immaterial question of choice between men."[10] This particular quality did not prevent Americans from sympathizing with republican movements in Europe. On the contrary, there was widespread approval in America for such movements. This is revealed, for example, by strong American sentiment to come to the support of republican France during the Revolutionary wars, and by American opinion concerning the later revolutions in France—in 1830, 1848, and 1870. Quite typical is the view expressed by Edward Everett, editor of the *North American Review*, who said of the 1830 monarchy that it was destined to go on toward an "inevitable republic."[11] And equally typical is a remark by President Grant, who spoke in 1870 against the "dynastic traditions of Europe" in favor of "representative government."[12] But what is most significant, during this period, is that American republicanism reflected a sense of confidence that mere historical progress would eventually replace the outmoded monarchies with republics;

[9]Louis Hartz, *The Liberal Tradition in America* (New York: Harcourt, Brace & Company, 1955), Chs. 1, 2, 10, 11.

[10]Quoted in Hartz, *op. cit.*, pp. 140-141.

[11]Quoted in Eugene N. Curtis, "American Opinion of the French Nineteenth-Century Revolutions," *American Historical Review*, 29 (January 1924), 251.

[12]Ibid., p. 268. For a more detailed examination of the American reactions to the Revolution of 1848, see Merle Curti, "The Impact of the Revolutions of 1848 on American Thought," in Edward N. Saveth, editor, *Understanding the American Past* (Boston: Little, Brown and Company, 1965), pp. 234-250.

conversely, it did not represent a sense of the need to propagate republican principles by deliberate and aggressive methods in Europe.

These qualities of American republicanism persisted into the early years of the twentieth century, but since then have been progressively altered by the nature of American reactions to and involvement in European political events. The older form of American republicanism reflected the isolation that President Washington urged upon the country in his Farewell Address. But the newer form reflects American involvement in both European and world politics. The transition from one form to the other has been a complex development. What concerns us here is the broad outline of how that transition took place with respect to growing involvement in the European ideological climate of thought.

Early American republicanism emphasized representative government, but in the course of the nineteenth century the emphasis shifted to the idea of democracy. The two ideas are not, of course, incompatible, but the former emphasizes the right of elected representatives to govern according to a constitution; the latter emphasizes the right of the people at large to determine policy by the direct expression of their will. Democracy, because of its belief in the rightness of the people's will, makes it possible to involve the mass of citizens in political conflicts more *directly* than in representative government. This makes it possible to more easily mobilize the will of the people, while bound by its pressures once that will is mobilized.

As America moved toward involvement in European politics early in this century, a European trend toward an emphasis on democracy paralleled that in America. But in Europe, as we have already seen, and above all in continental Europe, the dominant pattern of politics was the century-old conflict between doctrinal republicanism and doctrinal monarchism. Hence, the European trend toward an emphasis on the idea of democracy reflected the doctrinal quality of European politics; and in the measure that America became involved in the fate of European democracy, it also became involved in the doctrinal characteristics of European politics.

The first stage of involvement was American participation in World War I. To most Americans, the conflict was one between the progressive forces of democracy and the retrograde forces of autocracy. The specific cause of the war was understood to be the militaristic and expansionist policies of Germany. But the general cause was the refusal of the autocratic rulers—above all those in Germany—to recognize and accept that the autocratic form of government was ultimately doomed by the progressive spread of democracy.[13]

In 1917, Elihu Root, Secretary of State under Theodore Roosevelt, analyzed the conflict in his treatment of the effect of democracy on international law. On one hand, he believed the conflict was inevitable and universal. He summoned up the spirit of Abraham Lincoln's famous "house-divided" speech when he said, "The world can not be half democratic and half autocratic." He berated the "designs of aggrandizement and ambition which have characterized the autocratic governments of the world," and conversely praised the dedication of democracies to peace and to the rule of international law. He concluded that because autocracy is necessarily both militaristic and despotic, democracies can give it no quarter.[14]

On the other hand, Root's analysis contains little concerning a specifically *doctrinal* conflict between democracy and autocracy. He understands Germany's militaristic expansion as the result of the despotic, arrogant personal character of the autocratic rulers, not as the result, for example, of their claim to a divine right to rule, or of a principled attack on liberal democracies.[15]

Nor does Root mention any doctrines peculiar to democracy which would give offensive force to its policies and thus bring it into direct attack upon the old autocracies. Instead, he posits the gradual spread of the general ethos of democracy. By this he means that all the peoples of the world slowly are becoming aware that it is their right and destiny to live under a democracy, which is characterized by a spirit of self-government, respect for law, and opposition to military aggrandizement. Thus Root interprets the conflict between Germany and the democracies less as one between doctrinally-based regimes than as one between an outmoded aggressive form of government and the spirit of the peoples of the world—even the German people—which is essentially pacific.

As the events of World War I became mingled with those of the Russian Revolution—and above all with the Bolshevik phase of the Revolution—a

[13]For a general discussion of this whole development, see Robert E. Osgood, *Ideals and Self-Interest in America's Foreign Relations* (Chicago: University of Chicago Press, 1953), Part 2.

[14]Elihu Root, "The Effect of Democracy on International Law," in Robert A. Goldwin, editor, *Readings in American Foreign Policy,* Second Edition (Chicago: American Foundation for Political Education, 1952), pp. 52-56.

[15]*Ibid.,* p. 56.

sense of the novelty and the threat of a truly doctrinal conflict began to emerge in America.[16] The first stage of the Russian Revolution in the spring of 1917 was greeted in America as a climactic stage in the "progress of the great world movement that has doomed autocracy."[17] The outmoded Czarist regime, it was believed, was finally being undermined by the spontaneous democratic actions of the masses of the Russian people—actions which would profoundly influence the future of Russian domestic politics. But far over-shadowing that prospect was the expectation that the democratic regime would enter into the last assault on the Prussian autocracy; the war was con-ceived of as having been converted into a coalition of democratic regimes fighting autocracy. This conception of the war made American participation seem all the more consistent with American principles.

Thus the stage was set for what Americans believed would be the last act in the great struggle between republics and monarchies. Instead, to the horrified astonishment of most of them, the center of the stage was suddenly seized by the Bolshevik Party.

The Bolsheviks' takeover of the Russian Provisional Government in Novem-ber, 1917, and their subsequent attempts to spread revolutionary civil war throughout Europe, transformed both the Revolution and the nature of the war. American reactions to these events marked the beginning of the second stage of the country's involvement in European politics. Early reactions re-flected the astonished, halting, perplexed, skeptical, yet passionate feelings of most Americans; Bolsheviks were described as anarchists, crack-pots, eco-nomic imbeciles, or German agents.[18] But deeper, they reflected a funda-mental ambivalence concerning the nature and prospects of doctrinally-based regimes. Americans were fascinated by the attempt at a total transformation of a vast society, an attempt guided by a body of strange, even mysterious, doctrines. But they were almost totally ignorant, especially at the beginning of the Bolshevik stage of the revolution, of the substance of these doctrines. Furthermore, they were profoundly and persistently skeptical that the doctrines could ever be effectively translated into practice. Americans therefore tended to decry the possibility of the Bolshevik or any similar

[16]The interpretation which follows draws heavily upon these works: Peter G. Filene, *Americans and the Soviet Experience 1917-1933* (Cambridge, Mass.: Harvard University Press, 1967); Christopher Lasch, *The American Liberals and the Russian Revolution* (New York: Columbia University Press, 1962); and Arno J. Mayer, *Political Origins of the New Diplomacy, 1917-1918* (New Haven: Yale University Press, 1959).

[17]The phrase is by Elihu Root, *op. cit.,* p. 56.

[18]See Filene, *op. cit.,* Ch. 1; Lasch, *op. cit.,* Ch. 5; Meno Lovenstein, *American Opinion of Soviet Russia* (Washington, D.C.: American Council on Public Affairs, 1941), pp. 1-50.

regime lasting or becoming powerful. At the same time, they recognized its immediate challenge and responded to it with political actions and interpretations of its development.

The most obvious political reaction was American intervention in the Russian Civil War. More significant, in the long run, was President Wilson's role, during the last winter of the war, in reformulating the war aims of the Western coalition. This reformulation was made public in Wilson's speech of January 8, 1918, which set forth his famous "Fourteen Points."

The "Fourteen Points" have been described by Professor Arno Mayer as "Wilson's Countermanifesto." He argues that the threat of revolution in Europe, supported by the Bolshevik regime, caused Wilson to attempt to seize the initiative from the Bolsheviks. He attempted to do this by radicalizing the war aims and turning the war itself into a crusade of principles.[19] The immediate object of such a crusade was, of course, to destroy the German autocracy—not just defeat Germany's war aims. But the more profound object was to mobilize a crusading version of the principles of liberal democracy against the armed doctrines of the Bolsheviks. The profound significance of this development was perceived by Albert Thomas, a French Socialist, who wrote an article with what Mayer calls the "then novel" title of "Democracy or Bolshevism." Thomas discerned in the new war aims a crystallization of the conflict into a new form. It was henceforth to be a conflict between democracy, based on the French Revolution but now to be led by the American republic, and the "primitive, incoherent, brutal forms of Russian fanaticism."[20]

In spite of this development, American interpretations of the Russian Revolution remained for some time fundamentally skeptical concerning the viability of such a radical, doctrinally based regime. One form of this skepticism was the attempt to interpret the Russian Revolution in terms of the French Revolution. The most doctrinaire and fanatical stage of the French Revolution had been succeeded, within a few years, by a violent reaction and then a more moderate regime; America expected the same course of events to take place in Russia. Just as the Jacobins had been drunk with utopian fancies, so were the Bolsheviks, and just as the former had been rather quickly succeeded by men who operated on the basis of the "realities of life," so would the latter be replaced.[21]

[19]Mayer, *op. cit.*, Ch. 9.
[20]Mayer, *op. cit.*, p. 386.
[21]See Lasch, *op. cit.*, pp. 155-157, 214-215.

There was also a widely-held view that the Bolshevik doctrines would eventually be revealed as worthless because they conflicted with the natural forces of economic and political activity. The New Economic Program, a major innovation in the evolution of the Bolshevik regime, was widely interpreted not as merely a tactical and doctrinally-consistent adjustment to the exigencies of the revolutionary situation, but as proof that Marxist-Leninist principles were invalid. Henry Ford voiced this notion when he said, "It makes little difference what theory is back of the real work, for in the long run, facts will control."[22]

Similarly, many American liberals felt that Bolshevik theories were absurd and dangerous, and would be rejected as the Russian people became better educated, and as the "transitory class dogma" was exposed to the effects of "life and history."[23]

These interpretations, dominant in the 1920s, reflected the reverse side of the deeply rooted belief in the naturalness, self-evidence and invincibility of American republican principles.[24] The Bolshevik regime was generally understood to be a puzzling intrusion into the course of world progress toward democracy—a dangerous but essentially transitory aberration. But there was also, among a minority of observers, a foreboding sense that a radical and probably irreversible change in political relations had taken place because of the Bolshevik regime's ability to maintain control. This was distilled by Elihu Root in 1926, when he said:

The Russian Bolsheviks hold to their communistic doctrine with a fierce religious fervor. They have a missionary spirit like the early followers of Mohammed. If the American people lose their sincere belief in their own institutions and fall into a weak milk and water attitude towards the principles upon which our government is based, we are going to have very serious troubles ahead of us.[25]

The implication is that a monumental struggle was under way—a struggle in which the fierce religious fervor of the Bolsheviks might require a corresponding change in the way Americans subscribed to and defended their own principles.

On the whole, however, the American response to European political developments in the 1920s and the early 1930s tended to ignore the possibility of a

[22]Quoted in Filene, *op. cit.*, p. 121.

[23]*Ibid.*, Ch. 5.

[24]See Lasch, *op. cit.*, Ch. 7.

[25]Quoted in Filene, *op. cit.*, p. 284.

general conflict among doctrinally-based regimes. This tendency was revealed
in American response to the 1922 appearance of the Fascist regime in Italy.
The Fascist movement was recognized as reacting against both Bolshevism
and liberal democracy. Articles in the *New York Times* in October of 1922,
however, interpreted it as a "throw-back" to the Rennaissance and an
attempt to rectify the "inefficiency" of democracy by the experiment of a
retrograde "oligarchic administration."[26] Even a mid-1930s article on Italian
government in the **American** *Encyclopedia of the Social Sciences* barely touched
on the nature of Fascist doctrine or its political effects. The author speaks of
the old categories of political conflict when he observes that the Italian "constitution has. . . changed from a democracy to a virtual autocracy."

A greater emphasis on the importance of doctrines appeared in reactions to
the early stages of the Nazi rise to power in Germany. But there was still a
strong tendency to belittle them in a manner similar to the treatment of
Bolshevism in Russia as a product of "transitory dogmas." The well-known
American journalist, Dorothy Thompson, wrote a book in 1932 in which she
said of Nazi doctrine: "This social and economic theory is to a halfway
educated person a tale told by an idiot."[27] The views of another American
journalist, Edgar Ansel Mowrer, were similar. In a book entitled *Germany
Puts Back the Clock* (1933), Mowrer characterized Germany as "militaristic
in spirit and despotic in form, not altogether unlike the Fatherland of 1914."
As for Nazi doctrine, Mowrer argued:

. . . the metamorphosis of a deep-lying itch for power into a full-fledged "philosophy"
was. . .copied from the Russians, the Italians and the pre-war German socialists. Moreover it corresponds to the great need for vast mental construction under which most
Germans like to disguise their appetites and instincts.[28]

Even American social scientists placed no particular emphasis on doctrinal
forces as a key element in political conflict as late as the early 1930s. An
article in the *Encyclopedia of the Social Sciences* on the "History and Theory"
of government, by Professor W. H. Shepard of Ohio State University,[29] includes a discussion of different ways of classifying governments. Most of the
categories are continuations or adaptations of ones which date back to
antiquity—monarchy versus republic or unitary versus federal. The final

[26]*New York Times,* Section C (October 20), p. 16; (October 31), p. 14; (December 19),
p. 18; and Pt. IX (March 29, 1925), p. 4.

[27]Dorothy Thompson, *I Saw Hitler!* (New York: Farrar and Rinehart, 1932), p. 29.

[28]Edgar Ansel Mowrer, *Germany Puts the Clock Back* (New York: William Morrow
and Company, 1933), p. 270.

[29]*Encyclopedia of the Social Sciences,* Vol. 7.

classification distinguishes constitutional from absolute or despotic governments, but it does not appear to involve any marked doctrinal element, as
such. On the contrary, it emphasizes the difference in the distribution of
power: in constitutional government there is a wide distribution of power;
and in absolute or despotic government, power is highly concentrated.

Shepard says that "The democratic state is the last phase of political evolution extending down to the present." He then draws a contrast between the
profound faith in democracy that prevailed in the nineteenth century and the
appearance of "opposing tendencies" since World War I. In this category,
Shepard refers to "an increasing feeling of political scepticism," the "arrival
of a number of dictatorships, that of Mussolini in Italy being the most important," and to the existence of the Communist regime in Russia. He refers to
communism as an experiment being closely observed; there is no sense that it
is directly engaged in a doctrinal conflict with constitutional or other regimes.
And as for democracy, Shepard concludes that it must rid itself of its "absolutist characteristics," which must "give place entirely" to a "pragmatic
approach to the problems of government."

A second article of interest is one on the "State"[30] by Professor George
Sabine of Cornell University, whose textbook on political theory has long
been considered a classic. His treatment of the contemporary state is strik-
ingly similar in tone to Shepard's treatment of contemporary government.
Sabine's discussion pays little attention to the role of doctrines in Fascist,
Nazi or Communist states, either in internal politics or in political relations
with other states. Instead, his analysis concentrates on the problem of the
degree to which the central government of the state is to control various
aspects of social and economic life. Referring specifically to Italy, Russia and
Germany, he concludes as follows:

> It is impossible to tell whether these experiments indicate the emergence of a new type
> of state. In the case of Russia it is possible communism is dependent on conditions
> peculiar to that country, the absence of which makes it improbable that other states will
> develop along similar lines. In the cases of Italy and Germany it is difficult to say
> whether Fascism is a new type or represents a reversion in modern disguise to the old
> type, dictatorship. What passes for a theory of the fascist state seems in part a psycho-
> logical compensation for social distress and in part an *ad hoc* mixture of nationalism,
> Hegelianism and Machiavellianism.[31]

To sum up thus far: During most of the period from the Bolshevik seizure of
power up until about 1934, Americans basically held fast to their late

[30]*Ibid.*, Vol. 14.

[31]*Ibid.*, Vol. 14, p. 330.

nineteenth-century vision that liberal democratic regimes would naturally and inevitably replace all of the old monarchies of Europe. The sudden, unexpected appearance of new types of revolutionary regimes which were fundamentally hostile to liberal democracy seemed to be a temporary phenomenon—an aberration of a serious kind, but not one which could ultimately overturn the progress that had been achieved by the turn of the century. Also, Americans felt that the doctrines of the revolutionary regimes were essentially false, although capable of mobilizing fanatical parties to seize governmental power. Conversely, the validity of the liberal democratic principles remained essentially unchallenged; these principles were considered essentially distinct from the "ideologies," or false doctrines, of the new revolutionary regimes.

Thus until about 1934, Americans tended to depreciate the significance of ideology as a political phenomenon. But as the ideological conflict in Europe deepened in the wake of the aggressive policies of the Nazis, a grave possibility began to be seriously suggested by informed observers. It was a possibility that had been partially articulated at various times from 1917 to 1935—as by Elihu Root—but had never controlled American perceptions. This was the possibility that the Communist and Fascist regimes might not be just temporary aberrations, or anachronistic reversions to autocracy or oligarchy. Instead, they might be new and fearful *types* of regimes: permanently revolutionary, armed with doctrines as well as physical and economic weapons, capable of indefinitely maintaining their control over powerful nations unless defeated in war, and dedicated to doctrinal warfare on liberal democracies and on each other. In short, they might be what soon came to be called totalitarian regimes.

The march of political events from 1934 onward made this possibility seem all too real: The Nazi accession to power was followed in quick succession by the destruction of the Weimar Republic, an attack on the provisions of the Versailles Treaty, and a call to ideological war against Communism. The Great Depression enabled the contending parties in Europe to capitalize on economic chaos and human misery. The Italian Fascists launched a brutal attack on Ethiopia, justifying it as an exemplification of the true spirit of Fascism. The Bolsheviks began a series of vast purge trials that brought prison, torture and death to thousands in the name of dedication to Communism. The left and right wing factions fell to killing each other in the Spanish Civil War, whereupon the Fascist and Communist regimes intervened while the liberal democracies looked on in grim apprehension.

These events interacted with developments in America to bring about the third and crucial stage of American involvement in the European type of political-doctrinal conflict. First, the grave economic dislocation and human misery of the Great Depression lent some credence to the claim of the American Communists that the old order was doomed. As a result, the Communist Party flourished in this country as it never had before. Second, diplomatic recognition of the Bolshevik regime in 1933 indicated the United States' reluctant admission that the center of world communism was now a power in its own right. Third, the resurgence of Germany under the Nazis inspired the militant German-American pro-Nazi organizations which sprang up in the mid-1930s. Fourth, in the wake of the vast changes in Central Europe, thousands of refugees fled to America. Their personal experience with the savagery of the political conflict being waged in Europe was a frightening reality, which reinforced growing American apprehension. Among these refugees were many intellectuals who were deeply aware of the con- flict's doctrinal aspects. Many of them secured teaching positions at American colleges, where their activities greatly contributed to a heightened American consciousness of those aspects. Fifth, a flood of published materials of all kinds dramatized the conflict. Some of this material was clearly Communist and Fascist propaganda, but much of it was serious reporting and scholarly work, at times deliberately intended to involve Americans in the European perspective on events. A notable example of this was the English translation of Mannheim's *Ideology and Utopia*. For the English edition, the translators and the author wrote special materials intended to introduce and involve readers in the ideological problem.

The effect of these developments was a transformation in American political and intellectual orientation. The external sign of this was that although the term ideology was still unknown to most Americans in the late 1920s, by the end of the 1930s it had become a key term in American political vocabulary. More decisive than the change in vocabulary was the change in perspective which it represented. This change began shortly after Hitler came to power. It consisted of a heightened sensitivity to the international and domestic politi- cal effects of the ideological contest in Europe, and to its extension in America.

In November 1936, American Ambassador William C. Bullitt spoke to an American Legion Thanksgiving Day dinner in Paris. He referred to the European conflict between the "new fashionable fanaticisms which impose their dogmas on enslaved peoples by secret police and firing squads," and constrasted it to America's "civilized virtues of good-will and tolerance."[32] A few months later, Elizabeth Yates published an article in the *Christian Science Monitor* entitled "Ideology," in which she said, "Conflict in the past has been based on the desire of a people for land, for wealth, for power over another people. The conflict now facing the world is one of ideology—one set of ideas opposing another."[33] In the fall of 1937, the American writer Stuart Chase referred to the recent eruption of a "blazing war between fascism and communism"—a war in which "abstract terms are personified to become burning, fighting realities."[34] A year later an editorial in the *New York Times* said: "We have seen in our own day millions of lives and the happiness and freedom of many more millions sacrificed to an idea, whether it is of the Black or Brown or Red variety."[35] And in 1939, Max Lerner published a book whose title reflected the contemporary climate of opinion. He called it simply *Ideas Are Weapons*.

The examination of liberal democracy's relationship to the totalitarian war of ideas also became a problem during these years. Practically, how could liberal democracies best respond to attacks by the Communists and Fascists? Theoretically, were the principles of liberal democracy also an ideology and if so, how did it differ from the totalitarian variety?

Two positions became evident in response to these questions. The first held that democracy was not an ideology and that its best means of defense was to remain steadfast in its dedication to its own intrinsic qualities. Lewis R. Miller, in an article in the *Christian Science Monitor* followed this line of argument. Miller said that the democratic form of government is "not an 'ism,' " and that the "democratic citizen has no theory of Marx or Mussolini to prove by experiment in a political laboratory." The democratic citizen adheres

not to an ideology, but to the divine idea of man self-governed. He hears the critics of his institutions describe themselves as realists and him as an impractical idealist. In fact, it is he who is the realist. He may be an idealist, but he is not, like his critic, an ideologist. The citizen of democracy has no desire to impose his political convictions on subjects of other nationalities by force.[36]

---

[32]*New York Times* (November 27, 1936), p. 11.

[33]*Christian Science Monitor,* Magazine (March 17, 1937), p. 7.

[34]Stuart Chase, "The Tyranny of Words," *Harper's* (November 1937), p. 566.

[35]*New York Times* (September 9, 1938), p. 20.

[36]*Christian Science Monitor,* Magazine (March 9, 1938), p. 7.

To instill in democracy a new militancy would be to shape it, according to Miller, in the mirror image of its adversaries.

Yet there was a need to resist these adversaries. One of the ways commonly suggested was to combine adherence to the traditional principles of toleration and self-government with legislative and administrative actions of two kinds. One action would be coping with the grave problems of the Great Depression. The other would be protecting the country against the danger of internal ideological subversion by restricting the activities of ideological enemies within the country.[37]

The second line of response still distinguished the principles of liberal democracy from an ideology, but called for their reformulation and aggressive application. The advocates of this reaction often called for a greater and stronger "faith" than that of the totalitarians—a faith reflecting the religious and secular heritage of Western democracies. George Norlin, President of the University of Colorado, said in 1938 that such a "fighting faith" should rest on the "belief that man is not a means to an end, not a tool to be exploited either by his neighbor or by his nation . . . but an end in himself—the belief in the worth and preciousness of human life and in the sacredness of the human personality. . . . "[38] Even though democracy remains distinct from the totalitarian ideologies by virtue of the source and the truth of its ultimate principles, there is a sense here of the need to meet the challenge of ideological attack with a similarly militant democratic faith.

As the decade wore on, the contest between these two positions sharpened in response to the urgency of the political situation. But there was a gradual shift in terminology: the principles of liberal democracy were more and more frequently referred to as ideology. This shift was partially due to the heightened political interest of Americans in the contest of ideas, and the consequent vague equation of ideas with ideologies,[39] but it was also due to the progressively greater impact of American scholarly interest in and adoption of European theoretical conceptions of ideology.

[37]See, for example, Karl Loewenstein, "Militant Democracy and Fundamental Rights," *American Political Science Review,* 31, No. 3 (June 1937), 417-432; No. 4 (August 1937), 638-658.

[38]George Norlin, "A Fighting Faith," *Rice Institute Pamphlet,* 25, 3 (July 1938), 125-143.

[39]See, for example, Max Lerner, *Ideas Are Weapons* (New York: Viking Press, Inc., 1939), p. 7 ff.

An early, isolated instance of this scholarly development was revealed in a book entitled *Making of Citizens*, published in 1931. The author, Charles E. Merriam—a leader of the "Chicago School" of political science—argued that in all modern political regimes the "interests, advantages, and survival values" of citizens are interpreted in terms of ideologies, which he defined as "systematically organized and developed theories or philosophies of group life." According to Merriam:

There is an ideology of the particular order whether it be democracy, or fascism, or sovietism, or autocracy, or monarchy, or federalism. . . . Political theory is full of multi-colored interpretations of all forms of political organization, setting forth in rational form its special and exclusive advantages and the difficulties and dangers of all other systems in any manner differing from them.[40]

In the following decade, the use of ideology to refer to all types of modern political regimes became widespread in American social science. But where Merriam had emphasized the "rational form" of interpretation provided by different political theories, the later usage tended to qualify, even to undercut this notion by emphasizing the "anti-intellectual" and "non-rational" characteristics of political doctrines. The tension between these two aspects is seen in Charles A. Beard's analysis in 1934. On one hand, the "modern usage" of ideology means

A way of thought, more or less *consciously* conceived, which presents *reasons* for believing that a particular country, community, or class possesses inherent virtues . . . and should not be disturbed in its privileges, claims and contentions.[41] . . . [But] in some respects it *can scarcely be called thinking.* It consists rather in 'exuding' ideas satisfactory and pleasing to the person who does it or to the country or community or class for which it is done.[42]

By the end of the 1930s, the tension evident in Beard's formulation had been largely resolved in the direction of emphasis upon the rationalization and subjectivity of all political ideologies, including those of liberal democracy. This was observed by a prominent political sociologist of the period, R. M. MacIver, who argued that the extensive use of the term ideology was "symptomatic of the conditions of our age." He then traced the earlier European usage of the term, noting in particular that the claim that theories are rationalizations had been "very congenial to men like Sorel and Pareto." He then concluded:

[40]Charles E. Merriam, *Making of Citizens* (Chicago: University of Chicago Press, 1931), p. 336. See also pp. 4, 24, 249, 255.

[41]Charles A. Beard, *The Nature of the Social Sciences in Relation to Objectives of Instruction* (New York: Charles Scribner's Sons, 1934), p. 17. Emphasis supplied.

[42]*Ibid.* Emphasis supplied.

For our own age, with its anti-intellectual tendencies, the concept of ideology is very convenient. To some it is the watch-word of a completely relativist position, from which all systems of thought are treated as valuational expressions of a particular social situation, having therefore only a pragmatic validity. To others it is an incentive to seek for the factors that condition our thinking, so as to explain our philosophies, at least in degree, as social products. Generally, the justification that any institutional system puts forward in its own defense or to secure allegiance may be classed as ideology. Thus ideology and propagandism are closely linked.[43]

The preceding statements by three distinguished American social scientists reveal how great and rapid a change took place in the meaning of ideology during the 1930s, in response to the concerted effect of political events and the spread of theories of ideology. Early in the decade, the term was rarely used by social scientists; at the end of the decade, it had become a standard part of their vocabulary. Early in the decade, it meant the substantive political principles of various regimes and parties; at the end of the decade, it meant the theoretical reduction of such principles to their allegedly more fundamental basis in the economic interests or psychological biases of human beings. It is hardly surprising that in this process of relativization and reduction of all political principles, the validity of the principles of liberal democracy should become as theoretically problematic as that of opposing principles. But it is curious—even paradoxical—that this development of the concept of ideology in American social science should take place just as the country was about to enter the political-military crusade against the false and evil principles of Fascism. In effect, a tension appeared between the social scientist's and the citizen's conceptions of the validity of political principles of liberal democracy—a tension which has since become a characteristic and troubling feature of American society.

By the end of the 1930s, America's concern with ideology had been established—concern which was expressed in the form of progressively greater involvement in and reaction to the political-doctrinal conflicts of Europe. At the beginning of the decade, the involvement and the reaction were still largely peripheral, reflecting the persistent American belief that the doctrinally-based regimes in Russia and Italy were only temporary phenomena. But by the end of the decade, the cumulative impact of events from 1917 to 1939 had created an uncertainty that liberal democracy was destined to spread everywhere. In fact, the totalitarian regimes, dedicated as they were to a radically ideological style of politics, had come to be perceived as a threat to the very existence of liberal democracy, in America no less than in Europe.

[43]R. M. MacIver, *Leviathan and the People* (Baton Rouge: Louisiana State University Press, 1939), p. 137. See also, Francis G. Wilson, "The Structure of Modern Ideology," *The Review of Politics*, 1 (October 1939), 382-399.

Conclusion

The two decades from 1917 to 1939 were decisive in the emergence in liberal Western democracies of what appears now to be a more or less permanent concern with the ideological style of politics. For during those years three related developments of the greatest importance took place. First, the internal development of the totalitarian states revealed the awesome potentialities and the tenacious hold of the new style of ideological politics. Second, that style of politics profoundly affected the nature and conduct of foreign policy in both the totalitarian and the liberal democratic states. Third, many of the liberal democracies discovered that they had to deal not only with totalitarian enemies abroad, but also with their agents, in the form of subversive parties, at home.

Since the 1930s, there have been important changes in the liberal democracies' involvement in and concern with the phenomenon of ideological politics. The military defeat of the Fascist regimes in World War II at first narrowed the focus of concern to the contest with the Communist regimes. But with the extension of that contest from Europe to the whole globe, coupled with the end of the old European colonial empires, a much more complex pattern of such politics has come into being. Abroad, liberal democracies must contend not only with the ideological politics of the Communist regimes, but also with various other versions of such politics in many of the states loosely referred to today as constituting the "third world." And at home, a number of the liberal democracies must contend both with the problem of persistently strong Communist parties and with a newer version of the ideological style of politics—"the politics of confrontation." Yet however important these changes may be, underlying them is a sense of concern and persistent crisis which has its roots in the 1930s. It is a sense of participating in an unfinished drama—a drama in which the various forms and degrees of ideological politics continue to unfold.

The materials in Chapters Seven through Eleven treat modern ideological politics critically. The primary interest of the authors is to analyze and evaluate the nature of, effects of, and alternatives to such politics. Such an interest is, in many ways, a scholarly extension of the practical perspective of political leaders and citizens in liberal democracies. For one of its basic intentions is to assist leaders and citizens by broadening and deepening their comprehension of the problems posed by ideological politics, thus facilitating deliberate, intelligent political action.

The materials in Chapter Twelve treat the role of ideology in politics from the perspective of contemporary social science. The primary interest of these authors is not to criticize ideological politics, but to examine the function of ideology in political systems. This kind of interest is derived from a concern with and emphasis upon (1) conceptual tools which are generally applicable to ideology neutrally defined; (2) empirical measurements of the existence and effects of ideology so defined; (3) means of integrating such measurements into a larger, theoretical framework of political analysis.

Chapter Seven

Ideological Politics versus Civil Politics

Professor Edward Shils' interest in and contribution to the study of ideology and politics extends over the last thirty years. In 1936, he collaborated with the late Louis Wirth on the English edition of Karl Mannheim's *Ideology and Utopia*. In 1968, the new *International Encyclopedia of the Social Sciences* published his essay "The Concept and Function of Ideology" as one of two lengthy articles on ideology. In between, he wrote a number of studies which deal in some way with the problem of ideology. Many of these studies are concerned with the role of the intellectual in modern society. In the essay reprinted here Shils deals with the way ideological politics has been peculiarly congenial to intellectuals in the modern world. In light of the events which have taken place since the essay's publication in 1958, his doubts concerning both the ending of ideology and the prospect of intellectuals practicing the alternative politics of civility are particularly striking.

Ideology and Civility: On the Politics of the Intellectual*

Edward Shils

I

An ideological outlook encircled and invaded public life in the Western countries during the 19th century, and in the 20th century it threatened to achieve universal dominion. The intellectual classes which concerned themselves with politics were particularly affected. The intensity of the attack has varied from country to country. It has been least severe in the United States and Great Britain; in France, Germany, Italy, and Russia, it possessed an overwhelming power. Wherever it became sufficiently strong, it paralyzed the free dialectic of intellectual life, introducing standards irrelevant to discovery and creation, and in politics it constricted or broke the flexible consensus necessary for a free and spontaneous order. It appeared in a variety of manifestations, each alleging itself to be unique. Italian Fascism, German National Socialism, Russian Bolshevism, French and Italian Communism, the *Action Francaise*, the British Union of Fascists—and their fledgling American kinsman, "McCarthyism," which died in infancy—have all, however, been members of the same family. They have all sought to conduct politics on an ideological plane.

What are the articles of faith of ideological politics? First and above all, the assumption that politics should be conducted from the standpoint of a coherent, comprehensive set of beliefs which must override every other consideration. These beliefs attribute supreme significance to one group or class—the nation, the ethnic folk, the proletariat—and the leader and the party as the true representative of these residences of all virtue, and they correspondingly view as the seat and source of all evil a foreign power, an ethnic group like the Jews, or the bourgeois class. Ideological politics have not been merely the politics of a dualistic faith which confines itself to the political sphere. The centrality of this belief has required that it radiate into every sphere of life—that it replace religion, that it provide aesthetic criteria, that it rule over scientific research and philosophic thought, that it regulate sexual and family life.

*Edward Shils, "Ideology and Civility: On the Politics of the Intellectual," *Sewanee Review,* 66 (1958), 450-480. Copyright by The University of the South. Reprinted by permission.

It has been the belief of those who practice politics ideologically that they alone have the truth about the right ordering of life—of life as a whole, and not just of political life. From this has followed a deep distrust of the traditional institutions—family, church, economic organizations, and schools—and the institutional system through which politics have been conventionally carried on in modern society. Ideological politics have required, therefore, a distrust of politicians[1] and of the system of parties through which they work. Insofar as ideological politics have been carried on by organizations calling themselves political parties, it has only been because that term has become conventional for organizations actively concerned with politics. It has not signified that their proponents were ready to participate constitutionally in the political system. Extra-constitutionality has been inherent in their conceptions and aspirations, even when their procedures have seemed to lie within the constitution—and by constitution, we mean not just the written constitution, laws, and judicial decisions, but the moral presuppositions of these. Ideological politics have taken up a platform outside the "system." In their agitation, ideological politicians have sought to withdraw the loyalty of the population from the "system" and to destroy it, replacing it by a new order. This new order would have none of the evils which make up the existing system; the new order would be fully infused with the ideological belief which alone can provide salvation.

Ideological politics are alienative politics. They are the politics of those who shun the central institutional system of the prevailing society. Ideological politicians feel no affinity with such institutions, and they participate in them for purposes very different from those who have preceded them in the conduct of these institutions.[2]

---

[1] The hostile attitude toward politicians, toward the "parliamentary talking shop," with its unprincipled compromise of interests, and toward the petty quality of personnel of civil politics is a continuing theme of the ideologist. Hitler said that politicians were "people whose only real principle was unprincipledness, coupled with an insolent and pushing officiousness and shamelessly developed mendacity." *Mein Kampf* (München: 1941 [583rd-587th ed.]) p. 72. "Parliament itself is given up to talk for the special purpose of fooling the 'common people.' " Lenin, *State and Revolution,* in *Towards the Seizure of Power,* Book II [*Collected Works,* Vol. XXI] (New York: 1932), p. 186. At the other pole of intellectual sophistication, Mr. Edmund Wilson, during his own ideological phase, once wrote, "Our society has . . . produced in its specialized professional politicians one of the most obnoxious groups which has ever disgraced human history — a group that seems unique in having managed to be corrupt, uncultivated, and incompetent all at once." *New Republic* (January 14, 1931), reprinted in *The Shores of Light,* (London: 1952), p. 529. The anti-political literature of the ideological intellectual is vast: Hilaire Belloc and G. K. Chesterton, *The Party System* (London: 1911) is representative.

[2] Mr. Aneurin Bevan, who has within him, together with other gifts, a powerful ideological strain, has written of the radical's entry into the House of Commons: "Here

For the ideological politician, membership in a parliamentary body or the acceptance of office involves only an opportunity to overthrow and destroy the system rather than to work within it and improve it.[3]

Ideological politics are the politics of "friend-foe,"[4] "we-they," "who-whom."[5] Those who are not on the side of the ideological politician are, according to the ideologist, against him.

Thus, moral separatism arises from the sharp, stable, and unbridgeable dualism of ideological politics which makes the most radical and uncompromising distinction between good and evil, left and right, national and unnational, American and un-American. Admixtures are intolerable, and where they exist they are denied as unreal, misleading, or unstable.[6]

Ideological politics have been obsessed with totality. They have been obsessed with futurity. They have believed that sound politics require a doctrine which comprehends every event in the universe, not only in space but in time. To live from year to year and to keep afloat, to solve the problems of the year and of the decade are not enough for ideological politics. Ideological politicians must see their actions in the context of the totality of history. They must see themselves moving towards a culmination of history, either a new epoch, totally new in every important respect, or bringing to a glorious fulfillment a condition which has long been lost from human life. Whether

he is, a tribune of the people, coming to make his voice heard in the seats of power. . . . The first thing he should bear in mind is that these were not his ancestors. His ancestors had no part in the past, the accumulated dust of which now muffles his own footfalls. His forefathers were tending sheep or plowing the land, or serving the statesmen whose names he sees written on the walls around him, and whose portraits look down upon him in the long corridors. . . . In him, his people are here for the first time and the history he will make will not be merely an episode in the story he is now reading. It must be wholly different, as different as the social status he now brings with him." *In Place of Fear* (New York: 1952), p. 6.

[3]Cf. Leon Trotsky, *Whither England?* (New York: 1925), pp. 111-112: "We Communists are by no means disposed to advise the . . . proletariat to turn its back on Parliament. . . . The question . . . is not whether it is worthwhile to use the Parliamentary method at all, but . . . is it possible to use Parliament, created by Capitalism, in the interests of its own growth and preservation, as a lever for the overthrow of capitalism."

[4]Carl Schmitt, *Der Begriff des Politischen* (München, Leipzig: 1932), pp. 14 ff.

[5]Striking evidence of the separatism of ideological politics may be found in N. Leites, *The Study of Bolshevism* (Glencoe, Ill.: 1953), pp. 291-309, 384-390, 430-442.

[6]Cf. Raymond Aron, *The Opium of the Intellectuals* (Doubleday, Donan and Co.: 1957), pp. 3-34. The deep-rootedness of the mythology of left and right among intellectuals of the Marxist tradition, and its penetration even into allegedly scientific research in sociology and social psychology are treated in my essay, "Authoritarianism 'Left' and 'Right'," in Richard Christie and Marie Jahoda, *Studies in the "Authoritarian Personality"* (Glencoe, Ill.: 1954), pp. 24-49.

totally without precedent or a renewal of the long lost, the ultimate stage will be something unique in history.[7] Everything else is a waiting and a preparation for that remote event.

II

What are the grounds for thinking that the age of ideological politics is passing? How can we summon the naiveté to think such a thing, when the world is frozen into a menacing division engendered and maintained by Bolshevik ideas, when the Communist Parties of France and Italy are among the largest in their countries, when in the Middle East, in Africa and Asia passionate nationalist and ethnic ideologies continuously encroach on rational judgment and reasonable moral action.

Yet the expectation is not simply frivolously optimistic. The very heart which has sustained ideological politics among intellectuals over the past century is gradually losing its strength. Marxism is decomposing. The mythology of Bolshevik Marxism, the true nature of which was seen at first only by Bertrand Russell, Waldemar Gurian, and a handful of European Social Democrats and liberals, began its own self-deflation in the mid-1930's, at the moment of its maximum appeal to the world's intellectuals. The Moscow Trials were the first major step in the breakdown of the Communist claim that in the Soviet Union the ultimate stage of human history, the true realm of freedom, was being entered upon. The Berlin uprising of June 17, 1953 was a step further. The realm of harmony through which mankind would transcend its conflict-ridden history was unveiled as a phantasm when Russian tanks shot down German workingmen in the streets of Berlin. According to Marxism, there could only be harmony between Socialist societies bound together by the solidarity of the proletariat, but the Soviet Union showed no compunction about suppressing the East German workers by force. The eagerness with which Hungarian and Polish intellectuals greeted their prospective emancipation from a compulsory Marxism and the Russian repression of the Hungarian Revolution of 1956 also contributed to the demythologizing of Marxism.

[7] The Communist Manifesto declared that in place of a class society with its classes and class antagonisms, there would be a new free society "in which the free development of each is the condition for the free development of all." In the first edition, this was regarded by its authors as an entirely unique condition: "The history of all hitherto existing society" being "the history of class struggles." In 1888, Engels added a footnote which corrected this view, saying "all written history" was the history of class conflict. There had been a prehistorical period of communally owned property which was free of class conflict. Communism would thus be a renewal on a higher plane of what had been lost since the beginning of history. Marx and Engels, *Historisch-kritische Gesamtausgabe* (Erste Abt., Bd. 6, Moscow/Leningrad), 1933, pp. 525-526; p. 546.

Political events alone have not discredited Marxism. Perhaps more important
is its sheer unresponsiveness to the multiplicity of life itself. People still have
a need to believe, but Marxism cannot satisfy it. Its formulae are too simple,
and it offers nothing to those who are attempting to establish their intellectual individuality in the face of large-scale organizations and their accompanying professional specialization. The humanitarian element in Marxism—
its alleged concern for the poor—can have no appeal when there are still many
very poor people in Communist countries, and the poor in capitalist countries
can now be seen not to be poor, not to be miserable, not to be noble—but to
be as comfortable and as vulgar as, if not more vulgar than, the middle classes.
Marxist utopianism has lost its power of conviction—the world is too tired
and even, in this respect, too wise to be aroused by promises of a future
which might be spurious and which would not be much different from the
present. Journals like *Dissent* in the United States and the *Universities and
Left Review* in the United Kingdom are valiant and touching efforts to save
something of the ideological heritage. But they show how much ideological
politics are now on the defensive, and how uncertain they are of the validity
of their position. They know that their myth has faded, and that with good
grounds, the intellectual spirit of the times is running against them. In every
sphere of intellectual life, in economic theory, in history, and in sociology,
Marxism has lost its power to attract because it is too simplistic, too thread-
bare intellectually and morally, and too often just wrong or irrelevant to the
problems of the contemporary mind.[8] The emergence of the social sciences as
major subjects of university research and teaching—even though they have
their serious limitations and even though they sometimes bear a Marxist
imprint—constitutes a major factor in the tarnishing of Marxism.

Nationalism too has lost its doctrinal grip on the intellectuals of the West. Its
deeper, primordial hold is very strong, but it does not reach into the plane
where it could provide a principle for political judgment and action, and even
less does it provide a criterion for regulating other spheres of life. In the 20th
century among Western intellectuals doctrinal nationalism has never been
long preponderant, although in France among the followers of Maurras and
Barrès there has been a persistent and virulent minority. In Germany, it for a
time suffocated reason, and in Italy under Fascism it found many willing
proponents. Now, however, it is dormant. It might even be said that it is at its
lowest ebb in Europe and America since the Risorgimento and the movement
for the unification of the Reich. The hideous example of National Socialism,

[8]Even Professor Merleau-Ponty, against whose ingenious efforts to fuse existentialism
and early Marxism Professor Aron directs an unsparingly detailed and devastating criticism,
has lost some of his confidence in Marxism in the past few years.

the terrible national intoxication, and the monstrous deeds committed in the name of the nation have for the time being at least exhausted the ideological passions of the German people—intellectuals and laity. The fatigue and waste of the past World Wars, and the ominous possibility of an even worse war to come add themselves to all the other elements in the constitution of the intellectual outlook to render nationalistic enthusiasm one of the least attractive of all the available alternatives of the present time.

The ideals of the European Enlightenment have quietly reasserted their validity without arousing intellectuals to passion on their behalf. It was from the ideals of bourgeois liberalism that they had turned away in the great long wave of political enthusiasm which the Russian Revolution of 1917 had raised to a flood. Now that they have come back to these ideals, they have come back soberly, circumspectly, and with moderation. They do not yet even acknowledge that they have come back to them.[9] The mildness of religious faith in the Western countries, no less than the relaxation of nationalist passion to an unspoken patriotism, and the desire that national sovereignty should give ground to effective control of nuclear weapons seem to provide plausible grounds for an affirmative answer to the question as to whether we are at the end of the ideological age.

Moreover, the asperities of the debate between socialism and capitalism seem to be fading. The achievements of the American and Western European economies since the war, together with the political equivocality of centrally planned economies, the failures of economic planning in the Soviet satellite states, the re-introduction of the principles of the market economy into their economies by some of the Communist states, and the modest and by no means glamorous achievements of nationalized industries in England and France, have cooled the fires of a century-long dispute between the proponents of socialism and the advocates of capitalism.

The more valid aspirations of the older humanitarian elements which were absorbed into Marxism have been more or less fulfilled in capitalist countries. The socialist and communist countries have neither realized their more grandiose ideals at all nor achieved their more reasonable aspirations any better than the capitalistic countries.

[9]Indeed, in the counterattack on ideological politics, recent writers like Professor J. L. Talmon, *The Origins of Totalitarian Democracy* (London: 1952), have not spared the French writers of the 18th century in their effort to trace totalitarianism to its most remote origins and to extirpate it. This view is not, however, shared by Professor Aron (*op. cit.*, p. 35).

The Negro problem in the United States of course arouses passions, but no doctrines, no principles offer an apparently easy way out. The "woman question" has settled down to being a perennial headache, curable by no enunciation or espousal of clear and unambiguous principles. The ideology of egalitarianism has left the fundamental precipitate of moral egalitarianism from which it originally arose, but as a universally applicable principle it has lost its glamor. It seems almost as if what was sound in the older ideologies has been realized and what was unsound has demonstrated its unsoundness so obviously that enthusiasm can no longer be summoned.

Of course, ideological politics, Marxist, Islamic, Arabic, Hindu, Pan-African, and other, still exist in the new states outside the West in a vehement, irreconcilable form and often with great influence. But many in the West who sympathize with the desires and deplore the excesses are inclined to believe that they too will pass when the new states in which they flourish become more settled and mature. Looking back from the standpoint of a newly-achieved moderation, Western intellectuals view the ideological politics of Asia and Africa, and particularly nationalism and tribalism, as a sort of measles which afflicts a people in its childhood, but to which adults are practically immune.

There seems to be no alternative ideology for the intellectuals to turn to now, nothing to absorb all their devotion, nothing to inflame their capacity for faith and their aspirations toward perfection. The conservative revival, though genuine, is moderate. People take Burke in their stride. They have become "natural Burkeans" without making a noise about it. The *National Review*, despite its clamor, is isolated and unnoticed, and the effort to create a "conservative ideology" which would stand for more than moderation, reasonableness, and prudence has not been successful.[10]

There seem to be no more grounds for ideological politics. Thus, it appears reasonable to think that the age of ideological politics is gradually coming to its end.

Does the present lull give us reason to believe that the tempests are now behind us and that we are now entering upon a pacific sea? An inspection of the traditions which have formed the outlook of the modern intellectual in the West and in the new countries is not entirely reassuring.

[10]Cf. Irving Kristol, "Old Truths and the New Conservatism," *The Yale Review* (Spring 1958), pp. 365-373.

III

One of the grounds for believing that the age of ideological politics is ending is its modernity.

Professor Aron inclines towards the view that ideological politics originated in the French Revolution.[11] There is much truth to this contention. Ideological politics did indeed come into the forum of public life only at the end of the 18th century in an outburst not hitherto experienced by the human race.

The reason for this relatively recent appearance of ideological politics on a grand scale is not far to seek. Until recent centuries politics were not public. In the aristocratic republics and in the ancient city democracies, politics did not engage the attention of the mass of the population. Politics were the concern of rulers and of those who aspired to become rulers. The aspiration was, however, spread over a relatively small section of the population. Tribal, feudal, and dynastic interests, which were uppermost in the political life of societies before modern times, did not nourish the ideological outlook. There was, moreover, no intellectual class as a major factor in politics. Where the educated were taken into the civil service, as in China, in ancient Rome, and in the European Middle Ages, the bureaucratic *ethos* and personal dependence on the prince, to say nothing of the type of education preparatory for the civil service career, discouraged the emergence of an ideological orientation. The intrigues of court politics did not foster the success of the ideologically minded man. There was no class of independent professional literary men and journalists, free of patrons and of the need to remain on the right side of the authorities.

The violent political struggles of the Greek city-states and of the last decades of the Roman Republic, even where they involved the bitterest class antagonisms, did not become ideological. They were fought on behalf of "interests." The notions of "justice" and of the "good social order" did not enter into them except peripherally.

The ideological orientation toward life existed, of course, as it must exist wherever human society exists. It passed judgment on all things, and so it passed judgment on political things. It censured the existing political order as a realm of iniquity, and counselled and predicted its destruction. This ideological attitude toward politics did not, however, enter the sphere of

[11] Aron, p. 42. The same view is put forward by Professor D. W. Brogan in his most interesting essay, "Was the French Revolution a Mistake?", *Cambridge Journal*, Vol. I, No. 1 (October 1947), pp. 43-55.

political activity, because the kinds of persons who espoused it or came under its influence were not admitted into the circles which discussed and decided on succession to political office and on the actions of governments.

As long as politics were not an instrument of justice or of the realization of the right social order and were concerned with the mere maintenance of order, the conservation of the power of dynasties and classes which already had or sought it, there was no room for ideological politics. Those who practiced politics were not susceptible to them, except on rare occasions, and they found no following even where great individual personalities were moved by ideological—above all, religious—considerations.

The invention of printing and the possibility arising therefrom of diffusing arguments to a wider public, the Protestant belief that the Bible and not the priesthood is the vehicle of the sacred, the Protestant belief that each man must make his own proper contact with the sacred by his study of the Bible, and the slow and gradual rising of the mass of European populations from their torpor—all of these had much to do with the creation of the necessary conditions for ideological politics. The crucial element, however, was the creation of a class of intellectuals no longer dependent exclusively on patronage or inheritance for their livelihood.

The body of intellectuals which came into existence in the 16th century was a new phenomenon in world history. It consisted of men whose sensibility, intelligence, and imagination carried them beyond the standards and requirements of everyday life; they were no longer forced inevitably to depend on church or state or princely, aristocratic, or mercantile patronage for their existence. Their capacity for loyalty thus liberated, they were endowed with the freedom to attach themselves to symbols beyond those embodied in existing ecclesiastical and governmental institutions. The steady growth in the scale and importance of this stratum of the population in modern European societies is perhaps the decisive factor in the "ideologization" which, on its better side, has been called the "spiritualization of politics." The intellectuals—who before the development of specialized technical training were co-terminous with the educated classes—have lived in a permanent tension between earthly power and the ideal, which derives from their nature as intellectuals. They have not, however, created from within themselves the imagery and passion of ideological politics. The numerous traditions which they have developed, e.g., the romantic tradition, the scientific tradition, the bohemian tradition, important though they have been in disposing intellectuals towards ideological politics, would scarcely have been sufficient to give to such politics their extraordinary attraction and compellingness.

Ideological politics are rooted in an ideological tradition which lives in our midst through invisible radiations coming down from the depths of our Western past. They are sustained by our Judaic-Christian culture, by passions which are part of our souls, and by the nature of society.

The millenarian tradition which is the oldest source of the ideological outlook is an ever-present potentiality in Christian teaching and experience; it is usually maintained, for most people, most of the time, in a state of latency. It has a living existence in the life of the Protestant sects and in the records of the saints of every Christian society. Even where religious belief has become attenuated or has evaporated, the millenarian expectations and judgments have persisted in an aromatic tradition which, on occasion, becomes crystallized in a sensitive and receptive person. Religious *enthusiasm*, as the late Ronald Knox[12] showed with such compassionate understanding and as Professor Cohn, writing from a very different point of view, has corroborated, has never been absent from Western civilization. As early as pre-Exilic times, Jewish prophets foretold the cataclysmic end of time and the world as we know it, a Day of Wrath and a Last Judgment, when sinners, individual and corporate, would be cast down, and a regenerated Israel would populate Palestine and a second Eden.

The expectations of a Last Judgment on a sinful temporal order took a deep root in the early Christian communities. The tradition did not die out as the Church settled down to live on as an institution. Manichaeism, with its basic distinctions between light and darkness and its conception of the universe as a field of irreconcilable struggle between the forces of light and the forces of darkness, found hospitality in the Christian circles where this chiliastic tradition persisted. No church, indeed, no established institution, could survive if its members expected an imminent end of the world and its subsequent replacement by the Kingdom of God. It was to meet this view that Saint Augustine elaborated his conception of the Church itself as the Kingdom of God on earth. But for those with a great sensitivity to the sacred, and without Saint Augustine's powerful and disciplined intellect, no living church could ever represent the Kingdom of God. Insofar as it refused to preach the proximate realization of the Kingdom of God, it rendered itself subject to their most anguished and harshest criticism.

Professor Cohn, who is not concerned either to support the Marxist view that millenarian sectarianism was merely the ideology of a class conflict expressed

---

[12]*Enthusiasm: A Chapter in the History of Religion, with Special Reference to the XVII and XVIII Centuries* (Oxford: 1950).

in a religious idiom or to espouse the anti-Marxist view which argues that millenarianism was solely an expression of a hypersensitive and perhaps disordered religiosity, is at his best when he shows how it fused with the animosities of class, of ethnic hatreds, and of phantasies of national glory. The hatred-filled phantasies of princes, lords, wealthy merchants, the Pope, Jews, Turks, Italians, Saracens were amalgamated with the frightful images of Satan and the Antichrist. In its meandering and tragic history, full of misery, persecution and violence, rabid and deluded yearnings, false Messiahs, deranged visions, persecutions, and pitched battles, a single complex theme runs unbrokenly. This is the central theme of the ideological orientation towards existence.

The ideological outlook is preoccupied with the evil of the world as it exists; it believes in the immiscibility of good and evil. It distinguishes sharply between the children of light and the children of darkness. It believes that no earthly action can ameliorate or attenuate evil. It exhibits a violent hatred of the existing cosmic order, and especially of its earthly beneficiaries, governmental, economic, and ecclesiastical authorities, indeed, of authorities of any kind. It regards authority as an agent of evil and as a compromise with evil.

The mass of mankind lives in constant temptation and seduction by evil; the petty concerns of daily work and commerce, attachment to family, loyalty to friends, and the quest of private advantage are all inextricably involved with evil. Those who take upon themselves to rule the world as it is are either corrupt in their very nature to begin with, or become so through their contact with authority, which is diabolical by nature.

The ideological outlook expressed by millenarianism asserts, however, that the reign of evil on the earth is of finite duration. There will come a moment when time and history as we know them shall come to an end. The present period of history will be undone by a cosmic act of judgment which will do justice to the wronged and virtuous by elevating them to eternal bliss, and equal justice to the powerful and wicked by degrading and destroying them for all time to come. The order which will be ushered in by the cosmic last judgment will be a new realm of perfect harmony and peace, in which all men will live in accordance with the ultimate criteria of justice and mutual love. No conflict will mar their existence; there will be no scarcity to degrade and cramp them.

To usher in this glorious epoch requires heroism on the part of the small number of consecrated persons who live strictly in accordance with the dictates of the highest judgment. Heroism is required, above all, to give witness to the truth of the standards which ultimately will come to prevail and to help to inaugurate this totally new phase of existence.

Despite its extraordinary persistence, the millenarian tradition has been no ordinary tradition transmitted by the elders of a society to their next generation. Its reception is not the ordinary reception of tradition as something given, but a search and a yearning. There is no evidence of continuity of the movement of this tradition from person to person, and it is not commonly taught in any society. It is a phenomenon of the sinks and corners of society, and it creates groups which, in a state of inflammation, are remarkably short-lived as compared with the long history of the Churches. The tradition, however, has a long and continuous history.[13] From the Near Eastern seedbed of enthusiastic religiosity, millenarian Christian sectarianism spread from the Near East into Southeastern Europe and North Africa, from Bulgaria into Northern Italy, from Northern Italy into Southern France, from Southern France into the Low Countries, from the Low Countries into Germany and Central Europe and then into England. Yet the mechanism of its transmission remains a mystery. There is some evidence of personal links of the founders and spreaders of particular variants of millenarianism, but this does not explain why the soil was so fertile for their labors.

Similarly, although the inner affinities of millenarianism and modern revolutionary politics are now perfectly obvious,[14] the lines of filiation are more difficult to trace. The German Marxists' discovery of their own ancestry in the Anabaptists of Münster, in the Levellers and the Diggers of the English Civil War,[15] is an acknowledgment of the affinity, but is not evidence of a directly received influence.[16]

[13]Cf. LeRoy Edwin Froom, *The Prophetic Faith of Our Fathers: The Historical Development of Prophetic Interpretation* (Review and Herald, Washington, D.C.: 1948), Vols. I-IV; Steven Runciman, *The Medieval Manichee: A Study of the Christian Dualist Heresy* (Cambridge: 1947); Dmitri Obolensky, *The Bogomils: A Study in Balkan Neo-Manichaeism* (Cambridge: 1948); Knox, *op. cit.;* I should like also to call attention to a very sympathetic article by Miss Storm Jameson: "The Dualist Tradition," *Times Literary Supplement* (6 August 1954).

[14]Aron, Ch. IX, "The Intellectuals in Search of a Religion," pp. 264-294; Erich Voegelin, *Die politische Religionen* (Stockholm: 1939), pp. 39-42; Fritz Gerlich, *Der Kommunismus als Lehre vom tausendjahrgen Reich* (Munich: 1920), esp. pp. 17-78.

[15]Cf. Friedrich Engels, *The Peasant War in Germany* (New York: 1926); Karl Kautsky, *Communism in Central Europe in the Time of the Reformation* (London: 1897); Edward Bernstein, *Cromwell and Communism: Socialism and Democracy in the Great English Civil Revolution* (London: 1930); Ernst Bloch, *Thomas Münzer als Theologe der Revolution* (München: 1921).

[16]The German working class movements of the 1840's and British working class radicalism did, it is true, thrive in areas which had been the scenes of Protestant

Perhaps the continuity of the millenarian outlook through many different situations arises not from a continuously handed down tradition but from the recurrent attachment to its sources—the Book of Daniel, the Book of Revelations, the Sybilline Books, and the Johannine prophecy, which are available on the edge of our culture to all those who have a need for them. To these, time and again, persons with a yearning for the end of earthly injustice and the transcendence of time in a new and purer realm, resplendent with harmony and love, have turned. In the past century, they have not had to go back to the original sources. Through the heirs of these sources, their transformations into the doctrines of contemporary ideological politics have been available in an idiom more acceptable to the contemporary mind.

Now, if this is no ordinary tradition, transmitted in the way ordinary traditions are transmitted, why then does it persist as such a recurrent theme in Western history? The answer must be sought in Christianity, which contains among its manifold potentialities the ever-present promise of a Second Coming and the unchanging imminence of the ultimate catastrophe which precedes the second coming of a Messiah. Although the central institutions of modern societies, out of the very necessities of their continuing existence and the nature of the human beings who live in them, preclude the widespread practice and observance of the ideological orientation, there are always some persons in these societies to whom the ideological orientation has an especial appeal. It is always there for those who have the ideological need to be in saving contact with the ultimate. Every society has its outcasts, its wretched, and its damned, who cannot fit into the routine requirements of social life at any level of authority and achievement. Max Weber said that salvationary religions are most commonly found among declining strata of handicraftsmen and small enterprisers. This proposition is capable of generalization. Those who are constricted, who find life as it is lived too hard, are prone to the acceptance of the ideological outlook on life. A society in which the lot of the many becomes more constricted, in which they feel more deserted and more uncared for as a result of the failure of their rulers, will encourage this proneness to seek realization.[17]

sectarianism from the 16th to the 18th centuries. It is a plausible hypothesis that the ideological traditions of sectarian life made for a receptivity to revolutionary and radical ideas by virtue of their correspondence; in turn, aided by theorists more deeply dyed by the revolutionary traditions of the French Revolution and the Hegelian (and ultimately Christian) idea of history, the tradition of religious enthusiasm was transformed into an apparently secular heroic doctrine of ideological politics.

[17]Bengt Sundkler, *Bantu Prophets in South Africa* (London: 1948); Georges Balandier, *Sociologie actuelle de l'Afrique noire* (Paris: 1955), pp. 417-486; and Peter Worsley, *The Trumpet Shall Sound: A Study of 'Cargo' Cults in Melanesia* (London: 1957), show the connection between salvationary, messianic religion and the deprivations arising from the disruption of traditional institutions.

Naturally, not all those who live in a broken and disadvantaged condition are drawn equally by the magnet of the ideological orientation. Special personal qualities are required.[18] It takes a hyper-sensitivity to ultimate standards, to the sacred, and this is a quality which, although rare in all populations, is found in some measure at all times and particularly at times of crisis. There are human beings who, by personal constitution, are sensitive to the ultimate grounds of existence, just as there are human beings with a need for and a capacity for abstract reasoning, for understanding the mysteries of the universe in accordance with the powers of their reason. Some become mystics, some become scientists, others philosophers. Others who are filled with the sense of injustice and of grievance against the earthly order in its various manifestations, political and ecclesiastical, as well as familial and sexual, reach out toward and seek fusion with the symbols of apocalyptic fulfillment. That is why the ideological orientation so frequently draws to itself madmen full of hatred and fear—the paranoids who play such an important role in Professor Cohn's interpretation. Ideological sensitivity, even if it did not draw on the accumulated hatred and aggressiveness of its followers, would be separatist and in tension with the "world" of normal traditional society. Its utopianism and its quest for perfect harmony would put it at odds with the world of conflicting interests, half-measures, and self-seeking. The addition of the hatred and fear of those who feel injured and neglected adds a highly combustible fuel to its fire. For this reason, the ideological outlook is full of the imagery of violence and destruction, and its practice is often crowded with

---

[18]Cf. Norman Cohn, *The Pursuit of the Millenium* (Essential Books: 1957). Professor Cohn declares that paranoid tendencies are a necessary condition for the expansion of millenarianism. His view is supported not only by the content of millenarian imagery and aspirations which his book so richly describes, but by contemporary experience of millenarian groups, religious and political. He does not claim that all members of such groups must be paranoid, but that the leaders must be such. ". . . there are always very large numbers of people who are prone to see life in black and white, who feel a deep need for perfect saviours to adore and wicked enemies to hate; people . . . who without being paranoiac yet have a strong tendency towards paranoid states of mind. At a time when such tendencies are being encouraged by external circumstances, the appearance of a messianic leader preaching the doctrine of the final struggle and the coming of the new age can produce remarkable results—and that irrespective of whether the leader is a sincere fanatic or an impostor or a mixture of both. Those who are first attracted will mostly be people who seek a sanction for the emotional needs generated by their own unconscious conflicts. . . . these first followers, precisely because they are true believers, can endow their new movement with such confidence, energy and ruthlessness that it will attract into its wake vast multitudes of people who are themselves not at all paranoid but simply harassed, hungry or frightened" (pp. 311-312). There is much truth in this well-balanced picture, but it seems to me that he omits the religious or ideological sensitivity—the sensitivity to remote things—which is not necessarily connected with paranoia, any more than imagination or curiosity is connected with it.

actual acts of brutality and a heartless asceticism, while preaching a message of an ultimate condition of love and peace enveloping all human beings.[19]

Ideological politics have their nerve in this need to be in contact with the sacred. They live from grievance and the feeling of injustice, and no conceivable society can attain the condition in which everyone could be permanently free from grievance and the feeling of injustice, any more than any society could live up to the standards affirmed by the most saintly prophets and maddest zealots of the apocalypse.

The tendency of intellectuals in modern Western countries, and latterly in Asian and African countries, to incline toward ideological politics does not, however, derive only from this permanent feature of the Judaic-Christian religious culture, which affects even those who do not accept its explicit articles of faith.[20] As intellectuals, they also live in the flowing stream of other traditions which are particular to them as intellectuals.

It is probably not an accident that most of the traditions of the modern intellectuals seem to dispose them towards an ideological outlook. It seems to be almost given by their attachment to symbols which transcend everyday life and its responsibilities. Some of these traditions have arisen as effluvial by-products of specific intellectual activities, as, for example, scientism has arisen from scientific research and analysis. Others, like the tradition of bohemianism, have arisen from the age and mode of life of persons whose inclinations drive them towards an effort to be independent of traditions and conventions and on whom their devotion to the symbols of artistic and literary creation, and the restricted market for the sale of their creations, enforces material poverty and uncertainty. And still others, like the tradition of Romanticism, are the complex products of a profound movement of the human spirit, so intricate and multifarious that it seems almost inexplicable.

[19]One need only read the pacifist press to see how the preaching of peace and love is combined with a pleasure in the contemplation of maimed bodies and universal destruction. Mazzini once wrote, "I am inclined to love men at a distance . . . contact makes me hate them." Bolton King, *Life of Mazzini* (London: Everyman edition, 1912), p. 55.

[20]Is it entirely an accident that Communism in India has achieved its greatest success so far in an area where previously Christian missionary education had reached a larger proportion of the population than in other parts of India? It is not intended, however, to explain Indian leftism solely by an ultimate derivation from a secularized Christian outlook.

Let us consider some of these traditions of the intellectuals, with regard to their contact with the ideological outlook and their inherent disposition towards ideological politics. Let us consider scientism first. Scientism entails the denial of the truth of tradition. It asserts that life, if it is to be lived on the highest plane, should be lived in accordance with "scientific principles," and that these principles should be achieved by the rigorously rational examination of actual experience, systematically confronted through the elaborate and orderly scrutiny and experiment which constitute scientific research. It regards the generally accepted traditions of society as impediments to the attainment of these principles, which are ultimately the principles immanent in the universe. As such, therefore, scientism constitutes a vigorous criticism of traditional and institutional life, and a refusal to accept authority on any grounds except those of scientific principle. It holds before mankind the ideal of a society in which scientists, and administrators and politicians guided by scientists, will rule and in which the ordinary citizens will hold no beliefs and perform no actions which are not sanctioned by scientific principles.[21] This rejection of the prevailing order, and its central institutions and traditions, and the appreciation of an ideal order governed by the ultimate principles of science, obviously possess close affinities with certain features of the millenarian outlook. The hostility towards the barrier which received tradition raises between the human being and the ultimate principles of the universe, the dispraise of the authority of institutions, and the vision of an ideal order (infused by and conducted in accordance with the ultimate principles of universal existence) are only a few of the lines of affinity which link these two traditions. It is therefore not difficult to understand how the acceptance of the scientistic tradition can prepare the way to the acceptance of a secularized millenarianism and thus lead on to ideological politics.

Romanticism too flows in the same direction, feeding into and swelling the sea of ideological politics. Romanticism too views any existing order as repugnant because it mediates, compromises, and deforms the ideal. The ideal of romanticism is the spontaneous and direct expression of the essential

---

[21]Cf. F. A. Hayek, *The Counter-Revolution of Science* (Glencoe, Illinois: 1952), which provides the best account of one of the most important sources of scientism, that which derives from Descartes and which reaches its fullest elaboration in the work of St. Simon and Comte. B. F. Skinner, *Walden II* (New York: 1948), is an extreme contemporary statement of the scientific position, to which there are numerous approximations, not the least the Marxist. Marxist scientism is best represented by Professor J. D. Bernal, who has written, "Science has put in our power the means of transforming human life to a degree at least as great as those provided by the technical developments of the origin of civilization but the change differs in one crucial respect in that they can be consciously undertaken. What we can see straight away is the possibility of the removal of most of the hindrances to full human and social life that exist in our civilization." "Science and Civilization," in C. Day Lewis, *The Mind in Chains* (London: 1937), pp. 194-195.

nature of the individual and the collectivity. Both the individualistic and the collectivistic variants of the Romantic tradition placed great emphasis on the direct and full experience of the ultimate value of individual creativity or of the spirit of the community (folk or national or local). Like the millenarian outlook, Romanticism regards immediate experience of the sacred as a touch-stone of the good. Whatever is mediated by calculation or contrivance, by organization or compromise is antithetical to it. That is why modern large-scale society as it has emerged since the end of the 18th century is abhorrent to those who live in the tradition of Romanticism. Civil society, which allows so much space for private concerns, and which permits neither the single individual nor the total community the complete realization of their essential potentialities, is seen by Romanticism as a system of arbitrary repression, in contrast with some ideal realm of freedom and fulfillment. Civil society requires compromise and reasonableness, prudent self-restraint, and responsi-bility, and these are all deviations from the unqualifiedness and spontaneity which Romanticism demands of all action. Romanticism is, as a result, at war with civil society.

The influence of Romanticism on the outlook of intellectuals runs far beyond those circles who knowingly acknowledge its sovereignty over them. It has become universally pervasive. It is a major determinant of the attitude of the intellectuals towards politics and the authority of institutions. And different though it is in content from the frightful and dazzling visions of millenari-anism, they both work to the same end—the rejection of the existing order in the name of a pattern of existence more infused with the sacred.

In their spiritual genealogy, the traditions of bohemianism and populism are closely related to Romanticism. Bohemianism had an older history before it developed an *ethos* of its own. The restless scholars of the medieval univer-sities[22] and the homeless minstrels and minnesingers who lived from begging, thieving, and the hope of selling their artistic wares were the ancestors of the modern bohemian. They were footloose; they were not incorporated into the routines and responsibilities which filled most of the medieval European social structure. They would not accept the burdens of family and vocation, and sought only to serve their own creative impulse and pleasure.

---

[22]Miss Helen Waddell, describing these forerunners of bohemianism, quoted the Council of Salzburg: "They go alone in public naked, lie in bake-ovens, frequent taverns, games, harlots, earn their bread by their vices and cling with inveterate obstinacy to their sect, so that no hope of their amendment remaineth." *Wandering Scholars*, 7th ed. (London: 1942), p. 188.

The development of printing and the appearance of a body of writers trying to maintain themselves from the sale of their written product added a substantial body of persons in Western Europe whose uncertain existence and whose intellectual sensitivity forced them into an irregular course of life. Bohemian practice and bohemian *ethos* were well under way in London and Paris before the beginning of the 19th century. The widened range of education and the increased reading public, fed by the romantic idea of the creative man, the lonely genius who knows no law, made the café intellectual, the bohemian writer and artist into a major figure of life in all the great capitals of the Western countries. Paris was the center of this life, but London, Berlin, Munich, St. Petersburg, Rome, and New York all had their bohemias. The traditions of the French revolutions of 1789, 1830, 1848, and the commune of 1871, and the tradition of anarchism, doctrinal and practical, found a warm reception in the Parisian bohemia, and with varying degrees of attenuation and adaptation to national political traditions, they found acceptance in the bohemias of the other countries as well. Antinomianism—moral, aesthetic, and political—was at home there, and the political police kept their eyes peeled for revolutionaries in bohemian intellectual circles. Bohemians were at war with society,[23] some on well-thought-out-grounds, seeking a free life less encumbered by traditional standards, others out of an incoherent and impulsive aggressiveness against any sort of authority, cultural or institutional, and an inability to live in a settled routine of work or life. There were many points at which bohemianism and millenarianism diverged. Bohemianism was usually against the Church as well as against Christianity; millenarianism was Christian and only hostile to the authority of the Church. Bohemianism was usually opposed to asceticism; millenarianism was often ascetic. They had in common, however, their repugnance for *mere* tradition and for the constituted authorities who were associated with it.

Populism—the belief in the wisdom and the supreme moral value of the ordinary man of the lower classes—is a new phenomenon. In some respects it was a creation of Romanticism, but it was also an outgrowth of the moral egalitarianism of the Christian sects and of life at the peripheries of Western culture. By its praise of the uneducated and the humble, it places itself in opposition to the great and mighty of the earth; it denies their cultural creativity while imputing true creativity to the lower classes. Populism charges academic science and scholarship with a preoccupation with bloodless symbols unconnected with the essence of life. When it becomes political,

[23] Baudelaire once wrote, "Usefulness to the community always seemed to me a most hideous thing in man." *The Essence of Laughter and other Essays, Journals and Letters,* edited by Peter Quennell (New York: 1956), p. 178.

populism asserts that the standards of the ordinary people should prevail
against the standards represented by the authoritative institutions of society
—the State, the Law, the Church, the Universities. Thus the populistic tradition, too, like the other traditions cited, expressed a deep alienation from
traditional culture and from the society ruled through civil politics and the
equilibrium of power.

Populism and millenarianism share many significant features. Both repudiate
the official traditions of learning, millenarianism declaring that the prevailing
interpretation of sacred texts falsifies their true meaning, and populism
charging the learned with the transfiguration of authority and with enmity
towards the truth expressed in the popular will. Both oppose the mediation
of contact with the highest values, by authoritative institutions, by priests,
professors, and parliamentarians. Both are against the cold-blooded and
impersonal rules of institutions; both are responsive to charisma. The conceptions of the people and of the proletariat easily merge, as do those of
people and nation, and so populism can turn without difficulty into an ideological political orientation.

These are not the only traditions of the modern intellectual, but most of the
others have the same tendency. Of course, these traditions are not accepted
equally by all intellectuals. They are most widely accepted among men of
letters and academic scholars and scientists. Nonetheless, although an
increasing proportion of intellectuals in the broader sense, i.e., persons who
have passed through colleges and universities, are engaged in practical tasks in
administration and technology which curb their ideological predispositions,
the atmosphere in which they acquire their qualifications, and the traditions
which adhere to their professions, give to many of them some impulsion in
this direction. The impetus to an ideological outlook inherent in the very
constitution of intellectual activities would probably not be enough to
account for the upsurge of ideological politics of the past century and a half.
It has required the confluence of numerous traditions and their common confrontation with the situation of modern society to release the flood.

IV

Traditions seldom die. They recede very slowly, yielding before new traditions which replace them by incorporating elements of their predecessors and
assimilating them to new elements. The new traditions can grow only by
attachment to older traditions which they expand and elaborate.

It seems excessively sanguine, therefore, for us to congratulate ourselves on
the end of the ideological age. We would be more realistic to speak of its

subsidence, rather than of its end. Old traditions, such as millenarianism, deep in the marrow of our intellectual bones, traditions such as Romanticism, which are at the very heart of the modern age, are not likely to disappear so soon after the fury and the disillusionment of the first fifty years of this century.

What we may legitimately hope for in the coming decades is a condition of quiescence of ideological politics and of the ideological disposition from which it springs. This quiescence can be sustained only if an effective alternative is available. Civil politics are this alternative.

Civil politics are based on civility, which is the virtue of the citizen,[24] of the man who shares responsibly in his own self-government, either as a governor or as one of the governed. Civility is compatible with other attachments to class, to religion, to profession, but it regulates them out of respect for the common good.

Civil politics do not stir the passions; they do not reveal man at the more easily apprehensible extremes of heroism and saintliness. They involve the prudent exercise of authority, which tries to foresee the consequences of that exercise while appreciating the undeterminable limitations of human powers and the uncertainties of foresight. The civil politician must be aware of the vague line between the exercise of authority and the manipulation of human beings as objects outside his moral realm. He must shun that line and yet on occasion go over it, realizing the moral costs of such crossing over and the difficulties and the necessity of crossing back into the domain of legitimacy. He must maintain a sense of affinity with his society and share with his fellow citizens their membership in a single transpersonal entity, while bearing in mind their unresponsiveness to the ideal and their incapacity to sustain a continuous and intense relationship with the sacred. He must maintain this sense of substantial affinity while being aware of their lesser willingness to be responsible for the common good and while keeping his own feeling of responsibility for it alive and taut.

The difficulties of civil political conduct are great in democracies. Their large size and the impossibility of direct contact between politicians and their

---

[24]Civility has meant more than good manners, and it is an impoverishment of our vocabulary as well as a sign of the impoverishment of our thought on political matters that this word has been allowed to dwindle to the point where it has come to refer to good manners in face-to-face relationships. Two recent books by eminent British writers —*Traditions of Civility*, by Sir Ernest Barker (Cambridge: 1948); *Good Behaviour: Being a Study of Certain Types of Civility*, by Sir Harold Nicolson (London: 1955)—show no awareness of the older meaning of the term.

constituents are strains on the sense of moral affinity which, lacking the support of personal relationships, must be self-sustaining. Civility was rare in aristocratic societies, partly because aristocratic virtue—the virtue of the warrior—and civil virtue—the virtue of the citizen—are so far apart in their inner constitutions and particularly because aristocratic systems by their nature restrict man's development of the empathic sense of affinity. Liberal democratic regimes place great burdens on the civil sense because they permit open conflict and acknowledge and thus encourage partisanship. The common good is always hard to define, but it is rendered even harder when it must gratify and reconcile opposing interests and simultaneously attempt to guard values for which no strong partisan contends, but which, nonetheless, are essential to a good society. The politician must be partisan himself, while civility requires a partial transcendence of partisanship, as well as an empathic appreciation of the other parties within the circle of the civil political order. Partisanship must be carried on with the simultaneous perception of the civil and moral order which embraces both one's opponents and one's allies.

Civil politics—which are by no means identical with democratic politics—are especially difficult in contemporary society. The complex tasks which governments undertake and which nearly everyone thinks they should undertake, make so great the amount of material that a politician who devotes himself to the matter must master, and so many the obligations to which he must attend, that reflection is deprived of the quiet and leisure which it needs to mature. The complexity of the tasks renders easy understanding of them beyond the power of most of the citizenry and encourages a depreciatory attitude towards the capacities of the electorate, thus inhibiting the vitality of the sense of affinity between citizens and leaders that is essential to civil politics. The deep and increasing penetration of populism in all countries results in a greater pressure on the politician for the immediate satisfaction of class and sectional ends. The development of techniques of mass communication and of chemical, surgical, and psychological modes of controlling human behavior presents continuous temptations to the politician to respond to the incessant demands by manipulation. Not that he always by any means yields or that the techniques would be successful if applied, but the mere existence of the putative possibilities creates an atmosphere which impedes the cultivation and practice of civility.

Civil politics entail judging things on their own merits—hard enough in any case where the merits and demerits in any complex issue are so obscure and intertwined—and they also require respect for tradition. Civility requires respect for tradition because the sense of affinity on which it rests is not momentary only but reaches into the past and future. As to the past, civil politics appreciate the factual reality of past achievements as well as the human quality of those who, by virtue of having once been alive, command our respect for their names and the things they valued; as to the future, civil politics see the unity, in essence, of the present generation and those which are to follow, not just in a biological sense, but in the order of value as well. The population of a civil polity is in its fundamental being a continuous procession of those living in the present, preceded by those who have lived, shading off into the obscurity of time past, and to be followed by those who have still to live, shading off into the even more shadowy obscurity of time still unelapsed.

The traditional consciousness is not, however, one which encourages the direct contemplation of the merits and demerits of things as they are. The utilitarian mind usually has little patience with the pastness of things and is even disposed to assume that the mere fact of having been appropriate to the past is a disqualification for relevance to the present and future. Yet both the need for continuity—i.e., the maintenance of affinity with the past—and the need to draw on the benefits of the intelligence and artfulness exercised in the past, render imperative an appreciation of tradition.

Above all, civil politics require an understanding of the complexity of virtue, that no virtue stands alone, that every virtuous act costs something in terms of other virtuous acts, that virtues are intertwined with evils, and that no theoretical system of a hierarchy of virtues is ever realizable in practice. It has been a major fault of ideological politics that they have made the mistake of thinking that a coherent, systematic doctrine could guide conduct unfailingly along a straight line which made no compromise with evil. Ideological politics believed that the more strictly one adhered to a virtue, the more intensely one was attached to it, and the more completely one fulfilled it, the better would be one's actions.

This was the basis of the idea of the political spectrum which ran from the pole of virtue—be it left or right—to the other pole, the extreme and complete negation of virtue. The realism and circumspection of civil politics cannot accommodate such a simplification.

Practicing politicians do indeed manage to avoid the excesses which are inevitable in such simplifications. As Professor Aron shows, French politicians in the 19th and 20th centuries, in one of the countries of the most extreme ideological politics among intellectuals, have in practice usually not been dominated by this distinction between "left" and "right."[25] Indeed, this has been one of the reasons why French intellectuals have been so alienated from the political practice of their country.

The practice of politics imposes some measure of civility, but it also stirs the temptation of demagogy and offers the easy solution of satisfying the most clamorous sectional interests. If intellectuals could settle down to a more reasonable political outlook, their concern for the more general and for what transcends the immediate advantages of particular "interests" would infuse a most precious ingredient into political life.

V

Is it plausible to expect intellectuals to renounce their attachments to anti-political traditions in which they have lived for centuries? Can it be expected that intellectuals will be drawn down from the heights of the ultimate ideal so that they could, while still remaining intellectuals, tolerate the burden imposed by the vicissitudes of maintaining themselves as politicians who have invested their future in the unpredictabilities of politics, and by the task of keeping a society going? Can intellectuals be brought to appreciate politics which are concerned to keep society on a steady course, as much concerned to keep it from becoming worse as to make it better? Can they be expected to affirm a political practice which provides no final solution and which does not promise to bring society or the human race to a resting point of perfect fulfillment?

The civil politics which must replace ideological politics in the affections of the intellectuals have many competitive disadvantages. Their traditions are fewer and frailer. Cicero, who preached and tried to practice the virtues of civil politics, has been called an opportunist, and his assassination by the side with which he compromised has been regarded as evidence of his failure as a politician. Tacitus spoke on behalf of civility through his censure of its degradation in the Empire.[26] Clarendon's civil wisdom was put on paper in

[25]The avoidance of ideological politics is not synonymous with the practice of civil politics. Politics practiced in accordance with the prevailing constellation of interests is a third alternative, and it is one which is most commonly pursued by politicians. If the "interests" are intractable, then the civil order can be as badly damaged as it would be by ideological politics.

[26]"So corrupted, indeed, debased was that age by sycophancy that not only the foremost citizens who were forced to save their grandeur by servility but every ex-consul, most of the ex-praetors and a host of inferior senators would rise in eager rivalry to propose shameful and preposterous motions. Tradition says that Tiberius as often as he left the Senate House used to exclaim in Greek, 'How ready these men are to be slaves.' " (*Annals,* Book III, Section 65).

the rueful melancholy of exile and with the distrust of power which is the destiny of the disappointed and disregarded counsellor to princes. The fate of More and Raleigh and the disillusionment of the humanists who sought to guide the conduct of princes have left bitter memories of the tribulations of the intellectual in politics. On the other side, the image of politics reflected by those "advisors to princes" whose names stand out in our minds, Machiavelli above all, Halifax, et al., have given an appearance of justice to the condemnation of politics which the intellectual, devoted to the ideal of his calling, has often expressed.

The intellectual who seeks the path of civil politics has little to cheer and fortify him in his quest. He has many of his own prejudices to overcome—the whole complex of the traditions of ideological politics, and, in America, his traditional aversion for the politics of the pork barrel and the patronage lists, and his image of the 42nd Ward Young Men's Democratic Club, with its smokers and its belching boorishness, and of the harsh selfishness of the Union League Clubs.[27] He has no feeling of standing in a great intellectual tradition. There is no equivalent civil tradition to counterpose to the subter- ranean pervasiveness of the millenarian tradition, to provide an atmosphere in which he can breathe. He has the memory of Woodrow Wilson and Thomas Masaryk, Disraeli and Gladstone, and Guizot, to set alongside the far more numerous intellectuals approving of bomb-throwing and assassination, them- selves engaged in wire-pulling and plotting, impatient and contemptuous of the political profession.

If civil politics depend on an acceptance of the limitations of human powers, their establishment in the second half of the present century will not be rendered easier by scientific developments. The advances in physiology, biochemistry, neurology, applied mathematics, cybernetics, and the foolish propaganda made by some of the enthusiasts of psychology and the social sciences, can hardly induce a feeling of modesty in man, nor can they be expected to promote that fellow-feeling necessary to civil politics.

Nor, for that matter, can the specialization of education which accompanies this scientific progress bring much support. Quite the opposite. It is not that the humanistic education of the past has provided much of a bulwark against

[27]This is by no means confined to capitalistic America or to bourgeois politicians. Ferdinand Lassalle once said, "I have a real horror of workers' delegations where I always hear the same speeches and have to shake hard, hot and moist hands." David Footman, *The Primrose Path* (London: 1946), p. 183. The intellectuals' attitude toward politicians, regardless of their class, is epitomized in: "I met Murder on the way. He had a mask like Castlereagh."

the ideological outlook. Extreme specialization, however, adds a further strain to the weak sense of affinity. It is true that extreme specialization which reduces the contact of the intellectual with the broad range of traditions of the intellectual life of the past also restricts this relationship with many of the ideological elements in the traditions of the intellectuals. In many fields, however, and particularly in those of increasing importance, it exposes him more fully to the scientistic tradition. Thus, while it increases his matter-of-factness, it also increases his pride, his contempt for the past, and his confidence in the boundless superiority of the future, and these are not so congenial to civility.

If ideological politics thrive in conditions of danger, what are we to think of the chances of civil politics in an age in which peace is maintained by a conscious fear of cataclysmic destruction by nuclear weapons? These awful possibilities cannot avoid stirring up latent apocalyptic images and expectations. These real dangers make the sober, moderate, small-scale measures of civil politics appear excessively puny alongside the monstrous tasks which nuclear weapons impose on governments.

It should not be thought that civil politics can be stifled only by ideological politics, or that millenarianism is the decisive determinant of radical alienation. Radical transformations in society can be undertaken without millenarian impulsion. Western and Oriental antiquity have known revolutions without ideologies. Every social order, even the most just, will have some victims, and every population will contain antinomian personalities. These alone instigate tendencies towards a sort of proto-ideological politics, even when there are no ideological traditions living in the open or under the surface.

Finally, civil politics are not the only alternative to ideological politics for the intellectuals. They have in some instances entered upon political careers like professional politicans, given up their intellectual concerns and attachments, and devoted themselves to the conventional round of vote-getting, interest representation, self-preservation, and self-advancement. They could yield to the customary temptations of the vain and egocentric, demagogy, flattery, and opportunism. They could, in short, conform to their own prevailing image of normal political life.

This, however, is not likely. What is far more likely is withdrawal—angry withdrawal or sad and serene withdrawal. The traditions of withdrawal among the intellectuals are among the profoundest in our intellectual inheritance. One can be anti-political without being ideological. This was the dominant trend among American intellectuals from the Jacksonian Revolution until the Russian Revolution; and it is unfortunately, despite the charges of conformity, of "other-directedness," and of being "organization men," still the prevalent current among American intellectuals today. The valiant effort to embrace "Our Country and Our Culture" is not a resounding success as far as civil politics are concerned.[28] The repudiation of ideological politics has not led to the espousal or practice of civil politics. The life of American society is affirmed, but its political life and the civil element in its political life are not.

The situation in Great Britain is not very different. Great Britain has a better record in civil politics than any other country in the world, and its intellectuals have their proper share in that record. What is the situation today? The post-war idyll has ended in disenchantment. "Butskellism" is in retreat. The "angry young men" are on the rampage. Even the most amiable Mr. Kingsley Amis, who says that he is, when he has to choose, a Labour Party man, cannot take politics seriously. His heart is not in it.[29] He, like those with whom his name is coupled, is distrustful of the "professional espouser of causes." The humiliation of the Suez fiasco and the danger of the hydrogen bomb have seriously damaged the British intellectuals' capacity for civil politics. Even a sober, responsible intellectual of long and honorable political experience, Mr. Christopher Hollis, tells his fellow intellectuals that the main task before the British electorate is to discredit the two major political parties, even though he expects no serious "Liberal revival."[30] Mr. John Osborne, who has no such background of experience of political responsibility, is far harsher in his anti-politics. "I can't go on laughing at the idiots who rule our lives. . . . They are no longer funny because they are not merely dangerous, they are murderers . . . they are stupid, insensitive, unimaginative beyond hope, uncreative, and murderous."[31]

VI

Can the intellectuals re-educate themselves to a civil state of mind? Can they keep the traditions of ideological politics quiescent while they modify their own outlook? Can they take advantage of the present lull in ideological politics in the West and develop and fortify the incipient impulses of civility which the harsh experiences of the past half-century stirred into movement?

[28]Cf. Newton Arvin, et al., *America and the Intellectual,* Partisan Review Series No. 4 (New York: 1953).

[29]*Socialism and the Intellectuals,* Fabian Tract 304 (London: 1957).

[30]"What Shall we do Next Time?" *The Spectator,* No. 6765 (February 21, 1958), pp. 225-226.

[31]"They Call It Cricket," in Tom Maschler (ed.), *Declaration* (London: 1957), p. 67.

One condition of the success of this effort at self-"civilization" is that we should not think that we can or should completely extirpate the ideological heritage. There are valuable elements in that inheritance which are worthy of conservation in any political outlook which lays claim to our respect. The demand for moral equality, the distrust of authority and of the institutions which it conducts for its own continuance, the insistence on justice, and the call to a heroic existence, even the belief in the earthly paradise and the realm of freedom, all have some validity in them. To deny them will only lay civil politics open to the charge—not unjustified—of being philistine politics in the worst sense, without feeling or sympathy, unimaginative, timorously clinging to what already exists. The ideological element in our intellectual classes will not die out so easily and so soon that its successors will be able to escape unscathed while conducting politics which, while called civil, are merely concerned with the maintenance of order and keeping things as they are.[32]

These impulses in the human heart will not be disregarded. The fact that they have been forced to an extreme and cast into the framework of unrealizable hopes does not mean that they are in themselves immoral. The discredit into which their doctrinaire proponents have deservedly fallen should not be extended to them. Life would be poorer without them, and a political system which sought to proceed entirely without them or entirely against them would find the most sensitive spirits of its society once more drawn up in embittered and irreconcilable opposition.

It has not been the substantive values sought by ideological politics which have done such damage. Rather it has been the rigidity, the exclusiveness, and the extremity with which particular values have been sought. There is nothing evil about loyalty to one's community, national or ethnic or cultural, nor is there anything wicked in the appreciation of equality or the devotion to any particular ideal. What is so malign is the elevation of one value, such as equality or national or ethnic solidarity, to supremacy over all others, and the insistence on its exclusive dominion in every sphere of life.[33]

[32]One of the dangers of the New Conservatism is that it fails to see that civil politics are as eager for improvement as they are ready to conserve what has come down from the past. Cf. Charles Parkin, *The Moral Basis of Burke's Philosophy* (Cambridge: 1956), Ch. VI, pp. 109-130; also Mr. Kristol's perspicacious essay in the *Yale Review*, mentioned earlier.

[33]Few writers have made this criticism of ideological politics, while retaining a compassionate sympathy for their ideals, as well as Conrad. Natalie Haldin says at the end of *Under Western Eyes*, "I must own to you that I shall never give up looking forward to the day when all discord shall be silenced . . . and the weary men united at least . . . feel saddened by their victory, because so many ideas have perished for the triumph of one. . . ."

Civil politics therefore will have a better chance to obtain more enduring devotion among intellectuals if their proponents do not disavow all continuity whatsoever with the substantive values of ideological politics. Correspondingly, their chances for success will be enhanced if the prudence they extol is exercised in finding a just balance among the contending values rather than in merely seeking self-maintenance, which will degenerate into unprincipled opportunism.

A complete disavowal of every line of affinity between civility and ideology will not only be false in fact but would turn civility into an ideology. Civility would become an ideology of pure politics concerned with no substantive values except the acquisition and retention of power and the maintenance of public order and with absolutely no other interest. Civility would take upon itself the onus of the very same moral separatism for which it criticizes ideological politics, if it denied its affinity with the substantive values which the ideological outlook holds and distorts.

VII

How can intellectuals retain those elements of Romanticism which prize spontaneity and genuineness of expression, and which aid the cultivation of individuality, while curbing their expansiveness? By excessive demands for individuality and the consequent exaggeration of the restrictions which institutional life imposes on it, Romanticism will discredit any social order and turn the intellectuals against it and arouse the custodians of order against the intellectuals. The "imperialism" which the late Baron Ernst Seillière bemoaned in so many volumes can disrupt any social order, and above all a liberal order. A way must be found to retain many of the values of Romanticism while restricting their expansiveness.

A renewal of the old idea, fundamental to modern liberalism, of a separation of the spheres is needed. It can, of course, be realized only very incompletely; economic life cannot be completely independent of government and politics and *vice versa*; religion and politics cannot be completely separated; culture and politics cannot be completely separated. Nonetheless, while acknowledging and accepting their necessary collaboration and affinity, it is very important that the guardians, practical and intellectual, of each of the spheres should be aware of the desirability, in principle, of their separateness. This would be a bulwark against the romantic—and ideological—insistence on the universal application of a single set of standards. The separation of the different spheres of life would not please those ideological politicians and intellectuals who seek complete consistency. Without it, however, civility would be extinguished and our best intellectual traditions would be frustrated.

It should be quite possible in practice to realize a far-reaching separation of the spheres while maintaining their overlaps and affinities. This is in fact done to a large extent in societies of the West, however imperfectly and unprincipledly. The real difficulty is to bring about the intellectual's acceptance of it as a reasonable policy. There is not such a completely unbridgeable antinomy between individuality and institutions as Romanticism insists—although there must inevitably be some tension. The intellectual's distrust of the ongoing life in the spheres outside his own arises from the defects in his sense of affinity.

The nature of the sense of affinity which binds the members of a society together is a mystery. It seems somehow connected with the empathic capacities of the individual—not just his empathy for persons whom he encounters in concrete form, in person, or through written or plastic symbols, but for classes of persons who must necessarily remain anonymous. Up to a certain point, it goes hand in hand with individuality, and societies which do not know individuality also live without a sense of civil affinity. It is shrivelled and shrunken by fear, and when it is restricted, it is in its turn conducive to fear of one's fellow men. If somehow the intellectuals could be got over their almost primordial terror of and fascination by authority, which, they fear, crushes their individuality, the movement for civility would make a tremendous advance.

Modern Western societies have witnessed a diminution in the moral distance separating the higher and the lower classes. This has in part been a result of the changes in the distribution of national income which have raised the lower strata and diminished the upper strata, so that standards of life are now very much nearer to each other than they have ever been before, however considerable the differences remain, and should, to some extent, still remain. But more significant, I think, is the change in the civil consciousness which has taken place in Western societies. This is in some measure a result of the inner development of the potentialities of the Protestant idea—the same complex of ideas and sentiments which has aggravated the millenarian disposition. The notion that every man has a spark of divinity in him, that all men participate in a common substance—sacred in the last analysis but civil in its concrete and mediated forms—has grown out of the conjunction of the modern national state and Christian protestantism. From this conjunction grew the idea of the citizen, and from it our modern idea of the civil order as a stratum of being in which all the members of a state participate.

The modest flowering of civility in the modern world is a new thing in history. Pericles' Funeral Oration foreshadowed its program. The great Roman forerunners were, however grandiose, no more than adumbrations of a human possibility, rather than indications of a well-functioning civility in ancient times. The growth of civility has been halting and very imperfect. Its growth has been attended by an exacerbation of ideology—and the two seem in the modern epoch to have some obscure and intricate interdependence. Yet it does seem that with the spread of individuality—imperfect now and never perfectly realizable—in the wider reaches of the population, the sense of civil affinity has increased its scope and power among the lower strata, who previously existed as objects of authority and economic power but did not dwell within the same moral and civil domain as their rulers. There is now in all strata, on the average, a higher civil sense than earlier phases of Western society have ever manifested—and this despite class conflicts and ideological separatism and irreconcilability. Even ethnic barriers seem slowly to be yielding to the rising tide of civility. Is it too much to hope that the intellectuals, who have provided such illustrious antecedents in the true "civilization" of politics, will themselves come more fully into this process, and thus, by one of the great continental drifts of history, bring the age of ideology to an end?

Chapter Eight

**Ideological Politics versus
Political Tradition**

One of the great themes developed during the critical reaction to the French
Revolution was that of the contrast between rationalistic plans and the
accumulation of political traditions as the basis for society. The great English
statesman Edmund Burke made the most acute presentation of that contrast
in a variety of works. The two essays which follow are by contemporary
English scholars, Michael Oakeshott and J. W. N. Watkins. Professor
Oakeshott readdresses the problem perceived by Burke over a century and a
half ago. He does so in the course of treating a larger theme: what sort of
political education is appropriate? His conclusion that such education should
be a deep grounding in "our tradition of political behaviour" follows from his
distinction between "ideological politics"—an essentially mistaken understanding—and knowledge of the political tradition of one's society.

Professor Watkin's critique of Oakeshott's distinction is taken from a longer,
more general appraisal of the latter's political philosophy. Both writers are
concerned with the relationship between politics and political philosophy—a
problem treated at length in Part I. The relationship between "ideological"
and "true" politics is a particular form of the larger question.

A Critique of the Ideological
Style of Politics*

Michael Oakeshott

I

. . . In the understanding of some people, politics are what may be called an
empirical activity. Attending to the arrangements of a society is waking up
each morning and considering, 'What would I like to do?' or 'What would
somebody else (whom I desire to please) like to see done?', and doing it. This
understanding of political activity may be called politics without a policy. On
the briefest inspection it will appear a concept of politics difficult to substantiate; it does not look like a possible manner of activity at all. But a near
approach to it is, perhaps, to be detected in the politics of the proverbial
oriental despot, or in the politics of the wall-scribbler and the vote-catcher.
And the result may be supposed to be chaos modified by whatever consistency is allowed to creep into caprice. They are the politics attributed to the
first Lord Liverpool, of whom Acton said, 'The secret of his policy was that
he had none', and of whom a Frenchman remarked that if he had been present at the creation of the world he would have said, *'Mon Dieu, conservons
le chaos'*. It seems, then, that a concrete activity, which may be described as
an approximation to empirical politics, is possible. But it is clear that,
although knowledge of a sort belongs to this style of political activity (knowledge, as the French say, not of ourselves but only of our appetites), the only
kind of education appropriate to it would be an education in lunacy—learning
to be ruled solely by passing desires. And this reveals the important point;
namely, that to understand politics as a purely empirical activity is to misun-
derstand it, because empiricism by itself is not a concrete manner of activity
at all, and can become a partner in a concrete manner of activity only when it
is joined with something else—in science, for example, when it is joined with
hypothesis. What is significant about this understanding of politics is not that
some sort of approach to it can appear, but that it mistakes for a concrete,
self-moved manner of activity what is never more than an abstract moment in
any manner of being active. Of course, politics are the pursuit of what is
desired and of what is desired at the moment; but precisely because they are
this, they can never be the pursuit of merely what recommends itself from
moment to moment. The activity of desiring does not take this course;

*From Michael Oakeshott, "Political Education," in *Rationalism in Politics* (London:
Methuen & Co., Ltd., 1962), pp. 114-127. Reprinted by permission.

caprice is never absolute. From a practical point of view, then, we may decry the *style* of politics which approximates to pure empiricism because we can observe in it an approach to lunacy. But from a theoretical point of view, purely empirical politics are not something difficult to achieve or proper to be avoided, they are merely impossible; the product of a misunderstanding.

II

The understanding of politics as an empirical activity is, then, inadequate because it fails to reveal a concrete manner of activity at all. And it has the incidental defect of seeming to encourage the thoughtless to pursue a *style* of attending to the arrangements of their society which is likely to have unfortunate results; to try to do something which is inherently impossible is always a corrupting enterprise. We must, if we can, improve upon it. And the impulse to improve may be given a direction by asking, 'What is it that this understanding of politics has neglected to observe?' What (to put it crudely) has it left out which, if added in, would compose an understanding in which politics are revealed as a self-moved (or concrete) manner of activity? And the answer to the question is, or seems to be, available as soon as the question is formulated. It would appear that what this understanding of politics lacks is something to set empiricism to work, something to correspond with specific hypothesis in science, an end to be pursued more extensive than a merely instant desire. And this, it should be observed, is not merely a good companion for empiricism; it is something without which empiricism in action is impossible. Let us explore this suggestion, and in order to bring it to a point I will state it in the form of a proposition: that politics appear as a self-moved manner of activity when empiricism is preceded and guided by an ideological activity. I am not concerned with the so-called ideological *style* of politics as a desirable or undesirable manner of attending to the arrangements of a society; I am concerned only with the contention that when to the ineluctable element of empiricism (doing what one wants to do) is added a political ideology, a self-moved manner of activity appears, and that consequently this may be regarded in principle as an adequate understanding of political activity.

As I understand it, a political ideology purports to be an abstract principle, or set of related abstract principles, which has been independently premeditated. It supplies in advance of the activity of attending to the arrangements of a society a formulated end to be pursued, and in so doing it provides a means of distinguishing between those desires which ought to be encouraged and those which ought to be suppressed or redirected.

The simplest sort of political ideology is a single abstract idea, such as Freedom, Equality, Maximum Productivity, Racial Purity, or Happiness. And in that case political activity is understood as the enterprise of seeing that the arrangements of a society conform to or reflect the chosen abstract idea. It is usual, however, to recognize the need for a complex scheme of related ideas, rather than a single idea, and the examples pointed to will be such systems of ideas as: 'the principles of 1789', 'Liberalism', 'Democracy', 'Marxism', or the Atlantic Charter. These principles need not be considered absolute or immune from change (though they are frequently so considered), but their value lies in their having been premeditated. They compose an understanding of *what* is to be pursued independent of *how* it is to be pursued. A political ideology purports to supply in advance knowledge of what 'Freedom' or 'Democracy' or 'Justice' is, and in this manner sets empiricism to work. Such a set of principles is, of course, capable of being argued about and reflected upon; it is something that men compose for themselves, and they may later remember it or write it down. But the condition upon which it can perform the service assigned to it is that it owes nothing to the activity it controls. 'To know the true good of the community is what constitutes the science of legislation,' said Bentham; 'the art consists in finding the means to realize that good.' The contention we have before us, then, is that empiricism can be set to work (and a concrete, self-moved manner of activity appear) when there is added to it a guide of this sort: desire and something not generated by desire.

Now, there is no doubt about the sort of knowledge which political activity, understood in this manner, calls upon. What is required, in the first place, is knowledge of the chosen political ideology—a knowledge of the ends to be pursued, a knowledge of what we want to do. Of course, if we are to be successful in pursuing these ends we shall need knowledge of another sort also—a knowledge, shall we say, of economics and psychology. But the common characteristic of all the kinds of knowledge required is that they may be, and should be, gathered in advance of the activity of attending to the arrangements of a society. Moreover, the appropriate sort of education will be an education in which the chosen political ideology is taught and learned, in which the techniques necessary for success are acquired, and (if we are so unfortunate as to find ourselves empty-handed in the matter of an ideology) an education in the skill of abstract thought and premeditation necessary to compose one for ourselves. The education we shall need is one which enables us to expound, defend, implement, and possibly invent a political ideology.

In casting around for some convincing demonstration that this understanding of politics reveals a self-moved manner of activity, we should no doubt consider ourselves rewarded if we could find an example of politics being conducted precisely in this manner. This at least would constitute a sign that we were on the right track. The defect, it will be remembered, of the understanding of politics as a purely empirical activity was that it revealed, not a manner of activity at all, but an abstraction; and this defect made itself manifest in our inability to find a *style* of politics which was anything more than an approximation to it. How does the understanding of politics as empiricism joined with an ideology fare in this respect? And without being overconfident, we may perhaps think that this is where we wade ashore. For we would appear to be in no difficulty whatever in finding an example of political activity which corresponds to this understanding of it: half the world, at a conservative estimate, seems to conduct its affairs in precisely this manner. And further, is it not so manifestly a possible style of politics that, even if we disagree with a particular ideology, we find nothing technically absurd in the writings of those who urge it upon us as an admirable style of politics? At least its advocates seem to know what they are talking about: they understand not only the manner of the activity but also the sort of knowledge and the kind of education it involves. 'Every schoolboy in Russia,' wrote Sir Norman Angel, 'is familiar with the doctrine of Marx and can recite its catechism. How many British schoolboys have any corresponding knowledge of the principles enunciated by Mill in his incomparable essay on Liberty?' 'Few people,' says Mr. E. H. Carr, 'any longer contest the thesis that the child should be educated in the official ideology of his country.' In short, if we are looking for a sign to indicate that the understanding of politics as empirical activity preceded by ideological activity is an adequate understanding, we can scarcely be mistaken in supposing that we have it to hand.

And yet there is perhaps room for doubt: doubt first of all whether in principle this understanding of politics reveals a self-moved manner of activity; and doubt, consequentially, whether what have been identified as examples of a *style* of politics corresponding exactly to this understanding have been properly identified.

The contention we are investigating is that attending to the arrangements of a society can begin with a premeditated ideology, can begin with independently acquired knowledge of the ends to be pursued.[1] It is supposed that a political ideology is the product of intellectual premeditation and that, because it is a body of principles not itself in debt to the activity of attending to the arrangements of a society, it is able to determine and guide the direction of

[1] This is the case, for example, with Natural Law; whether it is taken to be an explanation of political activity or (improperly) as a guide to political conduct.

that activity. If, however, we consider more closely the character of a political ideology, we find at once that this supposition is falsified. So far from a political ideology being the quasi-divine parent of political activity, it turns out to be its earthly stepchild. Instead of an independently premeditated scheme of ends to be pursued, it is a system of ideas abstracted from the manner in which people have been accustomed to go about the business of attending to the arrangements of their societies. The pedigree of every political ideology shows it to be the creature, not of premeditation in advance of political activity, but of meditation upon a manner of politics. In short, political activity comes first and a political ideology follows after; and the understanding of politics we are investigating has the disadvantage of being, in the strict sense, preposterous.

Let us consider the matter first in relation to scientific hypothesis, which I have taken to play a role in scientific activity in some respects similar to that of an ideology in politics. If a scientific hypothesis were a self-generated bright idea which owed nothing to scientific activity, then empiricism governed by hypothesis could be considered to compose a self-contained manner of activity; but this certainly is not its character. The truth is that only a man who is already a scientist can formulate a scientific hypothesis; that is, an hypothesis is not an independent invention capable of guiding scientific inquiry, but a dependent supposition which arises as an abstraction from within already existing scientific activity. Moreover, even when the specific hypothesis has in this manner been formulated, it is inoperative as a guide to research without constant reference to the traditions of scientific inquiry from which it was abstracted. The concrete situation does not appear until the specific hypothesis, which is the occasion of empiricism being set to work, is recognized as itself the creature of knowing how to conduct a scientific inquiry.

Or consider the example of cookery. It might be supposed that an ignorant man, some edible materials, and a cookery book compose together the necessities of a self-moved (or concrete) activity called cooking. But nothing is further from the truth. The cookery book is not an independently generated beginning from which cooking can spring; it is nothing more than an abstract of somebody's knowledge of how to cook: it is the stepchild, not the parent of the activity. The book, in its turn, may help to set a man on to dressing a dinner, but if it were his sole guide he could never, in fact, begin: the book speaks only to those who know already the kind of thing to expect from it and consequently how to interpret it.

Now, just as a cookery book presupposes somebody who knows how to cook, and its use presupposes somebody who already knows how to use it, and just as a scientific hypothesis springs from a knowledge of how to conduct a scientific investigation and separated from that knowledge is powerless to set empiricism profitably to work, so a political ideology must be understood, not as an independently premeditated beginning for political activity, but as knowledge (abstract and generalized) of a concrete manner of attending to the arrangements of a society. The catechism which sets out the purposes to be pursued merely abridges a concrete manner of behaviour in which those purposes are already hidden. It does not exist in advance of political activity, and by itself it is always an insufficient guide. Political enterprises, the ends to be pursued, the arrangements to be established (all the normal ingredients of a political ideology), cannot be premeditated in advance of a manner of attending to the arrangements of a society; *what* we do, and moreover what we want to do, is the creature of *how* we are accustomed to conduct our affairs. Indeed, it often reflects no more than a discovered ability to do something which is then translated into an authority to do it.

On August 4, 1789, for the complex and bankrupt social and political system of France was substituted the Rights of Man. Reading this document we come to the conclusion that somebody has done some thinking. Here, displayed in a few sentences, is a political ideology: a system of rights and duties, a scheme of ends—justice, freedom, equality, security, property, and the rest—ready and waiting to be put into practice for the first time. 'For the first time?' Not a bit of it. This ideology no more existed in advance of political practice than a cookery book exists in advance of knowing how to cook. Certainly it was the product of somebody's reflection, but it was not the product of reflection in advance of political activity. For here, in fact, are disclosed, abstracted and abridged, the common law rights of Englishmen, the gift not of independent premeditation or divine munificence, but of centuries of the day-to-day attending to the arrangements of an historic society. Or consider Locke's *Second Treatise of Civil Government*, read in America and in France in the eighteenth century as a statement of abstract principles to be put into practice, regarded there as a preface to political activity. But so far from being a preface, it has all the marks of a postscript, and its power to guide derived from its roots in actual political experience. Here, set down in abstract terms, is a brief conspectus of the manner in which Englishmen were accustomed to go about the business of attending to their arrangements—a brilliant abridgment of the political habits of Englishmen. Or consider this passage from a contemporary continental writer: 'Freedom keeps Europeans

in unrest and movement. They wish to have freedom, and at the same time
they know they have not got it. They know also that freedom belongs to man
as a human right.' And having established the end to be pursued, political
activity is represented as the realization of this end. But the 'freedom' which
can be pursued is not an independently premeditated 'ideal' or a dream; like
scientific hypothesis, it is something which is already intimated in a concrete
manner of behaving. Freedom, like a recipe for game pie, is not a bright idea;
it is not a 'human right' to be deduced from some speculative concept of
human nature. The freedom which we enjoy is nothing more than arrangements, procedures of a certain kind: the freedom of an Englishman is not
something exemplified in the procedure of *habeas corpus*, it *is*, at that point,
the availability of that procedure. And the freedom which we wish to enjoy is
not an 'ideal' which we premeditate independently of our political experience, it is what is already intimated in that experience.

On this reading, then, the systems of abstract ideas we call 'ideologies' are
abstracts of some kind of concrete activity. Most political ideologies, and
certainly the most useful of them (because they unquestionably have their
use), are abstracts of the political traditions of some society. But it sometimes
happens that an ideology is offered as a guide to politics which is an abstract,
not of political experience, but of some other manner of activity—war, religion, or the conduct of industry, for example. And here the model we are
shown is not only abstract, but is also inappropriate on account of the irrelevance of the activity from which it has been abstracted. This, I think, is one
of the defects of the model provided by the Marxist ideology. But the important point is that, at most, an ideology is an abbreviation of some manner of
concrete activity.

We are now, perhaps, in a position to perceive more accurately the character
of what may be called the ideological *style* of politics, and to observe that its
existence offers no ground for supposing that the understanding of political
activity as empiricism guided solely by an ideology is an adequate understanding. The ideological style of politics is a confused style. Properly
speaking, it is a traditional manner of attending to the arrangements of a
society which has been abridged into a doctrine of ends to be pursued, the
abridgment (together with the necessary technical knowledge) being errone-
ously regarded as the sole guide relied upon. In certain circumstances an
abridgment of this kind may be valuable; it gives sharpness of outline and
precision to a political tradition which the occasion may make seem appropriate. When a manner of attending to arrangements is to be transplanted
from the society in which it has grown up into another society (always a

questionable enterprise), the simplification of an ideology may appear as an asset. If, for example, the English manner of politics is to be planted else-where in the world, it is perhaps appropriate that it should first be abridged into something called 'democracy' before it is packed up and shipped abroad. There is, of course, an alternative method: the method by which what is exported is the detail and not the abridgment of the tradition and the work-men travel with the tools—the method which made the British Empire. But it is a slow and costly method. And, particularly with men in a hurry, *l'homme à programme* with his abridgment wins every time; his slogans enchant, while the resident magistrate is seen only as a sign of servility. But whatever the apparent appropriateness on occasion of the ideological style of politics, the defect of the explanation of political activity connected with it becomes apparent when we consider the sort of knowledge and the kind of education it encourages us to believe is sufficient for understanding the activity of attending to the arrangements of a society. For it suggests that a knowledge of the chosen political ideology can take the place of understanding a tradi-tion of political behaviour. The wand and the book come to be regarded as themselves potent, and not merely the symbols of potency. The arrangements of a society are made to appear, not as manners of behaviour, but as pieces of machinery to be transported about the world indiscriminately. The complex-ities of the tradition which have been squeezed out in the process of abridg-ment are taken to be unimportant: the 'rights of man' are understood to exist insulated from a manner of attending to arrangements. And because, in prac-tice, the abridgment is never by itself a sufficient guide, we are encouraged to fill it out, not with our suspect political experience, but with experience drawn from other (often irrelevant) concretely understood activities, such as war, the conduct of industry, or Trade Union negotiation.

III

The understanding of politics as the activity of attending to the arrangements of a society under the guidance of an independently premeditated ideology is, then, no less a misunderstanding than the understanding of it as a purely empirical activity. Wherever else politics may begin, they cannot begin in ideological activity. And in an attempt to improve upon this understanding of politics, we have already observed in principle what needs to be recognized in order to have an intelligible concept. Just as scientific hypothesis cannot appear, and is impossible to operate, except within an already existing tradition of scientific investigation, so a scheme of ends for political activity appears within, and can be evaluated only when it is related to, an already existing tradition of how to attend to our arrangements. In politics, the only concrete manner of activity detectable is one in which empiricism and the ends to be pursued are recognized as dependent, alike for their existence and their operation, upon a traditional manner of behaviour.

Politics is the activity of attending to the general arrangements of a collection of people who, in respect of their common recognition of a manner of attending to its arrangements, compose a single community. To suppose a collection of people without recognized traditions of behaviour, or one which enjoyed arrangements which intimated no direction for change and needed no attention,[2] is to suppose a people incapable of politics. This activity, then, springs neither from instant desires, nor from general principles, but from the existing traditions of behaviour themselves. And the form it takes, because it can take no other, is the amendment of existing arrangements by exploring and pursuing what is intimated in them. The arrangements which constitute a society capable of political activity, whether they are customs or institutions or laws or diplomatic decisions, are at once coherent and incoherent; they compose a pattern and at the same time they intimate a sympathy for what does not fully appear. Political activity is the exploration of that sympathy; and consequently, relevant political reasoning will be the convincing exposure of a sympathy, present but not yet followed up, and the convincing demonstration that now is the appropriate moment for recognizing it. For example, the legal status of women in our society was for a long time (and perhaps still is) in comparative confusion, because the rights and duties which composed it intimated rights and duties which were nevertheless not recognized. And, on the view of things I am suggesting, the only cogent reason to be advanced for the technical 'enfranchisement' of women was that in all or most other important respects they had already been enfranchised. Arguments drawn from abstract natural right, from 'justice', or from some general concept of feminine personality, must be regarded as either irrelevant, or as unfortunately disguised forms of the one valid argument; namely, that there was an incoherence in the arrangements of the society which pressed convincingly for remedy. In politics, then, every enterprise is a consequential enterprise, the pursuit, not of a dream, or of a general principle, but of an intimation. What we have to do with is something less imposing than logical implications or necessary consequences; but if the intimations of a tradition of behaviour are less dignified or more elusive than these, they are not on that account less important. Of course, there is no piece of mistake-proof apparatus by means of which we can elicit the intimation most worth while pursuing; and not only do we often make gross errors of judgment in this matter, but also the total effect of a desire satisfied is so little to be forecast, that our activity of

[2]E.g. a society in which law was believed to be a divine gift.

amendment is often found to lead us where we would not go. Moreover, the whole enterprise is liable at any moment to be perverted by the incursion of an approximation to empiricism in the pursuit of power. These are features which can never be eliminated; they belong to the character of political activity. But it may be believed that our mistakes of understanding will be less frequent and less disastrous if we escape the illusion that politics is ever anything more than the pursuit of intimations; a conversation, not an argument.

Now, every society which is intellectually alive is liable, from time to time, to abridge its tradition of behaviour into a scheme of abstract ideas; and on occasion political discussion will be concerned, not (like the debates in the *Iliad*) with isolated transactions, nor (like the speeches in Thucydides) with policies and traditions of activity, but with general principles. And in this there is no harm; perhaps even some positive benefit. It is possible that the distorting mirror of an ideology will reveal important hidden passages in the tradition, as a caricature reveals the potentialities of a face; and if this is so, the intellectual enterprise of seeing what a tradition looks like when it is reduced to an ideology will be a useful part of political education. But to make use of abridgment as a technique for exploring the intimations of a political tradition, to use it, that is, as a scientist uses hypothesis, is one thing; it is something different, and something inappropriate, to understand political activity itself as the activity of amending the arrangements of a society so as to make them agree with the provisions of an ideology. For then a character has been attributed to an ideology which it is unable to sustain, and we may find ourselves, in practice, directed by a false and a misleading guide: false, because in the abridgment, however skilfully it has been performed, a single intimation is apt to be exaggerated and proposed for unconditional pursuit and the benefit to be had from observing what the distortion reveals is lost when the distortion itself is given the office of a criterion; misleading, because the abridgment itself never, in fact, provides the whole of the knowledge used in political activity.

There will be some people who, though in general agreement with this under-standing of political activity, will suspect that it confuses what is, perhaps, normal with what is necessary, and that important exceptions (of great con-temporary relevance) have been lost in a hazy generality. It is all very well, it may be said, to observe in politics the activity of exploring and pursuing the intimations of a tradition of behaviour, but what light does this throw upon a political crisis such as the Norman Conquest of England, or the establishment of the Soviet *régime* in Russia? It would be foolish, of course, to deny the possibility of serious political crisis. But if we exclude (as we must) a genuine cataclysm which for the time being made an end of politics by altogether obliterating a current tradition of behaviour (which is *not* what happened in Anglo-Saxon England or in Russia), there is little to support the view that even the most serious political upheaval carries us outside this understanding of politics. A tradition of behaviour is not a fixed and inflexible manner of doing things; it is a flow of sympathy. It may be temporarily disrupted by the incursion of a foreign influence, it may be diverted, restricted, arrested, or become dried-up, and it may reveal so deep-seated an incoherence that (even without foreign assistance) a crisis appears. And if, in order to meet these crises, there were some steady, unchanging, independent guide to which a society might resort, it would no doubt be well advised to do so. But no such guide exists; we have no resources outside the fragments, the vestiges, the relics of its own tradition of behaviour which the crisis has left untouched. For even the help we may get from the traditions of another society (or from a tradition of a vaguer sort which is shared by a number of societies) is conditional upon our being able to assimilate them to our own arrangements and our own manner of attending to our arrangements. The hungry and helpless man is mistaken if he supposes that he overcomes the crisis by means of a tin-opener: what saves him is somebody else's knowledge of how to cook, which he can make use of only because he is not himself entirely ignorant. In short, political crisis (even when it seems to be imposed upon a society by changes beyond its control) always appears *within* a tradition of political activity; and 'salvation' comes from the unimpaired resources of the tradition itself. Those societies which retain, in changing circumstances, a lively sense of their own identity and continuity (which are without that hatred of their own experience which makes them desire to efface it) are to be counted fortunate, not because they possess what others lack, but because they have already mobilized what none is without and all, in fact, rely upon.

In political activity, then, men sail a boundless and bottomless sea; there is neither harbour for shelter nor floor for anchorage, neither starting-place nor appointed destination. The enterprise is to keep afloat on an even keel; the sea is both friend and enemy; and the seamanship consists in using the resources of a traditional manner of behaviour in order to make a friend of every hostile occasion.

A depressing doctrine, it will be said—even by those who do not make the mistake of adding in an element of crude determinism which, in fact, it has no place for. A tradition of behaviour is not a groove within which we are destined to grind out our helpless and unsatisfying lives. . . . But in the main the depression springs from the exclusion of hopes that were false and the discovery that guides, reputed to be of superhuman wisdom and skill, are, in fact, of a somewhat different character. If the doctrine deprives us of a model laid up in heaven to which we should approximate our behaviour, at least it does not lead us into a morass where every choice is equally good or equally to be deplored. And if it suggests that politics are *nur für die Schwindelfreie*, that should depress only those who have lost their nerve.

A Critique of Oakeshott's Distinction*

J. W. N. Watkins

The conception of moral and political activity which Professor Oakeshott evolves from his understanding of practical knowledge and activity in general is clearly interesting and important. I shall not stay to applaud its merits but shall move on to consider what seems to me to be a central weakness whose removal, far from causing the structure to collapse would, I think, leave it more securely based.

The supposition that 'rational politics' means establishing a comprehensive conception of the ideal (and of the method of attaining it) in advance of political reform has been criticised on the grounds that it is not, in fact, a *rational* method of politics at all, since there are cogent reasons for supposing that the cost of a single-minded application of it will far outweigh any possible gain.[1] But Professor Oakeshott claims that it is an impossible form of politics and, as a corollary, that 'the pursuit of intimations' is not so much the most desirable form politics can take as 'the form it takes because it can take no other'. In other words, when revolutionary leaders, say, or political parties believe themselves to be practising ideological politics they labour under a misapprehension. They are actually relying, not on speculative ideas, but on other people's and their own practical experience, since ideologies always are abridgements of some practical experience and because no one ever does work out a comprehensive system of ends and means before

*The original form of this critique appeared in J. W. N. Watkins, "Political Tradition and Political Theory: An Examination of Professor Oakeshott's Political Philosophy," *Philosophical Quarterly*, 2 (1952), 333-337. Professor Watkins has revised the selection included here. Reprinted by permission.

[1] By Professor [Karl] Popper, for instance, in *The Open Society*, Vol. I, Ch. 9. He calls this method "Utopian engineering."

embarking upon a long-term activity—we all work things out ambulando in the course of our activity.

Thus, apart from the assumption that it is foolish to try to behave in a way in which it is impossible to behave, there is, Professor Oakeshott claims, nothing merely ethical in his critique of ideological politics. Purely ideological politics, he says, are impossible, an illusion; and if the ordinary pursuit of political intimations is overlaid and distorted by an ideology then the mongrel form of quasi-ideological politics which results is undesirable simply because its practitioners misconceive what they are doing and therefore do it worse than they would otherwise have done.

No one, I think, would assert that politics could ever be nothing but an a priori application of abstract principles worked out in vacuo; yet to say that politics can never be one hundred per cent ideological but must always owe much to experience is not to say, as Professor Oakeshott does say, that politics can never be influenced by political speculations containing genuinely novel elements. He claims that politics can never be genuinely ideological in this weaker sense because a genuine political ideology, i.e. a political theory which is more than a formalised abstraction from some experience in practical activity, is impossible.

This seems to me the central weakness in his argument; and in the remainder of this article I shall try to show that his attempt to criticise soi-disant ideological politics simply on the ground that they essay the impossible and to commend political traditionalism simply on the ground that there is no genuine alternative, lies at the centre of a nest of difficulties which would vanish if he evaluated the roles of reason and tradition in politics in the light of a normative political philosophy.

First, in order to support his contention that ideologies are nothing but abridgements of some traditional manner of doing things, he has to deny that there can ever be any real novelty or originality in speculative thought. An ideology, however, may surely express a reaction from some dominant experience. Marxism, he claims, is an abridgement of experience in war and industry applied to politics, but I confess I do not find this altogether convincing. Marxism, surely, has largely speculative origins—in German metaphysics, British economics and French socialism, and the last of these was a repudiation, rather than an abridgement, of eighteenth century commercialism. No doubt an ideology must, in a loose sense, 'follow' some practical activity, but its debt may be largely negative, and it may lead to a transformation of the activity. His thesis that ideologies leave out the complexities of some practical activity without ever adding anything significantly new presupposes what seems to me to be an unduly restrictive theory of imaginative thinking.

Consistency requires him to carry this denial of the novelty of all speculative thought into the field in which it would seem least tenable, the field of scientific enquiry. For he recognises an analogy between the relation of an ideology to a political tradition and the relation of a scientific hypothesis to a scientific tradition. We can agree with him when he says 'that only a man who is already a scientist can formulate a scientific hypothesis', but we may demur when he adds that a hypothesis is 'a dependent supposition which arises as an abstraction from within already existing scientific activity', an abstraction from '*traditions* of scientific enquiry'.[2] A strange kind of back-dating of scientific discoveries and inventions is implied by the suggestion that every new scientific hypothesis is no more than an articulated abridgement of something *already there*. For it cannot always have been there: people must have brought it into existence at some earlier period. If Kepler's three laws, say, are no more than an explicit summary of pre-existing material, the question arises: when and by whom was the earlier and genuinely creative work done, of which Kepler subsequently gave a digest?

This leads me to a second difficulty: it seems to me that Professor Oakeshott's traditionalism spoils his account of traditional activity. To make my objection plain I must draw a distinction between the way in which a decision is reached and the external character of the action decided upon. A person who disregards moral considerations has an amoral outlook, but this does not imply that he commits immoral acts. Similarly, someone who disregards precedents and who tries to decide what to do in the light of independent principles may be said to have an 'a-traditional' outlook, but his actions may nevertheless fit comfortably into a tradition of behaviour. On this terminology, 'a-traditional' is the contrary of 'traditionalist' and each of these terms denotes a certain frame of mind. The point I want to make is that the men who have really fostered vigorous traditions have not been mere traditionalists. In his *Memoirs*, Mr. Churchill describes how, in 1941, he decided to send a convoy of tanks through the Mediterranean to Wavell, instead of sending it by the much longer and safer Cape route. I think his state of mind then could fairly be called 'a-traditional'. He was not harking back to Pitt or Canning, or pondering what his father would have done. He had to argue the merits of his proposal before his colleagues, and to convince them that it was right to take the risk and that it would be wrong to delay re-inforcements. I

---

[2] Michael Oakeshott, *Political Education,* An Inaugural Lecture (Cambridge: Bowes and Bowes, 1951), pp. 14-15 (my italics).

reckon that he could have stated pretty definitely the criteria by which he judged these alternatives right and wrong, and I am convinced that such principles as loyalty to military commanders, and the need to save British lives, impressed themselves on him as objective obligations. But to say that he reached a decision which he believed to be nationally defensible in the light of what were felt by him as objective criteria is not to say that his decision was untraditional. On the contrary, it is decisions like this which are the stuff of the best tradition of British wartime leadership, just as the work of men like Galileo and Einstein, neither of them traditionalists, is the stuff of the scientific tradition.

But Professor Oakeshott's conception of mental activity allows no room for any genuinely a-traditional component. People who resort to supposedly general principles, he says, are in fact resorting to distorting simplifications of a tradition. It clearly follows that such people are more likely to corrupt their tradition than to foster it. Now the person who does not resort to such principles is the traditionalist; and a sort of sympathetic sensitivity towards his tradition will enable him, according to Professor Oakeshott, to pursue what it intimates. The tradition gives and he takes. I have argued that in fact vigorous traditions are largely generated by men doing what is intimated by the principles in which they believe; there is a mutual give-and-take between them and their tradition. I believe that Professor Oakeshott's assumption that traditional behaviour implies a traditionalist outlook is another consequence of what I consider the central weakness in his thesis: namely, his insistence that ideological politics, properly so-called are impossible because there can be no genuinely a-traditional component in a person's thinking.

The third difficulty is that it is impossible to read Professor Oakeshott without gaining the impression that there are very definite values implicit in his writings which often place him in strong opposition to current tendencies and proposals which seem to be 'intimated' by the contemporary 'flow of sympathies'—for instance, the decline of the apprentice-system, and the extension of the discretionary powers of government. True, when he criticises such tendencies he usually avoids words like 'bad', 'wrong', 'undesirable', and uses words like 'corrupting', 'eccentric', 'unhealthy', 'damaging', i.e. words which, if used literally in a narrow context, might have a purely descriptive connotation; but he uses them metaphorically in a political context, and here they undoubtedly express evaluations.

Lastly, it must be remembered that only thinking can teach us the dangers and limitations of speculative thought. That Professor Oakeshott does believe that the only cure for bad theory is better theory is implicit in the fact that he systematically criticises ideological politics; but he sometimes says that the cure for bad political theory is to stop theorising and to submit to habit and tradition and inherited belief instead. Now although he attributes the prevalence of political ideologising partly to the fact that the modern politician has to justify himself before an audience (i.e. to the fact that he works within a parliamentary or democratic framework), Professor Oakeshott does not seem to have reckoned with the full implications of this. It is perhaps significant that he does not mention an obvious and important difference between activities like cooking, and political activity: a cook may be taciturn yet good at his job, but a politician in the highly vocal, argumentative, Western political world cannot be. Having to answer questions and meet criticisms he is inevitably a rationaliser, and his rationalisations obviously invite critical scrutiny. It is really non-ideological politics which have become impossible in the West, because a process of increasing critical awareness cannot reverse itself. We cannot consciously make ourselves more naive, or argue ourselves into habit and tradition. Eating the forbidden fruit may teach us that we should be happier if we had never plucked it, but it cannot teach us how to restore it to the tree. Intemperate 'rationalistic' attacks on tradition can only be criticised from the standpoint of a more mature and catholic rationality. The philosophe must be answered by the philosopher. Acceptance of this is, as I have said, implicit in the way Professor Oakeshott goes about his task; and I believe that if he brought this acceptance into the open and admitted that in criticising ideological politics he was trying to advance to a more comprehensive political philosophy and not simply to revert to traditionalism, and if he adopted the moral standpoint which is in any case implicit in his criticisms, then all the difficulties I have indicated would disappear. Needing only to maintain that ideological politics are largely undesirable in their rejection of historical experience, but not impossible, he would no longer need to deny the occasional novelty, and power, and even fruitfulness of speculative thinking. Having officially recognised his own moral position he could recognise the a-traditional principles to which the creators of a tradition adhere, and he would also be justified in discriminating between antithetical traditions, and in criticising the turn a tradition was taking. And having admitted that genuine speculation is possible, his own political philosophy would no longer be in danger of refuting itself.

His critique of ideological politics would then be less sweeping; but it would be based, not precariously on a mixture of sceptical relativism and dubious psychological assumptions, but solidly on principles and arguments with which many would sympathise and agree.

Chapter Nine

The Limiting Case of Ideological
Politics: Totalitarianism

More than fifty years have passed since the first of the twentieth-century
totalitarian regimes was established. But only in the aftermath of the Second
World War did scholars begin to make a concerted effort to analyze the
nature of these regimes. Hannah Arendt has contributed greatly to this effort.
Her well-known book, *The Origins of Totalitarianism*, first appeared in 1951
and was re-issued in a revised edition in 1966. The Preface to the first edition
reveals her apprehension that the appearance of totalitarian regimes marks a
decisive turning point in man's historical experience. The essay which follows
was added to the revised edition as the concluding chapter. In it, Miss Arendt
analyzes the ideological basis of totalitarian regimes. That analysis reflects the
importance of understanding both the political history and the political
thought of the West as a foundation for the evaluation of this paradigmatic
form of ideological politics.

Ideology and Terror*

Hannah Arendt

I

The following considerations have grown out of a study of the origins, the elements and the functioning of that novel form of government and domination which we have come to call totalitarian. Wherever it rose to power, it developed entirely new political institutions and destroyed all social, legal and political traditions of the country. No matter what the specifically national tradition or the particular spiritual source of its ideology, totalitarian government always transformed classes into masses, supplanted the party system, not by one-party dictatorships, but by a mass movement, shifted the center of power from the army to the police, and established a foreign policy openly directed toward world domination. Present totalitarian governments have developed from one-party systems; whenever these became truly totalitarian, they started to operate according to a system of values so radically different from all others, that none of our traditional legal, moral, or common sense utilitarian categories could any longer help us to come to terms with, or judge, or predict its course of action.

If it is true that the elements of totalitarianism can be found by retracing the history and analyzing the political implications of what we usually call the crisis of our century, then the conclusion is unavoidable that this crisis is no mere threat from the outside, no mere result of some aggressive foreign policy of either Germany or Russia, and that it will no more disappear with the fall of Soviet Russia than it disappeared with the fall of Nazi Germany. It may even be that the true predicaments of our time will assume their authentic form—though not necessarily the cruelest—only when totalitarianism has become a thing of the past.

It is in the line of such reflections to raise the question whether totalitarian government, born of this crisis and at the same time its clearest and only unequivocal symptom, is merely a make-shift arrangement, which borrows its methods of intimidation, its means of organization and its instruments of violence from the well-known political arsenal of tyranny, despotism and

*Hannah Arendt, "Ideology and Terror: A Novel Form of Government," *The Review of Politics,* 15 (July 1953), 303-327. Reprinted by permission.

dictatorships, and owes its existence only to the deplorable, but perhaps accidental failure of the traditional political forces—liberal or conservative, national or socialist, republican or monarchist, authoritarian or democratic. Or whether, on the contrary, there is such a thing as the *nature* of totalitarian government, whether it has its own essence and can be compared with and defined like other forms of government such as Western thought has known and recognized since the times of ancient philosophy.

Questions of this sort have been out of fashion for a long time and for reasons which may have more than a little to do with those modern developments which eventually brought about a crisis of Western politics no less than of Western political thought. More specifically, such questions have been thought superfluous, if not meaningless, ever since the social sciences established their rule over the whole field of politics and history. Interesting in this development, which easily can be traced back to Marx, was that sociology from its beginnings showed a marked tendency to explain political institutions and historical developments in terms of psychological types; all the well-known clichés of the lower middle classes, the bureaucracy, the intelligentsia have already that particular tinge of typification which shows itself openly in categories such as "the authoritarian personality." More recently, with the growing disappointment in the strictly Marxist explanation of history, psychology itself with its new Freudian concepts of super-ego, father-image, and oedipus complex, has invaded the social sciences and continues to provide them with their chief tools of "evaluation" to such an extent that it has become difficult to tell the two sciences from each other.

This new-fangled mixture of sociology and psychology is no accident. Both sciences have their origin in a liberalism that viewed politics (and more or less all human affairs) under the dual category of society and individual. Men became mere parts of a society that conditioned or determined the individuals, as the whole determines its parts. In this sense, sociology and psychology have always been two sides of the same medal, the one dealing with the functioning of the whole (society), the other with the functioning of the parts (individuals). The trouble came when psychology, notwithstanding its respect for society, discovered that even these individuals, whose whole interior life was supposed to be conditioned by, or to react against, social circumstances, possess a "soul." But we have souls only as long as we are more than mere members of society where this psychological side of our being has always created disturbances. Manners and conventions, all public morals and *mores* help us to control our souls so that we can function on a merely social level. Individual psychology, since it looked on man as though he were nothing but an individual part of society, has developed into a science which deals mostly with abnormal behavior patterns: all "psychological" attitudes become abnormal when they occur in society because they have been stripped of the privacy in which alone a man's soul can function "normally." Individual psychology became fashionable wherever customs and conventions, the whole texture of morality which is the lifeblood of society, lost their authority. The modern individual is the surviving member of a society which no longer exists; it is a part that lost its place in the whole. In this situation, the psychological sciences have become increasingly social-minded and direct their greatest efforts toward the re-adjustment of isolated individuals. The trouble is that society as a whole, that is, as something which is greater than the sum total of its parts, no longer exists. The best demonstration of this is that the social sciences can conceive of society now only in terms of individual behavior patterns, which they indiscriminately apply to collective bodies where such behavior never occurs.

The great merit of this confusion is that it somehow has awakened us to the fact that political bodies, to quote a long-forgotten remark of Plato, do not spring from oak and rock. (Rep. viii, 544D) Yet, they do not spring from within our particular and individual selves either. The old Roman distinction between *res publica* and *res privata* is still valid. Political forms of organization concern matters which are of equal concern to each of us because they occur *between us*. Our question whether there is such a thing as the nature of totalitarian domination means actually whether the entirely new and unprecedented forms of totalitarian organization and course of action rest on one of the few basic experiences which men can make whenever they live together, and are concerned with public affairs. If there is a basic experience which finds its political expression in totalitarian domination, then, in view of the novelty of the totalitarian form of government, this must be an experience which, for whatever reason, has never before served as the foundation of a body politic and whose general mood—although it may be familiar in every other respect—never before has pervaded, and directed the handling of, public affairs.

If we consider this in terms of the history of ideas, it seems extremely unlikely. For the forms of government under which men live have been very few; they were discovered early, classified by the Greeks and have proved extraordinarily long-lived. If we apply these findings, whose fundamental idea, despite many variations, did not change in the two and a half thousand years that separate Plato from Kant, we are tempted at once to interpret totalitarianism as some modern form of tyranny, that is a lawless government where power is wielded by one man. Arbitrary power, unrestricted by law, yielded in the interest of the ruler and hostile to the interests of the governed, on one hand, fear as the principle of action, namely fear of the people by the ruler and fear of the ruler by the people, on the other—these have been the hallmarks of tyranny throughout our tradition.

Instead of saying that totalitarian government is unprecedented, we could also say that it has exploded the very alternative on which all definitions of the essence of governments have been based in political philosophy, that is the alternative between lawful and lawless government, between arbitrary and legitimate power. That lawful government and legitimate power, on one side, lawlessness and arbitrary power on the other, belonged together and were inseparable has never been questioned. Yet, totalitarian rule confronts us with a totally different kind of government. It defies, it is true, all positive laws, even to the extreme of defying those which it has itself established (as in the case of the Soviet Constitution of 1936, to quote only the most outstanding example) or which it did not care to abolish (as in the case of the Weimar Constitution which the Nazi government never revoked). But it operates neither without guidance of law nor is it arbitrary, for it claims to obey strictly and unequivocally those laws of Nature or of History from which all positive laws always have been supposed to spring.

It is the monstrous, yet seemingly unanswerable claim of totalitarian rule that, far from being "lawless," it goes to the sources of authority from which positive laws received their ultimate legitimation, that far from being arbitrary it is more obedient to these suprahuman forces than any government ever was before, and that far from wielding its power in the interest of one man, it is quite prepared to sacrifice everybody's vital immediate interests to the execution of what it assumes to be the law of History or the law of Nature. Its defiance of positive laws claims to be a higher form of legitimacy which, since it is inspired by the sources themselves, can do away with petty legality. Totalitarian lawfulness pretends to have found a way to establish the rule of justice on earth—something which the legality of positive law admittedly could never attain. The discrepancy between legality and justice could never be bridged because the standards of right and wrong into which positive law translates its own source of authority—"natural law" governing the whole universe, or divine law revealed in human history or customs and traditions expressing the law common to the sentiments of all men—are necessarily general and must be valid for a countless and unpredictable number of cases, so that each concrete individual case with its unrepeatable set of circumstances somehow escapes it.

Totalitarian lawfulness, defying legality and pretending to establish the direct reign of justice on earth, executes the law of History or of Nature without translating it into standards of right and wrong for individual behavior. It applies the law directly to mankind without bothering with the behavior of men. The law of Nature or the law of History, if properly executed, is expected to produce mankind as its end product; and this expectation lies behind the claim to global rule of all totalitarian governments. Totalitarian policy claims to transform the human species into an active unfailing carrier of a law to which human beings otherwise would only passively and reluctantly be subjected. If it is true that the link between totalitarian countries and the civilized world was broken through the monstrous crimes of totalitarian regimes, it is also true that this criminality was not due to simple aggressiveness, ruthlessness, warfare and treachery, but to a conscious break of that *consensus iuris* which, according to Cicero constitutes a "people," and which, as international law, in modern times has constituted the civilized world insofar as it remains the foundation-stone of international relations even under the conditions of war. Both moral judgment and legal punishment presuppose this basic consent; the criminal can be judged justly only because he takes part in the *consensus iuris*, and even the revealed law of God can function among men only when they listen and consent to it.

At this point the fundamental difference between the totalitarian and all other concepts of law comes to light. Totalitarian policy does not replace one set of laws with another, does not establish its own *consensus iuris*, does not create, by one revolution, a new form of legality. Its defiance of all, even its own positive laws implies that it believes it can do without any *consensus iuris* whatever, and still not resign itself to the tyrannical state of lawlessness, arbitrariness and fear. It can do without the *consensus iuris* because it promises to release the fulfillment of law from all action and will of man; and it promises justice on earth because it claims to make mankind itself the embodiment of the law.

This identification of man and law, which seems to cancel the discrepancy between legality and justice that has plagued legal thought since ancient times, has nothing in common with the *lumen naturale* or the voice of conscience, by which Nature or Divinity as the sources of authority for the *ius naturale* or the historically revealed commands of God, are supposed to announce their authority in man himself. This never made man a walking embodiment of the law, but on the contrary remained distinct from him as the authority which demanded consent and obedience. Nature or Divinity as the source of authority for positive laws are thought of as permanent and eternal; positive laws were changing and changeable according to circumstances, but they possessed a relative permanence as compared with the much more rapidly changing actions of men; and they derived this permanence from the eternal presence of their source of authority. Positive laws, therefore, are primarily designed to function as stabilizing factors for the ever changing movements of men.

In the interpretation of totalitarianism, all laws have become *laws of movement*. When the Nazis talked about the law of Nature or when the Bolsheviks talk about the law of History, neither Nature nor History is any longer the stabilizing source of authority for the actions of mortal men; they are movements in themselves. Underlying the Nazis' belief in race laws as the expression of the law of Nature in man, is Darwin's idea of man as the product of a natural development which does not necessarily stop with the present species of human beings, just as under the Bolsheviks' belief in class-struggle as the expression of the law of History lies Marx's notion of society as the product of a gigantic historical movement which races according to its own law of motion to the end of historical times when it will abolish itself.

The difference between Marx's historical and Darwin's naturalistic approaches has frequently been pointed out, usually and rightly in favor of Marx. This has led us to forget the great and positive interest Marx took in Darwin's theories; Engels could not think of a greater compliment to Marx's scholarly achievements than to call him the "Darwin of history." If one considers, not the actual achievement but, the basic philosophies of both men, it turns out that ultimately the movement of History and the movement of Nature are one and the same. Darwin's introduction of the concept of development into nature, his insistence that, at least in the field of biology, natural movement is not circular but unilinear, moving in an infinitely progressing direction, means in fact that nature is, as it were, being swept into history, that natural life is considered to be historical. The "natural" law of the survival of the fittest is just as much a historical law and could be used as such by racism as Marx's law of the survival of the most progressive class. Marx's class struggle, on the other hand, as the driving force of history is only the outward expression of the development of productive forces which in turn have their origin in the labor *force* of men. Labor, according to Marx, is not a historical but a natural-biological "force," namely man's "metabolism with nature" by which he conserves his individual life and reproduces the species. Engels saw the affinity between the basic convictions of the two men very clearly because he understood the decisive role which the concept of development played in both theories. The tremendous intellectual change which took place in the middle of the last century consisted in the refusal to view or accept anything "as it is" and in the consistent interpretation of everything as being only a stage of some further development. Whether the driving force of this development was called nature or history is relatively secondary.

In these theories, the term "law" itself changed its meaning: from expressing the framework of stability within which human actions and motions can take place, it became the expression of the motion itself.

II

By lawful government we understand a body politic in which positive laws are needed to translate and realize the immutable *ius naturale* or the eternal commandments of God into standards of right and wrong. Only in these standards, in the body of positive laws of each country, do the *ius naturale* or the Commandments of God achieve their political reality. In the body politic of totalitarian government, this place of positive laws is taken by total terror, which is designed to translate into reality the law of movement of History or Nature. Just as positive laws, though they define transgressions, are independent of them—the absence of crimes in any society does not render laws superfluous but, on the contrary, signifies their most perfect rule—so terror in totalitarian government has ceased to be a mere means for the suppression of opposition, though it is also used for such purposes. Terror becomes total when it becomes independent of all opposition; it rules supreme when nobody any longer stands in its way. If lawfulness is the essence of non-tyrannical government and lawlessness is the essence of tyranny, then terror is the essence of totalitarian domination.

Terror is the realization of the law of movement; its chief aim is to make it possible for the force of Nature or of History to race freely through mankind, unhindered by any spontaneous human action. As such, terror seeks to "stabilize" men in order to liberate the forces of Nature or History. It is this movement which singles out the foes of mankind against whom terror is let loose, and no free action of either opposition or sympathy can be permitted to interfere with the elimination of the "objective enemy" of History or Nature, of the class or the race. Guilt and innocence become senseless notions; "guilty" is he who stands in the way of the natural or historical process which has passed judgment over "inferior races," over individuals "unfit to live," over "dying classes and decadent peoples." Terror executes these judgments, and before its court, all concerned are subjectively innocent: the murdered because they did nothing against the system, and the murderers because they do not really murder but execute a death sentence pronounced by some higher tribunal. The rulers themselves do not claim to be just or wise, but only to execute historical or natural laws; they do not apply laws, but execute a movement in accordance with its inherent law. Terror is lawfulness, if law is the law of the movement of some suprahuman force, Nature or History.

Terror as the execution of a law of movement whose ultimate goal is not the welfare of men or the interest of one man but the fabrication of mankind, eliminates individuals for the sake of the species, sacrifices the "parts" for the sake of the "whole." The suprahuman force of Nature or History has its own beginning and its own end, so that it can be hindered only by the new beginning and the individual end which the life of each man actually is.

Positive laws in constitutional government are designed to erect boundaries and establish channels of communication between men whose community is continually endangered by the new men born into it. With each new birth, a new beginning is born into the world, a new world has potentially come into being. The stability of the laws corresponds to the constant motion of all human affairs, a motion which can never end as long as men are born and die. The laws hedge in each new beginning and at the same time assure its freedom of movement, the potentiality of something entirely new and unpredictable; the boundaries of positive laws are for the political existence of man what memory is for his historical existence: they guarantee the pre-existence of a common world, the reality of some continuity which transcends the individual life span of each generation, absorbs all new origins and is nourished by them.

Total terror is so easily mistaken for a symptom of tyrannical government because totalitarian government in its initial stages must behave like a tyranny and raze the boundaries of man-made law. But total terror leaves no arbitrary lawlessness behind it and does not rage for the sake of some arbitrary will or for the sake of despotic power of one man against all, least of all for the sake of a war of all against all. It substitutes for the boundaries and channels of communication between individual men a band of iron which holds them so tightly together that it is as though their plurality had disappeared into One Man of gigantic dimensions. To abolish the fences of laws between men—as tyranny does—means to take away man's liberties and destroy freedom as a living political reality; for the space between men as it is hedged in by laws, is the living space of freedom. Total terror uses this old instrument of tyranny but destroys at the same time also the lawless, fenceless wilderness of fear and suspicion which tyranny leaves behind. This desert, to be sure, is no longer a living space of freedom, but it still provides some room for the fear-guided movements and suspicion-ridden actions of its inhabitants.

By pressing men against each other, total terror destroys the space between them; compared to the condition within its iron band, even the desert of tyranny, insofar as it is still some kind of space, appears like a guarantee of freedom. Totalitarian government does not just curtail liberties or abolish essential freedoms; nor does it, at least to our limited knowledge, succeed in eradicating the love for freedom from the hearts of man. It destroys the one essential prerequisite of all freedom which is simply the capacity of motion which cannot exist without space.

Total terror, the essence of totalitarian government, exists neither for nor against men. It is supposed to provide the forces of Nature or History with an incomparable instrument to accelerate their movement. This movement, proceeding according to its own law, cannot in the long run be hindered; eventually its force will always prove more powerful than the most powerful forces engendered by the actions and the will of men. But it can be slowed down and is slowed down almost inevitably by the freedom of man, which even totalitarian rulers cannot deny, for this freedom—irrelevant and arbitrary as they may deem it—is identical with the fact that men are being born and that therefore each of them *is* a new beginning, begins, in a sense, the world anew. From the totalitarian point of view, the fact that men are born and die can be only regarded as an annoying interference with higher forces. Terror, therefore, as the obedient servant of natural or historical movement has to eliminate from the process not only freedom in any specific sense, but the very source of freedom which is given with the fact of the birth of man and resides in his capacity to make a new beginning. In the iron band of terror, which destroys the plurality of men and makes out of many the One who unfailingly will act as though he himself were part of the course of History or Nature, a device has been found not only to liberate the historical and natural forces, but to accelerate them to a speed they never would reach if left to themselves. Practically speaking, this means that terror executes on the spot the death sentences which Nature is supposed to have pronounced on races or individuals who are "unfit to live," or History on "dying classes," without waiting for the slower and less efficient processes of Nature or History themselves.

In this concept, where the essence of government itself has become motion, a very old problem of political thought seems to have found a solution similar to the one already noted for the discrepancy between legality and justice. If the essence of government is defined as lawfulness, and if it is understood that laws are the stabilizing forces in the public affairs of men (as indeed it always has been since Plato invoked Zeus, the God of the boundaries, in his *Laws*) then the problem of movement of the body politic and the actions of its citizens arises. Lawfulness sets limitations to actions, but does not inspire them; the greatness, but also the perplexity of laws in free societies is that they only tell what one should not, but never what one should do. The necessary movement of a body politic can never be found in its essence if only because this essence—again since Plato—has always been defined with a view to its permanence. Duration seemed one of the surest yardsticks for the goodness of government. It is still, for Montesquieu, the supreme proof for the badness of tyranny that only tyrannies are liable to be destroyed from within, to decline by themselves, whereas all other governments are destroyed through exterior circumstances. Therefore what the definition of governments always needed was what Montesquieu called a "principle of action" which, different in each form of government, would inspire government and citizens alike in their public activity and serve as a criterion beyond the merely negative yardstick of lawfulness, for judging all action in public affairs. Such guiding principles and criteria of action are, according to Montesquieu, honor in a monarchy, virtue in a republic and fear in a tyranny.

In a perfect totalitarian government, where all men have become One Man, where all action aims at the acceleration of the movement of Nature or History, where every single act is the execution of a death sentence which Nature or History has already pronounced, that is, under conditions where terror can be completely relied upon to keep the movement in constant motion, no principle of action separate from its essence would be needed at all. Yet as long as totalitarian rule has not conquered the earth and with the iron band of terror made each single man a part of one mankind, terror in its double function as essence of government and principle, not of action, but of motion cannot be fully realized. Just as lawfulness in constitutional government is insufficient to inspire and guide men's actions, so terror in totalitarian government is not sufficient to inspire and guide human behavior.

While under present conditions totalitarian domination still shares with other forms of government the need for a guide for the behavior of its citizens in public affairs, it does not need and could not even use a principle of action strictly speaking, since it will eliminate precisely the capacity of man to act. Under conditions of total terror not even fear can any longer serve as an advisor of how to behave, because terror chooses its victims without reference to individual actions or thoughts, exclusively in accordance with the objective necessity of the natural or historical process. Under totalitarian conditions, fear probably is more widespread than ever before; but fear has lost its practical usefulness when actions guided by it can no longer help to avoid the dangers man fears. The same is true for sympathy or support of the regime; for total terror not only selects its victims according to objective standards; it chooses its executioners with as complete a disregard as possible for the candidate's conviction and sympathies. The consistent elimination of conviction as a motive for action has become a matter of record since the great purges in Soviet Russia and the satellite countries. The aim of totalitarian education has never been to instill convictions but to destroy the capacity to form any. The introduction of purely objective criteria into the selective system of the SS troops was Himmler's great organizational invention; he selected the candidates from photographs according to purely racial criteria. Nature itself decided, not only who was to be eliminated, but also who was to be trained as an executioner.

No guiding principle of behavior, taken itself from the realm of human action, such as virtue, honor, fear, is necessary or can be useful to set into motion a body politic which no longer uses terror as a means of intimidation, but whose essence *is* terror. In its stead, it has introduced an entirely new principle into public affairs that dispenses with human will to action altogether and appeals to the craving need for some insight into the law of movement according to which the terror functions and upon which, therefore, all private destinies depend.

The inhabitants of a totalitarian country are thrown into and caught in the process of Nature or History for the sake of accelerating its movement; as such, they can only be executioners or victims of its inherent law. The process may decide that those who today eliminate races and individuals or the members of dying classes and decadent peoples are tomorrow those who must be sacrificed. What totalitarian rule needs to guide the behavior of its subjects is a *preparation* to fit each of them equally well for the role of executioner and the role of victim. This two-sided preparation, the substitute for a principle of action, is the ideology.

III

Ideologies—isms which to the satisfaction of their adherents can explain everything and every occurrence by deducing it from a single premise—are a very recent phenomenon and, for many decades, this played a negligible role in political life. Only with the wisdom of hindsight can we discover in them certain elements which have made them so disturbingly useful for totalitarian rule. Not before Hitler and Stalin were the great political potentialities of the ideologies discovered.

Ideologies are known for their scientific character: they combine the scientific approach with results of philosophical relevance and pretend to be scientific philosophy. The word "ideology" seems to imply that an idea can become the subject matter of a science just as animals are the subject matter of zoology, and that the suffix *-logy* in ideology, as in zoology, indicates nothing but the *logoi*, the scientific statements made on it. If this were true, an ideology would indeed be a pseudo-science and a pseudo-philosophy, transgressing at the same time the limitations of science and the limitations of philosophy. Deism, for example, would then be the ideology which treats the *idea* of God, with which philosophy is concerned, in the scientific manner of theology for which God is a revealed reality. (A theology which is not based on revelation as a given reality but treats God as an idea would be as mad as a zoology which is no longer sure of the physical, tangible existence of animals.) Yet we know that this is only part of the truth. Deism, though it denies divine revelation, does not simply make "scientific" statements on a God which is only an "idea," but uses the idea of God in order to explain the course of the world. The "ideas" of isms—race in racism, God in deism, etc.— never form the subject matter of the ideologies and the suffix *-logy* never indicates simply a body of "scientific" statements.

An ideology is quite literally what its name indicates: it is the *logic of an idea*. Its subject matter is history to which the "idea" is applied; the result of this application is not a body of statements about something that *is*, but the unfolding of a *process* which is in constant change. The ideology treats the course of events as though it followed the same "law" as the logical exposition of its "idea." Ideologies pretend to know the mysteries of the whole historical process—the secrets of the past, the intricacies of the present, the uncertainties of the future—because of the logic inherent in their respective ideas.

Ideologies are never interested in the miracle of being. They are historical, concerned with becoming and perishing, with the rise and fall of cultures, even if they try to explain history by some "law of nature." The word "race" in racism does not signify any genuine curiosity about the human races as a field for scientific exploration, but is the "idea" by which the movement of history is explained as one consistent process.

The "idea" of an ideology is neither the eternal essence grasped by the eyes of the mind nor the regulator of reason—as it was from Plato to Kant—but has become an instrument of explanation. To an ideology, history does not appear in the *light* of an idea (which would imply that history is seen *sub specie* of some ideal eternity which itself is beyond historical motion) but as something which can be *calculated* by it. What fits the "idea" into this new role is its own "logic," that is a movement which is the consequence of the "idea" itself and needs no outside factor to set it into motion. Racism is the belief that there is a motion inherent in the very "idea" of race, just as deism is the belief that a motion is inherent in the very notion of God.

The movement of history and the logical process of this notion are supposed to correspond to each other, so that whatever happens, happens according to the logic of one "idea." However, the only possible movement in the realm of logic is the process of deduction from a premise. Dialectical logic, with its process from thesis through antithesis to synthesis which in turn becomes the thesis of the next dialectical movement is not different in principle, once an ideology gets hold of it; the first thesis becomes the premise and its advantage for ideological explanation is that this dialectical device can explain away factual contradictions as stages of one identical, consistent movement.

As soon as logic as a *movement* of thought and not as a necessary control of thinking—is applied to an idea, this idea is transformed into a *premise*. Ideological world explanations performed this operation long before it became so eminently fruitful for totalitarian reasoning. The purely negative coercion of logic, the prohibition of contradictions, became "productive" so that a whole line of thought could be initiated, and forced upon the mind, by drawing conclusions in the manner of mere argumentation. This argumentative process could be interrupted neither by a new idea (which would have been another premise with a different set of consequences) nor by a new experience. Ideologies always assume that one idea is sufficient to explain everything in the development from the premise, and that no experience can teach anything because everything is comprehended in this consistent process of logical deduction. The danger in exchanging the necessary insecurity of philosophical thought for the total explanation of an ideology and its *Weltanschauung*, is not even so much the risk of falling for some usually vulgar, always uncritical assumption as of exchanging the freedom inherent in man's capacity to think for the straightjacket of logic with which man can force himself almost as violently as he is forced by some outside power.

The transformation of an idea into a premise and the use of the logic of deduction as only demonstration for truth, is certainly only one of the total-itarian elements in ideologies. Another is obviously the claim of all *Weltan-schauungen* to offer total explanations of everything, mainly, of course, of past, present and future. And the emancipation from reality this method always implies, since it pretends to know beforehand everything that experience may still have in store, might, psychologically speaking, be even more important. Yet, we insisted on this peculiar logicality of ideologies because the true totalitarian rulers (Hitler and Stalin, not their forerunners) used it more than any other element when they converted ideologies—racism and the premise of the law of nature, or dialectical materialism and the premise of the law of history—into foundation stones for the new totalitarian body politic.

The device both totalitarian rulers used to transform their respective ideologies into weapons with which each of their subjects would force himself into step with the terror movement was deceptively simple and inconspicuous: they took them dead seriously, took pride the one in his supreme gift for "ice cold reasoning" (Hitler) and the other in the "mercilessness of his dialectics," and proceeded to drive ideological implications into extremes of logical consistency which, to the onlooker, looked preposterously "primitive" and absurd: a "dying class" consisted of people condemned to death; races that are "unfit to live" were to be exterminated. Whoever agreed that there are such things as "dying classes" and did not draw the consequence of killing their members, or that the right to live had something to do with race and did not draw the consequence of killing "unfit races," was plainly either stupid or a coward. This stringent logicality as a guide to action permeates the whole structure of totalitarian movements and governments. It is exclusively the work of Hitler and Stalin who, although they did not add a single new thought to the ideas and propaganda slogans of their movements, for this reason alone must be considered ideologists of the greatest importance.

What distinguished these new totalitarian ideologists from their predecessors was that it was no longer primarily the "idea" of the ideology—the struggle of classes and the exploitation of the workers or the struggle of races and the care for Germanic peoples—which appealed to them, but the logical process which could be developed from it. According to Stalin, neither the idea nor the oratory but "the irresistible force of logic thoroughly overpowered (Lenin's) audience." The power, which Marx thought was born when the idea seized the masses, was discovered to reside, not in the idea itself, but in its logical process which "like a mighty tentacle seizes you on all sides as in a vise and from whose grip you are powerless to tear yourself away; you must either surrender or make up your mind to utter defeat." (Stalin's speech of January 28, 1924; quoted from Lenin, *Selected Works*, vol. I, p. 33, Moscow, 1947.) Only when the realization of the ideological aims, the classless society or the master race, were at stake, could this force show itself. In the process of realization, the original substance upon which the ideologies based themselves as long as they had to appeal to the masses—the exploitation of the workers or the national aspirations of Germany—is gradually lost, devoured as it were by the process itself: in perfect accordance with "ice cold reasoning" and the "irresistible force of logic," the workers lost under Bolshevik rule even those rights they had been granted under Tsarist oppression and the German people suffered a kind of warfare which did not pay the slightest regard to the minimum requirements for survival of the German nation. It is in the nature of ideological politics—and is not simply a betrayal committed for the sake of self-interest or lust for power—that the real content of the ideology (the working class or the Germanic peoples), which originally had brought about the "idea" (the struggle of classes as the law of history or the struggle of races as the law of nature), is devoured by the logic with which the "idea" is carried out.

The preparation of victims and executioners which totalitarianism requires in place of Montesquieu's principle of action is not the ideology itself—racism or dialectical materialism—but its inherent logicality. The most persuasive argument in this respect, an argument of which Hitler like Stalin was very fond, is: You can't say A without saying B and C and so on, down to the end of the murderous alphabet. Here, the coercive force of logicality seems to have its source; it springs from our fear of contradicting ourselves. To the extent that the Bolshevik purge succeeds in making its victims confess to crimes they never committed, it relies chiefly on this basic fear and argues as follows: We are all agreed on the premise that history is a struggle of classes and on the role of the Party in its conduct. You know therefore that, historically speaking, the Party is always right (in the words of Trotsky: "We can only be right with and by the Party, for history has provided no other way of being in the right."). At this historical moment, that is in accordance with the law of History, certain crimes are due to be committed which the Party, knowing the law of History, must punish. For these crimes, the Party needs criminals; it may be that the Party, though knowing the crimes, does not quite know the criminals; more important than to be sure about the criminals is to punish the crimes, because without such punishment, History will not be advanced but may even be hindered in its course. You, therefore, either have committed the crimes or have been called by the Party to play the role of the criminal—in either case, you have objectively become an enemy of the Party. If you don't confess, you cease to help History through the Party, and have become a real enemy.—The coercive force of the argument is: if you refuse, you contradict yourself and, through this contradiction, render your whole life meaningless; the A which you said dominates your whole life through the consequences of B and C which it logically engenders.

Totalitarian rulers rely on the compulsion with which we can compel ourselves, for the limited mobilization of people which even they still need; this inner compulsion is the tyranny of logicality against which nothing stands but the great capacity of men to start something new. The tyranny of logicality begins with the mind's submission to logic as a never-ending process, on which man relies in order to engender his thoughts. By this submission, he surrenders his inner freedom as he surrenders his freedom of movement when he bows down to an outward tyranny. Freedom as an inner capacity of man is identical with the capacity to begin, just as freedom as a political reality is identical with a space of movement between men. Over the beginning, no logic, no cogent deduction can have any power, because its chain presupposes, in the form of a premise, the beginning. As terror is needed lest with the birth of each new human being a new beginning arise and raise its voice in the world, so the self-coercive force of logicality is mobilized lest anybody ever start thinking—which as the freest and purest of all human activities is the very opposite of the compulsory process of deduction. Totalitarian government can be safe only to the extent that it can mobilize man's own will power in order to force him into that gigantic movement of History or Nature which supposedly uses mankind as its material and knows neither birth nor death.

The compulsion of total terror on one side, which, with its iron band, presses masses of isolated men together *and* supports them in a world which has become a wilderness for them, and the self-coercive force of logical deduction on the other, which prepares each individual in his lonely isolation against all others, correspond to each other and need each other in order to set the terror-ruled movement into motion and keep it moving. Just as terror, even in its pre-total, merely tyrannical form ruins all relationships between men, so the self-compulsion of ideological thinking ruins all relationships with reality. The preparation has succeeded when people have lost contact with their fellow men as well as the reality around them; for together with these contacts, men lose the capacity of both experience and thought. The ideal subject of totalitarian rule is not the convinced Nazi or the convinced Communist, but people for whom the distinction between fact and fiction (*i.e.*, the reality of experience) and the distinction between true and false (*i.e.*, the standards of thought) no longer exist.

IV

The question we raised at the start of these considerations and to which we now return is what kind of basic experience in the living-together of men permeates a form of government whose essence is terror and whose principle of action is the logicality of ideological thinking. That such a combination was never used before in the varied forms of political domination is obvious. Still, the basic experience on which it rests must be human and known to men, insofar as even this most "original" of all political bodies has been devised by, and is somehow answering the needs of, men.

It has frequently been observed that terror can rule absolutely only over men who are isolated against each other and that, therefore, one of the primary concerns of all tyrannical government is to bring this isolation about. Isolation may be the beginning of terror; it certainly is its most fertile ground; it always is its result. This isolation is, as it were, pretotalitarian; its hallmark is impotence insofar as power always comes from men acting together, "acting in concert" (Burke); isolated men are powerless by definition.

Isolation and impotence, that is the fundamental inability to act at all, have always been characteristic of tyrannies. Political contacts between men are severed in tyrannical government and the human capacities for action and power are frustrated. But not all contacts between men are broken and not all human capacities destroyed. The whole sphere of private life with the capacities for experience, fabrication and thought are left intact. We know that the iron band of total terror leaves no space for such private life and that the self-coercion of totalitarian logic destroys man's capacity for experience and thought just as certainly as his capacity for action.

What we call isolation in the political sphere, is called loneliness in the sphere of social intercourse. Isolation and loneliness are not the same. I can be isolated—that is in a situation in which I cannot act, because there is nobody who will act with me—without being lonely; and I can be lonely—that is in a situation in which I as a person feel myself deserted by all human companionship—without being isolated. Isolation is that impasse into which men are driven when the political sphere of their lives, where they act together in the pursuit of a common concern, is destroyed. Yet isolation, though destructive of power and the capacity for action, not only leaves intact but is required for all so-called productive activities of men. Man insofar as he is *homo faber* tends to isolate himself with his work, that is to leave temporarily the realm of politics. Fabrication (*poiesis*, the making of things), as distinguished from action (*praxis*) on one hand and sheer labor on the other, is always performed in a certain isolation from common concerns, no matter whether the result is a piece of craftsmanship or of art. In isolation, man remains in contact with the world as the human artifice; only when the most elementary forms of human creativity, which is the capacity to add something of one's own to the common world, are destroyed, isolation becomes altogether unbearable. This can happen in a world whose chief values are dictated by labor, that is where all human activities have been transformed into laboring. Under such conditions, only the sheer effort of labor which is the effort to keep alive is left and the relationship with the world as a human artifice is broken. Isolated man who lost his place in the political realm of action is deserted by the world of things as well, if he is no longer recognized as *homo faber* but treated as an *animal laborans* whose necessary "metabolism with nature" is of concern to no one. Isolation then becomes loneliness. Tyranny based on isolation generally leaves the productive capacities of man intact; a tyranny over "laborers," however, as for instance the rule over slaves in antiquity, would automatically be a rule over lonely, not only isolated, men and tend to be totalitarian.

While isolation concerns only the political realm of life, loneliness concerns human life as a whole. Totalitarian government, like all tyrannies, certainly could not exist without destroying the public realm of life, that is, without destroying, by isolating men, their political capacities. But totalitarian domination as a form of government is new in that it is not content with this isolation and destroys private life as well. It bases itself on loneliness, on the experience of not belonging to the world at all, which is among the most radical and desperate experiences of man.

Loneliness, the common ground for terror, the essence of totalitarian government, and for ideology or logicality, the preparation of its executioners and victims, is closely connected with uprootedness and superfluousness which have been the curse of modern masses since the beginning of the industrial revolution and have become acute with the rise of imperialism at the end of the last century and the break-down of political institutions and social traditions in our own time. To be uprooted means to have no place in the world, recognized and guaranteed by others; to be superfluous means not to belong to the world at all. Uprootedness can be the preliminary condition for superfluousness, just as isolation can (but must not) be the preliminary condition for loneliness. Taken in itself, without consideration of its recent historical causes and its new role in politics, loneliness is at the same time contrary to the basic requirements of the human condition *and* one of the fundamental experiences of every human life. Even the experience of the materially and sensually given world depends upon my being in contact with other men, upon our *common* sense which regulates and controls all other senses and without which each of us would be enclosed in his own particularity of sense data which in themselves are unreliable and treacherous. Only because we have common sense, that is only because not one man, but men in the plural inhabit the earth can we trust our immediate sensual experience. Yet, we have only to remind ourselves that one day we shall have to leave this common world which will go on as before and for whose continuity we are superfluous in order to realize loneliness, the experience of being abandoned by everything and everybody.

Loneliness is not solitude. Solitude requires being alone whereas loneliness shows itself most sharply in company with others. Apart from a few stray remarks—usually framed in a paradoxical mood like Cato's statement (reported by Cicero, *De Re Publica*, I, 17): *numquam minus solum esse quam cum solus esset*, "never was he less alone than when he was alone," or never was he less lonely than when he was in solitude—it seems that Epictetus, the emancipated slave philosopher of Greek origin, was the first to distinguish between loneliness and solitude. His discovery, in a way, was accidental, his chief interest being neither solitude nor loneliness, but being alone (*monos*) in the sense of absolute independence. As Epictetus sees it (*Dissertationes*, Book 3, ch. 13) the lonely man (*eremos*) finds himself surrounded by others with whom he cannot establish contact or to whose hostility he is exposed. The solitary man, on the contrary, is alone and therefore "can be together with himself" since men have the capacity of "talking with themselves." In solitude, in other words, I am "by myself," together with my self, and therefore two-in-one, whereas in loneliness I am actually one, deserted by all others. All thinking, strictly speaking, is done in solitude and is a dialogue between me and myself; but this dialogue of the two-in-one does not lose contact with the world of my fellow-men because they are represented in the self with whom I lead the dialogue of thought. The problem of solitude is that this two-in-one needs the others in order to become one again: one unchangeable individual whose identity can never be mistaken for that of any other. For the confirmation of my identity I depend entirely upon other people; and it is the great saving grace of companionship for solitary men that it makes them "whole" again, saves them from the dialogue of thought in which one remains always equivocal, restores the identity which makes them speak with the single voice of one unexchangeable person.

Solitude can become loneliness; this happens when all by myself I am deserted by my own self. Solitary men have always been in danger of

loneliness, when they can no longer find the redeeming grace of companionship to save them from duality and equivocality and doubt. Historically, it
seems as though this danger became sufficiently great to be noticed by others
and recorded by history only in the nineteenth century. It showed itself
clearly when philosophers, for whom alone solitude is a way of life and a
condition of work, were no longer content with the fact that "philosophy is
only for the few" and began to insist that nobody "understands" them. Characteristic in this respect is the anecdote reported from Hegel's deathbed
which hardly could have been told of any great philosopher before him:
"Nobody has understood me except one; and he also misunderstood." Conversely, there is always the chance that a lonely man finds himself and starts
the thinking dialogue of solitude. This seems to have happened to Nietzsche
in Sils Maria when he conceived of *Zarathustra*. In two poems ("Sils Maria"
and "Aus hohen Bergen") he tells of the empty expectation and the yearning
waiting of the lonely until suddenly *"um Mittag wars, da wurde Eins zu
Zwei . . ./ Nun feiern wir, vereinten Siegs gewiss,/ das Fest der Feste;/Freund
Zarathustra kam, der Gast der Gäste!"* ("Noon was, when One became
Two . . . Certain of united victory we celebrate the feast of feasts; friend
Zarathustra came, the guest of guests.")

What makes loneliness so unbearable is the loss of one's own self which can
be realized in solitude, but confirmed in its identity only by the trusting and
trustworthy company of my equals. In this situation, man loses trust in himself as the partner of his thoughts and that elementary confidence in the
world which is necessary to make experiences at all. Self and world, capacity
for thought and experience are lost at the same time.

The only capacity of the human mind which needs neither the self nor the
other nor the world in order to function safely and which is as independent
of experience as it is of thinking is the ability of logical reasoning whose
premise is the self-evident. The elementary rules of cogent evidence, the
truism that two and two equals four cannot be perverted even under the conditions of absolute loneliness. It is the only reliable "truth" human beings can
fall back upon once they have lost the mutual guarantee, the common sense,
men need in order to experience and live and know their way in a common
world. But this "truth" is empty or rather no truth at all, because it does not
reveal anything. (To define consistency as truth as some modern logicians do
means to deny the existence of truth.) Under the conditions of loneliness,
therefore, the self-evident is no longer just a means of the intellect and begins
to be productive, to develop its own lines of "thought." That thought processes characterized by strict self-evident logicality, from which apparently

there is no escape, have some connection with loneliness was once noticed by Luther (whose experiences in the phenomena of solitude and loneliness probably were second to no one's and who once dared to say that "there must be a God because man needs one being whom he can trust") in a little-known remark on the Bible text "it is not good that man should be alone": A lonely man, says Luther, "always deduces one thing from the other and thinks everything to the worst." (*"Ein solcher (sc. einsamer) Mensch folgert immer eins aus dem andern und denkt alles zum Argsten."* In: *Erbauliche Schriften*, "Warum die Einsamkeit zu fliehen?"*) The famous extremism of totalitarian movements, far from having anything to do with true radicalism, consists indeed in this "thinking everything to the worst," in this deducing process which always arrives at the worst possible conclusions.

What prepares men for totalitarian domination in the non-totalitarian world is the fact that loneliness, once a borderline experience usually suffered in certain marginal social conditions like old age, has become an everyday experience of the evergrowing masses of our century. The merciless process into which totalitarianism drives and organizes the masses looks like a suicidal escape from this reality. The "ice-cold reasoning" and the "mighty tentacle" of dialectics which "seizes you as in a vise" appears like a last support in a world where nobody is reliable and nothing can be relied upon. It is the inner coercion whose only content is the strict avoidance of contradictions that seems to confirm a man's identity outside all relationships with others. It fits him into the iron band of terror even when he is alone, and totalitarian domination tries never to leave him alone except in the extreme situation of solitary confinement. By destroying all space between men and pressing men against each other, even the productive potentialities of isolation are annihilated; by teaching and glorifying the logical reasoning of loneliness where man knows that he will be utterly lost if ever he lets go of the first premise from which the whole process is being started, even the slim chances that loneliness may be transformed into solitude and logic into thought are obliterated.

If it is true that tyranny bears the germs of its own destruction because it is based upon powerlessness which is the negation of man's political condition, then, one is tempted to predict the downfall of totalitarian domination without outside interference, because it rests on the one human experience which is the negation of man's social condition. Yet, even if this analogy were valid—and there are reasons to doubt it—it would operate only after the full realization of totalitarian government which is possible only after the conquest of the earth.

Apart from such considerations—which as predictions are of little avail and less consolation—there remains the fact that the crisis of our time and its central experience have brought forth an entirely new form of government which as a potentiality and an ever-present danger is only too likely to stay with us from now on, just as other forms of government which came about at different historical moments and rested on different fundamental experiences have stayed with mankind regardless of temporary defeats—monarchies, and republics, tyrannies, dictatorships and despotism.

But there remains also the truth that every end in history necessarily contains a new beginning; this beginning is the promise, the only "message" which the end can ever produce. Beginning, before it becomes a historical event, is the supreme capacity of man; politically, it is identical with man's freedom. *Initium ut esset homo creatus est*—"that a beginning be made man was created" said Augustine. (*Civitas Dei, Book* 12, ch. 20) This beginning is guaranteed by each new birth; it is indeed every man.

Chapter Ten

Ideology and the Conduct
of Foreign Relations

One of the profoundly mischievous effects of the French Revolution, according to Edmund Burke, was its transformation of the principles of diplomatic conduct. It converted conflicts of interest and policy between governments into doctrinal conflicts which could not be compromised. To Burke, this meant the appearance of a "new principle of alliances and wars"—a principle derived from "theoretic dogmas." Its goal was to render the traditional purposes and means of diplomacy obsolete.

This transformation provided a background for the most zealously-conducted foreign policies of the twentieth century. Louis Halle is one of the men who has done most both to clarify the dangers of, and suggest alternatives to, an ideologically-based foreign policy. His experience as a member of the State Department, joined to his scholarship, has created a body of work at once reflective and practical. The following selection is taken from an essay written in the 1950s, in which his immediate purpose was to discuss United States policy toward Yugoslavia. But his larger purpose was to contrast the ideological style of foreign policy and diplomacy to the style of "strategy." In editing the essay, I have retained those portions which dwell on the general principles involved.

From *Strategy versus Ideology* *

Louis Halle

. . .The difference which chiefly accounts for our disunity on foreign policy
. . . I think, is that between those who tend to give primacy to ideological
considerations and those who are disposed to put strategical considerations
first. The men who said we ought to deny our support to Tito's Yugoslavia
because we should have no dealings with Communists, however expedient
such dealings might be, were ideologists. Those who said we should grant it
were strategists.

This is stating the philosophical difference crudely. When we come to
examine it more closely we shall, perhaps, be disposed to give a more subtle,
refined, and complicated account of it. I am struck, however, by the fact that
essentially this difference, however we may come to define it, appears to
underlie much of our latter-day controversy over foreign policy. One finds it
in the disagreement during the Second World War between those who favored
dealing with officials of the Vichy government in order to make difficulties
for the Nazis in France and to facilitate our North African landings, and those
who opposed it on grounds of principle. One finds it in the disagreement,
right after the war, between those who advocated that we enter into mutual
security arrangements with all the Latin American governments, whatever
their character, and those who wished to exclude the more flagrant dictatorships on the grounds that coöperation with them would represent a policy of
expediency opposed to the democratic ideals which we professed.

Do we not detect essentially this same difference, again, in the following
exchange that took place in the English House of Commons during the
Second World War, on May 24, 1944? Prime Minister Churchill had just been
saying a good word for the government of Spain, expressing appreciation of
the restraint exercised by the Spanish dictator, General Franco, in not taking
advantage of the opportunity which had been his to interfere with prepara-
tions at Gibraltar for the North African landings.

The Prime Minister: . . . Internal political problems in Spain are a matter for the Spaniards
themselves. It is not for us—that is, the Government—to meddle in such affairs—

*Louis J. Halle, "Strategy versus Ideology," *The Yale Review*, Vol. 46, No. 1, pp. 3-9,
12-16, 19-21. Copyright by Yale University Press. Reprinted by permission.

Mr. Shinwell (Seaham): Why then in Italy? My right hon. Friend did remark, as regards the restoration of the Government in Italy, that it could not be Fascist. That was his declaration. Why not in Spain?

The Prime Minister: The reason is that Italy attacked us. We were at war with Italy. We struck Italy down. My hon. Friend, I am sure, will see that a very clear line of distinction can be drawn between nations we go to war with, and nations who leave us alone. . . . There is all the difference in the world between a man who knocks you down and a man who leaves you alone. . . . we pass many people in the ordinary daily round of life about whose internal affairs and private quarrels we do not feel ourselves called upon to make continued inquiry. . . .

It was during this same debate that Mr. Churchill remarked: "As this war has progressed, it has become less ideological, in my opinion." This prompted some of his critics to charge that he was incapable of understanding the real nature of the war, which should be regarded (and conducted) as an ideological crusade for the destruction of fascism everywhere rather than as a mere continuation of strategic power politics.

It is one thing to make a distinction by citing examples and another to define it. The word "ideology" has different meanings for different minds or in different contexts, so that its unqualified use may lead to semantic confusion. The reader who makes it synonymous with "philosophy," for example, may well maintain that, in the exchange just quoted, Mr. Churchill represented "ideology" as much as Mr. Shinwell. He simply represented a different "ideology." Yet it is evident, in the context of his reference to the lessening ideological character of the war, that he was referring to a development of which he approved. The claims of ideology were repugnant to him.

I surmise that Mr. Churchill was thinking of ideology as something tending, essentially, to fanaticism, narrowness, and intolerance, something opposed to that easy-going freedom of thought for which the liberal democracies have stood. I propose to use the word in that sense. It is one of those words that have come up late in the day to claim jurisdiction where their absence had never been felt. The articulate people of our democracies had always been conscious of having a philosophy and ideals, but they never thought of themselves as having an "ideology" until, in our century, the word was borrowed from another usage to describe what Marxists and fascists took pride in having. Then some of them began to wonder whether we were not deficient by contrast with these people—or, alternatively, whether we did not also have an "ideology" of our own in those concepts of freedom and self-government to which our Montesquieus, our Burkes, our Jeffersons, and our Lincolns had given such eloquent expression. The impulse to be like one's opponent is deep-seated. If our opponents had an "ideology," then we too must have one to pit against theirs in "the battle for the minds of men." However, when some of us began to think of our traditional philosophy as a sort of official "ideology" like any other, only better, then we broadened the meaning of the term, or we constricted the philosophy to which we fitted it, or we did both.

In the narrower sense to which I propose to hold the term here, an ideology is more systematic, more explicit, more doctrinaire, more rigid, more pretentious, and more demanding of its votaries. It generally has a bible of some sort which represents authority not to be questioned: "Das Kapital" or "Mein Kampf." It tends to impose conformity. (For example, if our traditional philosophy were an ideology in this sense our leaders would be under compulsion to hand down an authoritative and official judgment on who was correct, Hamilton or Jefferson.) Finally, an ideology is generally associated with a rather explicit program of social action. In operative terms, the ideological attitude is essentially fervent, intransigent, contemptuous of calculation, more concerned with abstract principles than with concrete circumstances, dissatisfied with half-measures, with compromises, and with limited victories.

We should note the inherent contradiction between ideological thinking, as we have defined it here, and our traditional philosophy of liberalism. Our traditional philosophy values diversity and the tolerance that protects it. It is hardly compatible, then, with the tendency toward intolerance and the drive for conformity that characterize ideological thinking. Freedom cannot be imposed. There is a difficulty here that has become apparent in the efforts of various groups on our own domestic scene to make us all conform to what they consider the American way of life or the ideals of our American Revolution. Associated with compulsion, Americanism loses its character. Freedom is no longer freedom. By making our traditional philosophy an ideology we tend to change it into something else.

We have defined "ideology" largely in terms of degree rather than in an absolutely categorical sense. Islam, we may say, represented a particularly fervent ideology in the first century after the death of its prophet; but with the passage of time it lost some of its zeal and learned to live in a more-or-less tolerant accommodation with the non-Islamic world. It became less ideological, although the ideological element remained strong among many Moslems, as it does today. On the other hand, Confucian China, accepting the principle of "many ways to one goal," was affably tolerant of Taoism, Buddhism, and Christianity for many centuries; but when the Christian West came to pose an overwhelming threat to its survival it developed manifestations

of that intolerant ideological passion which found one expression in the
Boxer Rebellion. The temperature of belief rises and falls; ideological
thinking is a matter of more or less.

In a sense, ideological thinking appears to be native to mankind. It is, at least,
more natural than strategical thinking to those of us who have not, through
long and poignant experience, learned to see our world as a world in which all
victories are temporary, as an inflammable world (today more so than ever) in
which destruction comes easier than creation, as a world that consequently
yields more to patience, moderation, and intellectual care than to fanatic
zeal. From earliest childhood we all learn to think in terms of absolute moral
distinctions, of conflicts between the good men and the bad, the cowboys
and the Indians, the saints and the sinners, the angels and the demons. To the
mind of almost any small boy in our society, for example, our present contest
with the Communist world is as simple as a game of cops and robbers. Is it
not unthinkable that the cops should ever compromise with the robbers or
make deals with them? Perhaps it can be said that we all begin life as honest
ideologists.

It is when we acquire direct responsibility for making this difficult world
work that we learn, if we had not learned before, how different the reality is
from that world of every child's imagination in which we had grown up. The
requirement of discharging a large practical responsibility successfully, of
averting failure, especially in the anarchic field of international relations,
makes most of us more disposed than we would otherwise have been to give
strategical considerations weight. This has been the repeated experience of
good men and true who enter government and find themselves participating
directly, for the first time, in the responsibility of conducting foreign relations. An example was cited by Mr. Arthur Krock in the New York "Times"
of November 17, 1942, when he reported official opinion in Washington on
our coöperation with Vichy's Admiral Darlan to facilitate our landings in
North Africa. "One of those [officials] questioned," he wrote, "said today:
'War has forced us idealists and democrats to quantitative, rather than qualita-
tive, morality as the test. If, for example, Goering should offer to come over
with a few planes, we don't want him. He will cost more than he will contribute. But if he can bring the Luftwaffe with him we'll receive him.' " Here
the pressure of governmental responsibility had strengthened the strategical at
the expense of the ideological attitude. In "The Nation" of November 21,
1942, its editor quoted this statement, expressing incredulity at the attitude
it reported. The editor's own view was that, if Darlan's "favors could really be
won only by setting him up as our Quisling in North Africa, we should have

done without them—even if lives were to be lost and military advantage forfeited as a consequence."

One of our fundamental disunities, then, takes the form of a conflict, generally disguised but never fully resolved, between government and the public; or, more precisely, between any governmental administration and those whose voices—in the newspapers, over television and radio, or in Congress—represent dominating elements of popular opinion.

One must not leave the impression that this difference of approach is categorical. While the discipline of continuous responsibility does generally impel governments to give preponderant weight to strategical considerations, governments are, after all, made up of the same human stock as the rest of us. The individuals of whom they consist, moreover, vary in the degree to which they share or feel the common responsibility. That is why there are bound to be these disagreements inside government as well as outside.

Within government an equally uncategorical distinction may be made, in this respect, between the professional career men and the transient political appointees of the administration in power. Years of intimacy with the external affairs of government, the discipline of accumulated experience, tends to emphasize strategical considerations in the thinking of the career men. The nonprofessional political appointees, on the other hand, represent the public in a more direct sense and are more responsive to public attitudes. But their experience of responsibility, once they achieve it, is even more immediate than that which ordinarily comes to the career men, so that they tend with the passage of time to acquire the same professional respect for strategical considerations, however little they may have had at the outset. Nevertheless, the distinction between these two elements of government gives some validity to that otherwise illogical instinct which leads the public to attack the professionals in the Department of State for such unpopular policies as that of coöperating with the Vichy government, even where such policies plainly represent the decision of the political chiefs.

The public, also, is not consistently or exclusively addicted to ideological considerations. Other elements beside ideology enter, time and again, into its common aversion to strategical considerations. When, as is so often the case, the strategical considerations imply unwelcome requirements of public behavior, sacrifices of comfort or peace of mind, the public ordinarily may be expected to resist them. The exceptions occur when it is aroused by what it recognizes as a great, a clear, and (above all) an imminent danger. Thus simple apathy may play an antistrategical role that in other circumstances is performed by ideological fervor.

Our human nature being contradictory, ideological zeal may actually conflict in the same breast with an aversion to the very dangers and exertions which it implies. Representative Americans, during the past five years, have sometimes been torn between their ideological animus against Communist China, which impels them to favor an uncompromising policy, and their desire to avoid such an expansion of war in the Far East as this threatens. We may recognize here one aspect of the common disposition to will great objectives in the field of external affairs while insisting on what may be, in strategic terms, an excessive economy of means for their attainment. . . .

Ideological thinking is a matter of degree. At the extreme you have those xenophobes who would not compromise our Americanism by coöperation with any country which, being foreign, was thus un-American. Short of this extreme are those who would coöperate with an England under the government of the Conservatives but not with an England in which the Socialists held power. Far more common—indeed, most abundant of all—are those who accept a range of diversity that stops short only of such dictatorships as exist in a number of Latin American countries, in Spain, and in Yugoslavia. Among these last we find some who can stomach a dictatorship of the left but not of the right and others who show the reverse predilection.

Strategical thinking also has its degrees. Few among us who tend to favor strategical thinking would not be disposed against close relations with any government that not only represented an alien ideology but, by its acts, consistently outraged the deepest moral sensibilities of mankind.

When all this is said, however, the gap between strategically-oriented governments and ideologically-oriented peoples remains, in its degree, as a challenge to statesmanship.

The statesmanlike way of meeting it, within the limits of possibility, is by persuading the public in each instance that the strategic course is right and necessary. But there are bounds to the possibilities of statesmanship in any particular situation, and the supply of statesmen is limited. In default of perfect statesmanship, political leaders often feel themselves constrained to bridge the gap by a rhetoric that is in some degree disingenuous. If they are adroit in this they can sometimes manage for long periods to meet the minimum requirements of strategy in their actions while affirming their ideological fervor in public speech, since the public is sometimes more critically aware of the words that are spoken than of the deeds that are done.

No party, faction, or political leader has been altogether above this sort of thing since George Washington's day, so that it is not necessarily invidious to cite as an example the President's words in his Address of February 2, 1953, on the State of the Union, when he announced the issuance of an order that our Seventh Fleet "no longer be employed to shield Communist China" from the Nationalist regime on Formosa. While he thus persuaded an aroused public that the anti-Communist Chinese forces were being "unleashed," his administration was soon to move, quietly but effectively, to meet the strategic necessity of bringing those forces under better control with a view to achieving a *modus vivendi* with the Communist Chinese. Foreign Service Officers who had been identified in the public mind with the abhorred strategic approach to Communism in the Far East were removed from the Service in order to reassure the public. At the same time the administration, dissociating itself from the evidences of strategical thinking in its predecessor, emphasized the theme of morality, publicly dedicating itself to "moral principles" and a "moral crusade."

Both of our administrations since 1948 have faced a choice of evils that should give them some claim to the sympathy of the knowledgeable. In default of the ability to bring about a prompt and radical change in the outlook of the people, they have had to choose between the degree in which they should permit themselves to dissemble and the degree to which they should risk the governmental paralysis that might otherwise ensue. Certainly both have had to dissemble in some degree, and both have suffered considerable paralysis in the development of our foreign policy.

Those of us who believe, albeit without mysticism, in the possibilities of democracy must look for our justification to a growth in public sophistication that will, with the passage of time, reduce the dimensions of this dilemma.

The point I have been making here is that this dilemma is a practical one consequent on our lack of a common and workable philosophy in dealing with our foreign affairs. The prime philosophical question has been debated in terms that are sometimes helpful but as often obfuscating. In the past few years we have been presented with the choice between "expediency" (or "realism") and "morality" (or "idealism"), the implication being that these terms are mutually antithetical, that "realism," for example, cannot be

"moral" and "morality" cannot be "realistic." On occasion one might almost
conclude that what is expedient is *ipso facto* immoral. This is a poor premise
on which to develop the foreign policy of a great democratic society, if the
objective of developing it is to insure that society's future.

It is also a poor basis for achieving that unity on which our strength depends,
since each of the two alternatives which it offers us as grounds for reunion
must, in the last analysis, be declared unacceptable. As a society we cannot
agree that morality is irrelevant to policy, and neither can we agree that
expediency is irrelevant. We are being asked to make a choice that, beside
being virtually impossible, is unnecessary.

The flaw in this presentation of alternatives is, I think, in the identification of
morality with ideological policies that represent an aversion to strategical
considerations. As we have seen, such policies may be manifestly inexpedient,
working against their own objectives. We must ask, then: Can a policy that
strengthens evil really be a moral policy, while its alternative which
strengthens the good is evil? Yet this has in some measure been the historic
experience with ideological policies regarded as moral and strategical policies
regarded as sinister.

The religious wars of the Reformation led to the devastation of half Europe
by the middle of the seventeenth century, without either side being able to
realize its objective of making its ideology supreme and universal. The totalitarian character of warfare in our own day, with all its consequences, is
essentially a product of ideological thinking. It corresponds with "people's
wars," wars of whole nations in arms, rather than of professional military
forces only.

Accepting the moral criterion for the moment, it can surely be said that the
historic crusaders for an ideology have released more evil passions, with
consequent social crimes, than they have ever succeeded in allaying or
controlling. And still, for all the cost, we have a world of diversity and
conflict. What, one may properly ask, is the worth of righteousness associated
with an inexpediency so extreme?

I think that the most moral among us are bound to prefer those occasions in
European history when strategical thinking prevailed. The relatively elegant
and limited wars of the late seventeenth and eighteenth centuries were
conflicts in which the issue was not so much any religious or political ideal as
it was the balance of power. Bismarck's wars in the nineteenth century had

the same character. When his Prussia fought Austria in 1866 the objective was not anything like conversion or extermination. It was simply to decide who should sit at the head of the table in the councils of the German union then being formed. When that question had been decided, with a minimum of moral and material destruction, the two countries shook hands, so to speak, and were friends.

It is true that no single party to a conflict can always determine, by itself, that the ideological element shall not predominate. The necessity of resisting the ideological pretensions of others, when they take the form of aggression, may generate a fervor in one's own nation against which reason will find it increasingly hard to prevail. But the historic role of states-manship has generally been to seek every opportunity to reduce the ideological element. The greatness of Queen Elizabeth I was nowhere more fully manifested than in her strategical policy of seeking to moderate the conflict between Catholics and Protestants rather than to gain total victory for her side.

When republican France went to war with monarchical England in 1793, President Washington insisted, on purely strategic grounds, that we remain neutral. He was consequently subjected to accusations of cynical immoral-ity and even treason for not coming to the aid of our ideological ally, France. President Lincoln, too, was not on the side of the ideologists. He was intent on saving the Union, whether slave or free, and like Elizabeth he sought to moderate the ideological passions.

These examples suggest that in the historical perspective the people identify statesmanship with strategic prudence, however much they abhor it in their moments of ideological excitement. Queen Elizabeth never aroused such fervor of approval among her contemporaries as Cromwell did, but history has preferred her example. In the same perspective Abraham Lincoln is morally superior to Carrie Nation. . . .

This emphasis on the ideological aspects of the present contest is, I think, adverse to the possibility of ever resolving it satisfactorily. It accords the principal role to the most intractable element. It assumes that the ideological choices made by the uncommitted peoples will irrevocably determine their choice of sides in the strategic conflict, thereby reducing the possibilities of diplomacy. It implies a world divided between two ideological blocs, the mutual opposition of which is bound to approximate totality.

The tacit and generally unpondered premise of the ideological school is that only like-minded nations can properly coöperate. Yet a large part of history suggests that this is not strictly so. After the devastation of Europe in the Wars of Religion it was discovered that Catholic and Protestant nations could, in fact, live and even work together. This lesson, so vivid to the Age of Enlightenment, has been largely forgotten with the lapse of centuries. We have less excuse for not appreciating Yugoslavia's demonstration of the fact that a Communist state does not have to be in the enemy's camp. Red China does not have to be the ally of Red Russia (which was our ally in 1941-1945). And if Vietnam should go Communist—as pray God it does not!—we need not suppose that it is thereby irrevocably committed to the policy of Moscow or the policy of Peiping. Here is where a strategic diplomacy might be effective.

I venture to say that we have never appreciated the risks that Moscow has taken in using nationalistic movements abroad, because it has never occurred to us as a people that our diplomacy could take advantage of those risks. This, in turn, has made the risks less.

But diplomacy, however indispensable it seems to the strategist, is an art for which the ideologists have little taste or patience. It is too expedient and too compromising.

We could hardly expect, however, to unite for long on any ideological policy that subordinates considerations of strategy. We would not remain united if the policy were unsuccessful, and we could have little hope for the success of any policy that held the expedients of diplomacy in contempt. When it began to fail, the spirit of recrimination would be aroused among us and we should then fall to warring with ourselves more bitterly than ever.

On the other hand, we could not unite on a Machiavellian policy, holding moral considerations in contempt; and even if we could unite on it such a policy would be as little likely to succeed as the anti-strategical policy. In other words, it could not even be justified as strategy in the long run, however "hard-headed" or "realistic" it claimed to be. Our solidarity depends on our remaining true to ourselves. What was proper to Machiavelli's prince is improper to the great democracies, above all to our own. Our position in the world is warranted by the ideals we represent. These ideals therefore consti- tute an essential basis of our power and influence among the nations. We could not effectively carry out a foreign policy of which we were morally ashamed, and a policy that the other nations recognized as being merely cynical would give us less claim to their support.

But our proper idealism, as I have suggested, does not consist in the idealization of conformity. It has, rather, diversity as its ideal and magnanimity as its outlook. Justice Oliver Wendell Holmes was explaining "the theory of our Constitution" when he wrote: ". . . when men have realized that time has upset many fighting faiths, they may come to believe even more than they believe the very foundations of their own conduct that the ultimate good desired is better reached by free trade in ideas—that the best test of truth is the power of the thought to get itself accepted in the competition of the market. . . ." When we are true to the best in ourselves we do not consider it immoral to accept the existence of those who do not conform to our own standards of political virtue, and to have dealings with them. We do not consider it immoral to sit at table with a Catholic if we are Protestant, or with a Jew if we are Gentile. We do not inquire into the morals of our local grocer before we buy from him, or ask the taxi-driver to pass suitable tests of belief and character before we ride with him. The condemnation of others for not being like oneself is not so much morality as it is that self-righteousness which was a fault in the Pharisees. Morality, in our own best tradition, is compassionate. It expresses itself in modesty and the charitable view. This charity and tolerance we carry to the ultimate limit allowed by what I may call the expediency of self-defense.

The expediency of self-defense, in the current situation, implies a distinction between states that represent an alien ideology and states that, whatever ideology they represent, threaten or commit aggression against us or against other independent countries upon which our safety depends. That is why we can live in mutual tolerance, if not liking, with Yugoslavia while we must set ourselves in determined opposition to the Soviet Union and Communist China as long as they manifest a policy of aggression. But within the limits of this necessity there is no moral reason why we should not practice a strategic diplomacy that holds a promise of coöperation with Communist states which, however ardent their nationalism, can otherwise have no alternative to dependence on Moscow or Peiping.

We must seek to avoid, in our American policy, those qualities of duplicity, conspiracy, and treachery that may have been suitable to Machiavelli's prince. We must be true to our proper morality. But within the limits of our proper morality there is room for ample flexibility in the conduct of a strategical policy based on magnanimity, tolerance, moderation, and the virtues of civility. Such a policy ought not be too difficult for us, the American people, to understand because it is essentially the liberal policy which we follow in our own daily lives, when we are not aroused to extremes of fear, hatred, and self-righteousness by either demagogues or well-meaning zealots. This, it seems to me, is the only basis on which we can really unite.

Chapter Eleven

Ideology and Politics in the Third World

Since World War II, the great colonial empires of Britain, France, Holland, and other European powers have disintegrated with startling rapidity. This process had many complex causes, one of which was the belated effect—especially on local leaders—of the spread of European political doctrines: nationalism, self-determination, democracy, socialism, and Communism. The ideological clash in Europe in the era after the Russian Revolution was an example for colonial people. And since World War II, the ideologically-oriented conflict between Communist and Western nations to direct political development in the scores of new states has had a considerable effect.

The interaction between European doctrines and foreign conditions and cultures is producing a set of hybrid developments and regimes in the so-called "third world." The character of that interaction, with respect to the pattern of revolution, and the uses and content of ideologies, are the themes of the following essay. Its author, Professor C. B. MacPherson, is a Canadian political theorist with a deep and continuous interest in the theoretical development of modern liberalism. This essay is the extension of an argument he presented a few years ago in an important book titled *The Political Theory of Possessive Individualism.*

Revolution and Ideology*

C. B. MacPherson

The revolutions and the ideologies likely to be most important in the second half of the twentieth century are those of the underdeveloped countries. This proposition does not denigrate the obviously great continuing importance of the Communist revolutions of the first half of the century or of the Marxist ideology. They will go on working themselves out. But the new revolutions, having altered the terms on which the senior revolutionary ideologies can continue to be influential, may be regarded as the critical new factor in the problems of revolution and ideology of the next several decades. The revolutionary and ideological currents in the underdeveloped countries, currents which are not formed entirely from either Marxist or liberal-democratic ideologies, are already having and will increasingly have an effect on the Communist and Western structures of power and of ideas.

Problem and Terms Defined

I want first to show that the new revolutions depend to an unusual degree on ideology, that the new states built on these revolutions will continue that dependence, and that their ideologies are not likely to conform either to the Communist or the Western pattern. I will then offer some speculations on the possible effects of this fact on the Western ideology.

Throughout I use *ideology* in a neutral sense, neither implying, with Marx, an idealist philosophy and "false consciousness," nor, with Mannheim, contrasting ideology and "utopia." I take ideology to be any more or less systematic set of ideas about man's place in nature, in society, and in history (i.e., in relation to particular societies), which can elicit the commitment of significant numbers of people to (or against) political change. This does not exclude a set of ideas essentially concerned with merely a class or a nation, if it relates the place and needs of that section of humanity to the place of man in general. Thus liberalism, conservatism, democracy (in various senses), Marxism, Populism, Nkrumaism, pan-Africanism, and various nationalisms are all ideologies. Ideologies contain, in varying proportions, elements of

*C. B. MacPherson, "Revolution and Ideology," in C. J. Friedrich, editor, *Revolution* (New York: Atherton Press, 1966), pp. 139-153. Reprinted by permission of the Publishers, Atherton Press, Inc. Copyright ©1966, Atherton Press, New York. All rights reserved.

explanation (of fact and of history), justification (of demands), and faith or belief (in the ultimate truth or rightness of their case). They are informed by, but are less precise and systematic than, political theories or political philosophies. They are necessary to any effective political movement, hence to any revolution, for they perform the triple function of simplifying, demanding, and justifying.

By *revolution* I mean a political overturn more far-reaching than a *coup d'état* or "palace revolution." I take revolution to mean a transfer of state power by means involving the use or threat of organized unauthorized force, and the subsequent consolidation of that transferred power, with a view to bringing about a fundamental change in social, economic, and political institutions. How long a period of consolidation is to be included in the revolution itself is a matter of theoretical convenience; here it will be convenient to consider the revolution to extend for as long as ideological zeal is needed (and is forthcoming) to secure a sufficient basis for the new institutions.

My interest in the revolutions and ideologies of the underdeveloped countries arises from my concern with the prospects of liberal-democratic political theory. The present widely-felt inadequacy of liberal-democratic justificatory theory is, I think, due to the possessive quality of its basic individualism. I have argued elsewhere[1] (a) that the philosophy of liberalism has been, from its origins in the seventeenth century, permeated by possessive individualism, which assumes that the individual is human *qua* proprietor of his own person, that the human essence is freedom from any but self-interested contractual relations with others, and that society is essentially a series of market relations between these free individuals; (b) that this individualism was ethically adequate for societies dominated and vitalized by competitive market relations; (c) that it becomes ethically inadequate once the natural rightness or inevitability of market relations is challenged or denied by substantial sections of the people (as it began to be in England and Europe from the middle of the nineteenth century); but (d) that possessive individualism cannot simply be discarded from the justificatory theory of liberal democracy because liberal democracy is still in our day coterminous with market-dominated societies, so that the assumptions of possessive individualism (though now ethically inadequate) are still factually accurate. The question about which I now speculate is whether the impact of the underdeveloped countries' revolutions and ideology may provide some basis for the requisite change in Western political theory or ideology.

[1] In my *Political Theory of Possessive Individualism* (New York: 1962).

Importance of Ideology in the Revolutions of the Underdeveloped Countries

Compared to the classic revolutions of the seventeenth to nineteenth centuries, the revolutions of the underdeveloped countries in our time depend to a much higher degree on ideology. Two reasons are evident:

(a) The new revolutions, in order to move toward their goal of bringing backward peoples rapidly into the modern world, must in most cases virtually create a nation. They must do in a few years what the classic European revolutions either did not have to do at all or were able to do with much less difficulty, that is, create a sense of primary loyalty to a political nation, rather than to local, tribal or feudal communities. The leaders of the new revolutions, themselves generally intellectuals,[2] politicized by training abroad, have had to bring a prepolitical people to a sense of nationality and national self-esteem, to create a political and national consciousness, and to infuse a hope and a faith that great things can be done by the new nation.[3] This is a task for ideology. And the leaders, being intellectuals, have been able to provide the ideology. They have generally proceeded by setting up the nation as the charismatic object, in place of the tribe, the kinship group, feudal or royal rulers, priests and magicians, in which the ordinary man hitherto had found the sacred quality.[4] But however the new ideology is brought into existence, its creation and spread are indispensable to the revolution.

(b) Just as the immediate aim of the revolution—the transfer of power from an outside imperial government to an indigenous national government—requires a high degree of ideology, so does the longer term but equally necessary aim of rapid economic development. The classic Western revolutions of the seventeenth to nineteenth centuries came, generally speaking, when there was already an enterprising *bourgeoisie* ready and able to press

[2]"The gestation, birth, and continuing life of the new states of Asia and Africa, through all their vicissitudes, are in large measure the work of intellectuals. In no state-formations in all of human history have intellectuals played such a role as they have in these events of the present century." Edward Shils, "The Intellectuals in the Political Development of New States," *World Politics* (April 1960).

[3]"Differences of caste, tribe, clan or religion must be integrated into the political process, and it is precisely because they loom so large as an obstacle to the creation of the modern nation-state that the leaders place great emphasis on the primacy of 'the nation' and the elimination of traditional status differentiations. . . . The first requirement is the implementation of the common ideal of universal participation in the nation." Paul E. Sigmund, Jr. (ed.), *The Ideologies of the Developing Nations* (New York: 1963), p. 7.

[4]See Edward Shils, "The Concentration and Dispersal of Charisma: Their Bearing on Economic Policy in Underdeveloped Countries," *World Politics* (October 1958), pp. 3-4.

ahead with economic development. In the new revolutions there is, generally speaking, no indigenous *bourgeoisie* and no indigenous accumulation of private capital. The desired economic development has therefore to be undertaken by state initiative, state accumulation and investment of capital, state planning and controls. The accumulation of capital, and the provision of incentives which will convert the ordinary people into a modern labor force, obviously require, and will require for a long time, heavy reliance on ideology.

In short, both of the practical objectives of the new revolutions—the change from colony to viable independent nation, and the promotion of rapid economic development—require and will continue to require a high degree of ideology. In the nature of the case, the ideology has to be developed by the political elite, who are at once the intelligentsia and the political leaders. They do not, of course, create ideologies out of nothing. Where they can, they find historical roots in the precolonial cultures and polities of their own lands. And they draw, of course, on the ideological traditions they find in the advanced countries, both Western and Communist. What sort of ideologies have resulted?

Revolutionary Ideologies Neither Communist Nor Liberal-Democratic

One may say in general of the new ideologies that they are neither Communist nor Western (using Western to mean pluralist, liberal-democratic, bourgeois-individualist). One may say also that it is not very useful to try to place them in a continuum stretching from Communist to Western. They see themselves as outside that continuum. For them, the polar division of the world is not between communism and liberal capitalism but between the rich nations and the poor nations. They know where they stand now in that division, and they know where they want to move. In order to move, they will take from both the Marxist and the liberal-democratic traditions whatever seems to them to go to the root of their problems.

As a brief analysis will show, they have, on the whole, taken something from Marxism, while refusing to identify themselves with Soviet Communism; they have rejected almost wholly the liberal individualist utilitarianism of the West, but have drawn heavily on its earlier democratic tradition, the tradition of Rousseau and Populism. Indeed, it is where Marxism and this original Western democratic ideology overlap that the leaders of the modern underdeveloped countries' revolutions find themselves ideologically most at home.

We may look first at what they have taken from, and what they
have rejected in, the Western ideology. The clearest thing about the new
ideologies is their rejection of the capitalist ethos. Whether or not they
accept, or how much they accept of, the thesis of Lenin's *Imperialism*,
they tend to have a strong moral aversion to the ethics of competitive
individualism. This goes deeper than the natural reaction of an exploited
colonial people to the ethos of their former exploiters and to any fear that
they may still be exploited economically even after winning political
independence. It goes back to their traditional culture, which saw no
intrinsic value in wealth getting and gave no respect to the motive of
individual gain.[5] These traditional roots might, of course, have been pulled
up, just as the traditional reliance on the prepolitical local community is
being uprooted. But there has been neither need nor inclination to try to do
so, for it has seemed clear to the revolutionary leaders that the rapid national
economic development they demanded could come only through social
control of the economy; to have left it to private capitalist enterprise would
have meant leaving it to foreigners, which would have negated the revolutionary goal of national independence.

Thus both the traditional ethos of the prepolitical society, and the political
needs of the revolution, have operated against acceptance of the Western
capitalist ethos. Added to this has been a strong moral egalitarianism, which
may be explained partly in traditional terms and partly as revulsion against
the dehumanizing contrast of poverty and wealth which they see in
capitalism. All these forces may be expected to continue to operate against
acceptance of the capitalist ethos.

At the same time that the economic ethos of capitalism has been rejected, so
has the political ethos of liberal pluralism. And here too, traditional outlook
has been reinforced by the requirements of a modernizing revolution. The
local, community-centered society traditionally made its decisions by discussion between equals. The more primitive the society, the less do plural
interests exist and demand recognition. In the underdeveloped societies
generally there was little basis for pluralism, or for the Western system of
competing political parties and pressure groups. Furthermore, the

[5]The "autonomous movement of the economic system is thought undesirable even if
possible." It "is believed that no intrinsic value resides in the economic sphere—in the
way in which the religious and political spheres possess the intrinsic value connected
with sacred things. The only truly respected motives are those generated by authority,
the exercise of that sovereignty, religious or political, which entails communion with
the sacred." Shils, *World Politics* (October 1958), p. 2.

requirements of the struggle for independence generally favored the emergence of a dominant single party or movement, and this has been carried into the postindependence structure in most cases as a single-party or single-party-dominance system.[6] The political leaders, as ideologists, find no difficulty in justifying one-party rule, both as fitting the indigenous traditional idea of democracy and as necessary for the task of making and consolidating the national revolution.

While the practical basis of the antipluralist ideology is the revolutionary need for unified command and unified popular support, the moral basis is found in a Rousseauan concept of a general will. This concept is the moral basis also of the economic side of the ideology—the rejection of competitive capitalist individualism. Just as Rousseau found the source of social ills, of moral depravity, of dehumanization and loss of human freedom, in the institution of inequality, and believed that the secular redemption of mankind could be got through a purified general will (which, to be operative, would require the institution of substantial economic equality and the absence of effective interest groups), so do the new ideologies. To them, the period of colonialism was the period of inequality forcibly or fraudulently imposed in place of an original equality. Inequality had destroyed the human dignity and freedom of the people. Dignity, freedom, and humanity could be restored by reestablishing equality. This required not only the political revolution but also a moral revolution—an assertion of the will of an undifferentiated people as the only legitimate source of power.

It is less important to stress the Rousseauan parallels than to notice that the essential assertion—the ultimate moral worth of the freedom and dignity of the individual, which can however only be realized by the operation of an undifferentiated popular or mass will—goes back to a preliberal democratic tradition. In England, the classic home of liberalism, democracy was feared, down to the middle of the nineteenth century and even later, by the most enlightened liberals, as being inconsistent with liberal society and the liberal estate. If the ideology of democracy was then inchoate, it was strong enough to be dreaded. It is this earlier tradition of democracy that the new leaders

---

[6]A recent study of new states in Africa shows that, of the independent states in which an indigenous majority participates in government (i.e., excluding the Republic of South Africa, Southern Rhodesia, etc.), all but four (Libya, Egypt, Sudanese Republic, and Ethiopia, in which no parties are permitted) have a single-party or single-party-dominance system. Single-party-dominance means that more than one party exists but one party has an overwhelming legislative majority and employs its legal, police, and political powers to restrict the competitive position of opposition parties and groups. M. L. Kilson, "Authoritarian and Single-Party Tendencies in African Politics," *World Politics* (January 1963), pp. 262-263.

have tapped. They have seen that, historically, it has as good a claim to the title democracy as has the now more familiar pluralist liberal democracy. This has given the leaders confidence that their regimes are in a genuine sense democratic. If they have deserted Rousseau in the matter of the representation of the general will, they have not deserted Robespierre; the party and its leaders are the bearers of the will of the people.

This egalitarian general-will ideology is likely to become firmly established. It feeds and is fed by the necessary nationalism of the underdeveloped countries' revolutions. And it is a highly valuable, if not indispensable, support to the position of the revolutionary leaders; it upholds their one-party or dominant-party state, and validates their authority as leaders of it. Without such authority they cannot hope to carry through the program of economic development necessary to consolidate the revolution. They may therefore be expected to use all the resources of state and party to strengthen that ideology.

We may say, then, that the leaders of the underdeveloped countries' revolutions, rejecting the ideology of contemporary Western liberal democracy, have anchored themselves in the earlier Western ideology of of preliberal democracy. Just as they have rejected alignment with either Western or Communist power blocs, and have seen themselves as outside the capitalism-communism continuum, so in rejecting contemporary Western ideology they have swung not to Communist ideology but to a position historically outside of both the dominant contemporary ideologies, a preliberal-democratic and pre-Marxist position.

It is in this light that the measure of their acceptance of Marxism may best be understood. Even the new nations whose ideology has come closest to Marxism, e.g., Sékou Touré's Guinea, can be seen to accept only those elements of Marxism that fit in with the pre-Marxian democratic position. Thus they gladly accept the basic moral position of Marx's humanism, which has its roots in the Rousseauan tradition. Although they may not be versed in the latest scholarly debates about the role of alienation in Marxism, they find immediately and deeply attractive the general thrust of Marx's analysis of the dehumanization of man by capitalism, and the Marxian belief that man can remake himself and can overcome his alienation, by concerted revolutionary action. But they do not accept as applicable to their countries or to the contemporary world the Marxian theory of class struggle as the motor of history, nor the theory of the state as essentially an instrument of class domination, both before the proletarian revolution and in the postrevolutionary dictatorship of the proletariat. Nor, consequently, are they interested in the withering away of the state. For they insist that their own countries are now classless societies, that the new national state (or the dominant party) consequently speaks for the whole of the people, and that its authority emanates directly from the whole of the people.

With this view of their own society as classless, they are able to accept what looks like the "vanguard" theory of Lenin's but which is not quite the same. Lenin argued, as early as 1902 in *What Is To Be Done?* that a working class by itself, under capitalism, could not reach more than trade-union consciousness, that only a vanguard of dedicated intellectual Marxists could see through to reality, and that it must therefore be their task, by building round themselves a tightly organized party, to lead and control the revolution. The vanguard, rather than the proletarian mass, was made the effective agent of the revolution. In thus clearly separating the function of the vanguard from that of the proletarian mass, and asserting that the vanguard could make a revolution before there was a thoroughly class-conscious proletariat, Lenin made it easier for the later underdeveloped revolutions to speak in Marxist terms. The fact that they had no industrial proletariat did not now matter; they had an intellectual vanguard.[7] Yet the theory and practice of the vanguard in most of the underdeveloped countries' revolutions is not exactly Leninist. The role of the vanguard is not to end class domination but foreign domination. It is to seize and wield power not in the name of a not yet fully conscious proletariat, but in the name of an undifferentiated people who are never to become a proletariat because industrialization is not to be allowed to take place under capitalist auspices.

Thus, in the matter of the vanguard, as in their beliefs about the sources of their people's dehumanization and the way to overcome it, the new ideologies have taken over less from Marxism or Leninism than from a pre-Marxist radical tradition, suitably reformulated to meet the needs of underdeveloped peoples in a highly developed world. The new ideologies may, in a sense, be said to have bypassed Marxism. For the conditions in which their revolutions are rooted are neither those envisaged by Marx nor those envisaged by Lenin. They have no industrial proletariat, and do not intend to have one. In the scales of Western economic history, they are peasants at most. Yet a colonial people may be called proletarian in a deeper sense. For, in the measure that

[7] This point was made by Eduard Heiman, "Marxism and the Underdeveloped Countries," *Social Research* (September 1952), who argued then that the addition of the vanguard theory had made Marxism readily transferable to the underdeveloped countries without distortion.

the colony was fully subject to the purposes of the metropolitan economy, the people were held to their economic position not, as the prerevolutionary Russian peasant, by feudal or precapitalist relations of production, but by capitalist relations of production, albeit imposed by an economic force from beyond their own borders. In this sense their revolutions might be called proletarian, for they have been made by peoples subjugated by capitalist relations of production in order to throw off those relations. But the classic Marxist and Leninist categories do not fit them exactly. An underdeveloped people caught up in capitalist relations is, so to speak, at once nonproletarian and more completely proletarian than the trade-union-conscious labor force of an advanced capitalist society. It is nonproletarian in that it has not the industrial worker's factory discipline and subordination to the machine (which Marx counted on to produce proletarian consciousness, and which Lenin counted on too, though with some impatience). It is more proletarian in that it, rather than the working classes of the advanced countries, has experienced the immiseration (*verelendung*) that Marx predicted for the latter, and in that virtually the whole people rather than just one class has been immiserized.

The attractiveness of Marxism to underdeveloped revolutionaries is no doubt due to this fact. Yet an underdeveloped people is not a Marxist proletariat even when they develop a consciousness of their common subjugation by capitalism, for their consciousness is not a class consciousness but a national consciousness. They intend as the immediate aftermath of their taking power, not a dictatorship of the proletariat (or of a vanguard in the name of the proletariat) over a *bourgeoisie*, but the dictatorship of a general will,[8] or of a vanguard in the name of the general will, over a people undifferentiated by class (for once the imperial power has been driven out, there is no *bourgeoisie* remaining to be dominated).

Yet if the ideologies of the underdeveloped nations have bypassed Marxism and rooted themselves in an earlier radical democratic tradition, it should also be noticed that recent Soviet Marxism has been making an effort to catch up. The Soviet leaders have abandoned the nineteenth-century Marxist view that

[8]Cf. Sékou Touré's concept of "democratic dictatorship." He begins by defining dictatorship as the exercise of sovereign power, so that all conceivable governments are dictatorships. Democratic dictatorship is then defined as government based on the sovereignty of the people. "A democratic state comes from the will of the people. Its program is therefore necessarily in conformance with the interests of the people. Likewise, its force, its authority, the powers it exercises, the discipline it imposes—in short, the dictatorship it exercises—arise exclusively from the interests, the requirements, and the principles of popular sovereignty." *La Lutte du Parti Démocratique de Guinée pour l'Emancipation Africaine* (1959), as translated in Sigmund, *op. cit.,* p. 163.

the world trend to communism must come through proletarian revolutions, and see it now as coming through colonial revolutions which, though they set up non-Communist systems, may be encouraged to move into the Soviet orbit. "It was no doubt with this prospect in view," Robert Tucker has written, "that Soviet doctrine was amended by Khrushchev in 1956 to provide for a 'peaceful' mode of 'transition to socialism.' In his report to the 20th Party Congress, he particularly singled out countries where capitalism is weak and relatively underdeveloped as the most likely places for the 'peaceful' mode of transition."[9]

One further factor must be taken into account in assessing the probability of Marxist penetration of the new ideologies. Most of the new nations have, from the beginning, taken a stand on non-alignment with either the Soviet or the Western powers. Whatever aid they receive from either bloc, they have remained uncommitted. They are likely to remain so, partly because their ideology has a strong moralizing element—a disapproval of power politics as such; partly because they hope, by remaining neutralist (even though not acting as a neutralist third bloc) to diminish the chances of conflict between the two great power blocs (an open conflict between which would finish their chances of economic development); and perhaps fundamentally because they are beginning to have some confidence that *they* see the long-range problem of a peaceful world order more realistically than those who are still caught up in the cold war. Whatever the reasons for it, their deliberate nonalignment with either bloc entails some reserve about Soviet theoretical principles, and thus throws up a barrier to their acceptance of a full Marxist ideology. Indeed, to the extent that the third of the reasons suggested above is operative, they will be apt to regard Soviet ideology (as well as Western) as less realistic than their own.

I have argued that the ideologies of the underdeveloped countries' revolutions are, and are likely to remain, neither liberal-democratic nor Communist; that while they may be said to have adapted elements both of Marxism and of liberal democracy, they may better be understood as having their roots in a pre-Marxist and preliberal notion of democracy. The new ideologies are not so much eclectic compilations of bits from the two competing ideologies of the advanced countries as they are growths from an earlier stem, with such grafts from the two modern plants as the original stem will take. Grafts are needed because the new soil is not entirely congenial to the old stem.

[9]Robert C. Tucker, "Russia, the West and the World Order," *World Politics* (October 1959), p. 18.

I have suggested also that the emergence of the new nations and the new ideologies has already had some effect on one of the two advanced ideologies —the Soviet theory has been adjusted to the fact and the prospects of the underdeveloped revolutions. Can Western ideology also be adjusted to them?

Possible Effects of the New Revolutions on Western Ideology

We may notice first that the requisite Western adjustment is not simply one that would make Western ideology more attractive to the underdeveloped countries. The notion of currying favor is as unnecessary as it is distasteful. What is needed is an ideology that would allow the West to maintain a position of world importance in a world one-third Communist, one-third uncommitted, and one-third Western (I assume that Western leaders will come to recognize that world dominance is no longer a feasible aim). I assume also that it is recognized by the leaders of both West and East (though not yet by the whole people or all the influential groups) that in the present and any future condition of nuclear armament no great power can maintain or improve its position in the world merely by a show of force. It follows that the West requires, beyond its military forces, a set of values or an ideology by which it can coexist with, while contesting with, the other two-thirds of the world. A viable Western ideology must be built on the recognition that the world is no longer a Western preserve. This is difficult but not impossible.

In the second place we may notice that the requisite adjustment of Western ideology does not involve altering or abandoning the values on which the West most prides itself. It would, however, be misleading to suggest that the Western adjustment would be simply related to means, not ends, as the Soviet theoretical adjustment has been. The Soviets have not given up any of their values. They are still Communist, and still intend to further the "transition to socialism" outside the Soviet bloc. They have merely dropped their insistence that class war and dictatorship of the proletariat are the only possible ways to achieve their ends. The Western adjustment would involve not only an alteration in the theory of means but some alteration in the theory of ends as well. For the Western ideology treats as ends not only the ethical values of liberal democracy but also the ethos of capitalist enterprise, or what I have called the values of possessive individualism. As stated above, possessive individualism regards the individual as human in his capacity as proprietor of his own person; the human essence is freedom from any but self-interested contractual relations with others; society consists of a series of market relations between these free individuals. I have argued that these assumptions have been built into the value system of liberal democracy, and they are no longer an adequate ethical basis for it. The point here is that a Western ideology that is to be internationally viable from now on will have to abandon this possessive individualism. The reasons may be reduced to two. First, it is, of all the Western values, precisely this possessive individualism which has been rejected by the uncommitted nations. Secondly, possessive individualism entails continual capitalist aggrandizement; a nation devoted to possessive individualism must be, in Harrington's phrase, "a commonwealth for increase," and this is what the Western nations can no longer expect to be.

The real question, then, is whether possessive individualism is so built into the Western ideology that it cannot be dropped or decisively modified. This is too big a question to try to deal with here in all its aspects, but we can consider one specific aspect: Is the fact of the underdeveloped countries' revolutions (added to the preceding fact of the Communist revolutions) itself a new force making for Western abandonment of possessive individualism?

To consider this question we must notice that Western ideology is not simply (as I have so far by implication defined it) a compound of pluralist liberal democracy and possessive individualism, but that it has defined itself increasingly in the last two decades as a cold-war ideology. It has done so by embracing the assumption that there is between East and West not merely a long-term contest for world influence but an implacable and absolute hostility, such that Western nations must bend their whole effort to forcibly defeating, or not being forcibly defeated by, the East. This assumption has fused with the other two elements in Western ideology to produce a new compound. *The* Western value becomes "the free way of life," a concept in which the values of liberal democracy, of possessive individualism, and of anticommunism, are merged. They are merged in such a way that, of the two original elements, one particularly, possessive individualism, draws much of its vitality from the hostility to communism.

To the extent that possessive individualism has been so fused with cold-war anticommunism, anything that produces a Western move away from the latter will also carry Western ideology away from the former. The emergence of the underdeveloped nations may alter the Western cold-war ideology in two ways.

First, in the measure that the world effect of the underdeveloped countries' revolutions is realistically assessed in the West, it must modify the cold-war attitude of the West. I assume that as neither East nor West can now hope to advance their power or influence by war, and as the two now have comparable technical and economic strengths (at least when rates of growth are taken into account), the future relative world strength of East and West depends mainly on who wins (or does not lose) the good will of the uncommitted parts of the world. On this assumption, a Western policy of peaceful coexistence with the East becomes the rational policy, for coexistence is the only policy the uncommitted nations can regard as rational for others as well as for themselves.

Second, the revolutions of the underdeveloped countries have already, as we have seen, led to substantial modification of the Soviet doctrine of class conflict. Soviet abandonment of the doctrine of the necessary class war and proletarian dictatorship should increase the possibility of peaceful coexistence between East and West. In both these ways the underdeveloped revolutions have set in motion forces tending to moderate the cold-war ideology and thus, on our earlier assumption, to carry Western ideology away from possessive individualism.

The possessive individualism of the Western ideology may be affected by the underdeveloped revolutions in a third way, operative even if cold-war attitudes are not greatly reduced. Even on cold-war assumptions, there is no ground for implacable hostility between the West and the underdeveloped new nations. Their ideology does not commit them to proletarian revolution or world revolution. Their goals are more modest. They seek only to realize an egalitarian humanism, and that only for their own countries. The West can coexist with these ideologies. The longer the West lives with them, and the more widely they are propagated, the more the ethical contrast between their egalitarian humanism and possessive individualism (which is already under wide attack by theologians, philosophers, and publicists in the West) will be borne in on the conscience of the West. In recognizing the merits of the new ideologies' humanism, the West would be going back to the roots of its own democratic tradition.

None of these prospects, it must be said, can be counted upon to reduce the possessive quality of our modern individualism to a point consistent with the requirements of twentieth-century liberal-democratic theory. But there is at least a possibility that Western recognition of the new world alignment of our time, in which the underdeveloped revolutions are playing the final decisive part, will be enough, coming as it does on top of the other new fact that individuals throughout the world are now equally insecure in face of the possibility of nuclear war,[10] to overcome the dominance of possessive individualism in Western ideology.

[10]The possible role of this new equality of insecurity in providing some part of a sufficient sense of equality to serve as an ethical base for a modern theory of liberal democracy is discussed in my *Political Theory of Possessive Individualism, op. cit.,* chap. VI, sect. 2.

Chapter Twelve

Scientific Analysis of the Role of Ideology in Politics: Three Perspectives

The authors of the following essays share a common concern: to advance the understanding of the role of ideology in politics by the application of scientific analysis. But the different perspectives of the essays reflect the differences in their theoretical premises and in their concepts of the scope and purpose of analytic treatment.

The first essay is by Léon Dion, a Canadian political sociologist whose basic concepts and modes of argument are greatly influenced by the sociological theories of Karl Marx, Robert Merton, and Karl Mannheim. The essay is an attempt to develop and clarify the meaning of an hypothesis that ideology may "mediate" between the "social and political structures." This hypothesis is derived from an avowed concern to treat society, and therefore the purpose and function of ideology, as a "whole," and in sociological terms.

Karl Loewenstein, a distinguished political scientist who came to America from Germany in the 1930s, also aims at a broad treatment of ideology. His argument is much less hypothetical than Dion's; he feels that by the time he wrote this essay in the 1950s, the basic features of the modern operation of ideology were apparent to the careful observer. Loewenstein ignores the distinction between social and political structure that is so important to Dion; he is concerned with the way in which ideologies represent the political institutions of a society, and with how that representation is understood and transmitted.

The third essay, by the American political scientist Samuel Barnes, is concerned with "empirical political inquiry." To Barnes, it is important to "operationalize" the concept of ideology, and to strive for precise methods by which to measure its presence and effect among political actors. His approach stands in marked contrast to the more theoretical, definitional treatments of the other two authors.

A careful and detailed comparison of the similarities and differences in definitions, purposes, and methods of these three arguments will reveal the range of perspectives among contemporary social scientists concerning the scientific treatment of the role of ideology in politics.

An Hypothesis Concerning the Structure and Function of Ideology*

Léon Dion

There is so little agreement concerning theories of political ideology that it may be appropriate to devote some preliminary remarks to the main orientations of recent research. I shall then state the approach to political ideology which is adopted in this paper.

"Political ideology" has different meanings in the two principal fields of knowledge in which it is used: sociology and political theory. The ambiguity which results is the greater because neither of these disciplines has as yet integrated this notion into the main body of its operational concepts. If the Marxist school of thought be excepted, one may well state that the notion of political ideology plays only a secondary and marginal role as a tool of sociopolitical analysis.

*Léon Dion, "Political Ideology as a Tool of Functional Analysis in Socio-Political Dynamics: An Hypothesis," *The Canadian Journal of Economics and Political Science,* 25, 1 (February 1959), pp. 47-59. Reprinted by permission.

Political theorists and philosophers generally view political ideologies as a part of the complex of forces which sustains the political structure or tends to its overthrow. For them, political ideologies are one of the means to power, or, as stated recently by Anthony Downs, of getting votes.[1] This approach is adequate so far as it goes, but in my view it narrows the notion of political ideology to one of its most manifest functions in democracies. Furthermore, most such treatments of political ideology assimilate it to a pseudo-philosophy. When this pseudo-philosophy is considered good, it is said to uplift and educate the people; when it is considered bad, it is held to mystify and corrupt them.[2] A new method of analysis must be devised in order to benefit from the invaluable contribution of sociology to the understanding of the genesis, structure, and functions of ideologies.

Sociologists, taking over with modifications the Marxist theory, have thrown much light on social ideology as a means of defining a situation and adjusting to it. They also have penetrated some distance into the dynamic process which ties ideologies to social structure and status. Unfortunately, they usually fail to distinguish between social and political ideologies except in terms of content and scale. They appear to assume that the frames of reference of political ideology are identical with those of social ideology. Many sociologists fail to recognize that political institutions and mechanisms constitute a structure different from, though dynamically interlocked with, the social structure, and this failure explains in part why political theorists have

---

[1]*An Economic Theory of Democracy* (New York: 1957). For his treatment of political ideologies, especially in a democratic context, see Part II, 96-142.

[2]However, it should be clear that the labelling of a given ideology as ethically good or bad may simply denote an ideological preference on the part of the thinker. The moral character of an ideology is a very important question but research of this kind should not be conducted in such a way as to give the impression that it is a study in functional analysis. Apart from the ethical viewpoint, political ideology may be considered from many different angles. From a logical viewpoint, ideologies raise the problem of their internal coherence; there is also the most fundamental question of their truth. That ideologies constitute a distorted knowledge of reality has been known since Francis Bacon's famous theory of idols which he developed in his *Instauratio Magna*. The problem of ascertaining the degree of truth of an ideology has been a hard one to solve. Mannheim, in his search for objective knowledge, was induced to postulate a universal class sufficiently free from social conditioning to transcend the bias resulting from limited perspectives. Indeed, some writers have gone so far as to lay themselves open to the suspicion that all knowledge is distorted by ideologies except their own. For a criticism of this position, see John H. Hallowell, *The Moral Foundation of Democracy* (Chicago: 1954), Part I. It is evident that there is finally only one way of ascertaining the objective truth of a given idea and it has been known for a long time: to apply to it the rules of logic, the forms of judgment, and the tests of scientific evidence. See Jeanne Hersch, *Idéologie et realité* (Paris: 1956). As to functional analysis, it is specifically concerned with the vitality and utility of a given ideology and it furnishes materials and perspectives for other kinds of research in ethics, logic, epistemology, etc.

found so little use for and interest in sociologists' discussions of political ideology.

Moreover this lack of analytical rigour is largely responsible for the fact that what theoretical knowledge we have about political ideology is not even integrated within sociology itself. In reality, there are two different and quite opposite branches of sociology which deal with political ideologies: the sociology of knowledge, and the sociology of mass communications. The basic postulates, the methods, the subject-matter, and the conclusions of the two differ essentially. Robert K. Merton, while deploring this situation, finds faults in both orientations.[3] He states that although the sociology of knowledge, which claims Karl Mannheim as its main systematizer, has contributed many important hypotheses, they are too general to be confirmed by systematic evidence. On the other hand, its American counterpart, the sociology of mass communications, tends to concentrate on partial aspects of the political structure, such as public opinion and electoral behaviour, to which are applied all the tests of the scientific method. It is neither Merton's contention nor mine that these orientations must be abandoned: on the contrary they must be given full credit for the light they have already thrown on so many obscure aspects of social and political phenomena. However, they fail to elucidate satisfactorily the structure and functions of political ideology.

My contention is that the possibility of making political ideology a useful tool of socio-political analysis depends initially on seeing it in the light of the total social structure. This global viewpoint is one of Marx's major contributions to social science. Marx then made the distinction between the sub- and the supra-structures, and Mannheim appropriated this distinction in the formulation of his sociology of knowledge. This fundamental assumption of a dynamic interaction within two levels of the social structure must be retained, though with modifications. The political theorist cannot elaborate his analysis from the notion of *société globale* which the anthropologist and even the sociologist are prone to postulate. In this paper, I will divide the total social structure into two different, though interdependent, elements, the social and the political. Political ideologies, like social ideologies, originate in the social structure and are generally grounded on a stratum or a group, but they differ from social ideologies in that their expression is conditioned by political objectives and their crystallization is

[3]*Social Theory and Social Structure* (Glencoe, Ill.: 1949; revised and enlarged, 1957). For relevant discussions by Merton see 1949 ed., Introduction to Part III and chaps. viii, ix.

effected within political institutions and mechanisms. Now political ideologies are elements of a given culture. Thus a political ideology may be considered as a more or less integrated cultural and mental structure.[4] A political ideology performs this mediation by tending to adjust groups and individuals to their situation, in so far as this situation is perceived in terms of political aspiration.

In the present essay, my aim is not to elaborate this hypothesis, but rather to illustrate and elucidate, by way of a few examples, some of its elements. In the next part, I shall discuss political ideology as a cultural and mental complex, and in the final part I shall endeavour to show what kinds of functions the hypothesis ascribes to political ideologies. Thus this essay should be considered as a general inquiry preliminary to the systematic testing of the hypothesis and eventually to its application in a case-study.

I

Our hypothesis is that political ideology is a cultural and mental complex which mediates between the norms associated with given social attitudes and conduct and the norms which the political institutions and mechanisms tend to crystallize and propagate. In other terms, political ideology is a more or less integrated system of values and norms, rooted in society, which individuals and groups project on the political plane in order to promote the aspirations and ideals they have come to value in social life. We shall now illustrate this conception by presenting two examples of the integration of given social norms and values into the ideological complex known as liberal democracy.

The first example deals with the processes by which the norms of public law were fixed by the men of the French Revolution. Groethuysen, Ripert, Garaud, and others have shown how the norms which were originally developed to govern the economic conduct of the bourgeoisie inspired the development of a new civil law, giving the sanction of natural law to private property, and endowing the contract with a sacred and obligatory character.[5]

[4] I originally derived the notion of "cultural and mental complex" from Ernst Cassirer's monumental treatise, *Philosophie der Symbolischen Formen* (3 vols., Berlin: 1923-9). Cassirer used the expression "symbolic form" to denote one or other of the constituent mental structures, such as language, mythical and rational thought, etc., by means of which reality is apprehended and reconstituted. By "cultural and mental complex," I mean a cultural pattern of norms and values which is both objective (i.e., an element of the total culture) and subjective (i.e., an element of the mental structure).

[5] Bernard Groethuysen, *Philosophie de la Révolution française: précédé de Montesquieu* (Paris: 1956), esp. 212 ff. Georges Ripert, *Le Régime démocratique et le droit civil moderne* (Paris: 1948). Marcel Garaud, *La Révolution et l'égalité civile* (Paris: 1953).

They thus were used as an authoritative model in the elaboration of the post-revolutionary public law. We may state in the following terms the ideological argument in which the intellectuals and politicians clothed the political struggle of the bourgeoisie: given the rational and universal character of natural law as applied to private property, would it not be also expedient to draw from it inspiration in matters of public law and in political life generally? As Groethuysen has pointed out, objective principles of public law were already established thanks to the previous partial restoration by the monarchy of Roman law, itself grounded on natural law. And this made the transition in terms of the new requirements easier.

This example appears to be significant because it expresses well the process by which specific social norms and values, by their being incorporated in civil and then public law, were transformed into an ideological complex able to mediate between the social and the political structures. It will suffice here to notice two peculiarities of this process: first, although the new political norms were derived from pre-existing social norms, they came to be virtually independent of them; second, whereas the social norms represented only the ethics and aspirations of a single class, the bourgeoisie, the new political norms governed the relations of all the social groups, in so far as these relations were subject to regulation by public policy. So long as such political norms mediate between the social and the political structure, not only do they determine the relations of the institutions and social groups among themselves and with the state, but also, by establishing the rules of the game, they condition the political expression of alternative norms, revolutionary or not, which are grounded in the situation of social groups other than the bourgeoisie.

The second example will deal with the transplanting into parliament of the economic conduct found in the "free market."[6] Parliaments, after having been used by monarchs as tools in their struggle with the feudal powers and the papacy, became the main institutional means of realizing the political ambitions of the mercantile classes.[7] In France this occurred through the

[6]This example is inspired by Frederick Watkins, *The Political Tradition of the West* (Cambridge, Mass.: 1946), 138 ff. See also Georges Ripert, *Aspects juridiques du capitalisme moderne* (Paris: 1957), and Harold J. Laski, *The Rise of European Liberalism* (London: 1936).

[7]During the Old Regime in France, the term *parlement* was applied to certain courts of justice. It was rather in the Estates General that the parliamentary function was lodged. However, since this body was not assembled from 1613 to 1789, one may say that the French parliament (National Assembly) was born from the revolutionary act of the third estate when it decided to hold its meetings independent of the two other orders.

revolutionary act of the third estate; in Great Britain, at the end of a long process of growth accompanied by many reforms. These classes, in adjusting the objectives and rules of parliamentarianism to their mentality and ends, drew their political norms and values from the ideologies they had developed concerning the relations of the market. In other words, compensating for their political inexperience by their economic training, they transposed into parliament the objectives and rules which presided over the relations of the market. They were led in this endeavour by thinkers as widely separated as Adam Smith, John Locke, Jeremy Bentham, and others, who translated into theoretical language and legitimated this evolving socio-political process.

Let us reconstitute some stages in this process as they were seen at the time. The relations of the market were then considered as a field of action in which an individual who offers a commodity, and another individual who wants to obtain the commodity for himself, will come to an agreement only if the bargain is considered advantageous by both. The relations of the market, then, have this peculiarity that they occur only when both parties, though motivated by contrary impulses, think they can gain from a reciprocal agreement: hence the principle of the natural harmony of diverging interests as immutably presiding over the relations of the market. Now if in conditions of free negotiation it has been possible to elaborate a rational mechanism that makes it possible for individuals, without renouncing their personal interests, to maximize the economic well-being of all, why should it not be possible to conceive a similar model of political relations which would guarantee at the same time the general welfare and the liberty of individuals? Such was indeed the ideological reasoning which inspired the bourgeoisie and which was systematized in the writings of philosophers and theorists of liberal democracy.[8] Then, when the practical necessity of political parties became evident, these were considered as reproducing in parliament the actors in the market. Parliamentary debates were conducted after the manner of the conventions and the postulates of the market, and were viewed as preliminary discussions leading to an eventual contractual agreement; they assumed the liberty and equality of the disputants, and were based on regard for the rules of the game as a condition for a decision in the interest of all. The same sacred and obligatory character was conceded to parliamentary decisions as to agreements between parties in the market. Nothing was left over and nothing was added, except that it was necessary, in parliament, to replace the rule of rationality by the rule of the majority, but to the latter was also attributed a rational character.

[8]Considering the fact that many of the principles and conventions of British parliamentarianism had actually developed before the theorists came to express them in terms of the liberal ideology, this process could well be viewed as one of social pseudo-morphism.

This second example demonstrates the process of taking certain norms, values, and conducts from social life and transplanting them in the political institutions and mechanisms of liberal democracy. It is important to note that during this process the rules and conventions which had originally been used to govern economic activities ("supply" and "demand," "discussion" and "conciliation," "agreement," "sacredness of the contract") were redefined independent of their previous context in order to fit the new political requirements; so that the day when the postulate of the free market would be discarded (and with it the liberal ideology of economic relations under capitalism) would not see the end of their effectiveness in the political sphere. When they became ineffective in the social structure, these rules and conventions none the less continued to animate the political structure. They owed their continued existence partly to the symbolism elaborated around the working of parliament but chiefly to the fact that they were incorporated in the cultural and mental complex of democracy.[9] Thus, having acquired a high degree of independence and autonomy, they could continue to mediate between the two structures.

We can now appreciate how these two examples illustrate our hypothesis. The first example has shown how a particular set of social norms that had been developed by the bourgeoisie—centring on the exaltation of private property incorporated in civil law—was raised by the men in the French Revolution above other sets of social norms and placed at the centre of the argument used to define and sustain the new public law, and, in general, the political relations of post-revolutionary France. The second example has indicated how the elements of social ideology that were developed around a type of social conduct—the relations of the market—were raised above all other types of conduct and became a directing model in the development of the political relations within parliament. In the light of these two examples we can elucidate our hypothesis in the following terms: from a genetic viewpoint, political ideologies originate from a social process of selection of norms and types of conduct; during this process the influence of a political aspiration comes to predominate, and to crystallize in political institutions and mechanisms; finally, political ideologies gain a relative independence and autonomy as regards the social norms and values which originally constituted their nucleus.

[9] In his *The Symbols of Government* (New Haven, Conn.: 1935), W. Arnold Thurman has studied the symbolism which has been elaborated in the United States about the Supreme Court. Thus he says, the Court is adorned with a majesty which it would not possess if it were judged from the character of the judges who compose it, the interests it serves, the notions that inspire the judicial decisions, etc. Most discussions of the Crown, parliamentary ritual, court procedures, etc., also stress the importance of symbolism in British political practice.

II

We have argued that political ideologies constitute a cultural and mental complex which mediates between the social and the political structures; let us
now consider, in the light of this hypothesis, what functions might be
ascribed to them.

From the very nature of the hypothesis, it is clear that we must derive the
functions from the general character of modern society. I shall develop my
argument from the central proposition which Merton established in his discussion of the sociology of science.[10] Studying the sources of and the reasons
for the resistance against scientific activity in Western civilization he argues
that the main opposition generally comes from groups which hold positions
of power in a given society. He points out that, owing to the socio-economic
evolution from the fourteenth century onwards which accelerated the secularization and rationalization of life, and thus of norms and values, the locus
of power shifted from the church to the state. In terms of our hypothesis, as
religion gradually lost its traditional dominant position at the centre of
power, it was no longer able to enforce its *Weltanschauung*; for it was substituted a new cultural and mental complex—political ideology—embedded in
the new dynamics of society and oriented toward and supported by the new
locus of power, the state. Political ideology became entrusted with the
political functions previously performed by religion.

Much has been written by historians and sociologists on the social functions
of religion in primitive and mediaeval societies. I shall note only two of them:
the function of defining ultimate purpose and the function of ensuring social
consensus. In primitive societies, purpose is given and consensus is guaranteed
by tribal religion. So long as tribal religion remains vigorous, it accomplishes
these functions so well that nobody sees in purpose and consensus any problem whatever since they impregnate the very norms and values incorporated
in religion itself and propagated by the priesthood. Extending its influence to
all spheres of thought and every field of activity, religion here must be viewed
as a *Weltanschauung*.

By contrast, when, as in classical Greece during the fifth century B.C., the
influence of tribal religion weakens as a consequence of changes in the social
order, men like Socrates begin to appear who raise the question of the ends of
the city. The philosophers question all traditional norms and values in the
light of universal and rational standards and substitute natural law for tribal

[10]*Social Theory and Social Structure* (1949 ed.), Part IV.

religion in their elaboration of a new cultural and mental complex able to perpetuate purpose and consensus on a higher plane.[11] Seen from this angle, natural law might be considered the first political ideology in so far at least as it sustained the Chinese, Egyptian, Hellenistic, and Roman empires before they disintegrated into feudalism.

From the fourteenth century onward, the Occident witnesses a similar process. A slow but continuous secularization of thought, accompanied by socio-economic changes, gradually affected the socio-political functions which the Christian religion had performed throughout the Middle Ages.[12] Up to Marsilius of Padua, William of Ockham, and Nicholas of Cusa, historical and political purpose as well as moral consensus had been easily integrated in the higher ends and solidarities of religion. Even emperors and kings, until Louis XI, in their political struggle against the papacy, did their best to use the theocratic arguments in favour of their own peculiar claims.[13] But whereas in the early Middle Ages religion had been used to hold in check the temporal power, in the sixteenth and seventeenth centuries it became, in the writings of James I of England, Richelieu, Bossuet, and Louis XIV in France, and the jurists and theologians of Spain and Germany, a tool placed at the service of absolutist political ambitions.[14] Religious purpose and consensus were preserved but their purveyor and beneficiary was no longer the church but the state, a clear indication that the seat of power had shifted.

What these apologists of absolutism essentially did was to elaborate a political ideology by selecting norms and values from the Christian religion and turning them into a cultural and mental complex able to mediate between the political and the social structures. But, as the principle *cujus regio ejus religio* indicates, it was the prestige and power of the king that sustained religion rather than the reverse. Furthermore, religion discredited itself as a consequence of the terrible wars conducted in its name and because, in certain

[11]Leo Strauss has thrown a great light on this function of natural law: see his *Natural Right and History* (Chicago: 1953), 86 ff. Also, Paul Janet, *Histoire de la science politique dans ses rapports avec la morale* (Paris: 1925).

[12]Georges de Lagarde, *La Naissance de l'esprit laique au déclin du Moyen-Age* (2 vols., Paris: 1947).

[13]Marcel David, *La Souveraineté et les limites juridiques du pouvoir monarchique du IXe au XVe siècles* (Paris: 1949). Also, Sidney R. Packard, *Europe and the Church under Innocent III* (New York: 1957).

[14]The classical presentations of the theological and philosophical background of the mediaeval church-state relations are contained in the numerous works of Otto von Gierke and Etienne Gilson. For an excellent general study see Hans Kohn, *The Idea of Nationalism* (New York: 1946), pp. 61-115.

regions, it opposed the socio-economical evolution of the ascending classes. Religion had inspired the political norms and values of a society in process of secularization but it had been found wanting.

It appeared for a time that the true support and justification of political life from then on would be, as Machiavelli had said and as Richelieu reaffirmed, *la raison d'état* or *real-politik*. Then, however, there developed the modern school of natural law headed by Grotius, Pufendorf, Burlamaqui, and others, who, having registered the defeat of religion, dedicated themselves to the search for a new universal and rational basis of purpose and consensus and again found it in natural law. In this manner, the doctrine of natural law was a catalyst in the development of many modern political ideologies. It sanctioned the conversion into political formulas of the doctrines of liberal economists, social traditionalists, racialists, and so on. It legitimatized revolutions and restorations. Declarations of the rights of man were written from its substance and belief in the common man was implicit in it. The Marxists, who have discarded all specific reference to natural law and have even ridiculed the doctrines derived from it, have nevertheless been induced to find a substitute in another absolute "law," dialectical materialism. Every modern political ideology has been nurtured in the culture of modern societies but each claims for itself a basis in the absolute. This claim is evidenced in the writings not only of the philosophers of liberal democracy but also of Marx and Lenin, and of the Nazi ideologists. The central questions they all raise in one form or other are still: "What is the end of the good life?" and "What is the common good?" But, with them, the answers are construed from a secular perspective.[15] This claim of all modern political ideologies to absoluteness must be seen as resulting from a "structural" necessity, since they have assumed in political life the place previously occupied by religion and have also been entrusted with the political functions so long exercised by religion.

Having shown in general terms the processes by which political ideologies inherited the position previously occupied by religion, it remains to illustrate the functional aspect of our hypothesis. Before we proceed further, however, it should be made clear that the fact of ascribing to political ideologies the two functions of defining purpose and promoting consensus does not imply

[15]The notions of nature and natural law furnished their fundamental sedimentations to most political ideologies, conservative or revolutionary, of the eighteenth and nineteenth centuries. See philosophical and historical discussions in Basil Willey, *The Eighteenth-Century Background* (London: 1949), and in René Rémond, *La Droite en France de 1815 à nos jours* (Paris: 1954), 27, n.

that they perform these functions in all cases or that there are no other cultural and mental complexes that accomplish the same functions. The hypothesis simply is that these are normal functions of political ideologies and that the search for these functions in actual ideologies would provide significant knowledge about their inner nature and social usefulness. I will first consider the function of purpose and then of consensus.

The first systematic endeavour in modern Western civilization to define and impose purpose by means of a secular political ideology was that of the Jacobins.[16] Saint-Just, Robespierre, and their followers were not long in realizing that the success of the Jacobin venture rested on the possibility of imposing secular substitutes for theology and the church: hence their efforts, on the one side, to formulate a syncretism of orthodoxy from the teaching of the philosophers, and, on the other side, to constitute a party on the basis of the then existing political clubs of discussion and action. This early experiment failed, first because the Jacobins, having been unable to create a dictatorial party, were forced to operate through the instrumentality of a state still influenced only slightly by their thought and of which, besides, they rapidly lost control; and, second, because they expected from the masses of the people a high degree of fervour and participation without being in a position to elaborate adequate techniques of influence, terror excepted, in order to ensure permanently the support of the population or even of a single group.

The example of Jacobinism, that preliminary abortive rehearsal of the great drama of modern politics, throws considerable light on our hypothesis. Jacobinism shows that the defining and enforcing of a political ideology cannot be entrusted to any one social institution or group; that rather, its success and perpetuation depend on its being able to reach to the very centre of political power and to partake of that power. Just as mediaeval Christian religion without the church would have evaporated, so a political ideology without some political mechanism will fail of acceptance. This view may be formulated in a general proposition: in a revolutionary situation or in an unstable society, political ideologies tend to crystallize in political parties and fail to impregnate the more institutionalized mechanisms of government, such as parliament, the courts, and the administration; whereas under normal conditions and in a stable society, they will penetrate the parties only slightly but will tend to crystallize in the more institutionalized mechanisms of

[16]The best study of Jacobinism from this angle is that of J. L. Talmon, *The Origins of Totalitarian Democracy* (London: 1952).

government. The first part of this proposition has been established by a few recent authors, among them Roche and Stedman;[17] the second part has as yet received little recognition.

Let us now illustrate how, in the light of this proposition and in terms of our hypothesis, the function of providing purpose may be accomplished in given conditions. I shall consider two extreme cases: Soviet Russia and the United States. In Russia, the problem of purpose is constantly raised in regard to all spheres of activity; in the United States it is seldom discussed at all. This contrast is generally explained by reference to the fact that the Soviet Communist ideology is totalitarian and Messianic whereas the American democratic ideology is pragmatic and diffuse. This explanation is true enough but it does not lend itself to functional analysis. Our hypothesis permits a more fruitful approach. The problem of purpose has to be constantly raised in Russia precisely because, like the Jacobin experiment, the Communist ideology has not impregnated the institutionalized mechanisms of government, that is, the soviets, the courts, the army, the police, and the administration, to such a degree as to ensure that these will always make their acts and decisions conform to the Communist purpose. Now, contrary to Jacobinism, Communism is supported by a strong party to whose central organs are entrusted the task of scrutinizing the acts of all state and social organizations from the standpoint of the line which the party itself defines in conformity with the Marxist-Leninist doctrine and the needs of the moment.

By contrast, the problem of purpose is seldom raised in the United States because the American people have been prone to believe that the Founding Fathers inscribed political purpose in the Constitution and, accordingly, that citizens will automatically behave in conformity with this purpose by respecting the political institutions and mechanisms created by the Constitution. Even among political theorists and philosophers, the search for purpose is usually manifested along with reflective comment on the Supreme Court, Congress, the Presidency, and so on.[18] The parties, which were not given a constitutional position, are, however, generally considered to be without much ideological content and thus to be simply means of getting votes for candidates.

Thus, political ideologies tend to crystallize in different institutions according to the manner in which the function of providing ultimate purpose is believed

[17] John P. Roche and Murray S. Stedman, Jr., *The Dynamics of Democratic Government* (New York: 1954).

[18] On this subject see Daniel J. Boorstin, *The Genius of American Politics* (Chicago: 1953, 1958). For an example of such an ideological valorization of political institutions and mechanisms in the United States see Harold F. Gosnell, *Democracy* (New York: 1948).

to be accomplished. And this belief itself reflects the social, economic, and cultural conditions. In the Communist case, the political ideology must necessarily preserve a high degree of transparency and consistency in order to be able to intervene on all occasions in political institutions and mechanisms thought to be fallible and imperfect; the function of purpose is here accomplished in a dramatic manner under the supervision of the party. In the United States, the supreme guarantee that the political ideology will exercise its function of purpose is found in the fact that it has been, so to say, incorporated in political mechanisms and institutions considered to be a close approximation to perfection.

The second function ascribed to political ideologies is that of achieving social consensus. At first sight, the bestowing of such a function on political ideologies seems a paradox, since most people attribute to them precisely the opposite function of bringing disunity. According to our hypothesis, however, political ideologies express social tensions and conflicts, and may at times aggravate them, but they do not create them.[19] These tensions originate in the social structure and the international situation. The function of political ideologies is to give social tensions and conflicts political expression and to canalize them on the political plane. The more acute the social tensions and conflicts, the more likely to be extreme the political ideologies that express them. I shall illustrate this by presenting two very different examples, first, socialism in Western Europe, second, present-day international tensions.

Let us establish first the case of socialism. Around the middle of the nineteenth century, the national bourgeoisies in the more advanced countries of Europe had appropriated for themselves political power or at least partook of it along with the aristocracies. Formally, most countries of Europe at that period were aristocratic or even absolutist. But it is an error to believe that the bourgeoisie occupies power only in democracies. From our point of view, a class holds power whenever the state serves its interests and is impregnated by its culture. By elevating certain norms and values of the bourgeois culture, philosophers and theorists had succeeded in formulating an ideology able not only to co-ordinate the energies and aspirations of the bourgeoisie, but also to mediate between the social and political structures. Already in Great Britain,

[19]That political ideologies canalize social tensions and conflicts has been recognized by some recent authors. See, among others, Robert A. Dahl, *A Preface to Democratic Theory* (Chicago: 1956), pp. 136-137; Roche and Stedman, *The Dynamics of Democratic Government*, 27; Hallowell, *The Moral Foundation of Democracy*, pp. 71, 79, 91. It is suggestive to note that C. B. MacPherson attributes the same function to political parties. See his paper entitled "The Role of Party Systems in Democracy" presented at the Third Congress of the International Political Science Association, August 1955, and his *Democracy in Alberta* (Toronto: 1953).

in France, and in Germany, the political structure had been increasingly permeated by a cultural and mental complex of bourgeois origin. As a consequence, the social conditions and aspirations of other groups had to be politically acknowledged and defined in terms of this particular complex. In particular, the capitalist definition of the relations of production in terms of the bourgeois civil law, and the political sanction of this definition by public law, not only contributed to maintain the industrial workers in a precarious situation but also prevented the development of a class-consciousness among them.

The theorists of socialism, themselves mostly of bourgeois origin, dedicated their lives to the analysis of this situation in order to identify the interests and formulate the socio-political objectives of the workers. However, in the field of practical action, they met the problem of justifying, in terms satisfying to the political leaders, demands for even the most elementary reforms, such as the recognition of the right of combination, legislation concerning the periods and conditions of work, and so on. The main difficulty came from the fact that the political leaders were responsive to the pressure of bourgeois interests and were themselves often imbued with bourgeois ideology. Thus in order to uphold even such demands, a new historiography and a new definition of culture in terms of the industrial class were required. Furthermore, since proletarian conditions could be appreciably improved only by political measures, socialist political ideologies based on proletarian historiography and aspirations were eventually formulated. The socialist movements of course diverged in their views of the nature and scope of the struggle to be waged. But whether the socialists were revolutionaries or reformists, socialist movements in all cases enabled the proletarian classes to find a unity of consciousness and a sense of destiny.

That socialism did perform for the proletarian classes a function of integration and unification can be readily seen. But, it might be objected, so much the worse, since socialism was a cause of the social conflicts and political struggles that darkened the last century. From our viewpoint, however, socialism is to be conceived as an expression of tensions and conflicts already present in industrial society. By formulating, from the proletarian's point of view, the social origin and character of the conflicts of the period, socialism transformed them from indistinct and obscure troubles into clearly oriented and powerfully stated claims. In all cases where the political structure was flexible enough to begin to accommodate socialist ideology, industrial conflicts underwent a gradual mitigation. In the course of this process which, in Burdeau's terms, goes from "la démocratie gouvernée" to "la démocratie gouvernante," or from "liberal" to the "welfare state," we witness, along

with a readjustment of political institutions and mechanisms, the development of a syncretism made of elements from the socialist and bourgeois
ideologies.[20] Thus the search for a more adequate way of mediating between
the social and the political structure has resulted in the development of a new
cultural and mental complex which exalts to a far less degree than previously
the norms and values of a single social class.

By contrast with this evolution, of which Great Britain furnishes the outstanding example, in all cases where a more inflexible political structure and
more intolerant political ideology opposed political recognition of the proletarian *Weltanschauung*, fear and cynicism on the side of the satisfied classes,
along with resentment and vengeful outbursts on the side of the mass of the
dissatisfied, created a climate of deep uncertainty. In such circumstances, not
a single social question or conflict can find any political expression, other
than a grotesquely distorted one, except through revolutionary means. It
would be as illusory to attribute the latent uneasiness in these societies to the
fact that socialist movements operate in the background, if not in the under-
ground, as to think that the dominant ideology can mediate the social
tensions and conflicts between the social and the political structure so as to
render revolutionary socialism anachronistic.

Our second case is taken from contemporary international political tensions.
Though many publicists and theorists assert that political ideologies constitute a cause of the tensions in international relations, we shall discard that
view for the moment and see what light if any, results from the application of
our hypothesis that political ideologies do not create but merely express
tensions and conflicts which have their origin in the social structure (in this
case in the international organization). We shall consider to what extent
political ideologies at present accomplish their supposed function of consensus. Then we shall suggest that a way of accomplishing this function is
perhaps within the reach of modern political ideologies, if we consider the
more and more noticeable process of socio-economic integration throughout
the world.

Considering the present state of international organization, it is not surprising
that the political ideologies that exist on that level constitute but the projection of norms and values which have been matured in national contexts.[21]

[20]Georges Burdeau, *La Démocratie* (Paris: 1956).

[21]In his *Scientific Man versus Power Politics* (Chicago: 1946), Hans J. Morgenthau has
suggested that, in contrast to national politics, international relations have never outgrown
the "pre-liberal" stage. Our own analysis of political ideology tends to confirm the radical
differentiation which Morgenthau establishes between the national and the international
spheres of politics.

These projected national ideologies are used, first, to assure national consensus and, second, to gain international consensus on the foreign policy followed by individual states. Here, the function of developing consensus labours under the constraint of the need for self-protection. This constraint is very evident when ideologies are used to discredit the foreign policies of other countries.

Thus we have here a case where political ideologies, far from permitting the mediation of social tensions and conflicts within the international political organisms tend, on the contrary, to place these organisms at the service of particular states. Political ideologies then constitute a factor in power politics. According to our perspective, this functional deviation is due to the fact that the norms and values which these ideologies convey to the international plane reflect the interests and aspirations of social groups within given socio-economic structures only in so far as they are represented in the national interests and aspirations of the single states or blocs of allied states. This is the case, for example, when ideological arguments are resorted to by national governments in order to sustain policies of economic assistance to under-developed countries.

Behind their manifest function, however, it is possible to perceive in national ideologies projected on the international plane a latent force making for consensus. This latent function of universal consensus at present is exercised only in a sporadic and erratic manner largely because political ideologies are cast in national moulds. Just as it was impossible to develop fully a socialist ideology with the nation as a frame of reference, so it is today useless to retain the national frame of reference in the task of formulating a truly international or world-wide ideology. The partial integration of the socialist ideology in older political structures disrupted, but did not abolish, the bourgeois conception of the nation as a cultural phenomenon and a political reality. In the country where socialism was accepted in its most extreme form, Russia, the socialist ideology invigorated or even created nationalism among the masses. In the same manner, national or regional cultures would not necessarily perish if the international political structures should come to be impregnated by the social norms and values which may eventually develop on a world-wide scale. Indeed such a development has recently been recognized by many observers.[22] Elements of a new and virtually universal social integration already exist as a result of the spread of industrial techniques, which tend everywhere to develop similar social statuses, interests, aspirations, and mentalities. As has often been said, the manager of a big Soviet state

[22]See, e.g., Emmanuel R. Posnack, *World without Barriers* (New York: 1956).

enterprise is closer in motivations, interests, and character to the executive of a large American firm than to a Russian worker or soldier. But existing political ideologies, because they largely reflect the particularisms of national social structures, are unable to embrace the socio-economic interests and aspirations which seek political recognition and expression on the international plane, and are thus inadequate as a means of establishing consensus in the international community.

I do not pretend to have validated in this essay my hypothesis concerning the character and functions of political ideologies. I have merely illustrated and elucidated it, and in this way have tried to suggest that the hypothesis, if proved valid, could be developed into an integrated conceptual model which would be a useful tool in the analysis of socio-political dynamics.

Political Ideology and Political Institutions*

Karl Loewenstein

. . . The specific emphasis of the study will be on the role played by the ideological factor in the formation and operation of political systems and the influence the ideological "infrastructure" exerts on the latters' institutions and techniques. The focus on ideology is justified by its actuality in our time which is spoken of as the "ideological age." The conflict between the West and the East is said to be basically the "ideological" anithesis between two political systems, generally described as democratic constitutionalism and totalitarian (communist or fascist) autocracy. However, it is prima facie evident that the antinomy of these two political systems is rather one of ideological content than of institutional arrangements since both of them make use, to a large extent, of identical political institutions and techniques such as constitutions, elections, parliaments, courts, political parties, and administrative procedures. It is submitted as the—as yet—inarticulate major premise of this study that in any political system it is the underlying political ideology which actually conditions the function and shapes the operation of the political institutions and techniques.

*Karl Loewenstein, "Political Systems, Ideologies and Institutions: The Problem of Their Circulation," *Western Political Quarterly,* 6 (1953), pp. 689-706. Reprinted by permission of the University of Utah, copyright owners.

The "Political System"

Society and Power

Society as a whole is a system of power relations. The term "political power" denotes the exercise of effective social control by the power-holders over the power-addressees. Within society, the state is the predominant, or, as historically the case may be, the paramount organization for the exercise of political power as social control. In this sense every state is a "political system." The core of every "political system," therefore, is the instrumentalities and agencies of the state for the attainment, exercise, and maintenance of political power. Under present-day democratic constitutionalism the essence of the political system consists in establishing an equilibrium between the various competitive plural forces of society. Under present-day totalitarian autocracy social control and political power are monopolized by a single sociopolitical group.

Political System, Political Ideology, and Political Institutions

In the dynamism of sociopolitical power ideologies are the motive forces, while institutions and techniques are the apparatus or mechanics through which the ideology transforms itself into the reality of political and social action. Ideologies and institutions (and techniques) are correlative and mutually interdependent. It is submitted that no political system, being the frame within which the process of social control and political power operates, has existed, nor can exist, without creating, consciously or subconsciously, a substructure for its institutionalized existence by an appropriate political ideology. In turn, each ideology is bound to create and utilize for its realization as sociopolitical action institutions and techniques commensurate to its ideological premises.

Political System and Form of Government

"Political system" is not coterminous with "form of government." Being a generic term, "political system" embraces, as a rule, various "forms of government," linked together by the same, or a similar, type of political ideology and the institutions corresponding to it. Thus, the political system of democratic constitutionalism includes various "forms of government" (presidentialism; parliamentarianism with legislative or with cabinet supremacy; directory government) as does the political system of totalitarian autocracy (assembly government of contemporary communism; the fascist "leadership" system; corporativism, etc.). . .

Definition and Elements of Ideologies

In this "ideological" age the concept and nature of the political ideology can be defined with a fair degree of general acceptance. An ideology is a

consistent and integrated pattern of thoughts and beliefs, or thoughts converted into beliefs, explaining man's attitudes toward life and his existence in
society, and advocating a conduct and action pattern responsive to, and
commensurate with, such thoughts and beliefs.

Qualifications of Contemporary Political Ideologies

To be effective in our time a political ideology must be: (a) formulated in
such manner as to be communicable to the mass of the power-addressees;
(b) carried by mass belief and not confined in its acceptance to a relatively
restricted circle of an elite or "the initiated"; (c) oriented towards a human
preference or social value, or a cohesive set of such values. These human
preferences or values refer to the exercise of social control and political
power. All political ideologies, therefore, are essentially related to political
power, even those which, like Ghandi's ideology of passive resistance, reject
resorting to physical force.

Ideologies and the Mass Society

The requirement of being capable of appealing to the masses of the power-
addressees and of being grasped and assimilated by them constitutes the characteristic aspect of ideologies in our contemporary mass society. In the need
of being mobilized for mass consumption lies the conspicuous difference of
the modern ideology from those operative in previous elitist or aristocratic
societies. For the purpose of mass articulation the manipulators of contemporary ideologies have developed, and apply scientifically, specific mass
techniques of simplification, generalization, popularization, and vulgarization.
This, in turn, is accomplished by the devices of symbolism, semantic and
verbalistic procedures, and, in general, by the techniques of dissemination
called propaganda. As used here the latter term is functional and non-
evaluative. The willingness of the masses of the power-addressees to accept
and share an ideology—a situation appropriately described as "receptivity"—is
largely conditioned by the effectiveness of the propaganda methods applied,
provided the ideology as such appears as the fulfillment of their desires and
aspirations. It is obvious that both the "mobility" or circulation of an
ideology and the "receptivity" of the power-addressees for it are primarily
dependent on the technology of the media of intercommunication.

Purpose and Function of Political Ideologies

The motive forces and incentives of political ideologies are either (a) the
desire for change of the existing sociopolitical order and a more equitable
distribution of the prevailing power potential among the various classes constituting the state-society, or (b) the desire for the maintenance and preservation of the existing sociopolitical status quo and the location of political
power resulting therefrom. In the former case the ideology evolves a thought

and action pattern intended to satisfy the needs of a class believing itself
excluded from its legitimate share in the exercise of political power. The
ideology of reform, as a rule, feeds on tangible grievances of the class discriminated against. In the second case, the ideology justifies the existing
social order, either to defend it against real or potential sociopolitical pressures, or, quite often, merely for the sake of self-glorification or self-
confirmation based on the belief that the prevailing political system has
achieved "finality." An illustration of the former ideological intent is the
political and economic liberalism of the rising bourgeoisie in the eighteenth
century; of the latter, the ideology of the divine right of kings in the seventeenth. There exist, of course, many intermediate situations in which motivations of attack and defense coincide and become mutually responsive.

Genesis of Ideologies

Recent cultural and sociopsychological research tries to clarify the complex
origin of current ideologies (religious, socioeconomic, political, and others),
assisted if not always helped by methods borrowed from individual psychology and psychoanalysis and applied to collective groups. Briefly summarized, ideologies derive from either rational or irrational sources; in most
instances, however, from both. They may originate with a member of the
intelligentsia, in many cases an individual political thinker, advanced either to
defend the status quo or, more frequently, to counsel reform. However, what
on the surface may appear invented or initiated by an individual theorist, in
historical perspective may prove to be the rationalization of a thought pattern
rooted in the past and shared, if subconsciously and without articulation, by
relevant sectors of the masses and public opinion of the period. Essential in
the formulation and concretization of the ideology is the function of the
intelligentsia, the support of which the disfavored class may find either in its
own ranks, or among outsiders, even among members of the ruling class who
side with the group discriminated against.

However, it should be noted that some of the truly world-shaking political
ideologists were originally time- and class-conditioned and served the specific
interests of the theorist articulating them. They acquired the quality of
absoluteness and universal validity only by becoming divorced from their
original setting. This can easily be demonstrated by projecting the ideological
"inventions" of men like Cicero, Polybius, Machiavelli, Bodin, Hobbes,
Locke, Rousseau, or Montesquieu against the particular historical background
from which they emerged, as was aptly pointed out by Harold Laski: "Every
great thinker is in part the autobiography of his age." Scientific analysis of

the dynamism of ideologies may also profitably distinguish between inventors and propagators, prophets and simplifiers, contrasting, for example, Rousseau with Sieyès and Jefferson; Montesquieu with Constant; Mussolini with Sorel and Pareto. Moreover, it occurred not infrequently that concrete historical situations were transubstantiated into abstract ideologies, as for example, the constitution of the late Roman republic by Polybius; the "Glorious Revolution" by Locke; the British constitution by Montesquieu; the Paris Commune by Marx and Lenin.

However, the main well-spring of ideologies is the irrational, supplied by religious beliefs; superstitions; the impact of the supernatural, mythologies; legends, folklore; and, in general, symbolizations and manifestations of national traditions and environmental conditions. In most cases an effective ideology is produced by the interaction of rational and irrational elements. Paradoxically it may be said that an ideology is the more effective the more it appeals to the irrational. Rationally conceived ideologies, such as Zionism and Marxism, by faith and belief turn into unchallengeable absolutes. On the other hand, an ideology primarily emerging from irrational and emotional motivations, such as nationalism, may gain currency only when consciously and rationally articulated by political theory. In some cases even concrete institutions, such as the American Constitution, or the Prussian civil service, could develop into valid ideologies.

Since any effective ideology requires mass acceptance and mass belief, and since the masses are drawn to an ideology more by belief than by reason, all contemporary political ideologies have strong religious overtones. It is characteristic of the religious that it does not admit degrees of acceptance. Being absolute by nature it must either be accepted or rejected; there are only believers and heretics. Most modern political ideologies have become religion-affected in the sense that a particular thought and belief pattern embodies values that are considered absolute by its adherents. To the masses the ideological belief is a substitute for eroded religious values. Even liberal ideologies whose specific value-content is tolerance and relativism, assume, when exposed to the competitive antithesis of totalitarianism, the absolutist coloration of the "either-or." Not without justification, therefore, many of the modern political ideologies are qualified as political religions. The historical shift from the religious to the sociopolitical value-content and the reconversion, under the impact of the mass society, of the socio-political programs into quasi-religious values is perhaps the most significant single feature in the contemporary ideological process.

Typology of Ideologies

As yet political science has not succeeded in establishing a systematically meaningful classification of the historically relevant types of political ideologies. The difficulty of establishing a tabulation of categories (*Kategorientafel*) arises from the complex and often contradictory character of most current ideologies—constitutionalism, liberalism, nationalism, socialism, and organicism, to name only a few. It may also seem well-nigh impossible to delineate political ideologies proper from those with religious, socioeconomic, moral, or cultural value-contents. Today most political ideologies are "total" or global in the sense that they claim to supply all answers to all questions. In previous more static periods of society ideologies were primarily religious; political and economic values were determined by, and subordinated to, the premises of the beyond-worldly, for example, those of Islamism, Catholicism, Puritanism, Calvinism, Buddhism, or Shintoism. On the other hand, considering the importance of socioeconomic factors for the life of the masses, in most contemporary ideologies the socioeconomic elements dominate and determine the intrinsically political components. The following listing of some of the historically most relevant political ideologies is merely exemplificative and does not imply any attempt at classification as to substance or causal correlation:

1.   Absolutism, as monarchism; dynasticism; legitimism; or, with a more religious accent, as theocracy and Caesaro-Papism.

2.   Constitutionalism, institutionalized in the ideologies of representative government; parliamentarianism; the rule of law (*Rechtsstaat*), and democracy.

3.   Individualism, in both its economic and political implications, as liberalism; free enterprise, capitalism; humanism.

4.   Social collectivism, as either democratic or proletarian socialism (communism); state capitalism; the ideology of the service or welfare state.

5.   Nationalism; imperialism; racism; internationalism; universalism.

6.   Elitist and organicist ideologies, such as aristocratism, agrarianism; managerialism; corporativism; and the modern variants of fascism.

Even the most elementary classification reveals that there are few if any "ideal types" of political ideologies and that most modern ideologies contain elements of collateral, complementary, and even antithetical thought and belief patterns. Nor can any political ideology be neatly separated fully from socioeconomic and ethical ingredients.

Political Ideology and Class Structure

If the premise is accepted that political ideologies refer to social values under-lying the relationship between power-holders and power-addressees the question arises: For whose interests is the ideology invoked and for whose benefit does it operate? Numerous historical situations are on record in which the beneficiary of power was an individual who, while pretending to represent generally desirable social values, in reality promoted nothing but his personal power aspirations. The weight of historical experience, however, tends to indicate that, as a rule, social values and, thus, the ideologies reflecting them, are generated by, and conditioned on, specific groups and classes. Religious ideologies, for example, served the rule of the priestly class. Economic ideol-ogies strengthened the rule of the propertied classes (landed wealth or mobile capital) or of the poor (proletariat). Elitist ideologies were mobilized and invoked to fortify the rule of a minority claiming to be specifically ordained. Most historically potent ideologies appear to have been class-invented and class-intended, be it by the priests, the military, the feudal landowners, the merchant and craft guilds, the manufacturing and trading bourgeoisie, the leisure class, the proletariat, the managerial elite, or other socially relevant groups. The ideology of nationalism may seem an exception to that rule because once embraced by the entire community it transcends class or group interests. On closer inspection, however, it can be demonstrated that in every individual case the nationalist ideology originated with a group or class (the intelligentsia, mercantile interests, or others) that expected to benefit from self-determination or independence.

It may seem a basic defect of present-day political science that political systems are analyzed and evaluated in terms of how their institutions func-tion, instead of the ideological causations responsible for these institutions. Political systems never are an "ideal type" or the "best" form of government, but concrete institutionalizations of the class rule and class interests of the power-holders, usually disguised, for their better "receptivity" by the masses of the power-addressees, by general or "objective" arguments of a moral char-acter, such as the "general welfare," "economic security," the "greatest happiness of the greatest number," the promotion of individual initiative, or similar semantic appeals.

Political Institutions and Techniques

Political Institutions

Ideologies must be sharply distinguished from institutions. Serving as the framework and apparatus necessary for the rational organization and orderly functioning of social life, they constitute established conduct and action patterns operating with a certain degree of permanency and reasonably predictable standards of regularity. Institutions may be described as the instrumentalities or agencies through which the sociopolitical functions of the state society are accomplished and the process of social control and political power is conducted. Institutions, therefore, are all the elements of the state machinery: governmental agencies in the widest sense of the term; parliaments; courts; the civil service; the military establishment; the political parties, but equally so, extraconstitutional agencies such as pressure groups and other associational forces of the pluralistically structured community.

Although all of these institutions are primarily functional, that is, designed for the rational operation of community life, in rare instances only are they indifferent to ideologies and the social values embodied by them. As a rule they are ideology-conditioned in the sense that they reflect a specific pattern of sociopolitical beliefs and purposes. There exist few wholly ideology-immune or ideology-neutral institutions, though in some instances the functional purpose of an institution may seem less ideology-affected than others, as are the military establishment or the administrative services without which no organized state society can exist. Many of the present-day misunderstandings of "political systems" arise from the excessive nominalism customary in political science which ignores the fact that different political systems utilize seemingly identical institutions with a different ideological intent. Instead, political institutions should be analyzed and evaluated in conformity with the ideological environment in which they operate, and the ideological purpose which governs them. The parliament, for instance, may be responsive to the democratic ideology of genuine representation of the popular will, or may be, in the case of a totalitarian (fascist or communist) ideology, merely a mechanism for the discharge of the legislative function dictated by the holders of power. Courts may be serving the ideology of the impartial rule of law, as under democratic constitutionalism, or merely enforcing the official state policy, as under absolutism and totalitarianism. Institutions that originated in a different ideological environment today are frequently being put to uses alien to their original *raison d'être*. Elections and plebiscites, parliaments, political parties, guarantees of individual rights—all these are institutions which stem from the ideological source of democratic constitutionalism. They lose their functional identity when attuned to, and perverted by, the ideological purposes of totalitarianism.

Political Techniques and Procedures

Institutions, in turn, should be distinguished from techniques and procedures. These are the devices and arrangements through which institutions perform their assigned functions. Most political institutions develop techniques and procedures commensurate to their functions. The distinction between institutions and techniques may not always seem easy. For example, political parties are both institutions and techniques. Western constitutionalism, hardly mentioning them in the constitutional documents, may consider them as techniques for mobilizing and crystallizing public opinion for political action, while under contemporary totalitarianism (fascism, nazism, communism) the single party is the paramount state institution and governmental agency.

Political techniques and procedures exist which are either strictly functional, or less ideology-conditioned than others. For example, the military establishment operates through the technique of command and obedience regardless of the ideological environment. Likewise, bureaucracy must accomplish its function through the techniques of hierarchy and rationality of office performance whatever ideology conditions the state society it serves. Parliaments everywhere must adhere to deliberative (discussion) and voting techniques whatever real political value may be attached to them. However, ideologies may condition and even pervert such inherent techniques to serve the ideological intent of the political system. A "parliament" remains a parliament only in the most nominal sense and is no longer a functional body when free discussion and voting are replaced by dictation, persuasion by compulsion.

The Correlation of Ideologies and Institutions

Political institutions and techniques, therefore, are, as a rule, responsive to, and reflective of, the specific ideology which governs the political system. The democratic ideology operates through institutions and techniques which promote the sharing of political power and favor the widest possible publicity to stimulate popular participation in political life. Totalitarian ideologies likewise are translated into institutions and techniques commensurate to them. They prefer, for example, appointive institutions and techniques to those based on election. In other words, to be effective a political system "institutionalizes" its political ideology. Ideologies materialize themselves in the political institutions and techniques corresponding to them. The ideology of democratic equality will rationalize itself in either referendal or genuinely representative institutions and techniques, both premised on universal suffrage and the free choice of alternatives. The ideology of the dictatorship of the proletariat, on the other hand, institutionalizes itself in the single party and the technique of compulsion applied to public opinion managed from above. The ideology of socialism resorts to planning institutions and nationalization techniques with the same intrinsic necessity as the ideology of private capitalism requires the specific institutions and techniques of competition and free enterprise.

However, here a curious phenomenon should be noted, namely the identification or the *quid pro quo* of the ideology and the institutions. Frequently an
institution reaches the point where it signifies and symbolizes the underlying
ideology. For instance, the constitution, historically merely the instrumentality of the thought and belief pattern that authority must be controlled
and government limited, becomes the epitome of the ideology itself. Hence
the frequently incongruous result that the introduction, by a nation, of
democratic institutions (constitution, universal suffrage, election procedures,
parliaments) is equated with the acceptance of the underlying ideology by the
bulk of that nation. The present-day lack of political stability in so-called
politically backward nations may be interpreted as the time-lag existing
between the adoption of the institutional framework and the commensurate
degree of implementing it by the corresponding ideology. This lack of
synchronization between ideology and institutions may help to explain the
disappointing progress and success of democratic constitutionalism in various
regions of the world. For example, the adoption of the separation-of-powers
institutions, signifying the preservation of individual liberties against governmental arbitrariness, in the Latin-American and Asiatic environments failed to
create the ideological climate for democratic constitutionalism and merely
served as the leverage of personalist dictatorship.

The "Ontology" of Political Systems as "Patterns of Governments"

If this approach of correlating sociopolitical institutions to their ideological
"infrastructure" is systematically applied it will necessarily lead to what may
be called the "ontology" of political systems or patterns of government, in
contrast to the customary institutional and functional analysis. For example,
the democracy of the Greek city-states can be interpreted as the rule of a
leisure class based on a non-technological slave society. The rule of the military caste and the corporate estates of the feudal period was conditioned by a
largely self-contained landed wealth economy. Representative constitutionalism of the classical period corresponded to the interests of the morally
self-reliant and economically competitive bourgeois manufacturing and
commercial class. Equalitarian socialism, in order to achieve a more equitable
distribution of wealth in a mass society, by necessity turns to planning techniques, and the latter, in turn, necessarily bring into play authoritarian
controls and management of socio-economic life. No analysis of political
systems, therefore, may seem satisfactory without consciously establishing
the causal relationship between its political ideological and the class interests,
class rule, and class-conditioned political institutions.

The "Mobility"—"Circulation"—of Political Systems and Ideologies

Definition of Terms

Political systems and the institutions evolved by them are disseminated primarily through the transmission belts of political ideologies. This process of diffusion will be spoken of hereafter as the "mobility" or "circulation." The process of the "penetration" of a political system into, or its "acceptance" by, an individual national environment will be called hereafter the "receptivity." The following discussion will confine itself to the problems of the *trans*national mobility and receptivity of political systems and ideologies without dealing with the conditions of the *intra*national "receptivity" of a national environment for indigenous political ideologies and institutions.

Stationary and Circulatory Ideologies

Past historical periods are characterized by the high degree of the *trans*-national uniformity of their political systems and the *intra*national similarity of their political institutions. Most state-societies were managed by an authoritarian form of social control and political power, mostly (though with the exceptions of aristocratic republics) as absolute monarchies which constituted the almost universal type of political rule. Political civilizations with a different rationale of government were exceptional, sporadic, and of relatively short duration. Of these, the historically most influential were the sociopolitical civilization of the Hebrews where royal absolutism was limited and held in check by the Law of the Lord propounded by the prophets, and the Greek city-states where political power was nominally exercised by the people or, rather, by the socially restricted group of the active citizens. The outstanding example of a non-authoritarian state society under the rule of law, the Roman Republic, was basically non-democratic and, after a glorious history, reverted to the universal pattern of absolutism under the Dominate. It was perpetuated, for another thousand years, as Caesaro-Papism in Byzantium.

Furthermore, past historical periods were distinguished by a high degree of intrastate social homogeneity and, consequently, of ideological stability. In spite of frequent—and frequently violent—changes in the personnel of the power-holders, the state-society of monarchical absolutism was socially static and stable. Similarly, the political rule of the aristocratic families in the republic of Venice lasted for almost one thousand years. Against the emergence of new ideologies with their corresponding political institutions militated the following factors: the forces of tradition; the governmental monopoly of certain ruling classes; the lack of contacts with other non-absolutist civilizations that could have stimulated change; the fusion of secular and religious values and institutions, and, correspondingly, the per-suasiveness of the "divine" justification of authority; and, most of all, the homogeneity and stability of the social stratification. Wherever a consciously articulated political ideology existed, as in Byzantium, it vindicated the wisdom of the "powers that be" and the status quo. Likewise the political institutions under medieval absolutism conformed to an almost universal pattern. Intellectual residues of ancient constitutionalism, derived from Greece and the Roman Republic, were imperceptible in the West and non-existent in the absolute state-societies of the non-Western world, Japan and China, India, and the Islamic dominions. Consequently, similar social condi-tions created more or less similar political institutions and their ideological justifications.

Diffusion and Convergence of Ideologies

Changes, however, did occur which appear as striking coincidences of political institutions and ideologies on transnational lines. Pertinent illustrations are the feudal agreements between the tenants-in-chief and the Crown in the early thirteenth century (England, Magna Carta, 1215; Hungary, Golden Bull, 1222; Germany, *Statutum in favorem principum* of Frederic II, 1231). Equally remarkable is the simultaneous emergence of representative institu-tions at the end of the thirteenth century in Spain, England, and France. It is still a celebrated controversy whether the apparent synchronization was caused by the indigenous conditions of the all-European feudal order, or was due to the transnational circulation of the ideology of representation. Pos-sibly the greater social mobility occasioned by the Crusades may have been an incentive added to local impulses. In this context it should be noted that no other feudal civilization (Byzantium, India, China and Japan, the Moslem world) did generate anything resembling representative institutions. For the sake of contrast another famous dispute may be referred to, namely whether the French Declaration of the Rights of Man was inspired by American precedents, or derived from indigenous French sources. While the prepon-derance of opinion favors the circulation of the ideology from the New World to France, native French motivations—the *rémonstrances*, for example, of the French *parlements* (courts)—constituted a strong contributory incentive.

The methodological problem involved in these illustrations is one familiar to cultural sociology, that is, to differentiate between the "diffusion" and the "convergence" of ideologies and institutions. The pattern of mobility called diffusion assumes that cultural attitudes circulate on transnational lines through imitation. Convergence, on the other hand, is premised on the assumption that similar social conditions in different national environments lead to similar ideological and institutional solutions without direct foreign influences. The problem is not confined to the circulation of political ideologies and institutions; it arises concerning the dissemination of any cultural phenomenon such as artistic styles (Romanesque, Gothic, baroque, rococo, "Empire," "functionalism"); literary fashions; musical modes.

The Accelerated Mobility of the Ideological Patterns

Since the fifteenth century the process of the circulation of ideologies and the institutions corresponding to them was immensely accelerated by the new techniques of intercommunication which broke down national isolation. First among them was the invention of the printing press. Knowledge, no longer confinable to the elite of the initiated, became accessible to a new intelligentsia other than the ruling classes in state and church. It was the printed word which placed education on a mass basis. Education, in turn, became both the cause and the effect of the mobility and circulation of ideas. On the transnational level ideational interpenetration and dissemination was promoted by the maritime discoveries and the closer cultural and economic contacts resultant therefrom. Finally, with the Reformation—a mass movement made possible only through the printed word—the circulation and mobility of religious ideologies, inextricably interwoven with sociopolitical thought and action patterns, became irresistibly transnational. State-societies heretofore stationary were intellectually "softened up" and ideologically linked together. With the disappearance of the educational monopoly of the professionals allied with the ruling classes in church and state an intellectual "open door" was established for nonconformist and revolutionary ideologies and institutions, climaxing finally in the great revolutions of the seventeenth and the eighteenth centuries.

The process of accelerated mobility and circulation of ideologies was repeated, on an even larger transnational scale, by the revolutionary inventions of telecommunications in the nineteenth and twentieth centuries. With the increasingly perfected technology of electronics (telegraph, telephone, radio, and television) and the unprecedentedly improved facilities of international transport (steam, electricity, the internal combustion engine) barriers to the transmission and circulation of ideas and techniques ceased to exist. Of particular importance, however, for the mobility of, and the receptivity for, political ideologies was the universal emergence of the political party as the instrumentality for mobilizing public opinion in a mass society. Political parties originated through both diffusion (from England to the Continent and to the New World) and convergence. Intensified ideological circulation acted as the dissolvent of the previously existing rigid class stratification. On the pattern first of England, thereafter of France, the various classes equipped themselves transnationally with appropriate socio-political ideologies. Diversification of class structures resulted in the diversification of class ideologies. The hour of the birth of the present-day ideological antithesis was the French Revolution, the intellectual progenitor of practically all modern political systems and ideologies, liberalism, democracy, and constitutionalism no less than nationalism, socialism, and totalitarianism. The process of ideological diversification gained its full momentum under the impact of the Industrial Revolution of the nineteenth and the chemical-biological revolution of the twentieth centuries.

The Circulation of Constitutionalism

In the circulation of the ideology and the institution of the written constitution the political scientist will find a particularly illuminating example of the mobility of political systems. To limit arbitrariness of dynastic absolutism the postulate of the written constitution, including the guarantees of individual rights inaccessible to public authority, had grown into the pervading ideology of liberalism and constitutionalism. The written constitution institutionalized and symbolized the ideology, first, of constitutionally limited, subsequently, of popularly expanded government. Transnationally it inspired all classes excluded from their legitimate share in political power. This explains the phenomenon of the "migration" or the "families" of constitutions, radiating, for example, from the American Constitution as the pattern of federalism and the separation of powers; British constitutionalism as party-operated cabinet government; the Belgian *Charte* as the model of the liberal monarchy by the will of the people; the Bismarck constitution signifying constitutionally disguised authoritarianism of the Crown; the French constitution of 1875 as the recognition of parliamentary supremacy; and, last but not least, assembly government (*gouvernement conventionnel*), invented by the French Convention of 1792 and revived, in our time, by the Soviet Union and its satellites as the pseudodemocratic camouflage of a totalitarian political system operated by single-party control.

The Transnational Character of Modern Political Ideologies

Since the French Revolution political ideologies have operated on a predominantly transnational scale. This phenomenon results primarily from the universalism of democratic ideologies and the institutions corresponding to them. In this process of dissemination the political parties became the qualified promoters and chosen transmission belts. Liberal parties spear-headed, and ultimately carried to victory, the revolt of the middle-class bourgeoisie and intelligentsia against the feudal order of absolutism. Subsequently, against the capitalist classes the Socialist parties organized themselves as the carriers of at first revolutionary, later revisionist Marxism in the First and the Second International. National variations, conditioned by specific environmental situations to the contrary notwithstanding, derived from common premises of the industrial civilization, identical socio-political institutions and techniques. The ideology of socialism followed almost standardized stratagems in the struggle for political power directed against the ruling bourgeois classes.

Transnational standardization is the natural history of contemporary totalitarian ideologies. Fascism, basically an elitist ideology with a mass basis, was at first experimentally applied in Hungary and Italy as a defense mechanism of the propertied classes against communist power aspirations. From there it circulated rapidly to, and penetrated into, national environments that possessed a similarly favorable climate of receptivity. Again, in spite of local variations, its basic institutions and techniques are imported from abroad, copied, imitated and adjusted, for the identical purpose of the conquest of power, to the specific environmental situations. Wherever fascism emerges, its ideologies, institutions, and techniques are stereotyped to the point of identity. Invariably the repertory includes: the leader and its followers; the party organization on military lines; the fifth column; martyrology; the "scapegoat" techniques; stagecraft and political symbolism; deliberately used exploitation of mass emotionalism to obtain the mass basis; and negation of the validity of democratic beliefs and institutions. Moreover, fascist movements are known to co-operate and to consult transnationally. Equally identical are the institutions and techniques of political control once a fascist movement has conquered power.

The highest degree, finally, of international mobility and transnational cohesion is evidenced by communism. Here an ideological world movement has arisen whose strategy and tactics in the struggle for the conquest of power appear centrally directed by transnational agencies (Comintern and Cominform). What had been, in the historical process, the spontaneous circulation of ideologies has now become converted into the rational planning of transnational mobility for moving the communist ideology across national boundaries. In this process international communism developed its specific power techniques, such as cells, action squads, infiltration into key positions in socioeconomic life and government, secrecy of operations, enforcement of blind party loyalty, and utter disregard for foreign sovereignties and of the principle of nonintervention. In contrast to the fascist technique of first establishing the mass basis for the subsequent conquest of power communism aims at accomplishing the *coup d'ètat* by minority action. Once the violent overthrow of the legitimate government has been consummated a definite action pattern is prescribed and followed for the intranational consolidation of the communist regime as evidenced by the standard procedures followed since 1945 in all states that succumbed to Soviet imperialism.

The Carriers of Political Ideologies

In former periods of less intensified transnational contacts the knowledge of foreign conditions and situations circulated accidentally and unsystematically. Travelers, merchants, diplomatic emissaries, political fugitives, possibly religious missionaries (such as the Irish monks preaching Christianity in Northern and Central Europe) may have been instrumental to the dissemination of foreign ideas, though such sporadic influences must have had a necessarily limited effect. On a broader front moved ideological interpenetration through conquest and occupation. Both could affect, and did affect, the political ideologies and institutions of the conquerors no less than of the vanquished as evidenced by Alexander's submission to the oriental environment, or the Romanization of the Teutonic invaders settled in the Roman Empire. More recent illustrations are the receptivity to French political ideologies and institutions in Southern and Western Germany, Italy, and elsewhere in the period of French expansion during the Revolution and under Napoleon, or, possibly, the impact of the Western political systems on occupied Germany and Japan, or of the Soviets on Eastern Europe. An example of the deliberate acceptance of a foreign political technique was the adoption of the Roman law in the fifteenth century when it provided the absolute monarchies of the rising nation states in Western Europe with the tool for centralized bureaucratic organization.

One may be tempted to ascribe the fact that today ideas and ideologies circulate in a vast and unbroken stream and no longer, as was the case formerly, merely sporadically and as an intermittent trickle, primarily to the technology of modern intercommunications. The Japanese could isolate themselves against foreign influences until Perry forced them to open themselves to the world. Ideas travel freely today, except to the Iron Curtain countries where the power-holders, through rigid control of the public opinion media, try to withhold them from the masses of the power-addressees. Possibly, however, this explanation of the present highly perfected mobility of ideologies may be insufficient. Under the impact of technological standardization and mechanization national diversities in culture have become leveled down and mutually assimilated. Forever social values and the ideologies representing them have been class-conditioned. Nowadays the class stratification is transnationally oriented. Specific class ideologies are shared by, or appeal to, a specific class such as labor, capital, agrarian and other professional interests, regardless of the national environment. A political ideology valid anywhere claims to be valid everywhere. Hence, the transnational solidarity of the social classes appears the most effective vehicle for the mobility and circulation of ideologies.

Some Summarizing Conclusions Concerning the Circulation of Modern Ideologies

The material submitted here may permit the following general if tentative conclusions concerning the circulation of political systems and the ideologies, institutions and techniques that constitute them:

1. The mass basis which any political ideology requires in this age necessitates a technological apparatus for its dissemination and acceptance. Being no longer accidental and sporadic, the process of circulation is carried on by professional agencies, particularly by political parties.

2. It is no longer feasible to differentiate political ideologies from those with other—economic, religious, moral—value contents. The modern ideology, mass-oriented and directed towards mass consumption, has become an all-inclusive, "gap-less," global thought and belief pattern. By virtue of being an encompassing systematization of the values of social life, the modern political ideology tends to become a "totalitarian" political theology.

3. To achieve its mass function the modern ideology can no longer consist of abstractions addressed to the initiated few and accessible only to the intellectual elite. Predigested for mass consumption it is now concrete, essentially externalized, superficial, simplified, and generalized.

4. In spite of its rational formulation, if not origin, the modern political ideology is emotion-generated and emotion-generating. Approximated, thus, to the religions as of old, it has become "monolithic" in the sense that it claims to be the only feasible explanation of man's life in society and the exclusive solution of man's sociopolitical dilemma. Paradoxically, even the ideologies of democracy and liberalism, historically inspired by the relativism of tolerance, have turned into an absolute and refractory dogma which, for

reasons of self-defense, can no longer admit the validity of other competitive ideological solutions.

5.   All political ideologies are now consistently directed towards concrete institutions and techniques embodying their social values. The establishment by the power-holders, and the acceptance by the power-addressees, of specific political institutions is believed to carry with it the fulfillment of the promises contained in the underlying political ideology.

Political Ideology and Political Behavior*

Samuel Barnes

Ideology is one of the most frequently cited and inadequately understood subjects of empirical political inquiry. It easily lends itself to diverse and conflicting usages and, with a few notable exceptions, research on it has been inconclusive and non-cumulative. If the theorist of ideology consequently faces many pitfalls, he also thereby gains considerable freedom of interpretation. I will take advantage of this freedom in order to criticize the utility of most usages of ideology and to suggest an alternative approach.

I assume that the most important problems facing the student of ideology are empirical; that is, they do not involve the analysis of the merits and short-comings of particular ideologies or the historical origins of contemporary ideological disagreements, though these important topics also merit attention. Rather, the most pressing problems concern how ideologies affect the structure of political conflict on the macro level and individual action on the micro level. They involve the relationship between political thought and behavior, and this relationship is primarily a problem of linkage. I maintain that this linkage takes place largely in the organizations in which elites and masses come together for political action, and that political organization is consequently the most promising focus for research on ideology.

There is mounting evidence that mass publics do not react in ideological terms. It seems equally true that much contemporary political conflict has an

*Samuel H. Barnes, "Ideology and the Organization of Conflict: On the Relationship Between Political Thought and Behavior," *The Journal of Politics,* 28 (1966), pp. 513-530. Reprinted by permission.

ideological dimension. This paper seeks to contribute towards the resolution of this seeming contradiction: It is presented not as a solution but as a beginning. In it, I (1) suggest a restricted usage of the term ideology; (2) review and criticize methods of operationalizing and measuring ideology and its dispersion; (3) propose political organization as the most promising focus for research on ideology; and (4) discuss how ideology relates to the organization of political conflict.

The Meaning of Ideology

Most difficulties in the operationalization of the concept of ideology can be traced to the meaning of the term adopted by the researcher. David Minar has reviewed these various usages and I do not want to retrace the field that he covered so well.[1] I agree with Minar that we need a definition "that reaches beyond mere attitudes, reasons stemming from the considerations of utility or suggestiveness, of historical identity, and communicability"; and we further agree on the need for a denotation that combines some of these elements with "a political theory of ideology that casts it as a sort of ideational background of politics, that conditions behavior and accounts for some of the basic continuities in political society."[2]

In this paper I will make a distinction between political belief systems and political ideologies. I will retain belief system as an open term referring to the set of political attitudes held by an individual, whether exhibiting constraint or not.[3] An ideology is a belief system that is internally consistent *and* consciously held. This approach rejects formulations that view ideology as a mere collection of political attitudes or policy preferences. Constraint must exist among components of an ideology; knowing one belief must increase the probability of guessing another correctly; components must "hang together." Most constrained belief systems undoubtedly relate directly or indirectly to one of the major traditions of political thought—the great isms—such as, for example, liberalism, communism, fascism, social Catholicism, or the several varieties of socialism. For the great isms are, among other things, attempts to work out the logical ramifications of some basic insight or insights; hence, at least originally and in their philosophical formulations, they are highly constrained systems of thought. But not everyone who claims

[1]David Minar, "Ideology and Political Behavior," *Midwest Journal of Political Science,* Vol. 5 (November 1961), 317-331.

[2]*Ibid.,* 326.

[3]For a discussion of belief systems, see Philip Converse, "The Nature of Belief Systems in Mass Publics," in David Apter (ed.), *Ideology and Discontent* (New York: The Free Press, 1964), pp. 206-261. My distinction between belief system and ideology is similar in many respects to Robert E. Lane's latent and forensic ideologies. See *Political Ideology* (New York: The Free Press, 1962).

to adhere to a particular ism necessarily accepts all of the logical consequences of his act of faith. Consequently, the degree of constraint in a belief
system is an empirical question; it must be demonstrated, not assumed, and
only constrained and consciously held belief systems will be labeled
ideologies.

To adopt a broader view of ideology would make it virtually synonymous
with political attitudes. Actually, a particular political system may contain a
wide range of political attitudes, many of which may be compatible with
several ideologies. Recognition of the distinction between political attitudes
and political ideology might clarify much of the present debate over the
decline of ideology. Even if political attitudes become increasingly similar,
their divergent ideological bases need not disappear.

To adopt a broader view of ideology would also complicate any discussion of
the relationship between the great isms and the belief systems of mass
publics. Although ideas do have consequences for the behavior of a small
portion of the population, evidence is accumulating that ideologies as consciously held, internally constrained systems of thought do not form part of
the mental equipment of mass publics anywhere. Retaining the limited view
of ideology resolves the problem of whether the beliefs of mass publics
should be considered ideological or not by converting the problem into an
empirical one. This is not to suggest that the belief systems of mass publics
are unrelated to traditional ideological concerns. They often have ideological
ramifications, but these are more likely to be super-imposed by the analyst
than consciously held by the subjects. Kaplan's warning that we not confuse
an act with an action is pertinent here: The meaning attached by the observer
to action should not be attributed to the actor.[4]

Nor does this formulation imply an absence of constraint in the belief
systems of mass publics. Socialization may give rise to coherent belief systems
without involving the consciousness of the subject. For example, socialization
in a closed society with a high consensus can cause mere traditionalists to
appear as ideologues.[5] And political organization can provide the functional

[4] Abraham Kaplan, *The Conduct of Inquiry* (San Francisco: Chandler Publishing Company,
1964), p. 122.

[5] For example, Mattei Dogan notes that Italian Christian Democratic women are tradi-
tionalists, not conservatives: "Le donne italiane tra il cattolicesimo e il marxismo." In
Joseph LaPalombara and Alberto Spreafico (eds.), *Elezioni e comportamento politico in
Italia* (Milan: Edizioni di Communità, 1963), pp. 406-474.

equivalent of ideology, or "ideology by proxy."[6] While these give rise to constraints in belief systems, their significance for ideology is vastly different. And it is these differences that we need to investigate. But we must first examine some methodological problems in the study of ideology.

Approaches to the Measurement of Ideology

Measurement is the handmaiden of science. It may not be the sole path to scientific significance, but it is certainly the principal route to greater precision. Without a concern for measurement it is difficult to make a meaningful statement about mass publics. And an examination of the ways in which ideology has been measured reveals that much work remains to be done. In the following discussion, examples are chosen as illustrative of emerging problems; I make no pretense at a thorough coverage. The measurement of ideology has two principal dimensions—the measure of individual ideology and the measure of its distribution within a population. Several approaches to the measure of individual ideology deserve mention here.

One approach involves the utilization of open-ended questions to construct a scale of ideological sensitivity, in which those "whose comments imply the kinds of conception of politics assumed by ideological interpretations of political behavior and political change" are separated out.[7] This method revealed that less than 12% of the American electorate exhibited any substantial ideological sophistication; it also demonstrated the importance of education, as almost one-third of the college educated were classified as ideologues or near ideologues. Comparable results are reported for the French electorate,[8] and for members of an Italian Socialist Federation.[9] It seems unlikely that the level of ideological sophistication, as measured in this manner, is very high among mass publics anywhere.

The above measure tells us something about ideological sophistication but nothing about the substance of the ideology. One way to get at substance is

[6]See Angus Campbell, et al., *The American Voter* (New York: John Wiley and Sons, 1960), p. 220; for the reconstructed logic of this process, see Anthony Downs, *An Economic Theory of Democracy* (New York: Harper, 1957).

[7]Campbell, et al., *op. cit.,* p. 227. See this chapter for a complete discussion of this approach, pp. 216-265.

[8]Philip Converse and Georges Dupeux, "The Politicization of the Electorate in France and the United States," *Public Opinion Quarterly,* Vol. 26 (Spring 1962), pp. 1-23.

[9]Samuel H. Barnes, "Participation, Education, and Political Competence: Evidence from a Sample of Italian Socialists," *American Political Science Review,* Vol. 60 (June 1966), pp. 348-354.

through depth interviews that probe into aspects of belief systems difficult to tap with more standardized tests. This was the method employed by Lane in his study of fifteen inhabitants of an Eastport housing development.[10] While this study sacrificed considerations of quantification and sampling in return for depth, it identified several significant features of American belief systems that should facilitate the design of larger projects in the future.

Another approach utilized in particular by social psychologists equates ideology with general attitude structure and deduces ideological patterns from responses to questions probing specific attitudes toward criminals, alcoholism, governmental intervention, authority, religion, etc.[11] This approach has several basic weaknesses from my point of view. The first is that it often barely touches on *political* ideology, the relationship between a factor such as tendermindedness, for example, and political behavior is not always clear. Secondly, this approach makes it difficult or even impossible to distinguish values (i.e., normative judgments) and opinions, whether salient, intensively held, or rationally examined, from ideologies. Finally, as will be clarified below, this approach evades what I consider to be a crucial question —whether or not there is a functional relationship between such specific attitudes and ideology.

An approach to the study of ideology that has the virtues of simplicity of operationalization and availability of data extracts ideology from the speeches and publications of individuals and organizations. This too involves several obvious pitfalls. If the writings largely concern proposals for public policy one is inferring ideology from policy; this is similar to inferring thought from action, or at least proposed action. Unless great care is devoted to sampling problems, which is rare, it is also difficult to avoid bias in the selection of "typical" statements. Through careful selection of sources and statements one can often show a group or an individual to be for or against almost anything at one time or another. And one can learn nothing in this way about the attitudes and beliefs of the inarticulate rank and file. Writing about the Christian Anti-Communist Crusade, Wolfinger et al conclude: "Failure to distinguish between the pronouncements of political leaders and the opinions of their supporters involves some grave risks in attempting to explain the appeal of the radical right."[12] This warning is relevant for most

[10]Lane, *op. cit.*

[11]For an example of this usage and a discussion of its origins, see Paavo Koli, "Ideology Patterns and Ideology Cleavages," *Transactions of the Westermarck Society,* Vol. 4 (1959), pp. 75-143.

[12]Raymond E. Wolfinger, Barbara Kaye Wolfinger, Kenneth Prewitt, and Sheilah Rosenhack, "America's Radical Right: Politics and Ideology," in Apter (ed.), *op. cit.,* p. 275.

individuals or groups deeply involved in political struggles. Finally, this approach is especially prone to assuming commitments on the part of the writer that may not be warranted. In politics, argument is often exaggerated for dramatic effect, advantages in bargaining, and other reasons, and one cannot assume that public pronouncements actually reflect the underlying belief system of an organization or individual.[13]

Especially suited to the study of conflict is an approach that utilizes responses to batteries of attitudinal questions to study consistency among the responses of individuals (constraint) and among members of a particular group (consensus). These attitudinal questions may involve public policy issues or they may probe more basic attitudes, but the pattern of responses is utilized as a measure of ideology.[14] Some researchers are aware of the many pitfalls involved in this method. Thus the authors of *The American Voter* write:[15]

At the very best, judgment on the presence or absence of a functional relationship between two or more attitudes demands some degree of inference on the part of the investigator. In most attitude studies, functional relationships are presumed to exist where it is found that knowledge of a person's belief on one issue helps to predict his belief on some other issue. It is important to recognize that an individual may hold attitudes that appear congruent from the point of view of the analyst when there is in fact no functional contact between them.

What seems significant about these approaches is their assumptions concerning the ideological origins of constraint. This approach tends to assume what needs to be demonstrated—the existence within mass publics of stable underlying patterns of attitudes toward political objects.

Yet, convincing evidence is accumulating that they do not exist. Using panel survey data, Philip Converse was able to confront the problem directly. He concluded that changes in attitudes over time towards a number of policy questions could not be adequately explained as resulting from genuine

[13]An otherwise useful work that exhibits all three of these weaknesses is Joseph Monsen, Jr., and Mark W. Cannon, *The Makers of Public Policy: American Power Groups and Their Ideologies* (New York: McGraw-Hill Book Co., 1965).

[14]For example, Herbert McCloskey, "Conservatism and Personality," *American Political Science Review*, Vol. 52 (March 1958), pp. 27-45; McCloskey, et al., "Issue Conflict and Consensus Among Party Leaders and Followers," *American Political Science Review*, Vol. 54 (June 1960), pp. 406-427; McCloskey, "Consensus and Ideology in American Politics," *American Political Science Review*, Vol. 58 (June 1964), pp. 361-382; Campbell, et al., *op. cit.*, pp. 188-215; Samuel J. Eldersveld, *Political Parties: A Behavioral Analysis* (Chicago: Rand McNally Co., 1964), pp. 183-219.

[15]Campbell, et al., *op. cit.*, p. 191.

conversions; rather, individuals must have responded at random.[16] As a consequence, they exhibited little more constraint in their belief systems than would be expected by chance alone. Elites, on the other hand, exhibited far more constraint. It must be emphasized that these questions concerned major contemporary issues. Had the individual respondents possessed stable underlying mechanisms for ordering their attitudes they would have exhibited greater constraint.

The measurement of the content of belief systems has not progressed very far. But it seems likely that mass publics are low in ideological sophistication and largely devoid of genuine constraints in their belief systems stemming from ideological considerations. And it is even more likely that mass publics do not exhibit constraints stemming from commitment to the isms of traditional political thought. As will be indicated below, it is likely that organizational ties are as important as ideology in the development of individual constraints within mass publics.

The second major dimension in the measure of ideology concerns its distribution within a population. This is primarily a sampling problem, but statistical sampling theory can resolve it only in part. However, careful attention to sampling in research design can eliminate the purely formal problems. National samples make possible reasonably accurate mapping of the distribution of belief systems within a population. This is especially important in democracies for the study of elections, for example, where elections determine the general orientation of public policy; and the distribution of opinion is an important subject in all polities. But the relationship between the national distribution of belief systems and the policy process is less clear as the election period recedes and new issues arise. The relationship is even more confusing in those polities, democratic or not, where the relationship between elections and the formation of a government is complex or even problematical, as in the French Fourth Republic. And this will probably prove even more obviously to be the case in developing countries where elite belief systems can be expected to diverge markedly from those of the mass.

These considerations suggest the need for a supplementary purposive sample designed to capture in greater detail the structure of the beliefs of "strategic elites."[17] In all polities these should include party, executive, legislative,

[16]Apter (ed.), *op. cit.*, p. 242.

[17]As developed by Suzanne Keller, *Beyond the Ruling Class: Strategic Elites in Modern Society* (New York: Random House, 1963).

bureaucratic, associational, and economic elites. The inclusion of others, the weight assigned to each, the degree of penetration into middle and lower strata (regional and local elites, for example), the amount of geographical spread desired, and the level of ideological sensitivity assumed—these will depend upon the structure of political conflict in the polity, the resources available to the researcher, and his judgment as to the payoff potential of various designs. It is necessary that we recognize that individual belief systems are not of equal importance in politics, and that the nonrandom aspect of sampling must be consciously confronted. Indeed, it may turn out that the best sampling unit is not the individual at all, whether within the elite or mass, but organizations, with a subsample of individuals that pays particular attention to their roles within the organization.

It is clear that any empirical approach to the study of ideology must deal with the measurement problem, for no generalizations about ideology and conflict can be better than the measurement techniques on which they are based. While many useful methods exist for measuring ideology and its dispersion, all have weaknesses, and considerable improvement is both desirable and possible.

Ideology and Organization

Tough-minded analysts of society and politics have tended to view ideologies as mere cloaks masking interests. For Marx, ideologies were rationalizations of class interest. For Bentley, they were "spooks." But for some, on the other hand, ideology is elevated to a leading position, guiding the actions of individuals and polities alike.

Most contemporary analysts of conflict take an intermediate position. Thus Dahrendorf writes, "Ideologies understood as articulated and codified manifest interests are again but a technical condition of organization. Ideologies do not create conflict groups or cause conflict groups to emerge. Yet, they are indispensable as obstetricians of conflict groups, and in this sense [act] as an intervening variable."[18] Dahl likewise views "patterns of attitudes and opinions" as intervening factors helping to account for variations in conflict and consensus.[19] Boulding, too, seems to take an intermediate position, though this must be inferred from scattered comments: "The extent to which ideological differences result in overt conflict depends mainly on the

[18]Rolf Dahrendorf, *Class and Class Conflict in Industrial Society* (Palo Alto: Stanford University Press, 1959), p. 186.

[19]Robert Dahl (ed.), *Oppositions in Western Democracies* (New Haven: Yale University Press, 1966), Chapter 13.

extent to which these differences are embodied in organizations designed for conflict," and "The conflict of ideologies . . . is partly ecological and partly organizational."[20] In addition, Coser, following Simmel, seems to view ideology, if not as an independent force, at least as a device for objectifying conflict so that individuals fight "not for self but only for ideals of the groups they represent."[21] And Mannheim sees a mutual interplay between ideology and interest in the role of intellectuals, who serve as apologists for interests but "in return for their collaboration with parties and classes" leave an ideological imprint on them.[22]

This middle position does indeed seem to be the only sensible one to assume. It would be absurd to argue, for example, that ideological considerations do not enter into the motivations of a communist intellectual; it would be equally foolish to assume that all peasant communists are ideologically motivated. The following general finding may serve to illustrate this point: Studies of communist movements in many countries, using a variety of research techniques, suggest that hard core ideologues are primarily middle-class professionals and intellectuals, few in number, who were attracted primarily by the ideological appeal of Marx; lower-class communists seem little affected by ideology.[23]

"The inevitable," Lenin is reported to have said, "requires a lot of hard work." No idea has ever made much headway without an organization behind it. And no organization has ever made much headway without satisfying the needs of substantial numbers of people. While small organizations and movements may have thrived on the ideological enthusiasm of their members alone, it is difficult to make a big impact without organizing large numbers of people.[24]

[20] Kenneth Boulding, *Conflict and Defense: A General Theory* (New York: Harper, 1962), p. 278.

[21] Lewis Coser, *The Functions of Social Conflict* (New York: The Free Press, 1956), p. 118.

[22] Karl Mannheim, *Ideology and Utopia* (New York: Harcourt, Brace & Co., 1946), p. 142.

[23] See, for example, Gabriel Almond, *The Appeals of Communism* (Princeton: Princeton University Press, 1956); Hadley Cantril, *The Politics of Despair* (New York: Basic Books, Inc., 1958); R. V. Burks, *The Dynamics of Communism in Eastern Europe* (Princeton: Princeton University Press, 1961), especially Chapter 2; Gene D. Overstreet and Marshall Windmiller, *Communism in India* (Berkeley: University of California Press, 1959); Arnold C. Brackman, *Indonesian Communism,* (New York: Praeger, 1963).

[24] For a recent statement of the reconstructed logic of the distinction between the motivations of members of large and small groups see Mancur Olson, Jr., *The Logic of Collective Action* (Cambridge: Harvard University Press, 1965). For an evaluation of the utility of Mansur's theory for empirical research see Samuel H. Barnes, "Party Democracy and the

It was pointed out above that the belief systems of mass publics seldom exhibit constraints among elements, and that elites are the hosts of ideologies. It is through organization that the ideologies of elites become politically relevant. The important question, What is the impact of the ideological preferences of elites on the goals of their political organizations? is often asked. But this is only half of the relationship. The opposite but related question is of at least equal significance: What is the impact of political organization on the ideologies of the elites? Numerous scholars have remarked upon the degeneration of charismatic and ideological movements into bureaucratic entities. This is perhaps an almost inevitable consequence of the necessities of organization, and it has profound consequences for the study of ideology. While ideological considerations relate largely to goals, organizations tend to develop internal dynamics of their own that include a multiplicity of goals. For participants they are instrumental organizations as well, often providing income and status in addition to the achievement of the organizational goal; in fact, organizational and individual goals may conflict. Moreover, organizations must come to terms with the belief systems of participants and clients, and ideological goals may become displaced in the process. Lenin and others have noted several advantages of small elite structures over mass organizations. His brilliant solution to the problem of the impact of organization on ideology was an elite party devoted to goal achievement working through other, primarily instrumental, organizations. This seems to have arrested but not prevented the disintegration of ideology in this case.[25]

Wherever ideologies seem to be important in politics they have a firm organizational basis. This seems to be true even in the United States where those who score high on ideological sensitivity and constraint also score high on party identification, and the least sophisticated ideologically flit from party to party if they vote at all.[26] And there is considerable evidence that American party elites are more ideological and also more extreme in their attitudes than the rank and file; these latter are, in fact, rather similar. Herbert McCloskey concludes the following:[27]

Logic of Collective Action," in William J. Crotty (ed.), *Approaches to the Study of Party Organization*, forthcoming.

[25]See Richard Lowenthal, *World Communism: The Disintegration of a Secular Faith* (New York: Oxford, 1964); Philip Selznick, *The Organizational Weapon* (New York: McGraw-Hill, 1952).

[26]Campbell, et al., *op. cit.*, pp. 263-265.

[27]McCloskey, "Consensus and Ideology in American Politics," *op. cit.*, p. 372. But Eldersveld casts some doubt on these conclusions (*op. cit.*, 188), and Edmond Constantini presents data that contradict them completely, "Intraparty Attitude Conflict: Democratic Party Leadership in California," *Western Political Quarterly*, Vol. 16 (December 1963), pp. 956-972.

Partisan differences are greater between the informed than between the uninformed, between the upper-class supporters of the two parties than between the lower-class supporters, between the 'intellectuals' in both parties than between those who rank low on 'intellectuality.'

And it equally seems likely that it is largely the elites dominating American political organizations, especially professional people, who are most strongly committed to the tenets of liberal democracy, the dominant American ideology.[28]

Countries such as France, Italy, the Netherlands, and Belgium—which are conventionally viewed as exhibiting great ideological cleavages—likewise feature extensive organizational underpinnings for their ideological debates. In these polities individuals are often socialized into subcultures rigidly separate from one another, and may belong solely to organizations reflecting the belief systems of that particular subculture. It is probable that organizational ties to parties, trade unions, and other associations are more important than ideology in imposing constraints on mass belief systems. Much evidence suggests that organized Catholics in the Netherlands, Belgium, France, or Italy, or communists in the latter two countries, for example, are much more strongly influenced by their organizational ties and face to face relationships than by considerations of ideology. Simmel and Coser have noted the association between extensive face to face relationships and intense conflict.[29] These ties and relationships, rather than ideology as such, may account for the seeming ferocity of "ideological" conflict in such countries.

These nonideological origins of constraint may turn out to be very important indeed, and especially so in polities characterized by deep cleavages, low education, and high levels of politicization. In such polities individuals may exhibit considerable constraint in their belief systems without being ideologically sophisticated.

Ideology and Political Conflict

I have indicated that it is through organizations that the ideologies of elites affect the belief systems of mass publics. I have also suggested that organizations respond to many types of motivation, of which ideology is only one. I will now examine some of the ramifications of this view of ideology for the structure of political conflict of a polity.

[28]See Robert E. Lane, "The Fear of Equality," *American Political Science Review*, Vol. 53 (March 1959), pp. 35-51.

[29]Coser, *op. cit.*, p. 62.

A discussion of ideology and conflict requires a basic distinction between levels of analysis. The discussion of polities as wholes entails macro analysis; the study of individual behavior involves micro analysis.[30] The functional role of an ideology or organization for the polity may be quite different from its role for individuals, and any linkage between the macro and micro levels must be demonstrated, not assumed.

At a given time, any particular polity possesses a given structure of conflict, and a particular political culture or cultures (as used, for example, in the works of Gabriel Almond). As components of culture, political belief systems are learned through socialization. A polity may have one or several significant belief systems; in the latter case we say that its political culture is fragmented. Generally when we refer at the macro level to an ism such as Soviet communism or Austrian socialism or Italian social Catholicism, we are utilizing a form of shorthand to identify a particular political culture or subculture that is conventionally identified with a particular ideology.

But if this shorthand leads us to make assumptions about the belief systems of individuals within the subculture we may be misled completely. For example, Gabriel Almond and Sidney Verba have demonstrated that in Italy the present constitutional parties (especially the Christian Democrats) are "supported in large part by traditional-clerical elements who are not democratic at all, and not even political in a specialized sense of the term," while the anti-constitutional left wing (mainly Communists) "at least in part and at the rank and file voter level rather than among the party elite, manifests a form of open partisanship that is consistent with a democratic system."[31] And to take a less dramatic example, the Netherlands is divided into Catholic, Protestant, Socialist, and Liberal subcultures, each with its own ideology, associational network, party or parties, and means of mass communications. Yet on many dimensions there seem to be few differences between the substantive political attitudes of working class members of these subcultures, though they vote for different parties and live in separate subcultures. Examples can be multiplied almost at will. I doubt that knowledge of macro- or micro-politics is furthered by the analysis of ideology independent of its organizational context.

[30]See Gabriel Almond and Sidney Verba, *The Civic Culture* (Princeton: Princeton University Press, 1963), pp. 32-36; V. O. Key, *Public Opinion and American Democracy* (New York: Knopf, 1961), chapters 16ff.

[31]Almond and Verba, *op. cit.*, p. 160.

While it may not be useful to speak of ideologies as wholes, analysis that makes use of ideological dimensions may be quite helpful. As Converse has noted, mass beliefs are formed in clusters.[32] This is probably especially true in democracies, for total ideologies require total commitments that are difficult to maintain amidst the conflicting pressures of pluralist societies. But one can meaningfully speak of a liberal-conservative economic dimension in studying American attitudes, or of the clerical-anti-clerical dimensions in French and Italian politics.[33] Yet it must be noted that attitudes toward these dimensions at the micro level may be formed by non-ideological considerations. And it is likewise true that any particular position on any single dimension may be compatible with several ideologies. Thus one can be an economic conservative for Burkean reasons, or because of a commitment to laissez-faire economics or to social Darwinism, or out of pure economic self interest, or for nationalistic reasons, or from irrational contempt for the poor, or any number of other reasons.

The discontinuity between the positions of individuals on different dimensions has often been noted. Many Burkean conservatives support civil rights and medicare, and always vote Democratic. In other words, individuals may possess seemingly inconsistent belief systems. While this may be a source of discomfort for intellectuals, most people seem unconcerned except when circumstances publicize the inconsistencies, as in the present confrontation between racism and the American creed. Even in this case some people do not admit their incompatibility, though it has become difficult to defend intellectually their inclusion in a single belief system.

Most people acquire the belief systems of those around them. Intellectuals are to some extent free of this determinism, for they are able to escape the limitations imposed on the imagination by time and place. But intellectuals can make contact with mass publics only with difficulty, and then only by working through organizations that have a largely instrumental character, such as schools, trade unions, and political parties. The degree to which

[32]In Apter (ed.), *op. cit.*, p. 211.

[33]Spatial models of party competition assume unidimensionality, whereas this is seldom the case, at least as the parties are perceived by mass publics. See Donald Stokes' criticism of spatial models: "Spatial Models of Party Competition," *American Political Science Review*, Vol. 57 (June 1963), pp. 368-377. On the other hand, the greater ideological sophistication of elites combined with the unequal saliency of ideological dimensions at the macro level should cause us to pause before discarding spatial models altogether. Where dimensions—for example, economic liberalism-conservatism, clericalism-anti-clericalism—tend to reinforce one another, as in Italy, spatial models may be quite useful at least at the macro level. Whether they are ever meaningful at the micro level remains to be seen.

ideological considerations intrude on instrumental ones varies greatly, of course, but it is probably not very high anywhere most of the time.

In Western society in general, and perhaps in Russian also, instrumental considerations have come to dominate. This is perhaps the consequence, if not always of democracy, at least of the importance of mass publics. For the belief systems of mass publics everywhere are increasingly similar; and in all cultures that have been touched by modernization, mass belief systems include a demand for greater material well-being. When mass publics are involved, ideologies of asceticism and self-denial do not do well in competition with those that promise more. An organization must adapt its ideology in order to enhance its chances of survival, whether it be the Communist Party of the Soviet Union, the Republican Party, or the Catholic Church.

The historical experiences of the Catholic Church serve to illustrate this contention. It has been noted that the instrumental needs of an organization have a tendency to dominate over ideological ones. The organizational structure of Catholicism and the instrumental functions the Church performed in a preindustrial society made it difficult for Catholicism to adapt quickly to the changed status of mass publics following the Industrial Revolution. As a result, new organizations espousing ideologies such as liberalism and socialism emerged to threaten its organizational survival. But the Church gradually adapted, and today in many countries has a full array of organizations for all social groups. Thus it has organized or sponsored trade unions, businessmen's clubs, democratic political parties, youth groups, and associations for almost every conceivable category of persons. It likewise has modified its ideology as reflected in Papal Encyclicals to accommodate to the belief systems of mass publics. Few organizations willingly disband. The continuity of the Catholic Church through numerous changes in social and political ideologies attests to the primacy of organization over political ideology, as does the prudence of Pope Pius XII during the Second World War.

In some countries, the necessity of coming to terms with the belief systems of mass publics has profoundly modified the ideologies of all political organizations so that they are quite similar on many dimensions, especially on the importance of the economic well-being of the masses. Marxist, Catholic, Protestant, and Liberal ideologies are generally compatible with most mass beliefs on this point. It is perhaps within this context that references are made to "the end of ideology." While there is growing consensus in Western countries, this is the result of convergence on some of the principal dimensions of political conflict, not of agreement on ideology. And other significant marginal differences become more important as organizational elites accentuate them to justify their survival. Note, for example, the importance of marginal differences between Democrats and Republicans in the United States, or Christian Democrats and Socialists in West Germany today. Differences on other dimensions may retain their significance despite convergence on the economic dimension. Thus in contemporary France attitudes towards clericalism, rather than economic or other outlooks, are still the best predictor of party allegiances.[34] And in the Netherlands, where subcultural and ideological differences coincide, the organizational networks developed within subcultures seem to guarantee the persistence of each, despite growing convergence in attitudes toward public policy on the part of two or three of the subcultures. With a complete structure of organizations to serve him, often combined with sanctions for nonparticipation, the individual today may be functionally isolated from deviant beliefs. Here, socialization into different political subcultures and organizational networks is as important as ideology as a basis for continuing cleavages in the polity.

These examples suggest that conflict that seems to be ideological is facilitated by the presence of structural discontinuities in the polity that encourage the maintenance of separate political and other organizations. Regional, linguistic, religious, ethnic, and economic seem to be the most important of these structural lines of division. These often coincide with one another, and the more they do so, the more likely are differences to be accompanied by elaborate ideologies. Economic development tends to reduce the importance of these differences because it tends to make for similar patterns throughout the polity, especially in the economic sphere. But development does not affect all areas equally, and some regions may lag behind others, as in the American South, Quebec, Southern Italy, and parts of France. Furthermore, development may merely add the dimension of industrial warfare to existing discontinuities in the political culture, though the circumstances under which this takes place remain somewhat obscure. Thus development may itself be a source of conflict. And there is increasing evidence that older lines of cleavage and conflict have an unexpected tenacity despite economic development; they may, in fact, be accentuated by it, as in Canada, Belgium, and the Netherlands. But in the absence of deep religious, linguistic, and regional cleavages, development does seem to contribute to the waning of the intensity of conflict, perhaps because of the growing similarity of ideologies on the subject of material well-being.

[34]Converse, in Apter (ed.), *op. cit.*, p. 248.

But, as pointed out above, organizations tend to persist. Despite growing convergence on many ideological dimensions, differences remain on others, and ideological debate among elites may continue. Mass publics may not be greatly affected by it, but their loyalties to primary and secondary groups and hence directly or indirectly to organizations persist. As a result, political conflict may retain an ideological dimension long after ideology has ceased to be of much significance for policy making or for mass publics.

This discussion of the importance of organization points up the crucial ideological role of the most important organization of all—government. For most political conflict focuses sooner or later on the institutions of government; governmental organizations are crucial, and like others, they have their own goals, elites, belief systems. Organizations such as legislatures, bureaucracies, commissions, etc., may or may not be broadly reflective of mass beliefs. The constitutional structure of the polity, and especially the electoral system, can facilitate or hinder the expression of particular ideological views. The relationship between mass beliefs and those of the governmental elites is thus crucial in understanding the actual role of ideology in politics. The distribution of mass beliefs may be only partially reflected in the formal organizations of the state. The electoral system may result in a legislature that does not adequately represent significant segments of the polity; the formation of the government may involve the exclusion of representatives of organizations and belief systems of great numerical importance within the polity. In this sense, too, belief systems are not of equal importance. While it is true that in the long run a polity can hardly ignore belief systems with strong organizational bases, the long run may be very long indeed. Thus the study of ideology and conflict must cope with the differential accessibility of the system to various ideologies.

The institutional structure of the polity is crucial not only for an understanding of the relationship between ideology and the outputs of the political system; it is also critical for the survival of particular ideologies. In ideologically well integrated polities the elites who dominate political organizations share most components of a common belief system; in other words, there is high consensus. These elites find it not only profitable but also possible to exclude proponents of deviant belief systems from important positions in the polity. Lacking visibility and legitimacy, the spread of deviant beliefs is greatly hindered. Political structure therefore greatly affects ideology. It makes a considerable difference whether the most influential organizations of the polity are accessible to or insulated from holders of deviant views. The differences between the United States and the Fourth French Republic are instructive on this point. Even partial success in capturing key positions greatly facilitates the growth of ideologically deviant organizations; this is exhibited by the parliamentary success of Communist parties in Italy and France. And the sharing of governmental positions seems to guarantee the perpetuation of the organizational bases of conflicting belief systems, as in Austria, Belgium, and the Netherlands.

Many unanswered questions remain in relation to ideology and the organization of conflict. How a particular structure of conflict arose is one of these. The dynamics of the formation and change of belief systems and ideologies at both the micro and macro levels is another. The role of ideology within a political organization is likewise poorly understood. But the importance of organization in mediating between ideology and behavior seems firmly established. Mass belief systems are part of the raw material of politics; they are a limiting factor but not a determining one. They condition elite behavior but do not determine it. Ideologies, on the other hand, require organization to render them politically significant, and organizations work profound transformations on ideologically motivated goals. Consequently, the best focus for the study of the relationship between political thought and behavior is the study of political organization.

Conclusion

I began this book by emphasizing the ubiquity and the protean character of the term "ideology" in contemporary treatments of politics. I shall conclude it by restating my perception of the two different but inseparable problems posed by the phenomenon of ideology.

The first is the problem of understanding the nature and significance of the phenomenon; the second is the problem of deciding whether political actions are called for by its existence, and, if so, what these actions should be. The first problem is primarily the responsibility of the student of political life; the second, that of the leader. These responsibilities merge, however, because the problems are complementary. Intelligent political action is impossible without a general understanding of political phenomena and a grasp of the particular situation. Conversely, general understanding of political phenomena is impossible without a sound sense of the nature of political action. This sense may be derived from personal experience in the conduct of political affairs or, more likely, from taking seriously the observations and experiences of actual political leaders and joining these to an awareness of what it means to live and act in political society.

Both of these problems are very difficult. They are difficult, first, because they are fundamental; they reach to the roots of political philosophy, on one hand, and to the essence of the proper conduct of political affairs, on the other. The resolution of such problems is certainly not guaranteed. Furthermore, to the extent that they are capable of resolution at all, they require excellence in one or both of the two complementary activities which comprise the essence of being human: thinking and acting.

The problems are difficult, secondly, because of their scale—a problem which is a striking feature of the political realm today. The ideological style of politics, generated in Western Europe about two hundred years ago, has now spread to most parts of the world.

Turning back to the problem of understanding—the main concern of this book—the student confronts a rapidly increasing mass of material on the subject as well as many conflicting definitions of and perspectives on the phenomenon. The basic problem, then, is this: By what principle or principles shall he select among these definitions and interpretations, especially when, as often happens, they conflict? Or should he say that there is no real problem because all the definitions and interpretations contribute to understanding? If he opts for this eclectic solution, does he not then have to supply a principle by which to justify it, and how does he evaluate the various contributions?

These questions lead to the heart of the great contemporary dispute over understanding social and political phenomena—the dispute between the philosophical and political senses. This dispute exists with respect to most social and political phenomena; therefore the problem of understanding the phenomenon of ideology is not unique. But because both the dispute and the phenomenon refer to the nature of theory and its relation to practice, it is a particularly revealing example of the difficulty under discussion. Reconsideration of the content and history of the original philosophical and political senses of ideology may clarify the issue.

The philosophical sense appeared first, as an extension and radicalization of the early modern critique of medieval and classical philosophy, natural and political. It was a reconstitution of all human sciences on the basis of a new theoretical understanding of the human mind. The application of this understanding to the realm of practice—even a radical transformation of practice— was intended from the outset. However, instead of the anticipated triumph of the new theoretical understanding, a vigorous political reaction to it occurred. Thus, within a short time, an unanticipated—and to the original *idéologues*, a wholly unwarranted and unwelcome—political sense of ideology came into being. The core of its meaning was that the theoretical pretensions of the science of ideas in general, and of the new science of politics in particular, are essentially incompatible with the nature of political life. What we see, then, at the origins of the appearance of ideology is that both the philosophical and the political senses focused on the problem of the nature of theory and its relation to practice.

That problem is still the fundamental one. Louis Halle's recent criticism of twentieth-century *idéologues* for their ill-conceived attempt to force political practice into the mold of theories is very much like John Adams' pithy condemnation, in 1814, of the original *idéologues*' attempts to do so. There have been, of course, important differences in the theories against which this political sense of the term has been directed. But those differences are less important than the persistence of a political sense that there is a profound and irreducible tension between modern theories and the proper conduct of political affairs.

This fundamental ideological problem is also apparent when one reflects on the character and the origin of the dominant contemporary philosophical senses of ideology. They are directly or indirectly derivative of earlier modern philosophic treatments of political life and of the nature of human understanding. More specifically, the present dominant philosophical senses are largely derivative of several *waves* of earlier modern thinkers' analyses. Thus, for example, Karl Mannheim's treatment draws upon and attempts to synthesize elements from the prior treatments of Francis Bacon, Destutt de Tracy, Hegel, Marx, Max Weber, Vilfredo Pareto, and Carl Schmitt, among others. Camus was profoundly influenced by certain thinkers of the French Revolution, but even more by Hegel and Nietzsche. Similar instructive patterns might be traced in the development of other contemporary philosophical senses.

I come, then, to a final question on the problem concerning ideology: Is it possible to understand that problem by relying upon contemporary, late-modern philosophical senses of the term? I doubt it. The historical origin of the phenomenon is rooted in an explicit rejection of the classical understanding of the nature of theory and its relation to practice. And the dominant contemporary philosophical senses of the term go back to the origin of the phenomenon. Thus a careful restatement of the problem as it appeared in the early-modern period is essential to proper understanding; but such a restatement is difficult. Either we accept the early-modern critical view or we reject it. If we accept it without making an independent examination of both positions, we defer to the authority of modern criticism. But it is doubtful that such deference constitutes understanding. If, on the other hand, we seek to achieve an independent understanding of both positions, we must go beyond the origin of the phenomenon toward a comprehensive restatement of the classical position. Such a restatement is difficult, but not impossible. But there can be no real incentive to achieve it unless the contemporary tendency to reduce philosophy to ideology is first called into question. Questioning that tendency is the beginning of understanding, although it is only the beginning.

Selected Bibliography*

Articles

Adams, James L., "Religion and the Ideologies," *Confluence*, 4 (April 1955), 72-84.

Arian, A., "The Role of Ideology in Determining Behavior," *Sociological Review*, 15 (March 1967), 47-57.

Aron, Raymond, "Nations and Ideologies," *Encounter* (Jan. 1955), 24-33.

Aron, R., "L'idéologie, Support Nécessaire de L'Action," *Res Publica*, 2 (1960), 276-286.

Banerjee, D. N., "Political Ideologies and Political Behavior," *Modern Review*, 92 (Dec. 1952), 444-450.

Bergmann, Gustav, "Ideology," *Ethics*, 61 (April 1951), 205-218.

Birnbaum, Norman, "The Sociological Study of Ideology, 1940-60," *Current Sociology*, 9 (1960), 91-172.

Boorstin, Daniel, "Our Unspoken National Faith—Why Americans Need No Ideology," *Commentary*, 15 (April 1953), 327-337.

*Many additional items will be found in the footnotes.

Carlton, W. G., "Ideology or Balance of Power?," *Yale Review,* 36 (Summer 1947), 590-602.

Chevallier, J. J., "Le 18ème Siècle et la Naissance des Idéologies," *Res Publica,* 2 (1960), 194-204.

Cohen, A. A., "Religion as a Secular Ideology," *Partisan Review,* 23 (Fall 1956), 495-505.

Crick, Bernard, "Philosophy, Theory, and Thought," *Political Studies,* 15 (Feb. 1967), 49-55.

Denninger, W. T., "Political Power and Ideological Analysis," *Il Politico,* 26 (June 1961), 277-286.

Dion, Léon, "Les Origines Sociologiques de la Thèse de la Fin des Idéologies," *Il Politico,* 27 (Dec. 1962), 788-796.

Galantiere, Lewis, "Ideology and Political Warfare," *Confluence,* 2 (March 1953), 43-54.

Halpern, Ben, "Myth and Ideology in Modern Usage," *History and Theory,* 1 (1961), 129-149.

Hodges, D. C., "End of the End of Ideology," *American Journal of Economics,* 26 (April 1967), 135-146.

Hudspeth, C. M., "A Telescopic View of Political Ideologies," *Rice Institute Pamphlet,* 44 (Oct. 1957), 47-69.

Hughes, H. S., "The End of Political Ideology," *Measure,* 2 (1951), 146-158.

Huntington, S. P., "Conservatism as an Ideology," *American Political Science Review,* 51 (Dec. 1957), 454-473.

Hu Shih, "Conflict of Ideologies," *Annals of the American Academy of Political and Social Science,* 218 (Nov. 1941), 26-35.

Jansson, J. M., "The Role of Political Ideologies in Politics," *International Relations,* 1 (April 1959), 529-542.

Jouvenel, Bertrand de, "Factors of Diffusion," *Confluence,* 2 (Sept. 1953), 69-81.

Kallen, H. M., "Social Philosophy and the War of the Faiths," *Social Research,* 20 (April 1953), 1-18.

Lane, R. E., "The Decline of Politics and Ideology in a Knowledgeable Society," *American Sociological Review,* 31 (Oct. 1966), 649-662.

Loewenstein, K., "The Role of Ideologies in Political Change," *International Social Science Bulletin,* 5 (1953), 51-74.

McKeon, Richard, "A Philosophy for UNESCO," *Philosophy and Phenomenological Research,* 8 (1948), 573-586.

McKeon, Richard, "Dialectic and Political Thought and Action," *Ethics*, 65 (Oct. 1954), 1-33.

Mabbott, J. D., "Conflict of Ideologies," *Philosophy*, 23 (July 1948), 195-207.

Minar, D. W., "Ideology and Political Behavior," *Midwest Journal of Political Science*, 5 (Nov. 1961), 317-331.

Morgenthau, H. J., "A Positive Approach to a Democratic Ideology," *Proceedings of the Academy of Political Science*, 24 (Jan. 1951), 227-238.

Murphy, A. E., "Ideals and Ideologies: 1917-1947," *Philosophical Review*, 56 (July 1947), 374-389.

Nott, Kathleen, "Notes on Feeling and Ideology," *Partisan Review*, 26 (Winter 1959), 64-71.

Nulle, S. H., "An Ecology of the Isms," *South Atlantic Quarterly*, 56 (Summer 1957), 350-360.

Ries, R. E., "Social Science and Ideology," *Social Research*, 31 (Summer 1964), 234-243.

Robinson, G. T., "The Ideological Combat," *Foreign Affairs*, 27 (July 1949), 525-539.

Rostow, W. W., "A Note on the 'Diffusion of Ideologies'," *Confluence*, 2 (March 1953), 31-42.

Roucek, J. S., and Charles Hodges, "Ideology as the Implement of Purposive Thinking in Social Sciences," *Social Science*, 11 (Jan. 1936), 25-34.

Roucek, J. S., "Ideology as a Means of Social Control," *American Journal of Economics and Sociology*, 3 (Oct. 1943), 35-45, 3 (Jan. 1944), 179-192, 3 (April 1944), 357-369.

Roucek, J. S., "A History of the Concept of Ideology," *Journal of the History of Ideas*, 5 (Oct. 1944), 479-488.

Roucek, J. S. "Scientific Claims and Methods vs. Ideological Claims and Methods," *Wisconsin Sociologist*, new series, 2 (Fall 1963), 1-6.

Rousseau, S. W., and J. Farganis, "American Politics and the End of Ideology," *British Journal of Sociology*, 14 (Dec. 1963), 347-362.

Schulze, R., "The Recession of Ideology?," *Sociological Quarterly*, 5 (Spring 1964), 148-156.

Schweitzer, A., "Ideological Groups," *American Sociological Review*, 56 (Aug. 1944), 415-426.

Schweitzer, A., "Ideological Strategy," *Western Political Quarterly*, 15 (March 1962), 46-66.

Shaw, Roger, "What Price Ideology?," *South Atlantic Quarterly*, 39 (July 1940), 344-349.

Shils, Edward, "The End of Ideology?," *Encounter*, 26 (1955), 52-58.

Stein, J. W., "Beginnings of Ideology," *South Atlantic Quarterly*, 55 (April 1956), 163-170.

Van Duzer, C. H., "The Contribution of the Ideologues to French Revolutionary Thought," *Johns Hopkins University Studies in Historical and Political Science*, 53 (1935).

Weidle, W., "Sur le Concept d'Idéologie," *Le Contrat Social*, 3 (March 1959), 75-78.

Williams, Bernard, "Democracy and Ideology," *Political Quarterly*, 32 (Oct. 1961), 374-384.

Books

Apter, David (ed.), *Ideology and Discontent*. Free Press of Glencoe, 1964.

Aron, Raymond, *The Opium of the Intellectuals*. Secker and Warburg, 1957.

Aron, R., *The Industrial Society: Three Essays on Ideology and Development*. Praeger, 1967.

Bell, Daniel, *The End of Ideology, or the Exhaustion of Political Ideas in the Fifties*. Free Press of Glencoe, 1960.

Cohn, Norman, *The Pursuit of the Millennium.* Harper Torchbooks, 1961.

Connolly, W. E., *Political Science and Ideology*. Atherton Press, 1967.

Corbett, P., *Ideologies*. Harcourt, Brace & World, 1966.

Friedrich, C. J., *An Introduction to Political Theory*. Harper & Row, 1967.

Germino, D. L., *Beyond Ideology*. Harper & Row, 1967.

Golob, E. O., *The "Isms": A History and Evaluation.* Harper & Bros., 1954.

Gregor, J. A., *Contemporary Radical Ideologies*. Random House, 1967.

Gross, Feliks (ed.), *European Ideologies: A Survey of 20th Century Political Ideas*. Philosophical Library, 1948.

Gyorgy, A., and G. D. Blackwood, *Ideologies in World Affairs.* Blaisdell, 1967.

Halevy, Elie, *The Era of Tyrannies*. Doubleday Anchor, 1965.

Hersch, Jeanne, *Idéologies et Réalité: Essai d'Orientation Politique*. Paris: Librairie Plon, 1956.

Jordan, Z. A., *Philosophy and Ideology*. Dordrecht, Holland: D. Riedel Publishing Co., 1963.

Lane, R. E., *Political Ideology*. Free Press of Glencoe, 1962.

Lenk, Kurt, *Ideologie*. Neuwied, Germany: Hermann Luchterhand Verlag, 1961.

Lerner, Max, *Ideas Are Weapons*. Viking Press, 1939.

Lichtheim, G., *The Concept of Ideology and Other Essays*. Random House, 1967.

Macrae, Donald, *Ideology and Society*. Free Press of Glencoe, 1961.

Naess, Arne, *Democracy, Ideology, and Objectivity*. Oxford: Basil Blackwell, 1956.

Shklar, Judith (ed.), *Political Theory and Ideology*. Macmillan & Co., 1966.

Sigmund, P. E. (ed.), *The Ideologies of the Developing Nations*. Praeger, 1968.

Weaver, R. M., *Ideas Have Consequences*. University of Chicago Press, 1948.

Parts of Books

Apter, David, "The Ideology of Modernization," in *The Politics of Modernization*, D. Apter (ed.), University of Chicago Press, 1965.

Feuer, Lewis, "Beyond Ideology," in *Psychoanalysis and Ethics*, C. C. Thomas, 1955.

Littunen, Yrjo, "Social Restraints and Ideological Pluralism," in *Cleavages, Ideologies, and Party Systems*, E. Allardt and Y. Littunen (eds.), Helsinki: Academic Bookstore, 1964.

Naess, Arne, "The Function of Ideological Convictions," in *Tensions That Cause Wars*, Hadley Cantril (ed.), University of Illinois Press, 1950.

Nevins, Allan, and Louis J. Hacker, "Revolutionary Ideologies between Two Wars," in *The United States and Its Place in World Affairs*, D. C. Heath & Co., 1943.

Partridge, P. H., "The Conflict of Ideologies," in *Paths to Peace: A Study of War; Its Causes and Prevention*, V. H. Wallace (ed.), Melbourne University Press, 1957.

Stankiewicz, W. J. (ed.), "The Problem of Ideology," in *Political Thought Since World War Two*, Free Press of Glencoe, 1964.